Persistent Object Systems

Principles and Practice

The Seventh International Workshop on Persistent Object Systems

Senior Editor   Diane D. Cerra
Editorial Coordinator   Marilyn Uffner Alan
Production Manager   Jodi Hauck, Omnipress, Inc.
Printer   Omnipress, Inc.

Editorial Offices:
Morgan Kaufmann Publishers, Inc.
340 Pine Street, Sixth Floor
San Francisco, CA 94104

ISBN 1-55860-447-2

Editors

Richard Connor   University of St Andrews, Scotland
Scott Nettles   University of Pennsylvania, USA

Programme Committee

Preface

The Seventh International Workshop on Persistent Object Systems took place at Cape May, New Jersey between the 29th and 31st of May, 1996. The workshop took place in the established POS tradition, with the emphasis on hard work and plenty of technical content. As usual, there was much active participation, with plenty of heated discussion both during the formal sessions and also at more informal times and places. Fifty papers were submitted, of which the program committee selected twenty-two for presentation; for the first time both submission and refereeing was conducted entirely electronically.

POS remains very much in the international domain, with papers submitted representing ten countries over five continents. From a UK perspective persistent systems are still not popular in England, with all of the seven UK submissions coming from Scotland!

As always, it is interesting to reflect on trends emerging at this biennial meeting of the persistent systems community. The trends of previous years continue, with an emphasis more on the implementation and optimisation of persistent object systems than on their design principles. A new development this year, particularly in discussion, was an increasing interest in the Java language, which appears likely to replace C^{++} as a foundation for many persistent system experiments.

Thanks are due to a number of people for the success of the workshop. Scott Nettles, my co-chair, must be thanked for his part in organising the refereeing process, the local organisation and the preparation of this manuscript. The members of the programme committee were extremely conscientious in refereeing papers to a very high standard in a short time. Peter Buneman must be thanked for securing significant funding from the NSF, and Elaine Benedetto handled most of the local organisation. The photographs are by courtesy of Alan Dearle. Finally Marilyn Alan of Morgan Kaufmann should be thanked for her eternal patience!

Richard Connor

Table of Contents

(continued)

Autonomous and Clustered Data Stores

Type-Safe Heterogeneous Sharing can be Fast

B. Liskov, A. Adya, M. Castro, Q. Zondervan
Laboratory for Computer Science,
Massachusetts Institute of Technology,
Cambridge, MA 02139

Abstract

Safe sharing is a desirable feature of an object oriented database because it protects valuable database objects from program errors in application code. It is especially desirable in a heterogeneous environment in which applications are written in various programming languages, many of which have unsafe features.

However, safe sharing is not without its potential performance costs. This paper explores these costs. It describes a number of techniques that improve performance without sacrificing safety, and presents results of experiments that evaluate their effectiveness. The results show that some of these techniques are very promising, allowing safe sharing to be achieved with essentially no performance penalty.

Keywords: Object-oriented databases, object-oriented languages, type-safe languages, heterogeneity, performance.

1 Introduction

Type-safe sharing is a desirable attribute for an object-oriented database since it means valuable database objects are less likely to be damaged by errors in application code that uses the database. It is even more desirable in a heterogeneous environment in which applications are written in various programming languages, many of which have unsafe features.

Type-safe sharing means that database objects are manipulated only by calling their methods. This provides the benefits of abstraction and modularity. Abstraction allows users to conceptualize objects at a higher level, in terms of their methods, and to reason about objects behaviorally, using their specifications rather than their implementations. Modularity allows local reasoning about correctness, by just examining the code that implements the abstraction, with the assurance that no other code can interfere. These properties have proved very useful in programming, especially for large programs. We believe that they are at least as important for object-oriented databases, where the set of programs that can potentially interact with objects in the database is always changing; type-safe sharing can ensure that none of this new code can cause previously written code to stop working correctly.

Both abstraction and modularity work only if backed up by an encapsulation mechanism that ensures that only the code that implements an object's abstraction has access to the representation of the object. The only practical way to ensure encapsulation is to limit the programming language used to implement database objects to be *type-safe*. Such a type-safe programming language must provide a mechanism for implementing data abstractions that limits access to object representations, and it must forgo various unsafe features such as unsafe casts, explicit memory management, and unchecked array indexing.

This research was supported in part by the Advanced Research Projects Agency of the Department of Defense, monitored by the Office of Naval Research under contract N00014-91-J-4136. M. Castro is supported by a PRAXIS XXI fellowship.

1

Although the language used to implement database objects must support safe sharing, it is desirable to allow applications to be written in whatever language is most congenial to the application programmer, e.g., C or C++. Many of these languages are not type-safe, and therefore application code written in them must not be allowed to run inside the database. Instead the application must run outside the database, and it must interact with database objects only by calling their methods (rather than manipulating them directly). Note that we require here both that the code run in response to the method calls be safe, and also that it be the right code for that object and method.

Support for safe sharing is not without its potential performance costs, and other systems have chosen to forgo safety for improved performance. Many systems, e.g., [CDF+, LLOW91, C+90] allow the application code to directly manipulate database objects; ODMG [Cat94] also follows this approach because it allows methods of shared objects to be written in various unsafe programming languages. O2 [D+90] and GemStone [MS87] store methods in the database, which means that it is possible to guarantee that the right code runs in response to application calls. However, the languages provided by O2 for method definition are not safe (for example, one of these languages is an extension of C). GemStone does better since programmers use a variant of Smalltalk to define the methods stored in the database, but GemStone exports an unsafe interface to client applications that allows direct access to an object's internal state.

This paper explores the performance penalty of supporting safe sharing. It describes techniques that improve performance without sacrificing safety. It also presents the results of experiments that indicate the effectiveness of the various techniques. Our results show that although some approaches are very slow, others provide excellent performance. They indicate that it is not necessary to abandon safe sharing to achieve good performance in a heterogeneous environment; instead you can have both. The experiments were done in Thor, a new object-oriented database system that supports safe sharing, and its type-safe language, Theta, but the results are applicable to other systems and languages.

This paper is organized as follows. We begin in Section 2 by briefly describing the context for our work. Section 3 describes the techniques that can be used to achieve safe sharing. Section 4 presents the results of our performance experiments. We conclude in Section 5 with a summary of what we have accomplished.

2 The Thor System Interface

Thor is a new object-oriented database system intended for use in heterogeneous distributed systems [ea96]. It provides highly-reliable and highly-available storage so that persistent objects are likely to be accessible when needed in spite of failures. It supports heterogeneity at the machine, network, operating system, and especially programming language levels. Thor makes it easy for programs written in different programming languages to share objects. Different client languages might be used for different applications, or even for components of the same application. Furthermore, even when client code is written in unsafe languages (such as C or C++), Thor guarantees the integrity of the persistent store.

Thor provides its users with a universe of objects. Each object in the universe is encapsulated: it has a state that is not visible to users, and can be accessed only by calling the object's methods. Each object also has a type that determines the signatures of its methods.

Applications can make use of Thor objects by starting up a *session* with Thor. Within a session an application carries out a sequence of transactions; our current approach starts up a new transaction each time the client terminates the previous one. Each transaction consists of one or more method calls. Clients can terminate a transaction by requesting a commit or abort. In the case of a commit, the system may not be able to commit the transaction, e.g., because the client has made use of stale data, and in this case the transaction aborts. If the commit succeeds, we guarantee that the transaction is serialized with respect to all other transactions, and that all its modifications to the persistent universe are recorded reliably [AGLM95].

Method calls return either *values* or *handles*. A value is an integer, boolean, character, or real. A

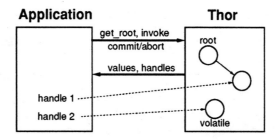

Figure 1: The Thor Interface

handle is a short-lived pointer to a Thor object. A handle is valid only for the current client session; an attempt to use it in a different session will result in an error.

Figure 1 illustrates the Thor interface. Note that Thor objects remain inside Thor, and the code for object methods is stored in Thor and runs inside Thor; this is an important way in which Thor differs from other systems. Code is implemented using a new programming language called Theta [DGLM95, L+94]. Applications are implemented in a programming language augmented by a *veneer* that makes it easy for the application to interact with Thor.

Theta is a strongly-typed language that guarantees that objects can be used *only* by calling their methods. In addition, all built-in Theta types do run-time checks to prevent errors, e.g., array methods do bounds checking. Theta is based on a heap with automatic storage management. It distinguishes between specifications (which are used to define the interface and behavior of a new type) and implementations (code to realize the behavior). It provides support for both parametric and subtype polymorphism, and it separates code inheritance from the subtyping mechanism. More information about Theta can be found in [DGLM95, L+94].

All type definitions and implementations are stored in Thor. The type definitions constitute a *schema library* that can be used for browsing, for compilation of Theta programs, and for producing programming language veneers as discussed next.

A *veneer* [BL94] is a small extension to a programming language that makes it easy for programs written in that language to use Thor. A veneer provides procedures that can be called to open a session or commit a transaction, and it provides translations between scalars stored in Thor (e.g., integers) and related types in the application language. It also provides a way of interacting with (non-scalar) Thor objects. This is accomplished by a *stub generator* for that language. A stub generator is a program that reads Theta type definitions and produces a *stub type* in the application language together with *stub operations* that correspond to methods of the Theta type. We refer to objects belonging to these stub types as *stub objects*. Stub objects are created in response to calls to Thor; when a call returns a handle, the application program receives a stub object containing the handle. When a stub operation is called on a stub object, it calls the corresponding Thor method on the object denoted by the handle in the stub object, waits for a reply, and returns to the caller.

When Thor receives a call from the veneer, it checks whether the handle is valid, whether the object has the method being called, and whether the call has the right number and types of arguments. This *dynamic type checking* is necessary for unsafe languages, since stub code can be corrupted or bypassed. If the client language were safe, checking would not be necessary, which would speed up the interaction between the application code and Thor.

We have defined veneers for C, C++, Perl, and Tcl, although only the C++ veneer will be provided in Thor0, the first Thor release. Experience shows that defining a new veneer is not very difficult. It is not necessary to modify the language compiler. Also veneers can be easily provided regardless of whether the application language provides support for objects. More information about veneers can be found in [BL94, L$^+$96].

3 Safe Sharing Techniques

The simplest way of achieving safe sharing is by keeping the application and the database in separate protection domains, which might run on the same or on different machines; we will refer to this as the *all-outside* approach. Each method call invoked by the application is then a cross-domain call. If the call performs a considerable amount of work (e.g., a complex query on a large set of objects), the domain-crossing costs are relatively unimportant. However, if the call does relatively little work, the domain-crossing costs dominate and can result in poor application performance. This scenario is the worst case for safe sharing and in the rest of this paper, we will analyze its costs along with techniques to reduce them.

The execution time of an application's transaction can be explained by the following model. Suppose the client invokes N methods on database objects. Each of these calls has an overhead of S seconds; S is the average cost of communicating the call from the client to the database, type checking the call at the database, and communicating the result from the database back to the client. (Thus S includes the cost of marshaling/unmarshaling arguments and results.) Also, suppose running the N calls requires X pairs of domain crossings, where each domain-crossing pair has an average cost of C seconds, i.e., C is the cost of a domain crossing round trip. Finally, let the remaining cost be R; R corresponds to the cost of running the transaction without cross-domain calls. Then the total elapsed time T will be:

$$T = X * C + N * S + R \qquad \text{(EQN)}$$

Note that the useful work done in the above equation is R; the rest of the time is the penalty paid for safe sharing. Note also that R includes concurrency control and persistency-related costs that are incurred while the application computation runs; however it does not included the cost of committing (or aborting) the application transaction, since we want to focus on the cost of the computation itself. R also includes safety-related costs incurred by Theta (such as array bounds checking).

Below we discuss techniques that reduce T. There are three techniques — *batching*, *code transfer*, and *sandboxing*.

3.1 Batching

Batching is a technique that reduces the total execution time by reducing the number of domain crossings. Rather than having a crossing for each call, calls are grouped into batches, and an entire batch is sent to the database in one crossing. Thus, X is divided by the average batch size.

Earlier work [BL94] investigated one way of doing batching, called *batched futures*. In this approach, whenever a method call returns a handle, the call is batched for future execution; this makes sense because the only thing that can be done with a handle is to make a subsequent call that uses the corresponding object. A batch is sent to the database when the application makes a call that requires an immediate response, such as a call that returns a value. Although this approach does improve performance (over an approach that has one domain crossing per call), experiments with OO7 [CDN93] showed that the average batch size was low (3.27), and this limited the amount of speed up.

This led us to investigate a second approach, *batched control structures*[Zon95], in which batches corresponding to entire loops can be constructed. This approach gives much higher batching factors, and thus reduces X substantially. It also reduces S. A batch describes a loop by containing a description of each call in a single iteration of the loop. It is type-checked when it is received by the database, and the type-checking cost is proportional to the size of the batch, rather than the number of calls that will occur when the batch runs in the database. Similarly, the marshaling and unmarshaling costs are also proportional to the size of the batch.

Both batched futures and batched control structures incur a higher cost C for each domain crossing. This extra cost is relatively unimportant for batched control structures since batch sizes are very large, but it can have a significant impact for batched futures.

3.2 Code Transfer

Code transfer moves a portion of the application into the database. The application then makes calls on the transferred code; thus code transfer effectively increases the granularity of the calls made by the application. Typically, the entire application computation is not moved into the database since there are certain operations that do not need the database, e.g. user interface operations. However, there is some computation/navigation that is done between such non-database operations; this computation can be captured in a procedure and transferred to the database. Queries are a code transfer technique; here we are interested in other kinds of code transfers that cannot be expressed in a query language such as OQL or extended SQL.

Clearly, we cannot just take a procedure written in an unsafe language like C++ and move it into the database. We need some safe ways of performing code transfer. Here are a few possibilities:

1. Write the procedure in the database language (Theta in the case of Thor). The only problem with this approach is that it requires the application programmer to know the database language.

2. Translate a piece of the application code into the database language. The piece being translated should correspond to a procedure that does not have any free variables, i.e., all communication with the environment is via arguments and results (and reads and writes of database objects). In addition, the language used to write such procedures would be limited to a simple (safe) subset of the application language. This approach has the disadvantage of requiring safe subsets of various application languages to be defined; a more serious disadvantage is that a compiler is needed for each application language.

3. Translate the application code to Java [LY96] byte codes. As in the previous approach, we assume that a procedure without free variables is being translated. It is possible that translators from various application languages to Java will be common in the future, and therefore this approach avoids the problem of needing translators to a non-standard language like Theta. A potential disadvantage is that Java byte codes are interpreted, which is unlikely to give performance competitive with the above two approaches. However, this problem can be overcome by compiling the Java byte codes.

These approaches reduce cost by reducing the number of calls N, which also reduces the number of domain crossings X. They can result in greatly improved performance because very large reductions are possible.

Each approach requires *validation* to ensure that the code being transferred to the database is legal. For the first two cases, the code that runs inside the database is object code produced by the Theta compiler. Therefore, we need to validate that the code really is produced by a legitimate Theta compiler. This can be accomplished by running the compiler inside the database, or running the compiler outside and communicating with it over a secure, authenticated connection. Validation is part of the methodology for loading Java byte codes; it is performed by the *byte code verifier*.

Validation can be very expensive, but it is not necessary to do it on every call. Instead, code can be validated and then stored in the database for future use; this is a kind of memoizing.

The transferred code makes calls to database code and we need to ensure that these calls are type-correct. In the first two approaches this *type checking* is done when the Theta code is compiled. In the third case the byte-code verifier does most of the type checking, although a few checks are left for runtime.

5

3.3 Sandboxing

The final technique for reducing the cost of safe sharing is to transfer object code into the database and use a sandboxing technique [WLAG93] to provide safety. This technique basically involves putting (unsafe) application code/data in a restricted range of virtual memory addresses and then allowing the application code to access only these addresses. The application's object code is *encapsulated*, i.e., augmented with runtime checks so that each jump/store/load operates only on valid addresses. Wahbe et al. have shown that the overheads of this approach are relatively low. With this approach the number of calls N remains the same, and furthermore each call requires a domain crossing. However, the cost of a domain crossing (C) is greatly reduced.

Sandboxing (like the code transfer techniques) requires both validation and checking. Sandboxed code is validated using an object code verifier [WLAG93]. Checking must be done on every call made from the sandboxed code to the database; thus each call still incurs a cost S. Checking costs have been ignored in earlier work on sandboxing; our experiments shed light on these overheads.

4 Experiments

To evaluate the approaches to safe sharing discussed in the previous section, we ran experiments that measured their performance. Our experiments were designed to highlight the costs of the various approaches.

The experiments ran on Thor. Thor has a distributed client-server architecture. Objects are stored persistently by a set of servers. Applications access these objects by communicating with a front-end (FE) process that caches copies of persistent objects. Both application and FE run on the client machine, in separate protection domains.

The experiments ran the FE and application on a DEC 3000/400 workstation, with 128 MB of memory and OSF/1 version 3.2. The code was compiled with DEC's CXX and CC compilers with optimization flag -O2. We found that the performance of our experiments was very sensitive to the layout of code in memory (we observed differences as large as 30%). Therefore, in order to reduce the noise due to misses in the code cache, we used *cord* and *ftoc* [Com], two utilities that reorder procedures in an executable by decreasing *density* (i.e. ratio of cycles spent executing the procedure to its static size). We used cord to obtain different executables optimized for each particular experiment.

The application and the FE communicate using a shared memory buffer with a simple synchronization based on spinning until a flag takes some desired value, and yielding the processor after each unsuccessful test. This gives us a very fast domain crossing. The cost of ping-ponging an integer between the client and the FE is $31\mu s$.

The experiments ran the single-user OO7 benchmark [CDN93]. The OO7 database contains a tree of *assembly* objects, with a height of 7; each non-leaf assembly has three children. The leaves point to three *composite parts* chosen randomly from among 500 such objects. Each composite part contains a graph of *atomic parts* linked by *connection* objects; each atomic part has 3 outgoing connections. The (*small*) database has 20 atomic parts per composite part and a total size of 7 MB. We implemented the database in Theta, following the specification of OO7 [CDN94] closely.

We report results for traversal T1, which performs a depth-first, read-only traversal of the assembly tree and executes an operation on the composite parts referenced by the leaves of this tree. This operation is a depth-first, read-only traversal of the entire graph of a composite part.

We ran the traversal 52 times within a single transaction; we report the average elapsed time of the 50 middle runs. The standard deviation was always below 1% for values above one second and below 6% for values below one second. We used an FE cache large enough to hold the entire database.

This experimental methodology strives to minimize the costs that are not related to safe sharing. In particular, it ensures that there is no disk I/O, no message passing across the network, and no commit cost in the measured traversal execution times. Therefore, the costs reflect only the computation at the application and FE, and the communication between them.

4.1 Results

The results of our experiments are shown in Figure 2. The experiment labeled all-outside ran the entire traversal in the application. In this experiment, the application called methods on database objects that simply fetched values of instance variables. The experiment labeled batching shows the performance when using the batched futures approach. The same-process experiment gives an approximation to what can be expected from a sandboxing technique. The remaining two experiments are code transfer techniques in which part of the application was written in Theta. In all-inside, the entire traversal ran inside the FE [1]. In part-inside, the assembly tree is traversed as in all-outside, but the composite parts and their associated graphs are traversed in the FE using Theta code. The figure shows that the all-outside approach performs much worse than all-inside (approximately 40 times slower). Note that this is a worst case, both because our experimental methodology avoids network and disk I/O overheads and because the methods called by the application are very simple and perform no computation. In fact, the figure shows that when methods perform some computation the overhead is significantly reduced (part-inside is only approximately 2 times slower than all-inside).

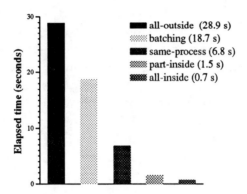

Figure 2: Performance comparison of different safe sharing techniques.

Experiment	X
all-outside	450886
batching	138020
same-process	450886
part-inside	9112
all-inside	1

Table 1: Number of cross domain calls.

To explain the experiments' results, we present some data that allows them to be analyzed using our equation *EQN*. The number of cross-domain calls performed in these experiments is presented in Table 1. Table 2 presents a breakdown of the execution time for the all-outside experiment; it shows that context switching is the dominant overhead in this case. The table allows us to compute the parameters of the analytic model presented in *EQN*, obtaining $C = 49\mu s$, $S = 13.5\mu s$, and $R = 0.7s$.

---

[1]This is in fact the way that the OO7 traversal is supposed to run according to [CDN94].

In Table 2, the context switching overhead was determined by comparing the elapsed time in all-outside with the elapsed time obtained by running the same code with the client and FE executing in the same process, and communicating using the same mechanism (labeled *same-process*). The safety and marshaling overhead was determined by subtracting the all-inside traversal time from the same-process time. This slightly underestimates this cost because the traversal code executes faster in C++ than in Theta as we will show. [2]

Context switching ($X \times C$)	22.1
Safety and Marshaling ($N \times S$)	6.1
Inside traversal (R)	0.7
Total	28.9

Table 2: Breakdown of elapsed time for the all-outside traversal (seconds).

The *batching* experiment reduces the number of pairs of domain crossings X from 450886 to 138020 but it does not change the number of calls N performed by the client. Therefore, the analytical model predicts an elapsed time of 13.6s. The difference between the predicted value and the observed value of 18.7s is due to the overheads introduced by the machinery to handle batched futures. This technique has the advantage that it is transparent to the programmer and portable. However, the experiment shows that its effectiveness is limited by the factor of reduction in the number of domain crossings (i.e. the size of batches) and the overhead introduced by the machinery to handle batching.

The same-process experiment represents an approximation to the cost of running the traversal using sandboxing. In this experiment, the application and FE execute in the same process. The traversal still makes $N = 450886$ calls to database object methods; each of these requires a *fault* domain crossing, but we have assumed that these crossings have zero cost ($C = 0$). We also neglect the overheads of running sandboxed client code; according to [WLAG93] sandboxed client code runs approximately 20% slower. Therefore we are only left with the cost S for making and type checking the calls. As expected performance improves noticeably over the all-outside case, but it is still significantly worse than running the entire traversal in Theta; this happens because sandboxing does not reduce the safety and marshaling/unmarshaling costs, i.e. $N \times S$, which can be significant for large N. [3]

We do not show any experiments that give the performance of the batched control structures mechanism, since it is not running in the current version of Thor. The part-inside gives an idea of what its performance might be (i.e., we could batch a loop for traversing each composite part). However, batched control structures would not perform as well as part-inside because it incurs additional overhead (the system translates the batch into a parse tree that is then interpreted to run the batch).

The results in Figure 2 show that code transfer techniques that run part of the application in the FE using Theta have the best performance. The all-inside value represents a best case for these techniques. To put this all-inside value in perspective we compare it with the elapsed time measured when running the same traversal using a C++ program that mimics the Theta code. The result of this comparison is presented in Figure 3. The C++ program does not incur any overhead for concurrency control and residency checks, but of course it ought to. Therefore, we break the all-inside execution time into overhead that is related to concurrency control and residency checks, and the actual cost of running the traversal in

---

[2]It is interesting to note that a significant portion of the safety cost, 2.6s, is due to a reference counting scheme that transparently garbage collects unused object handles. We have designed and implemented a scheme that eliminates this cost but forces the client to free object handles explicitly.

[3]The figure shows sandboxing to be 9.4 times worse than all-inside, but this experiment was done with garbage collection of handles; the same experiment done with explicit freeing of handles performs 5.8 times worse than all-inside.

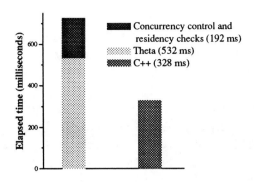

Figure 3: Cost of providing safety in Theta.

Theta. We conclude that Theta is 62% slower than the corresponding C++ implementation that provides no safety guarantees.

Table 3 presents a more detailed breakdown of the execution time for the all-inside traversal. The array bounds cost is necessary for safe sharing since it prevents violations of encapsulation. The remaining cost is not necessary for safe sharing. Here we are generating and checking exceptions for such things as integer overflow. Although safe sharing is still possible without these checks, it is worth noting that overall system safety is improved by having them: they will prevent erroneous transactions from committing that might commit in their absence. Furthermore, we have already designed a scheme that will reduce a large part of this cost.

Concurrency control	120
Residency checks	72
Exception generation/handling	156
Array bounds checking	36
Traversal time	340
Total	724

Table 3: Breakdown of elapsed time for the all-inside traversal (milliseconds).

Thus the only cost in the all-inside case that is intrinsic to safe sharing is the array bounds checking. This introduces an overhead of approximately 11% relative to the observed elapsed time for the C++ code. These results show that it is not very expensive to provide safe sharing of objects using a type-safe statically typed language like Theta. Furthermore, our Theta compiler is an experimental prototype, and therefore it does not generate highly-tuned code. We expect overheads to be reduced by using common compiler optimization techniques such as code motion.

5   Conclusions

Safe sharing is a desirable feature of an object-oriented database because it protects valuable database objects from program errors in application code. It is especially desirable in a heterogeneous environment in which applications are written in various programming languages, many of which have unsafe features.

However, safe sharing is not without its potential performance costs. This paper has explored these costs. It describes three techniques — batching, code transfer, and sandboxing, that improve performance without sacrificing safety, and presents results of experiments that evaluate their effectiveness. The results show that code transfer techniques are especially promising, allowing safe sharing with almost no performance penalty.

Code transfer techniques provide good performance because they reduce domain-crossing costs by reducing the number of domain crossings, and allow the checking of most method calls to happen prior to runtime, either when the code is compiled, or (in the case of Java byte codes) when it is verified.

The problem with code transfer techniques is that they require either an application programmer to write code in the unfamiliar database language, or they require compilers from arbitrary unsafe languages to the database language. The one exception here is translations to Java byte codes; this approach is promising because we may expect these translators to come into existence for other reasons (e.g., Web applets). Although running an interpreter for the byte codes inside the database is unlikely to produce performance comparable to what can be achieved when translating directly into the database language, this problem can be overcome by compiling the byte codes. This way we should be able to achieve the best possible performance (equivalent to the all-inside experiment).

References

[AGLM95] A. Adya, R. Gruber, B. Liskov, and U. Maheshwari. Efficient optimistic concurrency control using loosely synchronized clocks. In *Proc. SIGMOD Int'l Conf. on Management of Data*, pages 23–34. ACM Press, May 1995.

[BL94] P. Bogle and B. Liskov. Reducing cross-domain call overhead using batched futures. In *Proc. OOPSLA '94*, pages 341–359. ACM Press, 1994.

[C+90] M. Carey et al. The EXODUS extensible DBMS project: An overview. In *Readings in Object-Oriented Database Systems*, pages 474–499. Morgan Kaufmann, 1990.

[Cat94] R. G. Cattell, editor. *The Object Database Standard: ODMG-93*. Morgan Kaufmann Publishers, Inc., San Mateo, CA, 1994.

[CDF+] M. J. Carey, David J. DeWitt, Michael J. Franklin, Nancy E. Hall, Mark L. McAuliffe, Jeffrey F. Naughton, Daniel T. Schuh, Marvin H. Solomon, C. K. Tan, Odysseas G. Tsatalos, Seth J. White, and Michael J. Zwilling. Shoring up persistent applications. In *Proc. SIGMOD Int'l Conf. on Management of Data*, pages 383–394, Minneapolis, MN, May 1994. ACM Press.

[CDN93] M. J. Carey, D. J. DeWitt, and J. F. Naughton. The OO7 benchmark. In *Proc. SIGMOD Int'l Conf. on Management of Data*, pages 12–21. ACM Press, May 1993.

[CDN94] M. J. Carey, D. J. DeWitt, and J. F. Naughton. The OO7 benchmark. Technical Report; Revised Version dated 7/21/1994 1140, University of Wisconsin-Madison, 1994. At `ftp://ftp.cs.wisc.edu/OO7`.

[Com] Digital Equipment Company. *OSF/1 Manual Page*.

[D+90] O. Deux et al. The story of O_2. *IEEE Transactions on Knowledge and Data Engineering*, 2(1):91–108, March 1990.

[DGLM95] M. Day, R. Gruber, B. Liskov, and A. C. Myers. Subtypes vs. where clauses: Constraining parametric polymorphism. In *Proc. of OOPSLA '95*, pages 156–158. ACM Press, October 1995.

[ea96] B. Liskov et al. The language-independent interface of the Thor persistent object system. In *Object-Oriented Multi-Database Systems*, pages 570–588. Prentice Hall, 1996.

[L+94] B. Liskov et al. *Theta Reference Manual*. Programming Methodology Group Memo 88, MIT Lab for Computer Science, Cambridge, MA, February 1994. Available at `http://www.pmg.lcs.mit.edu/papers/thetaref/`.

[L+96] B. Liskov et al. Safe and efficient sharing of persistent objects in Thor. In *Proc. of SIGMOD*, 1996.

[LLOW91] C. Lamb, G. Landis, J. Orenstein, and D. Weinreb. The ObjectStore database system. *Comm. of the ACM*, 34(10):50–63, October 1991.

[LY96] T. Lindholm and F. Yellin. *The Java Virtual Machine*. Addison-Wesley, Englewood Cliffs, NJ, May 1996.

[MS87] D. Maier and J. Stein. Development and implementation of an object-oriented DBMS. In B. Shriver and P. Wegner, editors, *Research Directions in Object-Oriented Programming*. MIT Press, 1987.

[WLAG93] R. Wahbe, S. Lucco, T. Anderson, and S. Graham. Efficient software-based fault isolation. In *Proc. 14th ACM Symp. on Operating System Principles*, pages 203–216. ACM Press, December 1993.

[Zon95] Q. Y. Zondervan. Increasing cross-domain call batching using promises and batched control structures. Master's thesis, Massachusetts Institute of Technology, Cambridge, MA, June 1995. Also available as MIT Laboratory for Computer Science Technical Report MIT/LCS/TR-658.

Toward Painless Polylingual Persistence

Alan Kaplan* and Jack C. Wileden

Convergent Computing Systems Laboratory†
Computer Science Department
University of Massachusetts
Amherst, Massachusetts 01003 USA

{kaplan,wileden}@cs.umass.edu

Abstract

Heterogeneity in persistent object systems gives rise to a range of interoperability problems. For instance, a given object-oriented database (OODB) may contain data objects originally defined, created and persistently stored using the capabilities provided by several distinct programming languages, and an application may need to uniformly process those data objects. We call such a database *polylingual* and term the corresponding interoperability problem the *polylingual access* problem.

While many of today's OODBs support multiple programming language interfaces (we term such systems *multilingual*), none provide transparent polylingual access to persistent data. Instead, present day interoperability mechanisms generally rely on external data definition languages (such as ODMG's ODL), thus reintroducing impedance mismatch and forcing developers to anticipate heterogeneity in their applications, or depend upon direct use of such low-level constructs as the foreign language interface mechanisms provided in individual programming languages. Using such mechanisms make polylingual access *painful*.

In this paper we introduce POLYSPIN, an approach supporting polylingual persistence, interoperability and naming for object-oriented databases. We describe our current realization of POLYSPIN as extensions to the TI/Arpa Open Object-Oriented Database and give examples demonstrating how our POLYSPIN prototype supports transparent, *painless* polylingual access between C++ and CLOS applications.

Keywords: Persistence, Interoperability, Polylingual, Name Management, OODBs

1 Introduction

Over the years, as information systems applications have grown larger and more complex, various kinds of *heterogeneity* have appeared in those applications. As a result, individuals and organizations involved in developing, operating or maintaining such applications have increasingly been faced with *interoperability problems* – situations in which components that were implemented using different underlying models or languages must be combined into a single unified application. To aid in overcoming such problems, a range of *interoperability approaches* have been

*Alan Kaplan is now with the Department of Computer Science; Flinders University; GPO Box 2100; Adelaide, SA 5001; Australia. (kaplan@cs.flinders.edu.au).

†This paper is based on work supported in part by Texas Instruments, Inc. under Sponsored Research Agreement SRA-2837024 and by the Air Force Materiel Command, Phillips Laboratory, and the Defense Advanced Research Projects Agency under Contract Number F29601-95-C-0003. The views and conclusions contained in this document are those of the authors. They should not be interpreted as representing official positions or policies of Texas Instruments or the U.S. Government and no official endorsement should be inferred.

employed. As interoperability problems evolve, due in part to evolution of the underlying models and languages used in information systems applications, interoperability approaches must also evolve.

In applications developed using traditional database technology, there have been two primary sources of heterogeneity. One of these is the need or desire to code different components of an application in different programming languages. The other is the need or desire to make use of two or more different databases in a single application. These have given rise to two corresponding classes of interoperability problems, which we refer to as the *multilingual access* problem and the *multiple database integration* problem.

One of the important extensions to database technology that has appeared during the last decade has been the introduction of persistent object systems (POS). By virtually eliminating impedance mismatch, POS technology can be viewed as a significant evolution of the underlying models and languages used in information systems applications and hence has many ramifications. Among these are new possibilities for heterogeneity and concomitant new interoperability problems, which necessitate the evolutionary development of new interoperability approaches. In particular, a given object-oriented database (OODB) may contain data objects originally defined, created and persistently stored using the capabilities provided by several distinct programming languages. We call such a database *polylingual*. This novel kind of heterogeneity induces new interoperability problems, such as the possibility that an application may need to uniformly process the data objects in a polylingual OODB. We term this interoperability problem the *polylingual access* problem. Existing interoperability approaches provide little or no support for polylingual access, so new approaches must evolve to provide such support.

While many of today's OODBs support multiple programming language interfaces (e.g., ObjectStore [LLOW91], GemStone [BOS91]), none provide transparent polylingual access to persistent data. Instead, present day interoperability mechanisms generally rely on external data definition languages (such as ODMG's ODL [Cat93] or CORBA's IDL [OMG92]), thus reintroducing impedance mismatch and forcing developers to anticipate heterogeneity in their applications, or depend upon direct use of such low-level constructs as the foreign language interface mechanisms provided in individual programming languages. In addition, many current approaches require that all the data in a polylingual database be stored using a single common representation, and thus force a substantial amount of data translation to precede their use. Others, while avoiding data translation through the use of so-called "wrapper" techniques, often support only a subset of the manipulations that would be available if the data were accessed from its native language. Because they impose significant additional burdens or restrictions on application developers, we consider such approaches *painful*. More detailed comparisons to alternative approaches can be found in [Kap96, BKW96].

In this paper we focus on the polylingual access problem for object-oriented databases. We begin by discussing heterogeneity and interoperability in OODBs, introducing an example that illustrates various interoperability and heterogeneity issues and identifying some important facets of OODB interoperability problems, particularly the polylingual access problem. We then describe POLYSPIN, a framework supporting **persistence**, **interoperability** and **naming** for **poly**lingual object-oriented databases, and its current realization as extensions to the TI/Arpa Open Object-Oriented Database [WBT92]. In addition, we show how POLYSPIN can facilitate aspects of interoperability in polylingual object-oriented databases, returning to our earlier example to illustrate POLYSPIN's capabilities. We believe that POLYSPIN represents an initial step toward *painless* polylingual persistence.

2   OODB Heterogeneity and Interoperability: An Example

As a simple illustration of heterogeneity and interoperability problems in object-oriented databases, consider the following example:

> At Hypothetical University, two colleges have independently developed information systems applications, using object-oriented database technology, for managing personnel information regarding their students and faculty. Although both colleges have in fact utilized the same OODB, the Arts College has built their application on a CLOS API while the Sciences College has built theirs on a C++ API. Figure 1 shows a portion of the C++ schema used by the Sciences College, a portion of the CLOS schema used by the Arts College, and the OODB containing instances of the personnel data object from both colleges implemented in their respective languages.
>
> The central administration at Hypo U would like to develop some applications making use of personnel information from both colleges. Naturally, they cannot hope to convince either college to translate its personnel information to a representation corresponding to the other's API. Nor can they expect to

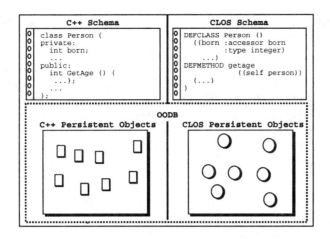

Figure 1: OODB Used By Hypothetical University

convince other colleges, when they develop their own personnel information systems in the future, not to use the API of their choosing (e.g., Ada 95 for the Engineering College, Object-Oriented COBOL for the Business College, etc.). Hence the administrators would like their application to be able to be oblivious to the implementation languages of individual persistent objects. They would also like to be able to employ either navigational access or associative access in processing the personnel information from the various colleges. An example of an OQL-style query (based on [Ins93]) that might be part of a C++ application, in this case seeking candidates for early retirement incentives, is shown in Figure 2. Note that the query should be able to be applied to *all* the personnel data residing in the OODB, i.e., independent of the language used to create the persistent objects.

```
setPerson = ...; // contains Person objects
Set<Person*> result = NULL;
Query {
   result = SELECT *
          FROM Person* matched IN setPerson
          WHERE matched->GetAge() > 45;
}
```

Figure 2: OQL-style Query

Despite the fact that the two college's personnel information schemas are clearly equivalent, existing OODBs, even those such as the TI/Arpa Open OODB that provide multiple APIs, do not support the kind of polylingual access desired by the Hypo U administrators. Several aspects of current OODB technology stand in the way of polylingual access. In the next section, we briefly discuss interoperability goals and issues in general. Later sections then indicate how these goals and issues are addressed in our POLYSPIN approach.

3 OODB Heterogeneity and Interoperability: Goals and Issues

Our work on interoperability is, and for several years [WWRT91] has been, motivated by a primary concern for the impact of an interoperability approach on applications developers. In our view, among the most important objectives for any approach to interoperability are the following:

- Developers should have maximum freedom to define types of objects that their programs manipulate. In particular, they should always be able to use the type systems provided by the language(s) in which they are designing and developing components of their applications.

- Whether a data object is to be shared among an application's components should have minimal impact on the components' developers. In particular, making (or changing) a decision about whether, or with what other components, a data object may be shared should not affect the definition of, or interface to, the object. As a corollary, interoperation should not result in an unnecessary reduction in the ways in which the (now shared) data objects can be manipulated.

Given these objectives, we have noted three major sets of issues regarding interoperability in OODB-based applications. Briefly, these are:

Naming How are objects in the persistent store accessed by applications that wish to interoperate through sharing those objects? Current OODBs typically rely on distinct and often incompatible name management mechanisms for each of the programming languages or application programming interfaces (APIs) they support. This results in disjoint persistent stores segregated according to the language used to define the persistent objects and also leads to inconsistent semantics for the name management capabilities provided by the various language interfaces.

Timing When is the decision to share data objects among an application's components made? This question has a dramatic impact on the suitability of different approaches to interoperability. Three distinct timing scenarios for interoperability decisions can be characterized by the relationship among the relative times at which the sharing or shared components are developed and the decision to share them is made, as illustrated in Figure 3. The salient features of each scenario are:

- **Easiest case:** The decision to share is made before any components are developed. In this case, a common (e.g., IDL) description of the shared data objects can be created prior to development of the components that will share them, language-specific descriptions can be directly created by mapping from the common description, and hence determination of type compatibility is trivial.

- **Common case:** The decision to share is made after one of the sharing components is developed but before any others are. In this case, a common (e.g., IDL) description of the shared data objects can be created by mapping from the language-specific description whose existence predates the sharing decision and then the remaining language-specific descriptions can be directly created by mapping from the common description, so determination of type compatibility is again trivial.

- **Megaprogramming:** The decision to share is made after the sharing components are developed. In this case, common (e.g., IDL) descriptions of the shared data objects can be created by mapping from each of the language-specific descriptions, but determination of type compatibility will then depend upon some kind of comparison of these synthesized descriptions and hence is nontrivial.

Typing How do developers determine whether the types of objects that they wish to share are of compatible types? For object-oriented database technology, most approaches to addressing this question have been based on use of a unifying type model [WWRT91], such as the ODMG ODL. While such approaches may suffice for the easiest and common interoperability scenarios, however, they are inadequate for the megaprogramming case. Since, as our example scenario suggests, that case is perhaps the most important and offers the greatest potential rewards, we have focused our research efforts on attempting to handle it.

4   PolySPIN

POLYSPIN is a generic, object-oriented framework that unifies persistence and interoperability capabilities in OODBs from a name management-based perspective.[1] POLYSPIN, in particular, provides a uniform name management mechanism that not only offers application developers a library of useful abstractions for organizing and

---

[1]Name management is the means by which a computing system allows names to be established for objects, permits objects to accessed using names, and controls the meaning and availability of names at any point in time in a particular computation [Kap96].

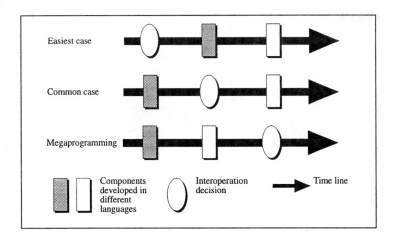

Figure 3: Interoperability Scenarios

navigating object-oriented databases but, as a byproduct, offers an interoperability mechanism providing transparent polylingual access to persistent objects, thus allowing applications to manipulate objects as though they were all implemented in the language of the application. In this section, we begin by briefly describing POLYSPIN's approach to name management. Next, we show how an application developer would use POLYSPIN to enable interoperability in an OODB. The section concludes with a discussion of the internal features of POLYSPIN. Throughout this section, we will refer to the scenario presented in Section 2 as a means of explicating various aspects of POLYSPIN. All the POLYSPIN features described in this section have been implemented as extensions to the TI/Arpa Open Object-Oriented Database [WBT92], using Sun C++ and the Lucid Common Lisp Object System (CLOS).

4.1 Name Management and Persistence in PolySPIN

While the benefits of orthogonal persistence capabilities offered by OODBs are widely known, relatively little attention has been to paid to how persistent objects should be organized (from an application's perspective) in an OODB. Typically provided by a name management mechanism, existing approaches in OODBs can be characterized as being relatively *ad hoc* and weak [KW93]. POLYSPIN addresses these various shortcomings by providing a uniform, flexible and powerful approach to name management. Although the details of its interface are beyond the scope of this paper, the name management mechanism in POLYSPIN allows names to be assigned to objects in binding spaces (where binding spaces are collections of name-object pairs) and names for objects to be resolved in contexts (where contexts are constructed from existing binding spaces) [KW94]. In addition, binding spaces may be assigned names, resulting in the ability to hierarchically organize the name space for objects (similar to directory structures found in almost all modern file systems). Coupled with the persistent store, this approach results in a name-based persistence mechanism where any object (including those in its transitive closure) bound to a name in a binding space reachable from a specially designated root binding space automatically persists. The approach is based on Galileo [ACO85] and Napier [MBC+93], where *environments* correspond to binding spaces. The name management mechanism in POLYSPIN is more general, however, since it supports objects defined in multiple languages.

To participate in this mechanism, an object's class definition must inherit from a common base class, designated the NameableObject class. By inheriting from this class, instances of the subclass can be, among other things, named and resolved using the operations supported by the various abstractions that make up the POLYSPIN name management mechanism. For example, Figure 4 shows a (partial) C++ definition for a Person class, a code fragment showing how a name might be assigned to an instance of Person, and a portion of a persistent store organization based on this approach.

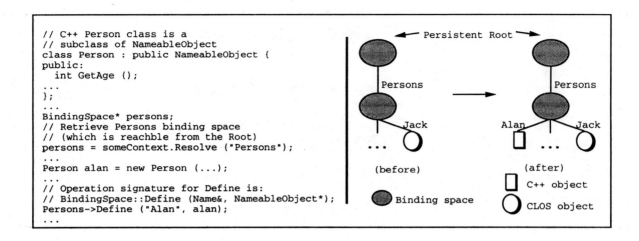

```
// C++ Person class is a
// subclass of NameableObject
class Person : public NameableObject {
public:
   int GetAge ();
...
};
...
BindingSpace* persons;
// Retrieve Persons binding space
// (which is reachble from the Root)
persons = someContext.Resolve ("Persons");
...
Person alan = new Person (...);
...
// Operation signature for Define is:
// BindingSpace::Define (Name&, NameableObject*);
Persons->Define ("Alan", alan);
...
```

Figure 4: Using PolySPIN's Name Management Mechanism

4.2 Name Management and Interoperability

As suggested above, having a class inherit from NameableObject could, and frequently might, be done quite independently of any intention to make objects interoperate. Inheriting from NameableObject does, however, also enable the use of the interoperability capabilities of POLYSPIN. First, having a uniform name management mechanism in place results in a language-independent method of establishing visibility paths to persistent objects (i.e., via their assigned names), regardless of the defining language of either the objects or the applications. Second, the name management mechanism serves as a useful place for capturing and recording language-specific information about objects, which can be used to support polylingual access. In particular, once an application has established an initial connection to a persistent object (via its name), the name management mechanism can provide the necessary information permitting the application to create a data path to an object. In other words, when resolving a name of some object (on behalf of some application), the name management mechanism can detect the defining language of the object and initiate the necessary communication medium for manipulating the object. The features supporting this capability are hidden from application developers within the internals of the POLYSPIN architecture, which are discussed in Section 4.3.

Given this interoperability mechanism, what is needed to achieve polylingual access is the ability to determine whether two class interfaces defined in different languages can indeed interoperate, and in the event they can, to instrument their implementations (including generating any necessary foreign function interface code) such that the interoperability features of POLYSPIN can be employed. As a step toward automating this process, we have developed a tool called POLYSPINNER. (A more detailed description of POLYSPINNER can be found in [BKW96].) The overall objective of POLYSPINNER is to provide transparent polylingual access to objects with minimal programmer intervention as well as minimal re-engineering of existing source code. The current prototype uses an *exact signature matching* rule [ZW95] in determining the compatibility between C++ and CLOS classes. It also encapsulates the foreign function interface mechanism for both Sun C++ and Lucid CLOS, as well as the various internal features of POLYSPIN. (Future versions of our approach can be generalized by replacing the exact signature matching rule with more relaxed and flexible ones [BKW96].)

To help illustrate how an application developer might use POLYSPINNER, we return to the scenario presented in Section 2. In this example, the OODB contains instances of a Person class, where some of the instances have been developed in C++ and others have been developed in CLOS. To take advantage of the naming facilities offered by POLYSPIN, we further assume that the original class definitions for each class already inherit from the NameableObject class, as defined in their respective languages. Thus, prior to any decision to interoperate, the objects resident in the OODB might be organized as shown in the left hand portion of Figure 5. In this scenario, the central administration at Hypo U wished to develop an application supporting queries of the kind shown in the right hand portion of Figure 5.[2] Specifically, the C++ OQL-style query shown here is embedded in a fragment accessing

---

[2]Although a query is given in this example, an update could be applied to the objects in a similar manner.

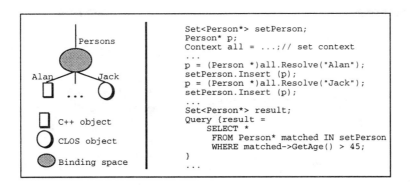

```
                          Set<Person*> setPerson;
         Persons          Person* p;
                          Context all = ...;// set context
                          ...
   Alan        Jack       p = (Person *)all.Resolve("Alan");
                          setPerson.Insert (p);
                          p = (Person *)all.Resolve("Jack");
                          setPerson.Insert (p);
                          ...
    C++ object            Set<Person*> result;
                          Query (result =
    CLOS object               SELECT *
                                FROM Person* matched IN setPerson
    Binding space               WHERE matched->GetAge() > 45;
                          }
                          ...
```

Figure 5: PolySPIN-based OODB

both the C++- and CLOS-defined objects and performing the desired query. Note that the implementation of each object is completely transparent to the C++ OQL-style query. That is, from the application's perspective both objects are instances of the C++ Person class, even though one is obviously implemented as a CLOS object. To accomplish this, the application developer would take the following steps:

1. Apply POLYSPINNER to the interfaces and implementations of both the C++ and CLOS Person classes. For example, Figure 6 shows the class definitions for the C++ and CLOS Person classes, where the plain face type represents the original source code and the boldface type represents the code generated by POLYSPINNER.

   (a) POLYSPINNER first determines whether or not the two Person classes are compatible by comparing the class interfaces. Using an exact match rule, it should be clear that the C++ and CLOS class interfaces shown in Figure 6 are compatible with one another.

   (b) Since the C++ and CLOS Person classes are deemed compatible, the tool next generates foreign function interface code corresponding to each of the operations associated with each of the classes. This permits calls from C++ to CLOS and vice versa. For example, foreign function interfaces corresponding to each of the "GetAge" operations provided by each of the classes must be generated.

   (c) The tool also modifies the implementations of each of the operations defined by a class. The modifications essentially wrap each operation with switching logic that determines the language in which an object is actually implemented and makes the callout to the code generated in the previous step, if need be. For example, if the C++ application invokes the "GetAge" operation on what is in reality a CLOS object, the CLOS "GetAge" operation should be invoked; otherwise the original C++ code implementing the C++ "GetAge" operation should be executed.

2. Re-compile the modified class (method) implementations and the generated source code.

3. Re-link the application.

As should be evident, neither the class interfaces nor the persistent data are modified by the POLYSPINNER tool. Only the class implementations must be re-compiled, along with the generated source code. In addition, the original application remains unchanged, although it must be re-linked to accommodate the changes made to the class implementations. Note that, in Figure 6, some of the POLYSPINNER generated code contains references to *CIDs* and *TIDs*. (We describe CIDs and TIDs more completely in Section 4.3.1.) Although transparent to applications, these abstractions enable polylingual access in POLYSPIN. In the remainder of this section, we describe these and other internals of POLYSPIN that enable polylingual access.

4.3 The Internal Features of PolySPIN

The fact that objects themselves may be implemented in different languages is completely hidden within POLY-SPIN's name management mechanism. To support this level of transparency in applications, the POLYSPIN framework utilizes the following components:

```
class Person : public NameableObject {        (defclass Person (NameableObject)
private:                                          ((born :accessor born
  int born;                                               :type Date
public:                                                   :initform "MM/DD/YY")
  int GetAge ();                                  )
};                                              )
// GetAge member function                       ;; GetAge method
int Person::GetAge () {                          (defmethod GetAge ((this Person))
  if (this->language == CLOS)                      (declare (return-values Integer))
    return                                         (cond  ( (EQUAL (language this) CLOS)
       (__Callout_CLOS_Person_GetAge(this->tidForObject));            (- Today (born this))
  else {                                                  ( (EQUAL (language this) C++)
    int result;                                            (__Callout_CPP_Person_GetAge (tid this)))
    result = 1995 - born;                           )
    return (result);                             );; Callout C++ Person GetAge
  }                                              (DEF-ALIEN-ROUTINE (" __Callout_CPP_Person_GetAge"
}                                                             __POLYSPIN_CPP_Person_GetAge)
// Callout CLOS Person GetAge                      int   (self TID )
extern "C" int __Callout_CLOS_Person_GetAge (TID this);   )
// Callout from CLOS into C++                     ;; Callout from C++ into CLOS
extern "C" int __Callout_CPP_Person_GetAge (TID self ) {   (DEF-FOREIGN-CALLABLE
  Person* object = (Person *) TidToCid (self);             (__Callout_CLOS_Person_GetAge
  return (object->GetAge());                                 (:language :c) (:return-type int))
}                                                           ( ( this TID) )
                                                    (GetAge  (tid-to-cid this))
                                                  )

              C++ Person Class                             CLOS Person Class
```

Figure 6: Results of Applying PolySPINner

- A three-level object identifier hierarchy.

- A common base class encapsulating language-specific information for transient objects.

- A universal object representation encapsulating language-specific information for persistent objects.

As we illustrate in the remainder of this section, these abstractions, together with their interactions with one another, form a suitable foundation for providing transparent polylingual access.

4.3.1 The Object Identifier Hierarchy

A common solution to the interoperability problem involves converting between data representation formats. For example, to achieve interoperability in the scenario described earlier, it might be possible to simply translate C++ Person objects into CLOS objects (and vice versa). Unfortunately, even when hidden from users and applications, such techniques can be prone to error and computationally expensive, especially for large and complex objects.

An alternative approach involves utilizing object references (or L-values) for identifying objects. This solution has the obvious benefits in terms of efficiency and maintainability. One drawback, however, is that different programming languages use distinct and incompatible object reference mechanisms. For example, native references to objects in C++ can not be interchanged with references to CLOS objects (and vice versa). Instead, a distinct mechanism must be used in a CLOS application to identify a C++ object. Languages supporting garbage collection (e.g., CLOS) present further complications since the value of an object identifier may change over the course of a computation. Although transparent to CLOS applications, garbage collection may cause subsequent accesses by a C++ application using a native CLOS object identifier to result in invalid or dangling references. The addition of persistence yields yet another identifier mechanism that must be managed despite the fact that persistent identifiers are generally hidden from applications. In particular, when an object is designated as being persistent, a persistent identifier is assigned to the object, where the persistent identifier is typically bound to some user-level name. When the object is retrieved from the database, the persistent identifier is first used to locate the object. A reference (i.e., an L-value) must then be created for the object so that the application can access and manipulate the object.

As a step toward relieving application developers from managing separate object identifier mechanisms or building special-purpose ones, the POLYSPIN framework maintains a three-level identifier hierarchy, as shown in Figure 7. The hierarchy, in order of increasing lifetime, consists of:

18

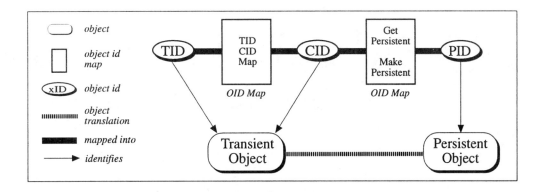

Figure 7: PolySPIN's Three Levels of Identifiers

- A *computation identifier* (or CID), which is an L-value or reference used by applications for identifying, accessing and manipulating objects defined in the same language. A CID for a particular object may change over the the course of a computation, although such changes are intended to be invisible to programmers. An object's (virtual) memory address is an example of a CID.

- A *transient identifier* (or TID), which is an active-computation-unique identifier for an object. Once assigned during some active computation, it is assumed that a TID does not change over the course of that computation's lifetime.

- A *persistent identifier* (or PID), which is a globally unique identifier for a persistent object. When an object is made persistent, a PID is assigned to the object. A PID is assumed to be immutable over the course of the object's lifetime.

In addition, for each language, POLYSPIN provides two-way TID↔CID and CID↔PID mapping mechanisms, where the former map can be implemented using a traditional hash table, and the latter map is often supplied by the underlying persistence mechanism provided by the OODB. POLYSPIN's maintenance of these identifiers, along with functions for mapping between them, means that applications can simply use CIDs to manipulate objects. Any required identifier translations are handled by POLYSPIN. For example, when an application retrieves an object from the persistent store (i.e., via name resolution), a CID identifying the object is returned to the application. As we will show in the following sections, the CID points to an object that, from the application's point of view, looks and behaves as if the object were defined in the same language as the application.

4.3.2 The NameableObject Class

As noted earlier, inheriting from the NameableObject class offers applications developers the ability to use POLY-SPIN's improved name management mechanism. At the same time, the NameableObject class encapsulates various language-specific information for an object including a defining language, a TID, and various type-related information. As shown in Figure 8, values for this information can be computed when an object (derived from NameableObject) is instantiated. For example, the constructors for the C++ Person and NameableObject classes in Figure 8 illustrate how this information is computed and recorded. (The same information is computed in an analogous fashion for CLOS.)

When an operation is invoked on an object, the data maintained by the NameableObject can be used to determine the actual implementation of an object. Since this is hidden from users, however, all instances of the class can be viewed and accessed through a single language interface, even though various instances may in fact be implemented in various languages. Returning to the C++ and CLOS classes shown in Figure 6, the "GetAge" operation for the C++ Person class first checks the value of the defining language for the object. If the object is implemented in C++, then the C++ implementation of the "GetAge" operation is used. If, on the other hand,

```
// NameableObject class
class NameableObject {
private:
  LanguageId language;
  TID tidForObject;
  ClassId classInfo;
public:
// Constructor for NameableObject
  NameableObject() {
    language = C++;
    tidForObject = CidToTid (this);
    ...
  }
// Constructor for Person class
Person::Person () {
// Implictly invokes NameableObject
// Then set type information
  classInfo = "Person";
  ...
}
```

Figure 8: The NameableObject Class

the object is implemented in CLOS, then the corresponding CLOS operation must be invoked (on the CLOS object). This involves making a call-out to a CLOS function (in this example, using the foreign function interface mechanisms of C++ and CLOS) and passing the CLOS object's TID and a value for the increment parameter. On the CLOS side, the TID is first mapped into its CID value and then the actual CLOS "GetAge" operation is invoked.

4.3.3 The Universal Object Representation

POLYSPIN unifies the persistent store by permitting the co-existence of objects implemented in different languages. Furthermore, access to the persistent store is provided by a name management mechanism that is uniformly available across multiple programming languages. To support polylingual access to persistent objects, POLYSPIN introduces a level of indirection in bindings between names and (persistent) objects called a universal object representation or UOR.

Like the NameableObject class, a UOR encapsulates various language-specific information about objects, including an object's PID. A UOR is created for an object when that object is assigned a name. In particular, the information stored by the NameableObject is transferred to the UOR. If the object is later designated as being persistent (as described above), then a value for the object's PID is also set in the UOR. Later, when the object is accessed (by resolving the name of the object), the name management mechanism can use the information stored in the UOR to return an appropriate object to the application.

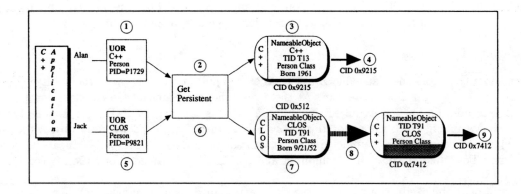

Figure 9: Accessing Objects Via UORs

For example, Figure 9 shows the various tasks POLYSPIN performs on behalf of a C++ application accessing two instances of the Person class, where one object, bound to the name "Alan," is implemented in C++ and the other, bound to the name "Jack," is implemented in CLOS. When the object named "Alan" is accessed, POLYSPIN examines the UOR for the object (1), determining the object's defining language and its PID. Based on this information, the object is retrieved from the store (2) and a transient, C++ version is constructed (3). Since the language of the application and the language of the object are the same, the object (i.e., its CID) is simply returned to the application (4). When the object named "Jack" is accessed, POLYSPIN again examines the UOR for the object (5), determining the object's defining language and its PID. Based on the information, the object is retrieved from the store (6) and a transient, CLOS version is constructed (7). Since the language of the application and the language of the object are in this case different, POLYSPIN creates a C++ Person object (8), which acts as a "surrogate" for its corresponding CLOS version. The surrogate's defining language is set to "CLOS" and its TID is set to the TID of the CLOS object. The rest of the data associated with the C++ Person surrogate is simply ignored (as indicated by the shaded portion of the surrogate object in the figure). Finally, the CID of the surrogate is returned to the application (9).

Subsequent accesses to both objects will (eventually) invoke the implementing object (as described in Section 4.3.2). For example, the query shown in Figure 5 calls the "GetAge" operation for both objects. As shown in Figure 6, for the object named "Alan," the original C++ "GetAge" operation is called, while for the object named "Jack," the CLOS "GetAge" operation is invoked. Thus, the query is able to access and process both objects, despite the fact that one object is implemented in C++ and the other in CLOS.

5 Conclusion

In this paper, we have described a new class of interoperability problem for OODBs, namely the polylingual access problem. We have also described POLYSPIN, an approach supporting persistence, interoperability and naming in OODBs, and we have shown how POLYSPIN can be used to painlessly overcome the polylingual access problem in OODBs. We have briefly described POLYSPINNER, a tool to help automate the use of POLYSPIN and illustrated its capabilities using a simple, but representative, example of a polylingual OODB application. Finally, we have discussed how our approach has been realized in a prototype implementation of POLYSPIN and POLYSPINNER supporting polylingual access between C++ and CLOS, built as an extension to the TI/Arpa Open OODB.

We believe the work reported in this paper represents an important extension to object-oriented database technology. While modern OODBs often provide multiple language interfaces, interoperating among the various languages can be a painful (i.e., cumbersome and complex) process, thus limiting their overall potential. POLYSPIN provides transparent, polylingual access to objects (of compatible types), even though the objects may have been created using different programming languages. Thus, application developers are free to work in their native languages without precluding the possibility of interoperating with foreign language objects or applications.

References

[ACO85]   Antonio Albano, Luca Cardelli, and Renzo Orsini. Galileo: A strong-typed, interactive conceptual language. *ACM Transactions on Database Systems*, 10(2):230–260, June 1985.

[BKW96]   Daniel J. Barrett, Alan Kaplan, and Jack C. Wileden. Automated support for seamless interoperability in polylingual software systems. In *The Fourth Symposium on the Foundations of Software Engineering*, San Francisco, CA, October 1996. (to appear).

[BOS91]   Paul Butterworth, Allen Otis, and Jacob Stein. The GemStone object database management system. *Communications of the ACM*, 34(10):64–77, October 1991.

[Cat93]   R. Cattell. *The Object Database Standard: ODMG-93*. Morgan Kaufmann Publishers, 1993.

[Ins93]   Texas Instruments. *Open OODB Query Language User Manual*. Texas Instruments, Inc., Dallas, TX, release 0.2 (alpha) edition, 1993.

[Kap96]   Alan Kaplan. *Name Management: Models, Mechanisms and Applications*. PhD thesis, University of Massachusetts, Amherst, MA, May 1996.

[KW93]   Alan Kaplan and Jack C. Wileden. Name management and object technology for advanced software. In *International Symposium on Object Technologies for Advanced Software*, number 742 in Lecture Notes in Computer Science, pages 371–392, Kanazawa, Japan, November 1993.

[KW94]   Alan Kaplan and Jack Wileden. Conch: Experimenting with enhanced name management for persistent object systems. In *Sixth International Workshop on Persistent Object Systems*, Tarascon, Provence, France, September 1994.

[LLOW91] Charles Lamb, Gordon Landis, Jack Orenstein, and Dan Weinreb. The ObjectStore database system. *Communications of the ACM*, 34(10):50–63, October 1991.

[MBC+93] Ronald Morrison, Fred Brown, Richard Connor, Quintin Cutts, Al Dearle, Graham Kirby, and Dave Munro. *The Napier88 Reference Manual (Release 2.0)*. University of St. Andrews, November 1993. (CS/93/15).

[OMG92]   OMG. Object management architecture guide, revision 2.0. OMG TC Document 92.11.1, Object Management Group, Framingham, MA, September 1992.

[WBT92]   David L. Wells, Jose A. Blakely, and Craig W. Thompson. Architecture of an open object-oriented management system. *IEEE Computer*, 25(10):74–82, October 1992.

[WWRT91] Jack C. Wileden, Alexander L. Wolf, William R. Rosenblatt, and Peri L. Tarr. Specification level interoperability. *Communications of the ACM*, 34(5):73–87, May 1991.

[ZW95]   Amy M. Zaremski and Jeannette M. Wing. Signature matching, a tool for using software libraries. *ACM Transactions on Software Engineering and Methodology*, 4(2), April 1995.

Operating System Support for Inter-Domain Type Checking

Alex Farkas, Alan Dearle and David Hulse

Department of Computing Science
University of Stirling
Stirling, FK9 4LA
Scotland

{alex,al,dave}@cs.stir.ac.uk

Abstract

Most existing file based operating systems tend to provide very little in the way of type related information about applications to the user. Instead, the user is required to construct applications that perform their own type checking, relying on information about existing programs and data to be obtained via other means, such as manual pages, or by visual inspection of source code. This lack of public type related information has, by and large, prevented the benefits of browsing technology as found in some persistent language systems to be delivered to the operating system level. A technique is examined in which detailed type information about operating system entities may be recorded, thus enabling more informative user interfaces, tools and applications to be constructed.

1. Introduction

The development of persistent systems has sparked the emergence of a variety of new programming techniques and tools. In particular, persistent store browsers [4,7,8,14] have been developed which permit users to discover the types of values contained in a persistent store, and the structure of values with respect to each other. In systems such as the Aberdeen programming environment [8] for Napier88 [17], the browser enables a user to quickly locate and execute programs in a persistent store without prior knowledge of the location of the data, programs or their interfaces. This is achieved by displaying graphical representations of the discovered values and their types. Using this information the programmer may manipulate data, invoke discovered programs, or construct new programs that use the browsed values in a type correct manner.

Until now, tools such as persistent store browsers have largely been language specific and the benefits of these tools have only been available from within the language environments that supported them. From the perspective of general purpose operating systems, corresponding tools have not been forthcoming due to the lack of type information about programs and data at the operating system level. Some operating systems do provide some of this functionality, for example, a tool called AppleScript [11] has been developed for the Macintosh system which enables applications to be invoked via textual scripts constructed by a programmer. Applications may provide a special interface which enables AppleScript to call functions within the application, such as the print option of a word processor. AppleScript even provides a simple browser which permits an application's AppleScript interface to be interrogated providing the programmer with a list of the permissible operations and their parameters.

However, the AppleScript language is not a general purpose programming language, and its specialised nature prevents it from being used to build complex applications. Furthermore, the interface information is not (readily) available to other applications and must be built separately into each application.

As most existing file based operating systems tend to provide very little in the way of type related information about applications, the user is required to construct applications that perform their own type checking. Information about existing programs and data must be obtained via other means, such as manual pages, or by inspecting source code. This has, by and large, prevented the benefits of browsing technology as found in systems such as Napier88, O_2 or Smalltalk from being delivered to the operating system level. This paper examines a user level architecture that permits detailed type information about operating system entities to be recorded, and later browsed and/or retrieved by the user. This architecture permits more sophisticated browsing and program development tools to be constructed. The operating system used in implementing the architecture described in this paper is the persistent operating system Grasshopper [6]. Section 2 gives an outline of this operating system and introduces the abstractions pertinent to the rest of the paper, as well as the IDL model used to represent types in the architecture. Section 3 describes the architecture, Section 4 examines the *G-shell*, a tool which is built using the architecture, Section 5 discusses some related issues and future work, and Section 6 concludes.

2. Grasshopper

The Grasshopper operating system has been expressly designed to provide support for orthogonal persistence. All entities in Grasshopper are constructed using three basic abstractions: an access and protection abstraction, the *capability* via which all Grasshopper entities are manipulated, an abstraction over all storage known as the *container* and an abstraction over execution known as the *locus*.

In order to operate on any Grasshopper entity, an appropriate capability must be presented. A capability in Grasshopper may be thought of as a pointer to an entity and a set of rights associated with that entity. Grasshopper implements a *segregated capability scheme* therefore all fields are protected from user access and are managed by the Grasshopper kernel [5]. For this reason, loci must refer to capabilities indirectly using a capability reference known as a *CapRef*. Capabilities in Grasshopper contain a number of different fields related to protection, however the conceptual view shown in Figure 1 is sufficient for the discussion in this paper. The system fields define various access rights and identify the entity to which the capability grants access. The user field is uninterpreted by the system and may be used for a variety of purposes; for example it could be used to identify a user or might be used as a tag mechanism in the implementation of a type system.

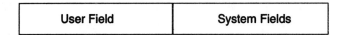

User Field	System Fields

Figure 1: The logical structure of a capability in Grasshopper

Containers are the only storage abstraction provided by Grasshopper and replace the notions of address spaces and file storage found in conventional file based systems. A container is a protected address space which may be used to store both programs and/or data. Containers are used in a variety of ways: as code repositories (like executable files or libraries in Unix), as data repositories (like data files in Unix) or as protected abstract data types containing both code and data and exporting a set of operations that operate on the encapsulated data.

In most operating systems, the notion of an address space is associated with an ephemeral entity, a process, which is the only entity that may access data within that address space. By contrast, Grasshopper containers and loci are orthogonal concepts: the longevity of containers and loci are independent of each other, containers may or may not have (multiple) loci executing within them and loci may migrate between different containers. A locus always executes in the context of some container, its *host container*, and when an address is generated by a locus it is always interpreted relative to its host container.

Grasshopper provides two facilities that allow the transfer of data between containers: *mapping* and *invocation*. Container mapping allows data in a region of one container to be viewed within a region of another container. Unlike the memory mapping mechanisms provided by other systems [1,2,22] containers may be arbitrarily (possibly recursively) composed providing considerably enhanced flexibility and performance [15].

Invocation is the process whereby a locus moves between containers. During invocation, a locus may supply a parameter block which contains data to be used in the destination container. There is no distinguished format for the data in the parameter block and it may be interpreted arbitrarily by the destination code. Typically a collection of data structures are marshalled into the parameter block and unmarshalled in the destination container.

All containers in Grasshopper possess a single entry point known as an *invocation point*. When a locus invokes a container, it begins executing code at this point. Since it is the invoked container that provides the code to be executed, it controls the execution of the invoking locus. Combined with the capability protection mechanism this allows hardware protected ADTs to be constructed [15].

2.1 Containers as ADTs

In Grasshopper, containers are commonly used to implement abstract data types exporting an arbitrary set of operations that operate on an encapsulated state; this is illustrated in Figure 2.

Client applications may access the container via the set of exported operations. However, as described earlier, a basic Grasshopper container only supports a single entry point at which execution commences if the container is invoked by a locus. This means that whenever a locus enters a container it always enters at the same location; whilst this enables the low level implementation to be lightweight and secure, it does not provide a direct method for enabling a collection of operations to be exported by a container.

Consequently, the following convention has been established to enable an invoking locus to specify more precisely a wider variety of container access points. Each invoking locus may carry with it a value called an *operation number*. Upon a locus's arrival in the destination container, the code at the invocation point examines the locus's requested operation number and branches execution to the appropriate section of code within the container. Thus, via an arbitrary set of operation numbers, a container may effectively export any number of operations. This is illustrated in Figure 3.

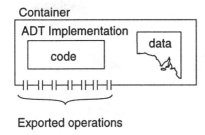

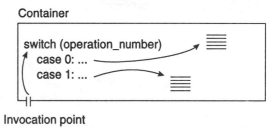

Figure 2: Conceptual view of an ADT implemented by a container.

Figure 3: Exporting multiple operations via the operation number convention.

The main difficulty of programming with the basic Grasshopper abstractions as described above is that considerable effort is required on the part of the programmer in implementing containers and clients; typically, a client program must marshall the relevant data to be sent to a destination container, establish the correct operation number value, and apply a system level operation to cause the locus to invoke the destination container. Similarly, the code in a destination container must inspect the incoming locus's operation number, unmarshall the parameters, and branch to the relevant piece of code.

Such code may be generated automatically by a tool, provided that a specification of the container interface is available. In our system, the interface definition language, IDL [19] is used to specify container interfaces in a machine and language independent manner. IDL is the interface definition language specified in the CORBA standard [18], and may be used to generate the following components for any given container interface definition:

°   code generated for use within a destination container,

•   client code which may be used to invoke a container, and

•   a structured representation of the container interface.

The first of these assists in the construction of a container supporting a specified interface. The generated interface code contains all the code necessary to unmarshall the parameters of an invoking locus and to transfer execution to the requested operation number. In addition, stub procedures for the various operation numbers are generated, the bodies of these procedures are the only parts of the program which need to be implemented by the programmer.

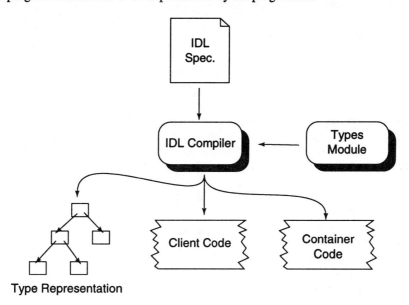

Figure 4: Generating components via the IDL compiler.

25

The second segment of code is intended for use by clients that wish to invoke any container with the given interface. This code may be mapped into a client's address space, allowing the programmer to invoke a container via a single function call, and removing the need for a programmer to implement the complex marshalling code otherwise required. The generated code performs all of the necessary marshalling of data and invoking, as well as the unmarshalling of any data returned.

Finally, a structured representation of an interface is generated which enables tools such as browsers to present information about an interface to the programmer. An independent library of operations for querying and constructing these representations is provided as part of the system, and they are analogous to those described for the Napier88 system in [3]. They are used by the IDL compiler, and may be accessed by any application to examine or manipulate the representations; for brevity, these operations are not described further here. The IDL compilation process is summarised in Figure 4.

The IDL specification technique described above provides an abstraction over the otherwise complex sequence of activities required to construct and use Grasshopper applications. Furthermore, the output from the compiler is made available in the Grasshopper system for use by browsers and other tools.

2.2   Containers as Libraries

In the section above, containers were described as providing a set of operations by which client applications could operate on encapsulated data. However, containers may also serve as data or executable code repositories, the contents of which are accessed via mapping rather than invocation.

As described earlier, a region of one container may be mapped into the address space of another, allowing, for example, a locus to execute code resident in another container. This does not require invoking the container which contains the code or data to be mapped, however the programmer must have knowledge about the internal composition of the container in order to know which regions to map. A somewhat crude solution is simply to document and make public the internal structure of a library, however, there are a number of drawbacks to this approach:

- it requires additional effort on the part of the library constructor,

- the method is open to error, especially if libraries are updated and documentation is not, and

- tools such as browsers or linkers are unable to determine the contents of libraries, making the implementation of such tools difficult.

Like the ADT style containers described above, libraries export a set of operations which may be described using IDL. The difference between these approaches is that generally containers providing an ADT interface are invoked, usually for protection reasons, whereas libraries are invoked by browsers or linkers and their contents mapped. Each library consists of a container containing the executable code, some linkage information describing whence the code may be mapped and an IDL specification of the exported operations.

3.   Name and Type Control

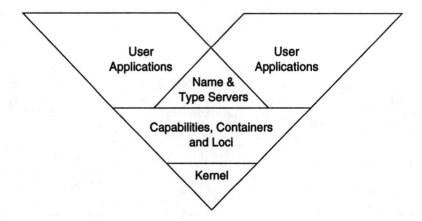

Figure 5: Name and type servers in the Grasshopper architecture.

Two abstractions are provided by Grasshopper to control names and types, namely *name servers* and *type servers*. The first abstraction is called a *name server*, and provides a mapping between textual names and capabilities. Name servers are similar in purpose to directories or folders in file based systems, but have the additional functionality that any number of labelled attributes may be associated with each name server entry. These attributes may be used to store arbitrary information about an entry in the form of integers, booleans, strings and even capabilities for other entities.

The second abstraction is known as a *type server*, and provides a repository for general type related information and executable code. Specifically, type servers store type representations of IDL interface definitions and code which may be used by a client to invoke containers with a given interface. Both name and type servers are intended for use by higher level applications, however they themselves are constructed using Grasshopper containers and capabilities and therefore reside in the domain of Grasshopper applications. This refined architecture is illustrated in Figure 5, which also indicates that in general, applications are not obliged to employ the name or type services.

3.1   Using Name and Type Servers

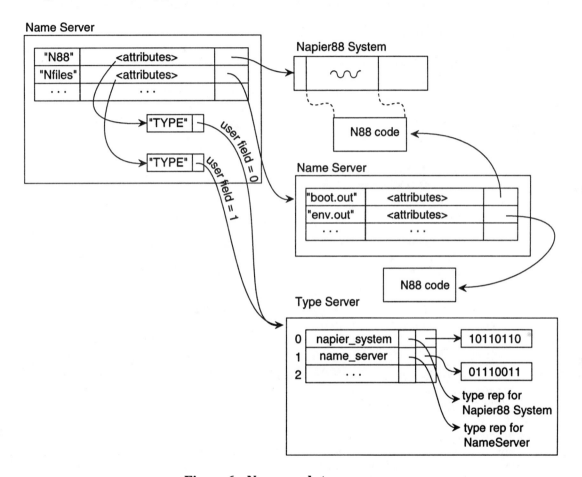

Figure 6: Name and type servers.

In general, name servers and type servers may be treated as independent entities. However, as shown in Figure 6, in Grasshopper they are used in conjunction with each other and permit applications to:

- obtain references to existing entities,

- determine the types of those entities, and

- to access executable client code required to call the entities.

The name server in the top left corner of Figure 6 contains entries for capabilities to two containers: a Napier88 programming system and another name server. These are associated with the names *N88* and *N88files* within the name server. In addition, each entry has been given an associated attribute, *TYPE*, which contains a reference to a type server that stores interface related data and client code appropriate to each container. In this case, each *TYPE* attribute is a capability for the type server shown on the bottom right of Figure 6. Encoded within the user field of each capability is a tag which may be used by the type server to locate the appropriate type representation.

To illustrate, consider the example where a client wishes to run a program using the Napier88 system. Figure 7 shows the IDL specification for the Napier88 container; a simplified representation of this interface type along with the client code are stored in the type server with the tag 0.

```
interface napier_system
{
        Status run_program( in CapRef program );
        Status initialise_store();
};
```

Figure 7: Specification of a Napier88 system interface.

In order to obtain a capability to the Napier88 system, the client performs a lookup operation on the name server with the name *N88*. This operation returns a capability for the Napier88 container with which it may be invoked, but does not provide the client with information about the operations exported by the Napier88 container. To determine the container's interface, the client retrieves the *TYPE* attribute associated with the entry *N88* in the name server. A capability for the type server is returned containing the tag for the *napier_system* entry. With this capability, the client may extract the type representation of the Napier88 system. Finally the client may request that the client code associated with the user field tag be mapped into the client's container, enabling the client to invoke the desired operations of the Napier88 system. As discussed below, this process may be performed at a variety of times.

3.2 Accessing Client Code

The example above has indicated broadly how name and type servers may be used co-operatively. The task of accessing the client code used to invoke a container may generally occur at three different times [9,13]:

1.   Firstly, it is possible for the programmer to interrogate a name and type server during client construction. The interfaces to the various required containers may be discovered, and code constructed to call the correct interface procedures. The client code may be copied from a type server into the client's address space. This process is analogous to static linking in Unix.

2.   The second possibility is similar to the first in that the programmer may interrogate a name and type server during client construction, and construct code to call the correct interface procedures. The client code is mapped into the host application. This may be performed statically when the application is being constructed or dynamically when the program is executed.

3.   The final method is the topic of example in the next section; via this method, the client may be constructed in such a way as to query name and type servers dynamically, and to dynamically construct a call to the appropriate client code.

The first two techniques have counterparts in most other operating system environments and are not discussed further. The third technique, however, is not generally supported at the operating system level, largely due to the fact that insufficient type information is available, thus inhibiting any form of dynamic type checking. Systems such as Multics [20] enable a style of dynamic linking, however no type checking takes place unless programmed explicitly by the programmer. The next section illustrates an application which uses this third technique to provide a dynamically type checked, general purpose user shell for Grasshopper.

4. A Typed Shell for Grasshopper

An example application of the architecture described above is a general purpose command line oriented shell for Grasshopper called G-shell. The G-shell was constructed as a simple user interface to many of the features of Grasshopper, but serves to illustrate how name and type servers may be used. More sophisticated, graphics oriented tools such as those provided by the Napier88 system could be constructed using the same techniques, but this is the topic of future work and is not discussed further.

Associated with each instance of the G-shell is a default name server which, like a home directory, provides a starting point from which other entities may be discovered. The G-shell itself supports a number of built in commands for navigating and manipulating a name server hierarchy, but these are not pertinent to the discussion and are ignored in this paper.

There are two major differences between G-shell and the shells provided by Unix, Macintosh or DOS:

28

1. G-shell is typed,

2. G-shell passes different types of values to applications rather than just strings.

When a Unix shell invokes an application it always passes strings to the application being invoked. Conventionally two parameters are passed to a Unix application *argc*: a count of the number of arguments to the application and *argv*: an array of strings containing the arguments. As a consequence, every application must check that the number of parameters being passed is correct and must decode the strings and reconstruct the appropriate values. During the last operation type checking is performed implicitly, for example the string "z23" cannot be decoded into a decimal integer.

In systems such as Unix, applications often present more than one interface, for example, they may present one interface to the shell and another to the network. Typically the code used to perform interprocess communication with the application will be generated from a specification written in RPCL [16] or some other specification language and will be type checked by programming language compilers. Furthermore, the values that are passed across the network to the application are generally more complex than strings.

In the approach described in this paper we are advocating the use of a single, type checked mechanism for specifying all interfaces to applications. Once such a mechanism has been established, it is natural to provide type checking in the user shell. In addition, it is natural for the shell to supply the application with values drawn from a richer domain than strings. By allowing type checking to be performed dynamically by the G-shell, the intellectual burden on the programmer to perform type checking in each constructed application is reduced.

4.1 Type Checking

We will continue to use the Napier88 example introduced in Section 3.1 to illustrate the techniques. Suppose that a user of G-shell wishes to run the (interpreted) Napier88 program called *boot.out* contained in the name server called *Nfiles*. When the following command is entered at the G-shell prompt, the G-shell performs the actions described below:

    N88.run 'Nfiles/boot.out

The first part of the line describes a command to be executed. In this case the user has specified that the *run* operation contained in the container denoted by *N88* is to be executed. Since the name *N88* does not refer to an intrinsic G-shell command, the name server associated with the shell is inspected to see if an entry with the name *N88* exists. Since it does, the type of the *run* operation must be ascertained in order to type check the invocation. This is achieved by querying the name server to obtain the capability associated with the *TYPE* attribute of the *N88* entry. The type representation for the *N88* interface may be obtained from the type server using this capability. The type of the *run* operation (if any) may be extracted from this type representation using library functions and in this case will yield the following type representation:

    Status run_program(**in** CapRef program)

From this type representation, the expected types of the operation's parameters may be extracted and used to type check the command line arguments. However, before doing so, the actual parameter list is parsed and a list of values and types is constructed. In this example, a single command line argument "'Nfiles/boot.out" has been supplied. The single quote symbol informs the shell to treat the next word (*Nfiles*) as a name and look it up in the current name server. When the shell parses the remainder of this argument and finds the slash symbol it will assume that the name *Nfiles* denotes a name server which it will verify from its *TYPE* attribute. Finally, the name *boot.out* is looked up in the name server denoted by *Nfiles* to yield a *CapRef*. Once the actual parameter list is constructed it may be compared to the expected type of the parameter list found from the IDL specification. In this case the comparison is trivial and the types would be found to match.

4.2 Dynamic Mapping of Invocation Code

As highlighted in the previous section, the code necessary to invoke a container could be constructed statically, and the client code mapped into the client container statically or dynamically and executed. The G-shell follows this course with name servers and type servers. In both cases, the shell knows in advance of the existence of these types and how values of these types are to be used.

However, the G-shell has no knowledge of types such as *napier_system* and must therefore perform all type checking dynamically as described above. Furthermore they do not and cannot contain the code necessary to invoke instances of types such as *napier_system*. For this reason, the final approach described in the previous section is used, in that once the parameters are type checked, the client code is mapped dynamically, the parameters placed onto the run-time call stack, and the mapped code executed.

5 . Discussion and Future Work

5.1 CORBA

The architecture described in this paper conforms to many aspects of CORBA [18]. The most obvious of these is the use of IDL as a specification language. Despite the fact that CORBA uses the active object model and Grasshopper the object-thread model, the way in which communication is effected is similar to CORBA. In CORBA all communication between address spaces is via an Object Request Broker. In Grasshopper this functionality is provided by the Grasshopper kernel. In both systems, the request to communicate with (CORBA) or invoke an object (Grasshopper) is independent of the object's location. This location transparency is also one of the corner-stones of persistent programming. The containers provided by Grasshopper are more powerful than CORBA objects in that, when viewed by a programmer, containers are persistent address spaces.

The name and type servers in our architecture resemble the functionality of instance and interface repositories in CORBA, however, the usage of these entities in our system differs from the CORBA repositories. For example, in our system, name and type servers may be used purely for browsing by a programmer constructing an application. Data or code may be extracted or linked to the final application, freeing it from any further dependence on the servers. This is not supported by the CORBA architecture.

In other ways, our architecture is a subset of the generic CORBA architecture. For example, only a subset of the IDL language (the interface definition part) is required to specify entities in the system. This further allows many of the kinds of tools described in the introduction to be constructed for general purpose use at the operating system level.

CORBA is designed to assist in the construction of distributed, object oriented application systems. Grasshopper benefits from this heritage, for example, a modified version of the Grasshopper IDL compiler may be used on a Unix system to generate a Unix based Grasshopper container interface. This permits Grasshopper services to be directly invoked from Unix application programs

5.2 OMOS

In the architecture described in this paper, name servers provide a mapping between names and implementations (containers), whilst type servers provide a mapping between interface specifications and code to access implementations exporting those interfaces. This system could be extended to enable a user to access multiple implementations of a particular interface depending on a specified set of requirements, as demonstrated by the OMOS system [21]. For example, in Unix, the *malloc* operation dynamically allocates blocks of memory. All applications requiring dynamic memory allocation, regardless of behaviour, use the same implementation of *malloc*, potentially retarding performance by preventing additional optimisation. Using an OMOS style linker, it is possible to request different implementations of *malloc* depending on the required behaviour. For example, one implementation could be optimised for memory intensive applications, and another for low memory usage applications.

In OMOS, a client specifies an interface and a number of desired properties for the implementation, and the linker returns an appropriate implementation. With judicious use of attributes in name and type servers, a similar style of programming could be obtained in our system. For example, multiple libraries could be implemented to support memory management routines optimised for a variety of circumstances. Each implementation could be tagged with a set of attributes denoting information such as garbage collection style, page alignment, whether free lists are used, and so on.

5.3 Hyper-Programming and Browsers

Hyper-programming has been described in various places [9,12,13], and is currently implemented in several Napier88 systems. The essence of hyper-programming is to allow a user to indicate that a program or value in the persistent store should be included directly within the source code of a program; this process is analogous to the way in which entities are linked in systems such as HyperCard [10] or Flex [23].

Using the architecture described in this paper, it is possible to construct language independent hyper-programming tools for Grasshopper. For example, a browser could be constructed to traverse name and type servers and display representations of the types of the stored entities. A simple tool could permit capabilities for discovered entities to be embedded in the source code of programs under construction. A more sophisticated program editor could directly map executable programs and data into the source code of a Grasshopper program under construction permitting the construction time binding of arbitrary program and data fragments. Furthermore, using the mechanisms described in this paper, this could be achieved in a programming language independent manner without the need to change language compilers.

6. Conclusion

The technique described in this paper is based on a number of mechanisms and conventions which have been constructed on top of the Grasshopper operating system. It was decided to incorporate the features as an additional layer on top of the existing abstractions rather than including them as operating systems abstractions in order to retain the flexibility and security offered by the basic operating system.

In the examples throughout this paper, only one type server has been shown associated with a few name servers; however, a running Grasshopper system will typically contain many name and type servers. Name servers are nested to form a hierarchy analogous to the way directories are nested in a file system. However, since capabilities are the only protection mechanism in Grasshopper, rather than a single hierarchy as found in Unix systems, each user is the owner of a hierarchy which may or may not be linked into other hierarchies. This approach lends itself to considerably more flexible and powerful high level protection regimes than is possible in systems such as Unix or NT.

A closer examination of name and type servers as described has revealed a wide range of possible applications for this technology; one consequence of combining a CORBA like approach with OMOS style libraries and linkers is to enable applications to link transparently to code on remote (possibly heterogeneous) systems.

As described in the introduction, the AppleScript system delivers the advantages of published application interfaces to the user. However, applications which do not export an AppleScript interface may not easily be accessed by AppleScript nor any other application. By contrast, all invokable containers in a Grasshopper system support an invocation point and (potentially multiple) operation numbers. These entry points are accessible to any application regardless of whether information about them is published in any form. Furthermore, arbitrary subsets of the operation numbers may be published via different name and type servers, permitting multiple views of containers.

Finally, our scheme provides a suitable platform for constructing a variety of general purpose tools to be constructed that were previously restricted to higher level, language specific environments. It is hoped these tools will provide programmers with more capabilities.

References

1. Cheriton, D. R. "The V Kernel: A Software Base for Distributed Systems", IEEE Software, Vol 1, No 2, pp. 9-42, 1984.

2. Chorus-Systems "Overview of the CHORUS Distributed Operating Systems", *Computer Systems - The Journal of the Usenix Association*, Vol 1, No 4., 1990.

3. Connor, R. C. H. "The Napier Type-Checking Module", Universities of Glasgow and St Andrews, Technical Report PPRR-58-88, 1988.

4. Dearle, A. and Brown, A. L. "Safe Browsing in a Strongly Typed Persistent Environment", *The Computer Journal*, Vol 31, No 6, pp. 540-545, 1988.

5. Dearle, A., di Bona, R., Farrow, J., Henskens, F., Hulse, D., Lindström, A., Norris, S., Rosenberg, J. and Vaughan, F. "Protection in the Grasshopper Operating System", *Proceedings of the 6th International Workshop on Persistent Object Systems*, Tarascon, France, Springer-Verlag, pp. 60-78, 1994.

6. Dearle, A., di Bona, R., Farrow, J., Henskens, F., Lindström, A., Rosenberg, J. and Vaughan, F. "Grasshopper: An Orthogonally Persistent Operating System", *Computer Systems*, vol Summer, pp. 289-312, 1994.

7. Deux, O. et al "The O_2 System", *CACM*, Vol 34, No 10, pp. 34-48, 1991.

8. Farkas, A. "Aberdeen: A Browser allowing Interactive Declarations and Expressions in Napier88", Honours thesis, Computer Science, University of Adelaide, 1991.

9. Farkas, A. M. "Program Construction and Evolution in a Persistent Integrated Programming Environment", Ph.D. thesis, Computer Science, University of Adelaide, 1994.

10. Apple Computer Inc. "HyperCard Reference Manual", 1993.

11. Apple Computer Inc. "AppleScript Reference Manual", 1994.

12. Kirby, G. N. C. "Reflection and Hyper-Programming in Persistent Programming Systems", Ph.D. thesis, Computing Science, St Andrews, 1993.

13. Kirby, G. N. C., Connor, R. C. H., Cutts, Q. I., Dearle, A., Farkas, A. M. and Morrison, R. "Persistent Hyper-Programs", *5th International Workshop on Persistent Object Systems*, San Miniato, *Persistent Object Systems*, Springer-Verlag, Workshops in Computing, pp. 86-106, 1992.

14. Kirby, G. N. C. and Dearle, A. "An Adaptive Graphical Browser for Napier88", University of St Andrews, Technical Report CS/90/16, 1990.

15. Lindstrom, A., Rosenberg, J. and Dearle, A. "The Grand Unified Theory of Address Spaces", *Hot Topics in Operating Systems (HotOS-V)*, Orcas Island, USA, IEEE Press, pp. 66-71, 1995.

16. Sun Microsystems "rpcgen programming guide", Technical Report Revision A, of March 1990.

17. Morrison, R., Brown, A. L., Connor, R. C. H. and Dearle, A. "The Napier88 Reference Manual", University of St Andrews, Technical Report PPRR-77-89, 1989.

18. OMG "The Common Object Request Broker: Architecture and Specification", OMG, Technical Report 91.12.1, 1991.

19. OMG "IDL Syntax and Semantics", *The Common Object Request Broker: Architecture and Specification*, OMG, pp. 45-80, 1991.

20. Organick, E. I. "The Multics System: An Examination of its Structure", MIT Press, Cambridge, Mass., 1972.

21. Orr, D. B. and Mecklenburg, R. W. "OMOS – An Object-Server for Program Execution", *Proc. International Workshop in Object-Orientation in Operarting Systems*, Paris, France, IEEE, pp. 200-209, 1992.

22. Rashid, R., Tevanian, A., Young, M., Golub, D., Baron, R., Black, D., Bolosky, W. and Chew, J. "Machine-Independent Virtual Memory Management for Paged Uniprocessor and Multiprocessor Architectures", *Proceedings of the Second International Conference on Architectural Support for Programming Languages and Operating Systems (ASPLOS II)*, Palo Alto, ACM Press, pp. 31-39, 1987.

23. Stanley, M. "An Evaluation of the Flex Programming Environment", RSRE Malvern, Technical Report 86003, 1986.

Design Issues for Persistent Java[1]: a type-safe, object-oriented, orthogonally persistent system

Atkinson, M.P., Jordan, M.J., Daynès, L. and Spence, S.

Department of Computing Science
University of Glasgow
Glasgow, Scotland, UK
{mpa, laurent, susan}@dcs.gla.ac.uk

Sun Microsystems Laboratories
2550 Garcia Avenue, UMTV29-112
Mountain View, CA, USA
mjj@eng.sun.com

Abstract

The object-oriented programming language Java is receiving much attention and is likely to become a popular commercial programming language because of its regular structure, safety features and modern constructs. It presents a novel opportunity, because of this safety and potential popularity, to make orthogonal persistence defined by reachability widely available. We report on a design for a system that provides such persistence with no changes to the Java language. The design includes ambitious goals for transactional flexibility but also includes simple transactional behaviour sufficient for many applications. We report on several issues that were encountered during the design which as yet have no obvious solution. An outline of the proposed implementation is also given.

1 Introduction

We report on the issues raised when designing the addition and implementation of orthogonal persistence to the Java language. The principles of orthogonal persistence are well known [AM95]. The first orthogonally persistent language, PS–algol [ACC+83] was conceived in order to add persistence to an existing language with minimal perturbation to its initial semantics and implementation. Our efforts to build a persistent system for Java have a similar motivation. Then the primary concern was to show that orthogonal persistence could be achieved at all and that it would have a beneficial impact on programmer productivity. Now we seek to achieve a much *broader set of facilities* in an *industrially supported language* to demonstrate that orthogonal persistence is beneficial for *large commercial programming projects*.

Typically such projects would currently be built from languages such as C and C++ and relational or object-oriented databases. This paper reports the first steps in an experiment to show that construction and maintenance of such persistent application systems (PAS) can be supported very effectively by an orthogonally persistent language.

We will support a general-purpose, orthogonally persistent system for the Java language [GM95, GJS96]. This system is called PJava. We will evaluate PJava by re-coding in PJava a PAS that is already being developed and supported by an OODB [JV95]. This requires a prototype persistent Java-runtime, called $PJava_0$, which will later be superseded by a complete, robust and well-engineered run-time, called $PJava_1$. Measurement of, and experience with, a redeveloped version of the PAS running on $PJava_0$ will provide design data for $PJava_1$.

1.1 Goals for PJava

The design of PJava seeks to provide an orthogonally persistent system that meets the following goals.

1   No loss of safety when utilising persistence and ideally, an increase in consistency.
2   No impact on the performance of programs that do not use persistence; minimum performance penalties and, if possible, performance gains for those that do.
3   Minimal changes to the language.
4   Simple, almost subliminal, use of persistence for many programmers that can be satisfied by a default model of transactions.
5   Sophisticated and precise control of transactional programming for those that require it.

Orthogonal persistence requires that all values, whatever their type or class, should have equal rights to longevity and brevity. Longevity requires adequate mechanisms for recovery after software or media failure and adequate facilities for system evolution. The use of such persistence permits arbitrary data structures to be preserved after one execution and to be re-used in later executions. If these data structures include bindings set up after verifying compliance with Java type rules and other safety mechanisms, then they are available for re-use in the subsequent executions without re-applying the checks. These and

[1] Java is a trademark of Sun Microsystems Inc.

other re-uses of the results of earlier executions may provide performance gains.

Goal 3 has been met in its entirety, as no changes are required to the language definition. New classes are provided and the Java Abstract Machine, JAM, will be modified in order to provide orthogonal persistence and transactional facilities. Goal 4 derives from a desire to make the transition to persistent programming easy. Goal 5 supports expert programmers who may want to satisfy end-users requiring particular forms of transaction, for design work, what-if experiments, CSCW, etc.

1.2   Features of Java Relevant to PJava

The Java language is currently receiving much attention [OSF95]. It therefore provides a golden opportunity to increase the industrial experience of using orthogonal persistence and hence to investigate the feasibility and benefits of orthogonal persistence in a wider range of applications, some of which may be expected to grow larger than the current generation of PASs built commercially. Java is particularly well suited to this because of the care that its designers have taken to make it safe [GJS96]:

- the type system is well defined and rigorously enforced and
- all pointers and all space are managed *implicitly* by the Java abstract machine and never explicitly by the application programmer.

The existence of native methods (which can be written in C) threatens this safety, but they are already excluded from many contexts and they will be kept away from persistent stores. The class loader already performs dynamic binding, necessary to enable new code to access persistent data and code [ABM88] and performs security checks to restrict the code to the required safety levels. This offers safe incremental construction of large PASs.

The type system, which determines the range of values that PJava must support, is a nice combination of simplicity based on regularity and completeness achieved via powerful type constructor rules. The base types are similar to those of C with the exception that booleans are properly differentiated and there are no pointer types. The only constructors are class, interface and array (denoted by []). The class constructor implements single inheritance, and provides for the definition of a set of labelled attributes of the class, which can have any combination of the following properties:

- public, protected, private or package — determining visibility outside the class definition (when no visibility modifier is provided, the default of package protection is assumed — visible to all classes in the same package);
- static or dynamic — determining whether the value is associated with the class or with each instance of the class;
- method or value — determining whether there is code associated with the attribute;
- final — which when present prevents the attribute from being over-ridden, or in the case of static variables, updated;
- base type or constructed type — determining whether *internally* a pointer is used to represent the value or whether it denotes itself;
- synchronized — when present it indicates that other threads should be refused access to the object or class while the attribute given this property is in use; and
- transient — which is defined as a reserved field modifier in the language definition but not allocated a function[2].

Interfaces provide a general mechanism for polymorphism. They define the signature of a set of object attributes. Any class that includes the attributes so defined, irrespective of what other attributes it offers, can then be used in any context that requires that interface type.

An extensive and growing library of classes is available with the existing Java system. Those that have to be treated specially during the implementation of orthogonal persistence (because they are not implemented in Java and perform operations relevant to persistence) are:

- Class — the class of all classes — instances of this class contain the definition of classes and provide access to the method code;
- Thread — the class that represents an independent thread of execution that may run concurrently with other threads;
- Lock — providing explicit locking when the implicit mutex provided by synchronized is insufficient; and
- a variety of classes concerned with IO, screen management, etc.

Other features of Java, such as packages, though relevant to our design and implementation, are not discussed in this paper.

2. Design Issues for PJava

This section presents some of the issues that were encountered during the design of PJava.

2.1 Principles and Desiderata

The three principles already well established for orthogonal persistence [ACC+83, AM95] are naturally re-applied in this context as follows.

The principle of **orthogonality** states that all values whatever their type have equal rights to persistence — longevity or brevity. In this context we need to identify carefully what constitutes all values. Clearly, all the base types and all values in the language constructed over those base types must be included. This naturally includes objects and arrays, and in our design it includes classes and code. JAM treats instances of the class `Class` specially, having special loading rules and different storage arrangements. We argue that instances of this class should be treated identically, for persistence purposes, with those of other classes so that if an object is in the stable store we can guarantee that the code to manipulate it is also available (see 2.3).

Treating classes consistently with other data results in a PJava store being self-contained and self-describing. In particular, there is sufficient information for garbage collection and schema edit. This can be compared with many OODBMS that have incomplete information about their contents; particularly those making C++ persistent which are usually forced to treat the class definitions (schema) and the code separately and specially.

The principle of **persistence independence** states that all code should have the same form irrespective of the longevity of the data on which it acts. This implies, for example, that transfers are not explicitly programmed. The essence of persistence independence is achieved for all PJava code as the semantics of the language does not vary as a consequence of variations in the longevity of data.

The principle of **persistence identification** states that there should be a straightforward and consistent mechanism for determining the longevity of values. In PJava, all values are either object instances or base-type values that are attributes of an object instance (`static` variables behave as attributes of instances of the class `Class`). Identifying persistence therefore reduces to identifying how long each object instance should persist as attributes of those instances will then persist as well. To maintain the pointer and space management safety of Java this has to be based on reachability [AM95]. PJava ensures that objects continue to exist for as long as they are transitively reachable from a distinguished persistent root for each store, an instance of the class `PJavaStore`[3].

Two additional considerations have influenced the overall design:

Safety may not be compromised by the introduction of persistence. It has been pointed out that the safety of Java is an essential foundation for security [OSF95] as well as being invaluable for programmer productivity. Type and pointer safety is not compromised in any way in PJava. This is a natural consequence of applying the principle of persistence independence.

Separation of policy and mechanism is already recognised as desirable in operating system design [RBF+89]. In the operating system context, this is generally achieved by allowing system programmers to supply code that defines policy. Not all application programmers can be expected to provide such code and the finer-grained mechanisms in a programming language implementation would be unacceptably costly if they made frequent referrals to application code. Nevertheless, some policies cannot be predetermined if PJava is to meet its goal of being general purpose. A compromise is achieved by building-in some mechanisms that could have been modifiable (storing classes in the stable store, for example) and allowing application programmer control for other issues, such as re-initialisation after recovery and the form that transactions should take. However, application programmers are not burdened with supplying this code as default policies are provided. Only when the default does not meet an application's needs does an application programmer need to supply policy defining code.

2.2 Stores and Orthogonal Persistence

A PJava program is normally started in conjunction with an existing and populated stable store specified by an environment variable, command-line parameter, default or similar mechanism. In exceptional circumstances, PJava may create a new, empty, stable store and begin to populate it. Certain objects and classes are needed by the implementation of persistence and are consequently in a stable store by default. Every PJava store will contain one object of the class `PJavaStore` and its `Class` instance containing static variables and the code to manipulate the `PJavaStore` object. PJava[0] arranges that this `PJavaStore` object and `Class` instance are accessible to code in the executing PJava program. Other objects and classes are faulted in as needed.

As already mentioned, `PJavaStore` is the root of persistence by reachability in the stable store that contains it. The method `registerPRoot(aName, anObject)` of `PJavaStore` will make `anObject` behave as a persistent root. It can be re-accessed, normally in subsequent executions, by `getPRoot(aName)`. All objects reachable from `anObject` are preserved.

[2.] We ignore the modifier `transient` but we suspect that the designers of Java intend it to indicate fields of an object that are to be set `null` as the object is stabilised or pickled because they can be reconstructed. We could support such semantics and we provide restoration call-backs that could be used for reconstructing derived data labelled in this way.

35

All objects reachable from a result of `getPRoot` will be made accessible by object faulting as data structures are traversed using the standard repertoire of Java operations. This mechanism enables a programmer to make any graph of objects and the values they contain have a lifetime extending beyond the current execution.

Objects are retained as long as they are reachable from `PJavaStore` via at least one registered PRoot. Their life will be terminated if subsequent program executions make them unreachable. This may occur through assignment to objects in the graph replacing one object reference with another or a `null`. It may also occur because the last connection to the `PRoot` index is severed by a call of `discardPRoot(aName)`. Space will eventually be recovered by garbage collection.

Other operations on the persistent roots are available, to test if they exist, to obtain all their names, etc. Further methods associated with `PJavaStore` are described below. Full details of the `PJavaStore` methods and the whole of the PJava system may be found in [ADS96].

2.3 Classes and Code

When an object, `c`, an instance of class `C`, is made persistent it is necessary to ensure that all information that may be needed to operate on `c` that isn't already persistent is simultaneously made to persist. This additional information includes the class C, any super-classes of class C, their methods, any objects reachable from any of their `static` variables and the classes and current values of all the fields of `c` including those derived from `c`'s super-classes.

Thus, *non*-persistent class X will be promoted to the persistent store if:

1. class X is directly referenced from a persistent object or from an object that's already been promoted,
2. an instance of the class X is being promoted to the persistent store for the first time,
3. class X is a superclass of the class being promoted,
4. an instance of the class X is a (static or instance) variable of the class being promoted,
5. an instance of the class X is a parameter of a method of the class being promoted,
6. an instance of the class X is a local variable of a method of the class being promoted or
7. a static variable of the class X is used by the class being promoted.

This is illustrated by the following:

```
class A {
    public static P p;
       ...
}

class C extends B {
    private D d;
    private E e[];
    static public F f;

    public void doSomething(G g, H h) {
        M m;
           ...
        m = A.p;
           ...
    }
    ...
}

class E extends J {
       ...
}

    C c = new C();
```

If the class C is not already persistent then, in accordance with rule 2 above, when object c of class C is made persistent, class C must also be made persistent. Since class B is the superclass of C then, in accordance with rule 3 above, class B must also be made persistent. Rule 4 means that classes D, E, and F must be made pesistent, as well as the values of the fields d, e and f. Rule 5 dictates that classes G and H must be made persistent and rule 6 dictates that class M must be made persistent. Since the method `doSomething` of class C uses the static variable p of class A, class A must also be made persistent, in accordance with rule 7. The promotion algorithm must recurse over all these additional classes and values until objects and

3. In PJava$_0$ only one store can be used per program run, so that only one instance of `PJavaStore` is visible at one time.

classes that are already persistent are reached. Thus, since class E is a subclass of class J, class J and its superclasses must also be made persistent if they are not persistent already.

An index of the classes that have been made persistent is maintained in each PJavaStore. There are methods to interrogate this index and a method may be provided to remove a class that no longer has any instances.

Whenever c is used, during some subsequent execution, the runtime system ensures that only the methods associated with C and its super-classes are run on c. This extends the guarantee of safety that Java gives for one execution to multiple executions. Any checks and verifications that were performed by the compiler and class loader validated the code that was stored with C. Since we ensure that only that code can operate on c all the original guarantees for the integrity of c are perpetuated throughout its persistent life.

This has benefits beyond safety but also some costs. The additional benefits include avoiding repeated checks and re-utilising optimisations introduced in earlier executions. The schema, i.e. the collection of class definitions in the store, will grow incrementally as new classes are needed by the application. But other aspects of schema evolution and support platform evolution need special support. For example, a special loader is needed to replace method code with revised code, perhaps to repair a bug. Additional mechanisms will be needed to alter the class definition in other ways: new fields, new methods, changed signatures for methods, etc. These will not be provided in PJava$_0$ and initially PAS implementors will have to achieve these effects by store re-builds.

2.4 Stabilisation, Initialisation and Restoration

2.4.1 Global Stabilisation and Durability

Stabilisation is the process of ensuring that data is durable. After a successful stabilise, the data concerned will be available on restart even if there is a subsequent software failure. It should also be available after media failure, but this depends on the number of redundant copies of the data and the extent of the media failure. In this section only the default form of stabilisation, global stabilisation, will be discussed. Partial stabilisation is via SnapShots (see 2.5).

A call of PJavaStore's stabilizeAll() method[4] will achieve a global stabilisation. This ensures that all changes since the start of the PJava program execution or the previous stabilise, are made durable. That is all of the objects that have been brought in from stable store and modified, all new objects that are reachable from these modified objects and any classes that are introduced via these new objects are all written atomically to disk. The registerPRoot call simply mutates the instance of PJavaStore. The PJavaStore object is then a modified object and the registered root object is the start of a graph of (possibly new) reachable objects.

2.4.2 Default Transactional Behaviour

The default transactional behaviour of PJava is an implicit call of stabilizeAll at the end of each successfully terminating program. A program that fails to handle an exception will terminate unsuccessfully and leave the stable store unchanged; thus an unhandled exception is, by default, equivalent to a transaction abort. Otherwise a PJava program behaves by default as a single transaction against the stable store with which it was associated.

Each object which was preserved by a stabilise holds its state at the last completed stabilise. This state determines the values of all its object variables when it is reloaded in a subsequent execution. However, in PJava an object may also have static variables which are effectively variables associated with the instance of that object's class.

2.4.3 Issues Arising with Static Variables

As their name suggests, static variables are only initialised once when the class is loaded, i.e. once per program execution in Java. In PJava we see the need for two different semantics for static variables:

1   persistently static variables, which are initialised when the class was loaded into some PJava program before it migrated to the stable store, or

2   transiently static variables, which are re-initialised according to their original initialisation code each time some execution of PJava causes them to be brought from stable store.

An example requiring a variable of the persistently static form would occur in a PAS that issues part numbers. A class Part would need a static variable in which to hold the last issued part number. A method would increment and issue the part number. If the part number variable were re-initialised each time a PJava program was run that used instances of class Part, the same sequences of part numbers would be re-issued repeatedly.

As an example requiring the transiently static form, consider an application that charges for the operations applied to instances of a particular class. Then it must start its variable holding the accumulated charge with the same initial value each time, and not the charge applied to the last customer.

---

4.   The "ize" spelling form is used for all identifiers introduced by PJava to be consistent with Java. As a result of habit we use the "ise" form in our text, although both forms are usually correct English spellings.

PJava supports both forms. By default, `static` variables are all persistently `static`. This supports well constants described in Java as `static final` variables. We contemplated allowing programmers to register in `PJavaStore` which classes should be transiently `static`.

This led to an unresolved concern as to whether the relationship between classes should be reflected in the static re-initialisation sequence. For example, suppose that classes B and D are specialisations of class A and that class C is a specialisation of class B. Suppose also that the application programmer includes C in the register of transiently `static` classes. Should this have any implications for classes B, A and D? For example, should classes B and A also be transiently `static` and should such inconsistency result in automatic registration of B and A or in an exception being raised? Such considerations led us to let the application programmers decide using the call-backs described next.[5]

2.4.4 Recovery and Initialisation Call-backs

PJava allows the application programmer to specify recovery and initialisation behaviour. As in Java, a PJava execution ultimately calls a `main` method of some class, often specified in the command-line. Before this call, PJava will run recovery code if the previous execution of PJava terminated unsuccessfully or there was a system or media failure during the final stabilise. After that, and before `main`, PJava will run an arbitrary sequence of call-backs supplied by the PAS programmer. PAS is emphasised here because those call backs must have been supplied during some previous successful execution.

There are two ways of setting the sequence of restoration call-backs. Both involve calling methods of `PJavaStore`. The method `setGlobalCallbacks(RestartCallback[] rc)` allows the application programmer to provide a sequence, `rc`, of call-backs, to replace any previous sequence. These call-backs are called by the PJava runtime in the order supplied in the array. The method `setClassCallbacks(RestartCallback[] rc, Class c)` provides a sequence of call backs for the specified class. These will be applied in order in any execution in which that class is loaded, after the global call-backs. Methods are provided to obtain the previous settings of these sequences.

Call-backs may be any implementation of the `RestartCallback interface`. They are called with a parameter which indicates whether PJava is performing a `restore`, a normal `restart` or a `retry`. A `restore` occurs after an incomplete stabilise or media failure. A `retry` occurs if, on a previous attempt at this bootstrap a call-back raised an unhandled exception or tried to perform an operation not allowed during the call-back sequence, such as `stabilizeAll`.

These call-backs can be used for many purposes, here are a few examples.

- To verify certain consistency constraints still hold in the store, and if they do not, to report this to an administrator, to warn the end-user and abort the execution. Call backs of this kind are likely to accumulate as successive classes are defined and may be generated by design tools.
- To establish the extent to which some previous execution completed a task.
- To create transient structures derivable from the stored structure. This might be "display and visualisation" data derived from the stable store and presented to suit the current user or context.
- To allow refinements of the initialisation policy for `static` variables.
- To permit an application team to develop a more sophisticated virtual machine on top of PJava and to initialise its state while working entirely within PJava.

2.5   Transactions in PJava

Three major issues were considered during the design of a flexible transaction model for PJava:

- how threads and transactions should compose,
- how to present a simple interface for programmers using *predefined* transaction models, and
- what primitives would best support programmers defining *new* transactional models.

2.5.1   Transactions and Threads

In order that code written independently can compose properly, it is necessary that nested transactions are supported. That is, some package may have been written using transactions. That package is then used from some other package that is also using transactions directly and they must compose correctly, i.e. with understandable and reasonable semantics.

Initially, we considered restrictive regimes, such as constraining a transaction to a single thread. At first sight, this appears to simplify the PJava programming model, but all the possible restricted models suffer the following drawbacks:

- they prohibit code that it seems reasonable to allow; and
- they will surely generate problems when independently written code is combined.

As an example of the former, consider a transaction that is required to obtain an edit to some complex value. That value might be displayed in several forms simultaneously in different windows, to allow the end-user to make changes to one form and visualise them in all views — e.g. a 3D manipulation or a graphical and textual view of a semantic data model schema. The

[5]. We observe that the field modifier `transient` could be used in conjunction with `static` to indicate a reinitialised static variable.

38

edits and feedback would then be organised in terms of several co-operating threads. But the whole edit would be within one transaction. On the other hand, a thread supporting a long editing session might run this as a series of transactions, so that the end-user can choose when to secure the work so far.

Similarly, we expect that the code in one package may utilise threads and in another utilise transactions, so that composition of PJava programs requires that a transaction may contain several threads and a thread may contain a sequence of, possibly nested, transactions.

This issue is not fully resolved. The principle of parsimony in language design appears to be violated. Both transactions and threads support concurrent operations. There is a nuance that the thread model is more concerned with programming where programmers have an overall understanding of the set of co-operating threads and their interactions, whereas the transactional model is more concerned with programming where the programmers are not aware of all the other simultaneous activities. However, as programs get larger, programmers are less able to visualise thread interactions and so have to write thread-safe code protected by synchronize or explicit locks anyway. Similarly, as longer transactions are supported, programmers need to become more supportive of constructive interaction between transactions. It may eventually prove possible to elide the thread and transaction constructs. However, our goal of minimising perturbations to existing constructs currently results in two constructs.

Perhaps, as the number of application programmers grow, and consequently the number of independently-written concurrent threads grows, it will become mandatory to make all code thread-safe. At which point, the replacement of threads by transactions will have little execution cost and will relieve programmers of managing most locks and synchrony.

All code in PJava is run within some transaction. If an encompassing transaction has not been explicitly initiated, then it is the implicit transaction associated with the whole program (see 2.4). This is also a contentious issue. It means that there is some write barrier monitoring updates for all threads at all times. There are clearly threads for which this is useless work, for example a thread that monitors the system clock and displays the time — you would not wish to restore its previous state on a restart. However, so far, we haven't been able to devise a scheme that will allow non-transactional threads that doesn't also potentially breach the safety and consistency requirements.

2.5.2 TransactionShells

It is apparent that a wide range of transactional behaviours are useful in different applications [BKK85, GS87, PKH88, CR91, KP92, GR93, KP95]. The support for transactions in PJava is an experiment to test whether a wide range of these transactions can be made available by providing a small set of primitives that can be composed to achieve the transactional behaviours. The logical properties of these compositions have already been explored [Day95, DG94, ADS96]. Only preliminary studies of their performance in real applications have been undertaken so far.

Because of the recursive structure of computations in a modern language like Java, some form of nested transaction [Mos81, HR93] will be required as a result of program composition and calls of code that contain transactions. There is, however, a choice of nested transaction semantics, for example:

- the effects of inner transactions may be propagated to parents and only made durable when the top transaction commits or may be made durable immediately;
- only sibling concurrency may be supported or parent-child concurrency may be available, and
- children may be constrained within the lifetime of their parent or may be allowed to escape.

The present design supports sibling and parent-child concurrency [HR93], it also defaults to non-escaping children with durability achieved only by top-level transactions, which may themselves be nested. However, the primitives provided allow a programmer to arrange for earlier durability and for escaping transactions. These primitives are also capable of supporting various forms of long-running transactions, such as SAGAS [GS87].

To achieve this flexibility, a TransactionShell class is provided. Specialisations of this class hold definitions of the transaction management policy to be used for transactions run under their control. Instances of these specialisations run individual transactions according to their policy. Transactions under different policy regimes may be executing concurrently with predictable behaviour. Two specialisations of TransactionShell are provided initially.

OLTPTransaction provides the typical flat ACID transaction model of many DBMS. It expects a brief transaction, suppresses the transaction operations of inner transactions. It makes all of its updates durable and releases all its locks at the terminal commit; and

NestedTransaction provides nested transactions with both parent-child and sibling concurrency. These transactions make their updates durable when the outermost transactions commit; inner transactions undo on abort and delegate their updates and locks to their parents on commit.

2.5.3 The External Transactional API

At present the division of the available transactional facilities into an "external" and an "internal" API is a matter of convention. In fact, all the transactional facilities are available to all programmers. We made need to review this reliance on convention.

It is intended that the standard, external transactional API provided by the instances of `TransactionShell` and its specialisations should satisfy most application programmers. This API hides implementation details from application programmers who program using a few `TransactionShell` methods. These methods allow the programmer to associate any object that satisfies the `Runnable` interface with an instance of a `TransactionShell`. Whenever the code in that `Runnable` object is activated, it is constrained to conform to the transaction model implemented by that `TransactionShell`. Programmers can then use its methods to:

- start its execution,
- enquire about the state of the execution (`running`, `aborted` or `completed`) and
- claim the results (synchronously or asynchronously).

By default transactions are run synchronously, that is, the transaction that performs the start operation is suspended until the initiated transaction completes. It is also possible to launch transactions asynchronously, making further methods useful. These can stop or kill a transaction and wait on an individual or group of transactions to achieve a certain state (all completed, one aborted, etc.).

2.5.4 The Internal Transactional API

Programmers who wish to define new transactional models by defining a specialisation of `TransactionShell` must use a more sophisticated internal transactional API which utilises a set of transaction building primitives.

`UpdateBookKeeper` Instances of this construct track the set of objects that have been updated by transactions associated with them. The internal API provides methods for creating `UpdateBookKeepers` and for binding `Threads` to a particular `UpdateBookKeeper`. Threads are always associated with precisely one book keeper. The two most important functionalities of `UpdateBookKeepers` are their ability to make a `Snapshot` and their ability to delegate some or all of their updates to another `UpdateBookKeeper`[6]. For example, this capability is used to pass updates to parents in nested transactions, so that they may later make durable, delegate or undo these updates. The `Snapshot` creation captures the state of this `UpdateBookKeeper`'s updated set of objects as a basis for undo and redo operations. This state can optionally be made durable as it is captured, thus guaranteeing its continued availability for two phase commit, long transactions, etc.

`AccessBookKeeper` These are similar to `UpdateBookKeepers` except that they do not have the capability to make `Snapshots`. They may be used where it is necessary to have available an identified set of the objects that have been accessed by a `Thread`. A typical use is to specify a set of objects whose locks and / or updates are to be delegated to another transaction.

`Snapshot` These are produced by `UpdateBookKeepers` which retain their ordering. It is then possible to apply a method of a `Snapshot` to perform a set of updates that restore the saved state. This implies application of any intervening `SnapShots`. After such an undo operation, application of the restore method of a later `SnapShot` would correspond to a redo operation. The `Snapshot` itself may be included in the set made durable as it is formed, or omitted from this set. `Snapshots` may be disabled. If a Snapshot is made durable and then disabled, the permanence of an ACID transaction is achieved. `SnapShots` are available for programmers wishing to build redo and undo in a command set as well as for transactional purposes.

`LockingCapability` These can be used within a transaction to represent locks accumulated by transactions. They provide a mechanism for specifying exclusion models other than the default of one writer or many readers and delegation. Delegation of locks can be used in a similar way to delegation of updates, in the definition of nested transactions for example. Normally delegation of updates and locks occur in step, but they may be separated; for example, in chained transactions a transaction that commits will pass its locks on, but not its updates which will have been stabilised [GR93].

Figure 1 illustrates how two of these constructs, `SnapShot` and `UpdateBookKeeper` may be combined. Update operations U_i and SnapShot operations Sn_i are shown for an execution history. In addition, a `SnapShot` stabilise is shown as a large arrow. It is possible to disable a sequence of `SnapShots` as a stabilisation is performed. The initial SnapShot, Sn_0, is formed implicitly as the `UpdateBookKeeper` is created and is the default point for a roll back. Rollbacks are automatically performed whenever a thread bound {e.g. by B (ubk, th) } to this `UpdateBookKeeper` fails to handle an exception. After B (ubk, th) every update made by th is logged by ubk, including updates to the threads stacks, to static and local variables, etc.

This internal API is more complicated than the external API which we expect to be sufficient for most of the programmers who are not content with the default transactional model. The goal is to allow application programmers an easily negotiated ramp of increasing transactional sophistication. Only evaluation of the use made of these facilities by independent application programmers will show whether the separation of the default behaviour, the external and internal APIs of `Transaction-Shells` has paid off. Reasonably efficient mechanisms to support the individual primitives are known, but our intuition that

---

[6.] The concept of delegation is formally described in [CR94].

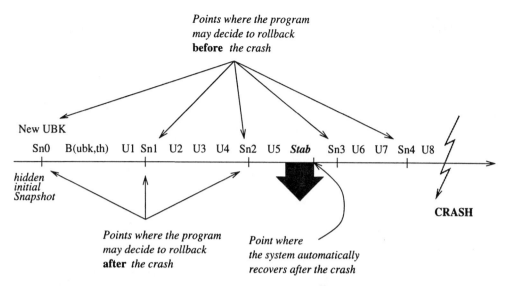

Figure 1 : a Program Execution Trace to show `UpdateBookKeeper` and `Snapshot` operations

it is feasible to compose them has yet to be tested.

3. Implementation Issues

Space only permits a very brief sketch of our implementation plans. PJava requires changes to the Java abstract machine (JAM), to the Java run-time and to the special classes provided with Java listed above (section 1.2). In addition we need to implement classes: `PJavaStore`, `TransactionShell`, `UpdateBookKeeper`, `AccessBookKeeper`, `SnapShot` and `LockingCapability`. These are implemented partly in Java and partly as C extensions to the Java run-time. A tutorial on the general mechanisms required to incrementally load and stabilise a persistent store using persistence by reachability is given in [AM95]. We use the same nomenclature here.

3.1 Architecture of PJava$_0$

The overall architecture of PJava$_0$ is represented in Figure 2. The main features to notice are given below.

- The existing JAM has been disturbed minimally, in particular its garbage collected heap and the handles it uses to access transient objects on that heap retain the format they have in standard Java. Also, the changes to the interpreter are minimal.

- All of the persistence activities are handled via structures in the Object Cache and the Buffer Pool. Every object in the Object Cache is addressed by the JAM via handles that are distinct from those for transient objects. These handles are collected together in the resident object table (ROT).

- The Object Cache is bootstrapped by loading the `PJavaStore` class and object instances. Thereafter, other objects are faulted into the cache whenever a PID that cannot be found in the ROT is dereferenced.

- Objects are promoted from the garbage collected heap and allocated new handles in the ROT, as well as PIDs, during the first part of a stabilise. They are then written to the stable store on disk.

- When an executing Java program requires a class that is not yet resident, a lookup in the Persistent Class Directory (PCD) is performed first. The standard class loading mechanism of Java is used only if the class is not found in the PCD.

- The Buffer Pool is implemented on top of RVM [MS94] using a no steal policy (i.e. dirty pages are not written back until commit)[7]. The dirtying of pages only begins during the final phase of stabilisation so that this will not pin pages for long. Objects are copied from the Buffer Pool to the Object Cache as they are faulted in and are copied back to the Buffer Pool during stabilise if they have been updated. This object copying policy is chosen to increase the density of active objects in the Object Cache [CAC+84, WW92, Mos92, KBC+88].

3.2 Swizzling & Faulting

Whilst from the Java application programmer's viewpoint, objects appear to reference each other directly, under the surface

[7] This is imposed by RVM which we are using for PJava$_0$.

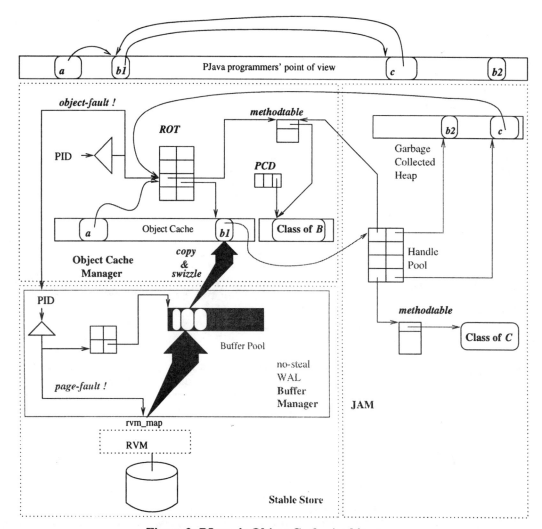

Figure 2: PJava₀'s Object Cache Architecture

a level of indirection is used. We have been able to exploit this existing indirection via handles in our faulting and swizzling mechanism. We have adopted eager indirect swizzling [Mos92] for objects and lazy swizzling for arrays and methods. A clustered technique, described below, is used for class data. The rationale behind these decisions is:

- objects are usually small, and therefore eagerly swizzling and allocating handles for their pointers is not expected to be expensive;

- arrays are potentially large and could require excessive handle space and processing time — it remains to be seen whether most accessed arrays then have all their elements accessed; and

- the code for operations within class data can be left unperturbed if we reconstruct the Java data structures as we fault a class before continuing.

When a program tries to *unhandle* a handle we need to test for residence and potentially fault in a non-resident object. As soon as an object is faulted into the Object Cache, all its PIDs are swizzled to point to handles in the ROT. If the referend hasn't been partially swizzled this far already, a new handle is added to the ROT. Each handle in the ROT holds the corresponding PID. Thus the swizzling horizon is maintained in the handles rather than in the objects.

For swizzling to be thread safe it is necessary to ensure that two threads do not concurrently fault in the same object as there would then be two images of that object potentially being updated independently. This is achieved by an optimistic policy. It is assumed that it will be relatively rare for two threads to attempt to unhandle the same handle simultaneously. The residency test is therefore performed once without any locking. Only if it is found that the object is non-resident is the object-faulting mutex acquired and the test re-performed. If the thread still finds the object non-resident it will be the only thread faulting that object. In this way all the residency checks for resident objects avoid the mutex overhead.

3.3 Clustered Class Loading

Observing the Napier88 system [MCC+96], we find that the same group of objects[8] are loaded at the start of every program. Without evasive action, this phenomena will be repeated in PJava, as the `PJavaStore` object and class and all the objects and classes on which they depend to perform the start up are brought in. We also require that when a class is loaded, all of its internal objects and related objects be loaded, so that we can avoid residency checks and object faults within the class `Class` implementation.

To avoid these repeated object faults and internal residency checks, classes will be treated specially. During a stabilisation, the whole of the class including internal objects and all of the classes and objects on which it intimately depends will be marshalled together and shipped as one store object. When faulted in, the reverse process reconstructs the internal data structures and the indirect links via handles to all these closely associated objects. A generalisation of this, with a slightly more extensive set of commonly used classes and objects, will be used to achieve fast program initialisation by clustering the extensive set in the stable store and loading all of these with the `PJavaStore` object and class.

3.4 Promoting New Objects

When a PJava program stabilises, new objects in the garbage collected heap are promoted. First, they are found by performing an application of Java's garbage collection scanner from the handles in the ROT that are identified as having been updated since the last stabilise. These are then copied into the Object Cache and allocated handles in the ROT.

The next step is to allocate them PIDs at the end of the stable store, i.e. beyond the point where the size of the stable store, recorded in the `PJavaStore` object, says the store ends. They can then be written directly to the disk in a single transfer, by-passing RVM. There is no need to put any information in the log at this stage. If a crash occurs before the end of the next stage, the recovery mechanism will behave as if they had never been written and the store was still its old size with those PIDs unallocated, as the updated `PJavaStore` object has not been written back.

The PJavaStore object is now updated with the new size, highest PID, etc. and an RVM transaction is used to write back all of the modified objects in the Object Cache. This will be logged. If it commits, the whole stabilise succeeds and the new objects are visible. If it aborts or a crash occurs, then the modifications to these objects will not be visible at the next restart. Since these include the change to the store size, the new objects will also be ignored. During a database load there is a very high rate of creation of new objects. The machanism above avoids writing to the log and avoids complex allocation for these new objects. We believe that, in consequence, database load will be significantly accelerated with no loss of stable store integrity. Other features of the implementation will be discussed in a later paper which will include performance measurements for the mechanisms introduced above.

4. Conclusions and Future Work

The design for the system PJava has been presented. It is an alternative platform for the Java language with provision of completely orthogonal persistence for data, meta data (classes) and code (methods). One of the goals of PJava is to attract wider use of this form of persistence and another is to support a wide range of applications.

To achieve both of these goals a simple transactional model is provided by default and composable primitives are provided for describing complex transactional behaviour. Normally, these more complex behaviours will be programmed by specialising the class `TransactionShell`. As these shells, including their specialisations, present a standard external API, the majority of application programmers should be able to code, even using ready made sophisticated transaction models, without being aware of details of transaction implementation.

The syntax of Java is unchanged and only minimal changes have been made to the semantics of certain operations. In particular, there is no reduction in the safety afforded by Java. At present, we envisage PJava being used mainly for server software and not for applets. For example a crossword server might be written in PJava and a crossword presenter applet in Java. When the presenter is used, the remote user can select a crossword and then view clues, etc. The user may also ask the presenter to preserve a partial solution and return to it later. The crosswords and clues would be stored at the server in the stable store. As users progressed with crosswords their solution increments would be shipped back to the stable store to preserve them. After some failure, or when returning on another occasion, the user could resume an earlier puzzle and its partial solution would be retrieved from the store and shipped to the presenter. The communication between the Java applet and the PJava server could be any protocol available in Java.

The implementation of the prototype, PJava$_0$, which presents only the default transactional behaviour and omits several planned optimisations, is in progress. It is anticipated that a preliminary report on experience with this prototype and on its performance, will be available at the POS-7 workshop.

The prototype will be followed by a succession of releases leading to the functionality described here. Experience with earlier versions will be used to identify the need for design changes. Testing applications during this phase will be the development

---

[8.]   About 670 according to some recent measurements [Bai96].

43

of CASE tools and some geographic information system (GIS) examples. Measurements with these loads will be used to identify which optimisations to focus on. An early task will be the development of a more integrated store management scheme, including disk garbage collection.

Design issues that are not easily resolved concerning the semantics of PJava include:

- when to re-initialise static variables in persistent classes;
- whether to take note of class relationships when organising static variable initialisation;
- whether to make top-level transactions of PJava analogous to UNIX processes (to maintain the analogy, each transaction would need to manufacture its own set of static variables to emulate the behaviour with respect to static variables of say two separate C++ programs run as transactions against a common database);
- whether to persevere with a combination of transactions and threads or to seek one construct that serves both purposes; and
- how to choose a good set of transaction primitives and implement them with minimal performance costs.

Our presently preferred solutions to these design issues are being implemented and will be tested for a few applications. It is hoped that other forms of persistent Java will be developed to exploit the novel opportunity of a language that is safe and which looks likely to become popular and commercially important. This will permit comparison of the various outcomes from these design choices, but much more importantly, it may enable many more application teams and industries to enjoy the benefits of persistent programming.

6.   Acknowledgements

This work was supported by a grant from Sun under their collaborative awards program. It builds on research and technology developed in the European Community Basic Research Action FIDE$_2$, 6093.

Bibliography

[Atk96] M.P. Atkinson, editor. *Fully Integrated Data Environments* Springer-Verlag 1996.

[ADS96] M.P. Atkinson, L. Daynès and S. Spence. *PJava Design 1.2* Working Document available via http://www.dcs.gla.ac.uk/~susan/pjava/

[AM95] M.P. Atkinson and R. Morrison. *Orthogonal Persistent Object Systems* in VLDB Journal, 4(3), pp319-401, 1995.

[ABM88] M.P. Atkinson, O.P. Buneman and R. Morrison. *Binding and Type Checking in Database Programming Languages* in Computer Journal, 31(2), pp99-109, April 1988.

[ACC+83] M.P. Atkinson, K.J. Chisholm, W.P. Cockshott, and R.M. Marshall. *Algorithms for a Persistent Heap* in IEEE Software, Practice and Engineering, 13(3):259--272, March 1983.

[Bai96] P. Bailey. Personal communication, University of Glasgow, February 1996.

[BKK85] F. Bancilhon, W. Kim, and H.F. Korth. *A Model of CAD Transactions* in Proc. of the 11th Int. Conf. on Very Large Database, pages 25--33, 1985.

[CA93] M. Chelliah and M. Ahamad. *Operating System Mechanisms for Distributed Object-Based Fault-Tolerant Computing* Technical Report GIT-CC-92-23, School of Information and Computer Sciences, Georgia Institute of Technology, Atlanta, Georgia, October 1993.

[CR94] P. Chrysanthis and K. Ramamritham. *Synthesis of Extended Transaction Models using ACTA* in ACM TODS, 19(3), pp450-491, September 1994.

[CR91] P.K. Chrysanthis and K. Ramamritham. *A Formalism for Extended Transaction Models* in Proc. of the 17th Int. Conf. on Very Large Database, pages 103--112, Barcelona, September 1991.

[CAC+84] W.P. Cockshott, M.P. Atkinson, K. Chisholm, P. Bailey, and R. Morrison. *Persistent Object Management Systems* in IEEE Software, Practice and Engineering, 14:49--71, 1984.

[Day95] L. Daynès. *Conception et réalisation de mécanismes flexibles de verrouillage adaptés aux SGBDO client-serveur.* Ph.D. thesis, Université Pierre et Marie Curie (Paris VI -- Jussieu). 29 September 1995.

[DG94] L. Daynès and O. Gruber. *Efficient Customizable Concurrency Control using Graph of Locking Capabilities* in M.P. Atkinson, V. Benzaken, and D. Maier, editors, Persistent Object Systems (Proc. of the Sixth Int. Workshop on Persistent Object Systems), Workshops in Computing, Tarascon, Provence, France, September 1994. Springer-Verlag in collaboration with the British Computer Society, pages 147--161.

[DGV95] L. Daynès, O. Gruber, and P. Valduriez. *Locking in OODBMS clients supporting Nested Transactions* in Proc. of the 11th Int. Conf. on Data Engineering, pages 316--323, Taipei, Taiwan, March 1995.

[GS87] H. Garcia-Molina and K. Salem. *SAGAS* in Proc. of the ACM SIGMOD Int. Conf. on Management of Data, pages 249--259, 1987.

[GM95] J. Gosling and H. McGilton. *The Java Language Environment -- A White Paper.* Sun Microsystems Computer Company, May 1995.

[GJS96] J. Gosling, B. Joy and G. Steele. *The Java Language Specification.* Addison-Wesley, 1996.

[GR93] J. Gray and A. Reuter. *Transaction Processing: Concept and Techniques.* Morgan-Kaufman, 1993.

[HKM+96] N. Haines, D. Kindred, J. Morisset, S.M. Nettles, and J.M. Wing. *Composing First-Class Transaction* to appear in ACM TOPLAS, 1996.

[HR93] T. Härder and K. Rothermel. *Concurrency Control Issues in Nested Transactions* in VLDB Journal, 2(1):39--74, 1993.

[JV95] M. Jordan and M. Van De Vanter *Software Configuration Management in an Object-Oriented Database* in Proc. of the USENIX 1995 Conference on Object-Oriented Technologies, Monterey, California, June 26-29, 1995.

[KP95] G.E. Kaiser and C. Pu. *Cooperative Transaction for Multiuser Environments.* chapter 20, pages 409--433, in W. Kim, editor. Modern Database System -- The Object Model, Interoperability and Beyond. Addison Wesley/ ACM Press, 1995.

[KP92] G.E. Kaiser and C. Pu. *Dynamic Restructuring of Transactions*, chapter 8, pages 266--295, in "Database Transaction Models for Advanced Applications", Data Management Systems series, Morgan-Kaufman, San Mateo, CA, 1992. A.K. El-magarmid, editor.

[KBC+88] W. Kim, N. Ballou, H. Chou, J.F. Garza, and D. Woelk. *Integrating an Object-Oriented Programming System with a Database System* in OOPSLA '88 Int. Conf., pages 142--152, September 1988.

[Kra85] G.L. Krablin. *Building Flexible Multilevel Transactions in a Distributed Persistent Environment* Chapter 14, pages 213--234, in Atkinson, M.P. and Buneman, O.P. and Morrison, R., Data Types and Persistence -- Proceedings of the First Workshop on Persistent Object Systems, Appin, Scotland, August 1985.

[MR95] C.P. Martin and K. Ramamritham. *ARIES/RH: Robust Support for Delegation by Rewriting History.* Technical Report 95--51, University of Massachusetts, Amherst, Massachusetts, June 1995.

[MS94] H.H. Mashburn, and Satyanarayanan. *Recoverable Virtual Memory.* RVM Release 1.3, CMU, January 1994.

[MSc94] F. Matthes and J.W. Schmidt. *Persistent Threads* in Proceedings of the Twentieth International Conference on Very Large Databases, pages 403--414, Santiago, Chile, 1994.

[MCC+96] R. Morrison, R.C.H. Connor, Q.I. Cutts, G.N.C. Kirby, D.S. Munro and M.P. Atkinson. *The Napier88 Persistent Programming Language and Environment* in chapter 1.5.3, [Atk96].

[Mos92] J.E.B. Moss. *Working With Objects: To Swizzle or Not to Swizzle?* IEEE Transactions on Software Engineering, 18(8):657--673, August 1992.

[Mos81] J.E.B. Moss. *Nested Transactions: An Approach to Reliable Distributed Computing.* PhD thesis, Massachussets Institute of Technology, April 1981.

[MCM+94] D.S. Munro, R.C.H. Connor, R. Morrison, S. Scheuerl and D.W. Stemple. *Concurrent Shadow Paging in the FLASK Architecture* in M.P. Atkinson, V. Benzaken, and D. Maier, editors, Persistent Object Systems (Proc. of the Sixth Int. Workshop on Persistent Object Systems), Workshops in Computing, Tarascon, Provence, France, September 1994. Springer-Verlag in collaboration with the British Computer Society, pages 16--42.

[OSF95] Open Software Foundation. *Java Mobile Code -- A White Paper*, December 1995.

[PKH88] C. Pu, G.E. Kaiser, and N. Hutchinson. *Split-Transactions for Open-Ended Activities* in Proc. of the ACM SIG-MOD Int. Conf. on Management of Data, pages 26--37, Los Angeles, California, August 1988.

[RBF+89] R. Rashid, R. Baron, A. Forin, D. Golub, M. Jones, D. Julin, D. Orr, and R. Sanzi. *Mach: A Foundation for Open Systems* in Proceedings of the Second Workshop on Workstation Operating Systems (WWOS2), September 1989.

[SM96] D. Stemple and R. Morrison. *Specifying Flexible Concurrency Control Schemes: An Abstract Operational Approach* in chapter 1.4.1, [Atk96].

[WW92] S. White and D. DeWitt. *A Performance Study of Alternative Object Faulting in Pointer Swizzling Strategies* in Proc. of the 18th Int. Conf. on Very Large Database, pages 419--431, Vancouver, British Columbia, Canada, 1992.

Modules and Type Abstraction in Persistent Systems

Richard Connor[†], Giorgio Ghelli[‡] and Paolo Manghi[†‡]

[†]School of Mathematical and Computational Sciences,
University of St Andrews, St Andrews, KY16 9SS, Scotland.

[‡]Dipartimento di Informatica, Università di Pisa,
Corso Italia 40, Pisa, Italy.

{richard, paolo}@dcs.st-andrews.ac.uk
ghelli@di.unipi.it
manghi@cli.di.unipi.it

Abstract

This paper contains an examination of the typings associated with the construction of persistent systems through the use of parametric abstract modules. Of particular interest are the class of dependent, potentially dynamic typings required as a consequence of diamond import. An example is introduced, including the diamond problem; solutions to it are shown in Fibonacci, using its module provision, and in Napier88, using more general existential types and dynamic typing. The dependent typings are highlighted in each language, and an abstract module algebra is introduced which makes such typings more explicit. The module algebra is shown to have the expressive ability of both systems, as well as the original SOL language, making it a candidate for a general language mechanism to express both module and abstract type programming paradigms.

1. Introduction

It is a matter of some debate as to whether an explicit module mechanism is required or desirable in an orthogonally persistent programming language. An original motivation for modules is to allow the separate compilation of program units, whereas some persistent systems achieve this orthogonally by the use of a general dynamic binding mechanism. Another major purpose of modules, that of providing abstract interfaces, can also be achieved through other general language mechanisms, notably that of existentially quantified data types [MP88].

In this paper the typing of module systems is examined. An example, including the "diamond import" problem, is described, and its typing shown in the Fibonacci [AGO95] and Napier88 [StA96] languages. The Fibonacci solution uses an explicit module mechanism, whereas the Napier88 solution uses general programming mechanisms: specifically those of existential types [MP88, CDM+90] and explicit dynamic typing [ACP+91, CBC+90]. The different typings are examined in detail through the introduction of a new abstract algebra designed to describe module typings. Module typing issues are essentially those of existential types, but with an extended (and sometimes necessarily dynamic) model of type equivalence.

The intention is not to provide an answer to the question of whether a module mechanism is a useful or required language mechanism, but simply to shed some light on the typing issues involved. We do however demonstrate that a single language mechanism may be used to capture the semantics of both modules and abstract data types.

2. Modules - background

It is well established that the development of large scale applications requires a mechanism to support the subdivision of the programming task into subtasks, whose implementations may be separately specified, and which may be mechanically linked together to form the application. Such mechanisms are ubiquitously referred to as module mechanisms, after early work by Parnas [Par72]. Many different mechanisms have been suggested, specified, and implemented; the common features are briefly presented.

2.1. Interface and implementation

A module is an entity containing data, metadata and programs, the use of which may be specified without reference to any realisation. This is achieved by the concepts of interface and implementation; the interface specifies what functionality is provided by a module, and the implementation gives a realisation of this. Thus the interface contains sufficient information for any use of the implementation to be defined, without dependence on the implementation itself.

The advantages of such dependency limitation are well-documented, and include the following:

- a matching of the normal refinement patterns of problem decomposition

- an understandable program structure

- the confinement of errors (both static and dynamic) to sub-units

- separate compilation of sub-units

Various relationships between interface and implementation are possible. The most flexible systems support both *multiple interfaces* and *multiple implementations*. The intuition supporting this derives from the correspondence of module instances to language values, and of module interfaces to types. Thus each interface can have any number of implementations; in a language with polymorphism, an implementation may belong to a number of interfaces.

2.2. Import and export

Applications composed of modules are structured as a set of controlled interactions:

- each module realises some functionality and *exports* its use to other modules

- each module, to realise its own functionality, can *import* from other modules

There are two kind of importation, *constant* and *parametric*:

Constant importation occurs when the binding from imported identifiers to their instances occurs at the same time as compilation. As the linking is effectively static, the subsequent modification of a module requires re-linking (and therefore re-compilation) of all dependent modules.

Parametric importation occurs when the compilation and binding phases of module construction occur separately. A module instance is yielded as a result of a function which is applied to other instances. Module implementations may be modified without a requirement to relink the code of dependent modules.

2.3. Abstract modules

Importing modules may use an exporting module only through its interface. By appropriately hiding the implementation of an interface, it is possible for a module to export abstract data types: the type's representation, as specified within the implementation, may not be seen outside the module. Thus code using the abstract module cannot refer to the concrete type, but only to its abstraction. Clearly there is an important duality between abstract modules and abstract data type packages as defined by Mitchell and Plotkin. The introduction of abstract modules gives rise to the diamond import problem.

2.4. Diamond import

The diamond problem occurs when a module depends on another abstract module through two different paths. An example is shown in Figure 1.

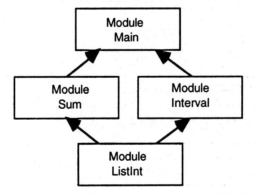

Figure 1 : The diamond import example

ListInt is an abstract module which exports an abstract type representing a package of integer list functions. The module interface exports an abstract type identifier, hiding the list representation, and a set of functions defined over it. The other three modules are parametrically defined, and they act as follows:

Interval imports an implementation of the module *ListInt* and exports a function which, given two integers representing an interval, returns a list of integers corresponding to that interval.

Sum also imports an implementation of the module *ListInt*, and exports a function which, given a list of integers, yields the sum of its elements.

Main imports the two modules *Interval* and *Sum* and exports a function which, given two integers, returns the sum of the interval between them.

The problem is that *Main* imports the same abstracted type, that provided by *ListInt*, by two different paths. If the module system allows interfaces to have more than one implementation, it may happen that *Main* imports two different implementations of *ListInt*. These implementations, although sharing a common interface, may be defined over different representations of the abstract type. Therefore the mixing of list values deriving from the different interfaces is a potential source of unsoundness within the system and can not be allowed without further checks.

The requirement is to preserve soundness without disallowing the flexibility allowed by the combination of abstract and parametric modules. Note that if we impose any of the restrictions of static importation, single module instances or concrete typing the problem can not occur.

The typing problem, in terms of existential typings, is as follows: there exist values *interval* of type $\exists i.\text{fun}(\text{int}, \text{int} \rightarrow i)$ and *sum* of type $\exists i.\text{fun}(i \rightarrow \text{int})$, and it may be possible to determine from knowledge of the system composition that *sum(interval(x,y))* is a meaningful combination. In the SOL [MP88] model of existential typing there is insufficient flexibility to type this expression; in general dynamic typechecking may be required at the time of the *main* module instantiation. We must therefore introduce sound, but potentially dynamic, type mechanisms to allow such combinations where they are appropriate. Importantly, the presence of dynamic typing at the time of system construction does not imply the possibility of dynamic type failure during system execution [DCC93].

We continue by showing codings of the above problem in the language Fibonacci, using a purpose-designed module mechanism, and in Napier88, using a general purpose abstract type mechanism. Although both achieve the same purpose, the typing of the intermediate levels is subtly different. We conclude by introducing an abstract module model which is able to subsume the semantics and typing of both models.

3. The example codings

In the module systems we describe, modules are first class values and the commands which link modules together are invocations of first class procedures. It should be noted that this model ony makes sense in the context of persistent higher-order languages, and is quite different from mechanisms employed by other module systems in which the modules do not form a part of the language's semantic domain.

System installation proceeds as follows:

1. Generator execution - linker installation phase. In this phase code which includes the definition of the generator functions is executed, making these functions available within the persistent context.

2. Linker execution - module installation phase. In this phase the generator procedures themselves are executed, resulting in module instances. These instances may in general be the input of subsequent linker procedures, modelling module import and export.

If subsequent changes to a module are required, only its generator is reinstantiated, hence producing a new linker for that module; for changes to be propagated throughout the system, all dependent linking phases must be re-executed. The basic requirement in such a system is that as many consistency checks as possible are carried out at installation time. It is therefore possible for "dynamic" checking to occur during linking phases without compromising static safety requirements of the resulting system.

Fully static module checking would mean that every consistency check takes place when the generators and their application are typechecked. Installation time checking means that every consistency check takes place by the end of the installation process. Installation only happens once (unlike general functions, which are typically compiled once and executed many times), hence, up to the point of the whole application being generated, static and dynamic type-checking are not very different.

3.1. Module ListInt

In all the examples of this paper, the existence of an orthogonal persistence mechanism is assumed. No account is taken of persistent binding and scoping issues, and the discussion concentrates solely on the typing of modules. The presence of orthogonal persistence is a requirement, as otherwise values of these types could not persist and be used as modules; however details of the persistence mechanism are by definition orthogonal to the discussion.

First the type (interface) of the *ListInt* module is given in the two languages:

Fibonacci	Napier88

Let ListInt =
<[
    T <: **Any**;
    empty : T;
    cons : **Fun**(v : **Int**; l : T) : T;
    isEmpty : **Fun**(l : T): **bool**;
    first : Fun(l : T) : **Int**;
    rest : Fun(l : T) : T
]>;
	type ListInt **is abstype**[T]
	(
	    empty : T;
	    cons : **proc**(int, T -> T);
	    isEmpty : **proc**(T -> bool);
	    first : **proc**(T -> int);
	    rest : **proc**(T -> T)
	)

The codings are almost identical, and serve mainly to point out the differences in the concrete syntax of the languages. The most important difference is that Napier88 adopts the SOL approach to existential types, while Fibonacci represents an existential type by a tuple type (or "module type") where every field may either be a value with a given type or a type with a given kind (*<: Any* is the kind which contains any type). The two approaches have the same expressive power, as should be apparent from the example above [CL90]. Another difference is that the Fibonacci function types include parameter names, whereas Napier88 do not.

We now proceed to make an instance of the type:

let listInt: ListInt =
<[
    Rec Let T =
        Choice
            Empty: **Null**
            Cons: [value: **Int**; next: T]
        End;
    let empty = **choice** Empty of T **end**;
    let cons =
        fun(v: **Int**; l:T):T **is**
            choice Cons of T **with** [v; l]
        end;
    let isEmpty = **fun**(l: T): **bool is** l is Empty;
    let first = **fun**(l : T) **is** (l **as** Cons).value;
    let rest = **fun**(l : T) **is** (l **as** Cons).next
]>;
	rec type T **is variant**
	(
	    Empty : **null** ;
	    Cons : **structure**(value : **int** ; next : T)
	)
	
	let listInt = ListInt[T]
	(
	    T(Empty : **nil**),
	    proc(v : **int** ; l : T -> T)
	        T(Cons : **struct**(value = v; next = l)),
	    proc(l : T -> **bool**) ; l **is** Empty,
	    proc(l : T -> **int**) ; l'Cons(value),
	    proc(l : T -> **int**) ; l'Cons(next)
	)

Once again there are no technical difficulties with the coding. Napier88 automatically overloads the definition of structured types as constructor functions for those types, but type equivalence is nonetheless structural in both systems. The use of *ListInt* as a constructor is parameterised by its specialising type; here the identifier *T* is used to correspond with the Fibonacci example and is not significant except for its consistent use throughout this program fragment.

3.2. Module Interval

We now make a first attempt to define the module *Interval*. Although the semantics of the following code are appropriate, it will become evident that the typings, although correct, are not sufficiently flexible to support the diamond application. In both languages the result of the *createInterval* procedure is a general existential type; more information than this is required to allow its subsequent matching with the *Sum* module.

```
Let Interval =                                     type Interval is abstype[ T ]
<[                                                 (
    T <: Any;                                          create: proc( left, right: int -> T )
    create: Fun( left, right: Int ): T             )
]>;
                                                   let createInterval = proc( m: ListInt -> Interval)
let createInterval = fun( m: ListInt ): ( Interval )    use m as M[ T ] in
is                                                 begin
<[                                                     rec let create = proc( left, right: int -> T )
    Let T = m.T;                                       if  left>right
    rec let create = fun( left, right: Int ): T is         then M( Null )
    if  left>right                                         else M( cons )(left; create(left+1; right))
        then m.null                                    Interval[ T ]( create )
            else m.cons(left; create(left+1; right) )  end
]>;
```

The body of the Napier88 *createInterval* procedure uses an abstract *use* clause[1], similar in intent to the SOL *open* mechanism, to create the required constant binding from the identifer *M* to the package *m*; Fibonacci uses more sophisticated static analysis [CL90] to achieve the same effect. Both languages introduce a denotation *T* for the witness type of the imported module *m* and proceed to declare a new procedure whose implementation uses the imported interface. The result of the execution is a new procedure which generates an *Interval* module implementation, based on the input implementation, and typed as $\exists i.(\ create : fun(\ int, int \rightarrow i\ )\ )$.

This typing requires to be enhanced in some way before the module *Main* will be able to successfully combine the applications of *Interval* and *Sum*. The typings required involve dynamic dependencies, as the correct typing of *Main* depends on the actual value supplied to the *Interval* and *Sum* generator functions. Each language has a different mechanism which may be used to achieve this.

3.2.1. *Fibonacci dependent typing*

The Fibonacci system of dependent types allows the description of a function where the type of the result depends on the value of a parameter, provided that the parameter is a tuple with a type component. For example, a function which receives a tuple *m* with type

> [T <: Any, a: T]

and extracts the *a* field from *m*, has type

> Fun(m : [T <: Any, a: T]) : m.T

This ability may be exploited to give a more precise type to the *createInterval* function, which statically specifies the fact that the witness of the abstract type of the created module is the same as the witness of the imported module:

```
let createInterval =
    fun( m: ListInt ): ( Interval with T = m.T ) is
    …
```

The notation *Interval with T = U* means "the same type as the tuple type *Interval*, but substitute *EQ(U)* to the kind of the *T* field" It does not add expressive power to the system, but enhances readability. *EQ(U)* is a kind whose only element is *U*, hence every type in this kind is equivalent to *U*. It is important to notice that the information representing the relationship between the witness types is explicitly arranged to be present.

3.2.2. *Napier88 dependent typing*

The syntax of Napier88 allows the description of the required type dependency as follows:

---

[1]It should be mentioned for the sake of completeness that the Napier88 syntax requires the body of a use clause to be void; in these examples they appear with non-void bodies for the sake of simplicity. The reason for this restriction is not connected with these examples, and each may actually be programmed by means of a variable declared in an outer scope being assigned to within the body.

```
use m as M[ T ] in
begin
    type Interval is proc( left, right: int -> T )

    rec let create = proc( left, right: int -> T ) ...
```

The type *Interval* is actually a dependent type, as the meaning of the identifier *T* depends on the value supplied as *m*. Unfortunately however it is not possible for the value *create*, which is typed as *Interval*, to be exported from the local scope with this type: it is impossible for a denotation of the type to exist outside the scope of the *use* clause. However Napier88 has an explicit dynamic typing mechanism, used to provide persistent binding capabilities, and this may be used to code the example. The dynamic typing respects the semantics of the value dependency[2], the use of abstract types in persistent bindings being earlier noted as otherwise overly restrictive [CM88, OTC+90].

The final version of the Napier88 module generator is as follows. Although the return value is typed as *any*, the required semantics have been achieved. In fact this dynamic typing will be factored out during the execution of the *Main* generator function; the typing of *Interval* thus represents a coarser-grain dynamic check than is required for maximum elegance, rather than an unnecessary dynamic check.

```
type Interval is any

let createInterval = proc( m: ListInt -> Interval )
use m as M[ T ] in
begin
    rec let create = proc( left, right: int -> T )
    if left > right
        then M( Null )
        else M( cons )( left, create( left+1; right ) )
    any( create )
end
```

3.3. Module Sum

The codings of the module *Sum* generators are included for completeness, and should not generate any issues other than those already covered in *Interval*:

`Let Sum =`
`<[`
    `T <: Any;`
    `sumlist: Fun( list: T ): Int`
`]>;`
 	
`let createSum =`
    `fun( m: ListInt): ( Sum with T = m.T ) is`
`<[`
    `Let T = m.T;`
    `let add = fun( l: T ): Int is`
    `if m.isEmpty( l )`
        `then 0`
        `else m.first( l )+add( m.rest( l ) )`
`]>;`
	`type Sum is any`
	
	`let createSum = proc( m: ListInt -> Sum )`
	`use m as M[ T ] in`
	`begin`
	    `rec let add = proc( l : T -> int )`
	    `if M( isEmpty )( l )`
	        `then 0`
	        `else M( first )( l ) + add( m( rest )( l ) )`
	    `any( add )`
	`end`

3.4. Module Main

In this module the threads are tied together and we introduce a final generator function which takes as parameters instances of *Interval* and *Sum* modules, and applies them to each other. Sufficient value dependency has been indicated in each system to allow appropriate dynamic checking to occur at the start of the generator procedure; if the diamond dependency is incorrect,

---

[2]This is true of Napier88 Releases 2.0 and afterwards; releases before this have the static model reflected in the dynamic typing semantics, and the *Main* generator function shown later would fail with a dynamic type error.

that is the implementations of *IntList* used in the generation of *Interval* and *Sum* are different, then the generation of the *Main* module will fail with an appropriate high-level type error. If the same module has been used then the generation will succeed, and the resulting module is statically safe.

Let Main =
 <[
       sumInterval: **Fun**(x,y: **Int**): **Int**
 ]>;
 	
 let createMain =
 fun(m1: Interval; m2: Sum **with** T = m1.T): Main
 is
 <[
       let sumInterval = **fun**(x, y : **Int**): **Int is**
           m2.sumList(m1.create(x, y))
 ]>;
	type Main **is** proc(int, int -> int)
	
	 let createMain = **proc**(m0 : ListInt;
	                  m1 : Interval; m2 : Sum
	                     -> **proc**(int -> int))
	 use m0 **as** M[T] **in**
	      project m1 **onto** proc(int, int -> T) **in**
	          project m2 **onto** proc(T -> int) **in**
	             proc(int x, y -> int)
	               m2(m1(x, y))

The Napier88 program is shown partly as pseudo-code. The reason for this is that, as Napier88 programmers will be aware, the collecting of persistent components as above is normally achieved with the environment binding mechanism. As our intention is to discuss typing issues only, an invented form of *project* is used in the example to reflect the typing underlying environment projection. Napier88 programmers will be able to mentally recode all the above examples to use environments instead of type *any*; and the elegance of the solution is actually enhanced. Readers who are not familiar with Napier88 may read the above example as simple projection from a dynamic typing.

The diamond import problem is solved in different ways in the two systems. In Napier88 dynamic typechecking is required to resolve the value dependency between the module *m0* and the dependent types of *m1* and *m2*, and an instance of the module *m0* is required as an operand to allow this check to be made. In typical use of the Napier88 system, the dynamic typechecks occur at the same time as dynamic binding checks, and the reliance on the *m0* module may be made implicit. In Fibonacci everything is statically typed, however the sharing constraints must be explicitly stated in the intermediate level modules. Once again, this exactly suits the typical system construction methodologies used in the Fibonacci environment. Thus there is a tradeoff in the way that the same information is transmitted up to the time of the final module creation.

The most important point, however, is that both systems give a statically checked final module. The presence of dynamic typechecking causes no problems so long as it occurs during the installation phase. The requirement to list indirectly imported modules or sharing constraints may be a serious burden on the programmer during the construction of large systems, and both Napier88 and Fibonacci methodologies may require to rely on automatic tools to insert this kind of information.

Finally we show the combination of all the module generators to produce the main program, making the second phase of module system construction as identified above:

let listPack = createListInt() **let** interval = createInterval(listPack) **let** sum = createSum(listPack) **let** main = createMain(interval, sum)	**let** listPack = createListInt() **let** interval = createInterval(listPack) **let** sum = createSum(listPack) **let** main = createMain(listPack , interval, sum)

Notice again how both systems eventually generate a statically typed and sound module; the dependency checking essential to the process has been entirely factored out during the module generation process.

To finish, we examine the typings present in both languages with respect to a more abstract module algebra.

4. The abstract module algebra

In this section the fundamental typings of the different language constructs are examined in a single conceptual framework, and the different typings of the Fibonacci and Napier88 solutions are described. This is achieved by the description of abstract module concepts as a language extension.

4.1. Outline

Dependent typings are unavoidable in flexible module mechanisms where the diamond problem can occur; a major purpose of the algebra is to explicitly decouple the type dependencies from the other operations of the language. To achieve this, in outline, a new type *ModuleWitness* is introduced; values of this type can also be treated as types. This is a similar approach to the witness type mechanism proposed by Ohori et al in [OTC+90]. In this context however values of type *ModuleWitness* are used to explicitly type general values, and replace the need for the *open* mechanism. Instead the concept of a pseudo-abstract type is introduced, such as in the following example:

type Concrete **is structure**(x : int, y : **proc**(int -> **string**))
type FullyAbstract **is Module**[i](x : i, y : **proc**(i -> **string**))
type PseudoAbstract **is structure**(x : w, y : **proc**(w -> **string**))

where *w* is a value of type *ModuleWitness*. The only operation defined on values of *Module* (fully abstract) types is their specialisation to pseudo-abstract types; values thus specialised may be used as concrete types so long as their *ModuleWitness* components may be statically deduced to be compatible.[3] Thus one property of the algebra is to disseminate the burden of static dependency checking from the abstract package to its components.

It is worth observing at this point that the intermediate modules *Sum* and *Interval* are typed as pseudo-abstract types in both languages in the above examples, and the difference in typechecking reflects a tradeoff between the time of checking and context of legal use.

4.2. Formal Description

For an arbitrary language the following constructs are added to the type and expression domains:

T ::= ... | **Module**[i](T) | **ModuleWitness** | E
E ::= ... | **mkModule**(E, T) | **mWitness**(E) | **repModule**(E, T)

In the types domain, *Module[i](T)* is the type of an abstract module, where *i* stands for the abstract (witness) type which, in non-trivial cases, will appear free in the type signature *T*. *ModuleWitness* is the type of an explicit dependent type; values of this type also appear in the type domain, explaining the presence of *E*. Notice however that this does not necessarily give rise to undecidable static checking, relying on static analysis techniques as mentioned above.

In the expression domain, the *mkModule* function is essentially a type-widening operation: its parameters are a value and an abstract module type; it returns the same value wrapped as an abstract module. It is at this point that the value of the module witness type is calculated, and also stored as part of the abstract module value. This is the value returned by the *mWitness* operation. The *repModule* operation takes a module instance and a module witness type (described as *T*, although *E* would be equally valid) and returns the abstract value in a pseudo-abstract instantiation. This operation is only defined if the module witness type provided is compatible with that of the module instance; we introduce the $\equiv$ operator to define this compatibility, and leave its definition until later.

The following type rules formalise the context of use of the new expressions and types. Within the type rules the syntax f(t) in place of a type variable is used to represent a type signature imposed over an arbitrary type, such that if T = f(x) then f(y) = [x $\leftarrow$ y]T (where x and y are themselves type expressions).

$$\frac{\pi \vdash e : ModuleWitness}{\pi \vdash e \in Type}$$

$$\frac{\pi \vdash e : f(t)}{\pi \vdash mkModule(e, Module[i](f(i))) : Module[i](f(i))}$$

$$\frac{\pi \vdash e : Module[i](T)}{\pi \vdash mWitness(e) : ModuleWitness}$$

$$\frac{\pi \vdash e_1 : Module[i](f(i)) \wedge \pi \vdash e_2 : ModuleWitness \wedge [[e_2]] \equiv mWitness(e_1)}{\pi \vdash repModule(e_1, e_2) : f(e_2)}$$

The last of these rules introduces two potential problems with the static typing of programs. The first is the re-typing of *e₁* as f(e_2), which gives the possibility of arbitrary expressions subsequently being typed as *ModuleWitness* types as discussed above. The second problem is more serious: that is, in general, the dynamic evaluation of e_2 is required before the rule can be applied, giving rise to dynamic checking on those occasions where the result of the $\equiv$ operator on the meaning of e_2 cannot be determined statically. This dynamic checking however is essential to provide the required flexibility seen in the

---

[3] Orthogonal mechanisms for achieving this are known, e.g. [CL90], and the issue is not discussed further here.

earlier examples. In cases where dynamic checking is not required for flexibility it is possible to factor the checking out statically.

A semantics for the new constructs is defined as follows:

$$[[\text{ mkModule}(E : f(t), \text{Module}[i](f(i)))]] = pair([[E]], formWitnessRep(t))$$

$$[[\text{ mWitness}(E)]] = snd([[E]])$$

$$[[\text{ repModule}(E_1, E_2)]] = fst([[E_1]])$$

In the semantic model, a module consists of a pair, the elements of which are a value and a witness type representation. The *mkModule* operation forms the pair with the value *[[E]]* and a witness type representation. The *mWitness* operation returns the witness type representation. The *repModule* operation dereferences the enclosed value from the E_1 module pair and allows it to be typed over the E_2 ModuleWitness type value. Notice that the type rule for this operation ensures that the value E_2 is compatible (using the $\equiv$ operator) with the witness type representation of E_1 .

The semantics hinges upon the meaning of the *formWitnessRep* and $\equiv$ functions; in fact a family of different semantic models may be specified by using different definitions. In the current context of use, we make the following definitions, where *unique()* generates a unique value and $\approx$ signifies equality over such values:

$$formWitnessRep(t) \quad = \quad t \qquad \text{if } t : ModuleWitness$$
$$unique() \qquad \text{otherwise}$$

$$t_1 \equiv t_2 \qquad = \qquad t_1 \approx t_2$$

The observation that the new language mechanisms capture type abstraction in SOL, without introducing dynamic typing, is straightforward and not elaborated further. We proceed to show how the examples of module construction given earlier above may be described.

4.3. Modelling module mechanisms

There is only a single typing of the base module *ListInt*, which is an abstracted record type containing both the data and functional components of the module:

type ListInt **is module**[T](**structure**(empty : T; ... - *as before* - ...))

let aListInt = **struct**
(
    empty = ListInt(Empty : **nil**),
    .. - *as before* - ...
)

let listInt = **mkModule**(aListInt, ListInt)

However there are two possible typings of the intermediate modules *Interval* and *Sum*. The first typing for *Sum* is:

Module[Rep](**proc**(Rep -> int))

and the other possiblility is:

proc(Rep -> int), where *Rep* = *mWitness*(aListInt)

These different types correspond to the terms *fully abstract* and *pseudo-abstract* introduced above. The essence of the different solutions is in the binding of the local abstract type variable *Rep*, which may be either closed in the fully abstract definition, or open and resolved as some value dependency in the pseudo-abstract definition. In the fully abstract model a new type closure is created as follows:

```
type Sum is Module[ Rep ]( proc( Rep -> int ) )

let createSum = proc( listImpl : ListInt -> Sum )
{
    let T := mWitness( listImpl )
    let m = repModule( listImpl, T )

    rec let sumList = proc( list : T -> int );
        if m.isEmpty( list )
            then 0
            else m.first( list ) + sumList( m.rest( list ) )

    mkModule( sumList, Sum )
}
```

Given the above definition of *formWitnessRep* the call to *mkModule* in the text gives the same model as *(Sum with T = m.T)* in the original Fibonacci definition, by ensuring the placement of sufficient dependent type information in the abstract module. However the dynamic semantics of this placement would allow the information to be (dynamically) recaptured in a different static environment, whereas the Fibonacci model is completely static.

The pseudo-abstract equivalent is as follows:

```
let createSum = proc( listImpl : ListInt -> proc( mWitness( listImpl ) -> int ) )
{
    let T = mWitness( listImpl )
    let m = repModule( listImpl, T )

    rec let sumList= proc( list : T-> int );
        .. - as before - ...

    sumList
}
```

Notice the explicit value dependency which appears in the procedure header. This general form of typing certainly removes the possibility of fully decidable static typing. Notice, however, that this particular procedure can be statically checked.

The definitions of *Interval* add no new typings and are not elaborated. The procedure *createMain* following in the fully abstract model is as follows:

```
let createMain = proc( m1: Interval, m2: Sum -> proc( int,int -> int ) );
{
    let W1 = mWitness( m1 )
    let X1 = repModule( m1, W1 )
    let X2 = repModule( m2, W1 )

    proc( x, y: int -> int );
        X2( X1( x, y ) )
}
```

If this code is compared with the Fibonacci solution above, it may be observed that the condition *(m2: Sum with T = m1.T)* in the original Fibonacci program is replaced by the call *repModule(m2, W1)*, which will succeed only if the modules share the same witness representation. However although the test is the same, it occurs in the procedure body rather than as part of the typing, giving a more general procedure type (notice that this is of particular importance in a system with first-class executable forms) at the expense of dynamic typechecking; however, as noted, this dynamic checking occurs before the end of the application construction phase.

With the pseudo-abstract model the definition is as follows:

```
let createMain = proc(      m0: ListInt;
                            m1: proc( int, int -> mWitness( m0 ) );
                            m2: proc( mWitness( m0 ) -> int )
                                                -> proc( int, int -> int ) );
        proc( x, y: int -> int ); m2( m1(x, y) )
```

Notice that it is possible to statically type this procedure. (We do not provide a general mechanism, only the observation that it is possible in this instance.) In fact it may be possible to statically type the whole creation of an instance of *Main*, as for example

```
let listPack = createListInt()
let interval = createInterval( listPack )
let sum = createSum( listPack )
let main = createMain( listPack , interval , sum )
```

Notice however that the static typing of the *createMain* procedure requires the base module *m0* to be explicitly provided as a parameter, unlike the fully abstract coding where it is not required. Given parametric polymorphism this can be avoided by defining *createMain* polymorphically and specialising the call appropriately from outside the context, as follows:

```
let createMain = proc[ t ](   m1: proc( int, int -> t );
                              m2: proc( t -> int )
                                              -> proc( int, int -> int ) );
        proc( x, y: int -> int ); m2( m1(x, y) )

let listPack = createListInt()
let interval = createInterval( listPack )
let sum = createSum( listPack )
let t = mWitness( listPack )
let main = createMain[ t ]( interval , sum )
```

The important difference here is that, instead of the specification of all module dependencies needing to be explicit, a single dependent type value may be used to check all diamond dependencies within a module system. Once again, it is possible to statically typecheck the above code, which may be interesting to compare with the Fibonacci system solution above.

The fact that these particular examples can be statically typed does not imply that pseudo-abstract forms are to be preferred in general; in fact their typechecking is much harder to automate and undisciplined use, if statically allowed, must generate implicit dynamic checks to preserve soundness. Fully abstract forms, on the other hand, while possibly requiring more dynamic checking in some cases, have a more understandable typechecking regime and generate only explicit dynamic checks.

5.   Conclusions

We have investigated the typing of module mechanisms in a persistent environment. The significance of orthogonal persistence is that the aspects of longevity and binding often associated with such mechanisms may be assumed to be orthogonal to their typing. The general-purpose abstract type mechanism of Napier88 was shown to go some way in the provision of module requirements, although some general restrictions in the language syntax mean that precise type definitions are sometimes lacking compared to equivalent solutions given in the Fibonacci module syntax. A more detailed examination of the typing issues involved has resulted the description of an abstract module mechanism which gives more flexibility, at the cost of less certain static typechecking. The new mechanism has been shown to capture both of the languages investigated, and may be a candidate for a combined abstract type / module mechanism.

6.   Acknowledgements

The *moduleWitness* type is a development of a dependent typing invented by Atsushi Ohori, and ideas generated from discussion with him have probably found their way into this paper. The implementation of the dependent witness types in Napier88 was carried out by Quintin Cutts. Thanks are due also for helpful comments from the anonymous referees. The authors are grateful for financial assistance from the Esprit III FIDE2 project (BRA 6309), which allowed Paolo Manghi to visit St Andrews for an extended period. Richard Connor is supported by EPSRC Advanced Fellowship B/91/AF/1921.

7.   References

[ACP+91]   Abadi M, Cardelli L, Pierce B and Plotkin G, "Dynamic typing in a statically typed language", ACM TOPLAS 13, 2 (1991) pp 237-268.

[AGO95]   Albano A, Ghelli G and Orsini R, "Fibonacci: a Programming Language for Object Databases", VLDB Journal 4, 3, (July 1995), pp 403-444

[CBC+90]   Connor R.C.H., Brown A.L., Cutts Q.I., Dearle A., Morrison R. & Rosenberg J., "Type Equivalence Checking in Persistent Object Stores", Proc. 4th International Workshop on Persistent Object Systems, Martha's Vineyard, Massachusetts, September 1990, in **Implementing Persistent Object Bases - Principles and Practice**, Morgan - Kaufmann, pp 154-170.

[CDM+90]   Connor R.C.H., Dearle A., Morrison R. & Brown A.L., "Existentially Quantified Types as a Database Viewing Mechanism", 2nd International Conference on Extending Database Technology, in **Advances in Database Technology - EDBT '90**, F. Bancilhon, C. Thanos & D. Tsichritzis (Eds), LNCS 416, Springer-Verlag, March 1990, pp 301-315.

[CL90]   Cardelli L and Leroy X, "Abstract Types and the Dot Notation", SRC Report 56, DEC Systems Research Center, Palo Alto (March 1990).

[CM88]   Cardelli L and McQueen D, "Persistence and Type Abstraction", in Atkinson, Buneman and Morrison (eds), **Data Types and Persistence**, Springer-Verlag (1988) pp 31-41.

[DCC93]   Dearle A., Connor R.C.H. & Cutts Q.I., "Using Persistence to Support Incremental System Construction", Journal of Microprocessors and Microsystems, 17, 3, 1993, pp 161 - 171.

[MP88]   J.C. Mitchell and G.D. Plotkin, "Abstract Types have Existential Type", ACM TOPLAS 10, 3 (July 1988) pp 470-502

[OTC+90]   Ohori A., Tabkha I., Connor R.C.H. & Philbrow P., "Persistence and Type Abstraction Revisited", Proc. 4th International Workshop on Persistent Object Systems, Martha's Vineyard, Massachusetts, September 1990, in **Implementing Persistent Object Bases - Principles and Practice**, Morgan - Kaufmann, pp 141-153.

[Par72]   Parnas, D.L., "On the Criteria to be Used in Decomposing Systems into Modules", CACM 15, 12 (1972) pp 1053-1058.

[StA96]   The St Andrews Persistence Research Group, http://www-fide.dcs.st-and.ac.uk

Dynamically Configurable Concurrency Control for a Persistent Store

*Michael Flanagan, *Alan Fekete, †Frans Henskens and *John Rosenberg

*Basser Department of Computer Science, F09,
University of Sydney, NSW, 2006, Australia.
email: {groo, fekete, johnr}@cs.usyd.edu.au

† Department of Management,
University of Newcastle, NSW, 2308, Australia.
email: mgfah@alinga.newcastle.edu.au

Abstract

A system is described, in which concurrent access to persistent data is controlled by a variety of alternative concurrency control mechanisms. Users can dynamically install a mechanism of their choice, by specifying it in a small stack-based programming language. Attempts to access data will then invoke execution of the installed mechanism, which may delay access or allow it depending on the situation. This system allows different data to be protected with different mechanisms. As an example, we show how the system would operate with the multigranularity locking algorithm as concurrency control.

1 Introduction

For fifteen years, the notion of orthogonal persistence has been investigated by the research community. There has been extensive work on type systems, protection, storage management, distribution, and other important topics. Perhaps because each of these is already very complicated, most papers and systems have been intended for a single-user environment. However, if a persistent system is to support real-world applications, and be a viable alternative to conventional database systems, it is essential that they support multiple users accessing data concurrently. There are well-known anomalies that can arise if arbitrary interleaving occurs between concurrent users: updates can be lost, queries can retrieve inconsistent results, and so on [GR93].

The operating systems and concurrent programming communities have generally adopted solutions based on semaphores. Here the system or language environment provides a building block, but it is the responsibility of the programmer to ensure that all the concurrent activities obtain and release the semaphores correctly. The database community has taken a different approach, in recognition of the likelihood that applications are written by inexpert programmers, who in any case can't be expected to know the full set of concurrent activity. Instead the transaction has been acknowledged as the central abstraction in preventing concurrent applications from corrupting the contents of a database [EGL+76]. Here, each application is written independently, and it is the responsibility of the system to determine when to set and release locks to ensure that the effect is serializable, that is, the same as if applications did not overlap at all. The original concurrency control algorithm, strict two-phase locking with shared and exclusive locks, is still widely used in practice, since it is simple to implement and guarantees serializability. Many alternative algorithms have been proposed: timestamps are well-studied but not used, while commercial systems have implemented variants of key-range locking to avoid phantoms, and escrow reads to improve throughput on hotspot data, as discussed in [GR93].

Besides algorithms which offer alternative implementations for the traditional transaction semantics (ACID properties), there have been many new models proposed, for use in advanced application domains where cooperation is needed between concurrent activities. A detailed survey of these new ideas is found in [Elm92]. Each new model needs one or more algorithms to provide concurrency control. It is important to note the distinction between an alternative transaction model and alternative concurrency control algorithms for a given model. Users can observe the impact of a change in model, since

60

applications will interact with different semantics; however, the choice of concurrency control algorithm is purely a matter of efficient execution, without semantic effect.

Traditionally, the choice of transaction model and concurrency control algorithm in a DBMS, and in those persistent stores which support concurrency, has been made when the system is designed. The system offers a fixed set of transaction management primitives, such as begin-transaction, or commit; also the lock manager has a fixed set of lock modes and unalterable rules for dealing with conflicts. For example, the lock manager described in [GR93] is hardwired so that a process blocks when another holds a conflicting lock. This is unable to deal with nested transactions or timestamp-based algorithms. This paper describes a system based on a different view. We offer a system architecture where the choice of transaction model and concurrency control algorithm can both be made at run-time; indeed different algorithms can be used simultaneously on different parts of the database.

The importance of flexible concurrency control in a persistent store can be seen in two different dimensions. First, the different transaction models are each useful in their own application domain; if a system supports only one model, then either its use will be restricted to the domain where that model is valid, or else the application programmers will need to waste time in finding work-arounds. For example, if classical ACID transactions are the only available model, then the store will be unsuitable for all the cooperative work applications that are described in [Elm92]; on the other hand the advanced transaction models do not meet the needs of traditional record processing commercial applications. Second, even within a single transaction model, such as classical ACID transactions, it makes sense to construct a system with a simple, easily-programmed concurrency control algorithm and later use data-type specific information to upgrade the performance for those items that are hotspots. A substantial body of theory has been developed to guide this process [Wei89].

The key idea of our design is that there is a "Conflict Manager" that fills the role of a traditional lock manager in a DBMS, but it contains an interpreter for a small stack-based language. When a particular algorithm is chosen to provide concurrency control for some part of the data, the user sends strings written in the language to the Conflict Manager, and binds them to certain function names. Later when access to the data is needed, the functions are executed in the Conflict Manager. This results in a range of outcomes such as blocking the requestor, allowing it to continue, or even sending a signal to a waiting process. Since many traditional algorithms are based on classes of conflicting locks, our system contains a "fast-path" so that a table of conflict rules may be expressed in a particularly simple fashion. Our design has been substantially implemented: the persistent store and Conflict Manager are running, and we have installed and tested Two Phase Locking, Multi-granularity Locking and Notification Locking algorithms all operating on different objects in the same store. The first two provide a classical transaction model, while the latter supports cooperative transactions. Thus we have demonstrated our design's flexibility. Complete details of our system can be found in [Fla96].

Among persistent systems reported in the literature, there have been a few with support for multiple concurrent users. The original PS-Algol language [ACC81] divided the store into discrete "databases" (with no inter-database references allowed), and it limited each application to open at most one of these for writing, at any time; the system obtained an exclusive lock on the writeable database. Thus atomicity is provided, at the cost of gravely restricting possible concurrency. There is no provision for users to alter the model or mechanism.

More recently, work at St Andrews has explored flexible multi-user access through the CACS specification language [SM92]. In CACS, one can describe different transaction models in terms of the events that take place, and dependencies between them; various access sets are maintained which allow different applications to use certain objects but not others, and events cause objects to move between access sets. CACS operates at a higher, more declarative level than our system; it. is suitable for describing transaction models, but it does not contain the stack based language which allows our system to also execute different algorithms within a single transaction model The infrastructure for the implementation of the CACS model is described in [Mun94]. Further work has concentrated on recovery algorithms rather than concurrency control [MCM+,SRM+96].

Considering the wider DBMS community, the prior work most closely related to ours is the Kala system [SG91], which also supports a range of concurrency control mechanisms. However, Kala provides a fixed collection of powerful primitives to allow and disallow sharing of versions, rather than a language executed at run-time, and so Kala is less flexible than our proposal. The ASSET system [BDG+94] and a similar system by Georgakoupolous [GHK+94] are based on formalisms similar to CACS, and are also appropriate for describing transaction models and providing simple, not necessarily efficient implementations of these, but they are not able to incorporate alternative mechanisms for a given model. For example neither [BDG+94] nor [GHK+94] suggests a way to model Multi-Granularity Locking.

The rest of the paper is structured as follows. Section 2 describes the overall architecture of our system, and especially the interaction patterns between the Conflict Manager and the rest of the system. Section 3 presents the calls that are supported and the stack-based language, in which the algorithm is expressed. Section 4 shows in detail how the Conflict Manager can be programmed to follow the multi-granularity locking algorithm.

2   System Overview

The system is designed to provide flexible concurrency control over data residing in an object repository, or *store* (the term object is used in a more generic manner than in object oriented paradigms). The system provides run time selection of concurrency control requirements by providing a layered structure in which different tasks can be selected, within certain layers, to provide the run time support for the chosen concurrency scheme. The system is divided into layers as depicted in Figure 1. The major components which make up the system are the Communications Manager, the Concurrency Managers, the Object Manager and the Conflict Manager.

The various components exist concurrently as multi-threaded tasks which communicate with each other via a message passing protocol. When an external process connects to the system to request data services its causes new threads to be spawned within the various layers of the system. These new threads combine to provide dedicated service to the external process. Thus each external process connects to what is effectively a vertical slice through the system. The term "manager" is used to refer to the task responsible for initialising and spawning new threads in each layer of the system. The threads which are spawned to handle client process services are referred to as "sessions". Thus the "Conflict Manager" and "Conflict session" implement the Conflict Management Module. The responsibilities and activities of each of the system components are described below.

The Communication Manager is responsible for all communication with client processes. The communication manager is responsible for managing the connection process and selecting a concurrency manager of the type appropriate for the client process. All issues of communication such as pipe or socket management reside within this part of the system. All internal communication between the system components is handled via an internal message passing protocol.

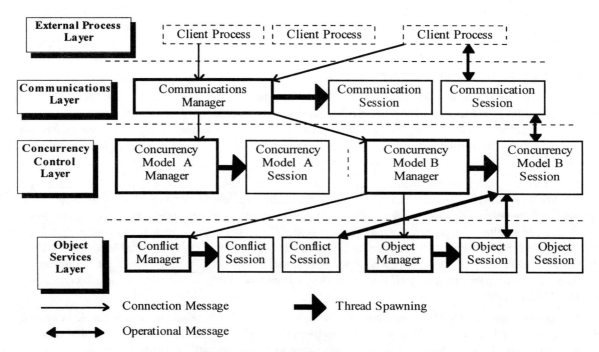

Figure 1: System Layers and Messages

The various Concurrency Model managers each implement a different concurrency control scheme. Concurrency Model managers register themselves with the communication manager and are activated when a client process requests a connection to the service corresponding to their registered name. The concurrency control manager and session are responsible for establishing a connection to the Conflict Manager and the Object Manager and providing any necessary initialisation, such as conflict tables or functions for the Conflict Manager. The Concurrency Model Session then receives messages from the client process which are appropriate to the scheme being implemented. The Concurrency Model Session must translate the client requests into requests for data services or conflict services. This involves such actions as translating simple read and write requests into requests for locks and access to the Object Manager. A more detailed example is given at the end of this paper to illustrate how a Concurrency Model Manager is coded.

The Object Manager provides an interface to a simple object store similar to those which are commonly found in persistent systems. The store implements a type of object which is simpler in structure to objects found in object oriented systems. Objects consist of a number of bytes of uninterpreted data and a collection of references to other objects. Concurrency Model Managers make requests of the Object Manager to perform tasks such as reading, writing, creating, deleting objects and version management.

The objects within the store are given object identifiers (OIDs) which are unique throughout the lifetime of the store. The Object Manager provides caching and garbage collection services transparent to the other modules.

The Conflict Manager provides a configurable conflict management service to the various Concurrency Model Managers. The Conflict Manager is initialised, by a Concurrency Model Manager, with the necessary tables and functions for a given concurrency scheme. The Conflict Manager then receives requests from a Concurrency Model Session and interprets the requests using the installed conflict resolution procedures. The initialisation of the Conflict Manager, the processing of requests and the language used to code the required functions and tables are described in detail in the next section.

3   The Conflict Manager Interface and Language

The role of the Conflict Manager is to provide services to the Concurrency Model Manager to handle tasks involving the determination of resource conflicts within the concurrency scheme. While the Concurrency Model Manager handles issues such as transactional structure, what should be locked, tagged or read and when such actions are performed, the Conflict Manager determines which associations cause conflicts or which requests cause the notification or blocking of other processes.

The Conflict Manager interface is divided into two sections. One section of the interface provides the facility for specifying a conflict scheme, i.e. initialising the Conflict Manager for a specific scheme. The other section of the interface accepts request messages which are interpreted using the tables and functions of the registered schemes.

The specification section of the Conflict Manager interface consists of functions for:

- gaining a connection to the Conflict Manager,

- installing the conflict table and the code for the functions of a concurrency scheme

- querying the Conflict Manager for the value of scalars and identifiers for registered functions.

A description of the process of gaining a connection to the Conflict Manager involves a description of the task management policy and message passing protocols of the system. This falls outside the scope of this paper. Part of this initialisation process involves the specification of a file name which identifies a file containing code for the Concurrency Model Manager. This code specifies the functions and tables necessary to implement the conflict resolution of the desired scheme. There are also functions used to query the values of scalars and function identifiers. These allow the Concurrency Model Manager to get numerical identifiers which are associated with the named functions or modes, thus avoiding repeated time consuming string comparisons.

The messages described above are used by a Concurrency Model Manager during the initialisation phase. When these initialisation procedures are completed, individual Concurrency Model sessions (child tasks of the Concurrency Model manager) can acquire a Conflict Manager connection and begin to perform association requests, free association etc. The messages which are used to perform the tasks are discussed below.

Messages may be sent from a concurrency model session to perform the following tasks:

- request an association on a resource

- free an association on a resource

- invoke a registered function to perform some action (e.g commit and abort).

To request an association a concurrency session sends the message:

Bool request_assoc(Resource res, **AssocMode** mode)

This message requests that the resource name *res* be associated with the requesting task in the supplied *mode*. This causes the Conflict Manager to invoke the registered function with the name *requestAssoc*. Note that this action does not necessarily result in the creation of a lock in the conventional sense. It can result in some alternative type of association being created between the session and the resource, which could for example result in the notification of some other sessions. Also note that the "resource" is just a string; it need not be directly linked to any object in the store (although it often is so linked).

Similarly a concurrency session may send the *release_assoc* message which will cause the invocation of a registered function This message requests the Conflict Manager to remove the requesting task from the list of tasks which hold associations with the resource. Concurrency models may allow multiple tasks to hold compatible associations with a single resource so a *release_assoc* message will not necessarily leave a resource free of all associations.

To cause a transaction to commit or to perform some other action appropriate to the current concurrency control model, as task may send the message:

Bool invoke_function(FunctionID action, **char** *format, ...).

This message will cause the Conflict Manager to invoke the function with the given id. The 'C' function which acts as a stub for this message takes a variable argument list and a format string similar to the 'C' I/O functions. This allows a variable collection of arguments to be passed to the Conflict Manager function. The *invoke_function* message allows a scheme to implement such actions as:

- freeing all locks in the case of commit or abort in conventional transactions

- passing all locks onto the parent transactions on completion of a nested transaction

- etc.

The above mentioned messages allow concurrency models to register functions with the lock manager and invoke functions. These functions are written in a small stack based language which is similar to Forth or Postscript. The language is designed to be applicable to the development of small functions which determine simple conflict states and keep track of associations between tasks and resources.

The language includes facilities for

- function definition,

- table definition,

- scalar definition,

- process control,

- function invocation,

- flow control,

- list manipulation,

- association structure access

- table access,

- arithmetic operations and

- stack manipulation.

In addition to this the language has a collection of built in functions.

Function definition is achieved through the use of the *def* operator, which has the form:

<name><codeBlock> **def**

This associates the code in the codeblock with the supplied name. The name, which is preceded by a '/' character as in PostScript, is associated with a numerical identifier which may be used to uniquely and efficiently identify the function from outside the Conflict Manager. Within the Conflict Manager code the function is referred to by its ASCII name. Scalar definition is similar

Tables are defined with the *tabdef* operator which has the form:

<name> <entry$_{00}$> ... <entry$_{NM}$> <width> <height> **tabdef**

This operator takes a collection of table entries and a width and a height and creates a two dimensional array with the supplied name. This array may then be accessed using the languages table manipulation operators.

Process Control in the language involves the concept of a task which is a connection to a Conflict Manager session from a Concurrency Model session. Task management is performed using the operators *block* and *wake*. The *block* operator allows a Conflict Manager session to suspend the invoking task (the concurrency model session to which it is connected) and label its suspension with a resource and an associated mode, so that it can later be awoken conditionally. The *wake* operator allows a Conflict Manager session to wake up another task. The structure of these operators is a follows:

<resource> <mode> **block**
<task> **wake**

Function invocation is performed by the *call* and *execTable* operators. The *call* operator takes a function id from the top of the stack and invokes the code associated with this function. As the language is stack based, parameters are passed and results returned by placing values on the stack before, and at the end of, invocation. The format of the *call* operator is simply:

<functionId> **call**

The *execTable* operator provides function invocation from a two dimensional lookup table. Its form is:

<index$_1$> <index$_2$> <tableID> **execTable.**

Another form of call is provided by the *callback* operator. When executed, the *callback* operator will invoke the callback function specified during registration of the scheme.

Flow control in the language is supported by the following operators:

<start> <inc> <stop> { *code_block* } **for**
{ code_block } **while**
{ code_block } **until**
<cond> { code_block } **if**
<cond> { btrue } { bfalse } **ifelse.**

The *for* operator steps through the integers from start to stop, using the incremental value inc, and executes the code block once for each integer after placing the integer on the top of the stack. The *while* and *until* provide loops by testing the top of stack and only executing the block of code if the value is true. The *if* and *ifelse* operators execute the code segment conditionally depending on the value of the top of stack.

List manipulation is performed by the use of the *makelist, addhead, addtail, head, tail* and *joinlist* operators. In addition to these operators the language provides operators for iterating over a list: lfor, land and lor. The *lfor* operator iterates over a whole list by placing subsequent elements from the list onto the stack then executing the specified code block. The *land* and *lor* operators provide short cut evaluation of a predicate over the contents of a list. The *land* operator executes the code block once for each element of the list (after placing the element on the top of stack as in *lfor*) until the code block returns a false value on the top of stack or the list is consumed. If the block of code returns true for all list elements the final value true is left on the top of stack otherwise a value of false is returned. The *lor* operator performs similarly with disjunction instead of conjunction.

The language supports a built in type called an association. This type represents a binding between a task (Concurrency Model session) and a resource which is tagged with a mode. Thus it contains the three fields: owner, resource, mode. The language has operators which allow the construction and separation of associations.

Operators exist for the manipulation of lists as single element arrays. These are *lget* and *lput* which behave similarly to their two dimensional counterparts. The language also contains operators which are similar to those provided by Postscript. They include: *dup, add, sub, neg, exch, rol, ndup, pop, <, >* etc.

To facilitate the specification of a conflict management scheme in the language, the Conflict Manager has several reserved names. These names are

- mode - the name of the scalar definition used to identify valid association modes

- releaseAssoc - the name of the function called in response to the *release_assoc* message.

- requestAssoc - the name of the function called in response to the *request_assoc* message.

- maxTable - the name of a table of association modes used by the predefined function *MaxMode*.

The language includes a number of predefined functions which have predefined function identifiers. These functions perform common tasks which are expected to be needed in most systems and are called through the use of the *call* operator in the same way as registered functions but all their function identifiers fall within a reserved range which will never be returned as the identifiers of registered functions. Some of these functions manipulate a built-in table shared among all Conflict Manager sessions, which stores all of the registered associations between resources and tasks.

The two functions for storing and removing associations from the builtin table are:

> <lock> *storeAssoc* **call**
> <lock> *deleteAssoc* **call**

The *deleteAList* function is called as follows:

> [lock$_1$...lock$_n$] *deleteAList* **call**

It examines each association record in the supplied list and removes the referenced association from all internal tables, thus freeing the resource from this association.

The *holds_list* and *blocked_list* functions return a list of all locks held on, or blocked during request of, a resource in a mode. The mode may be replaced by the reserved mode **any_mode** to get a list of all locks held on 'res'. The *max_mode* function uses the lock maximisation table registered with the name *maxTable* to determine the upper bound of the modes of all locks on a resource. This function is used in schemes such as Multi Granularity Locking to determine if a requested lock is compatible with the locks already granted. There is also a function *task_locks* which returns a list of all locks held by the task with given identifier which hold a resource in the given mode. Again the reserved mode **any_mode** may be used in place of a specific mode. The language includes predefined functions which make use of parent/child relationships between tasks using the Conflict Manager. These functions include *is_ancestor* and *parent*.

The next section shows how the language features and functions described above, may be used to implement a Multi-granularity locking scheme.

4 An Example: Multi-granularity Locking

The multi-granularity locking example presented here is a very simple one. It assumes a system consisting of two levels of objects. When a client locks more than a given threshold number of sub-objects then the parent object is locked.

4.1 Conflict Manager Functions

To implement Multi-granularity locking we must register a group of functions with the Conflict Manager.

The function Gproc is called from a jump table to grant a lock. It makes use of the built in function *store_lock* which adds a lock to the granted queue for a given resource. It assumes that a lock structure exists on the argument stack which contains the necessary lock details. The text of the Gproc function is:

```
Gproc {
    STORE_LOCK call
    false
}
```

It leaves **false** on the stack which will be used in other code as an indication that the lock request did not block.

The Bproc function, as with Gproc, is called from a jump table when the requested mode conflicts with the currently granted mode of a resource. It uses the predefined function BLOCK to cause the current thread to suspend execution until it is awoken using the WAKE function. The BLOCK function takes a resource and a lock mode so that threads may be selectively reactivated depending on the resource and mode provided when they executed a BLOCK call. Bproc extracts the resource and mode from the lock structure which it assumes is on the stack. Bproc and Gproc must assume the same stack contents when invoked as they are both called from the same jump table. The text of Bproc is:

```
Bproc {
    dup             // copy the lock structure on the TOS
    lockres exch    // get resource and swap with
                    // lock structure on TOS
    lockmode     // TOS now holds res, mode
    BLOCK call
    true
}
```

The Bproc function returns the value **true** to indicate that blocking took place.

The GetLock function is used to process a lock request. It first determines the maximum lock mode under which the requested resource (r_res) is currently locked by calling the predefined function MAX_MODE. It then uses this value and the value of the requested mode as indices to the LockRequestTable (below) to select either Gproc or Bproc depending on the lock compatibility. If a block occurs the function called from the LockRequestTable will leave the value **true** on the stack which will cause the while loop to repeat when the thread is awoken. In this manner the process will continue until the lock is successfully acquired. As GetLock will be called from outside the interpreter (i.e. in direct response to a concurrency model manager request) it makes use of the external argument symbols r_owner, r_res and r_mode. The text of the GetLock function is:

```
GetLock {
    {
        // create lock structure as arg for Gproc or Bproc
        r_owner  r_res  r_mode  makelock
        // find maximum current mode
        r_res MAX_MODE call
        r_mode
        // index jumptable using requested and maximum modes
        LockRequestTable exectable
    } while
};
```

In the above code the symbol *LockRequestTable* would be replaced by the identifier returned when the table was registered. The registering of this table is discussed below.

The FreeLock function is used to wake any processes which are blocked waiting for the given lock. The processes will then compete to acquire the lock. The text of the FreeLock function is:

```
FreeLock {
    dup DELETE_LOCK call
    lockres ANY_MODE BLOCKED_LIST call
        { lockMode wake }
    lfor
}
```

The function assumes a lock structure is on the stack indicating which lock is to be freed. It duplicates this lock structure (dup) then frees it using the built in operator *delete_lock*. The function then uses the built in operator *lockRes* to extract the resource name from the lock structure and wakes any tasks which are in the list of tasks blocked on this resource. Note this implementation is inefficient in that many processes may be wakened while only one may successfully get the lock. Note also that this method does not support fifo granting of lock requests. If fifo granting is desired, or if efficiency is required, the wake operator could be applied only to the head of the list returned by BLOCKED_LIST.

The EndProc function is used to clean up after a transaction has committed or aborted. It simply gets the list of locks held by the current transaction using the predefined function TASK_LOCKS and then frees all locks in the list using the FreeLock function.

```
EndProc {
    r_trans ANY_MODE TASK_LOCKS call
    { FreeLock call } lfor
}
```

4.2 Concurrency Model Manager code

Rather than present the Multi-granularity Model Manager code in full, a summary will be given, outlining how the code works and giving some fragments.

Firstly the abovementioned Conflict Manager functions must be registered. This is done by passing a character string to the function *register_function* and storing the result in a variable of type FunctionID. For the Gproc function this would be:

```
char gproc_text[] = "{STORE_LOCK call false}";
...
FunctionID gproc_fn, bproc_fn, endproc_fn,
        getlock_fn, freelock_fn;
...
gproc_fn = register_function(gproc_text);
```

Next the tables for lock maximisation (Figure 2) and the jump table called *LockRequestTable* (Figure 3) are registered using the *register_table* function.

Having registered all required functions and tables the Concurrency Model Manager can register the scheme with the Conflict Manager by a call to the new_control function, as in:

```
new_control("MGL",
  MODE_X,               // maximum mode (Defined in enum)
  mgl_max_table,        // returned by register_table()
  getlock_fn,           // from register_function()
  freelock_fn,          //
  (FunctionID) NULL);   // no callback required
```

Multi Granularity Lock Maximisation							
	None	**IS**	**IX**	**S**	**SIX**	**U**	**X**
None	None	IS	IX	S	SIX	U	X
IS	IS	IS	IX	S	SIX	U	X
IX	IX	IX	IX	SIX	SIX	X	X
S	S	S	SIX	S	SIX	U	X
SIX	SIX	SIX	SIX	SIX	SIX	SIX	X
U	U	U	X	U	SIX	U	X
X	X	X	X	X	X	X	X

Figure 2: Multi Granularity Lock Maximisation Table

68

MGL Lock Request Table						
	Requesting Mode					
Granted Max Mode	IS	IX	S	SIX	U	X
None	Gproc	Gproc	Gproc	Gproc	Gproc	Gproc
IS	Gproc	Gproc	Gproc	Gproc	Bproc	Bproc
IX	Gproc	Gproc	Bproc	Bproc	Bproc	Bproc
S	Gproc	Bproc	Gproc	Bproc	Gproc	Bproc
SIX	Gproc	Bproc	Bproc	Bproc	Bproc	Bproc
U	Bproc	Bproc	Bproc	Bproc	Bproc	Bproc
X	Bproc	Bproc	Bproc	Bproc	Bproc	Bproc

Figure 3: Muti Granularity Lock Request Table

In addition to registering the functions and tables needed for conflict management the code for the Concurrency Model Manager must include functions to handle connections, disconnections and requests for reads and writes to objects. A simplified code fragment below demonstrates how the main message loop of the Concurrency Model Manager is written to support a simple MGL protocol which uses a two level object hierarchy with simple reads and writes of second level objects. If more than a certain number (threshold) of locks are requested for a group of siblings then a lock is taken out on their common parent. In the following code segment the bold face function names indicate functions which use facilities of the Conflict Manager. All other functions are implemented internally to the Concurrency Model Manager.

```
read_object(TID tid, OID parent, OID child)
{
  int lcount;        // number of locks currently held
                     // on children of parent
  LMODE mode;        // current lock mode of parent
  LMODE max_cmode;   // max mode a child of parent is held

  lcount = current_lock_count(tid, parent);
  held_modes(tid, parent, &mode, &max_cmode);

  if (lcount >= THRESHOLD)
  {
     if (mode < MODE_S)
     {
        request_lock(tid, parent, MODE_S);
        // when locking parent, pass 0 as parent ID
        register_lock(tid, parent, (OID) 0, MODE_S);
     }
  }
  else
  {
     if (mode < IS)
     {
        request_lock(tid, parent, MODE_IS);
        register_lock(tid, parent, (OID) 0, MODE_IS);
     }
     request_lock(tid, child, MODE_S);
```

69

```
        register_lock(tid, parent, child, MODE_S);
  }
}
write_object(TID tid, OID parent, OID child)
{
  int lcount;        // number of locks currently held
                     // on children of parent
  LMODE mode;        // current lock mode of parent
  LMODE max_cmode;   // max mode a child of parent is held

  lcount = current_lock_count(tid, parent);
  held_modes(tid, parent, &mode, &max_cmode);

  if (lcount >= THRESHOLD)
  {
     if (mode < MODE_X)
     {
        request_lock(tid, parent, MODE_X);
        register_lock(tid, parent, (OID) 0, MODE_X);
     }
  }
  else
  {
     if (mode < MODE_IX)
     {
        request_lock(tid, parent, MODE_IX);
        register_lock(tid, parent, (OID) 0, MODE_IX);
     }
     request_lock(tid, child, MODE_X);
     register_lock(tid, parent, child, MODE_X);
  }
}
void message_loop()
{
  ...
  receive_message(&m);
  switch (m.type) {
     case CONNECT:
        if (!is_registered("MGL"))
           register_mgl();
        tid = start_transaction();
        break;
     case DISCONNECT:
        perform_action(endproc_fn);
        end_transaction(tid);
        break;
     case READ:
        read_object(tid, m.parent, m.child);
        break;
     case WRITE:
        write_object(tid, m.parent, m.child);
  }
}
```

5   Conclusions

We have proposed a system design that can support flexible, and even dynamic, choice of concurrency control algorithm and transaction model. The key idea is to have a programmable Conflict Manager that maintains "locks" that are associations between a transaction and a resource name. The Conflict Manager can interpret a small stack-based language. When a concurrency control scheme is chosen, one can register appropriate functions to obtain and release locks. Later, when an application is running, these functions are executed, which results in transactions being blocked, allowed to proceed, or woken up, as specified by the concurrency control algorithm. The system has been implemented; we have demonstrated its flexibility by showing how a multi-granularity locking algorithm is expressed.

Acknowledgements

The authors gratefully acknowledge the support provided by the Australian Research Council under grant number A49232246 for this project. We also wish to thank Fred Curtis for his assistance with the implementation of this system and Anders Lindström for presenting the paper at the Workshop.

References

[ACC81]   M. Atkinson, K. Chisholm, W. Cockshott, "PS-Algol: An Algol with a Persistent Heap" in *ACM Sigplan Notices:*17(7):24-31, 1981.

[BDG+94]   A. Biliris, S. Dar, N.Gehani, H. Jagadish, K. Ramamritham, "ASSET: A system for supporting extended transactions" in *Processdings ACM Sigmod: 44-54, May 1994.*

[Elm92]   A. Elmagarmid (ed), *Database Transaction Models for Advanced Applications*, Morgan Kauffman 1992.

[EGL+76]   K.Eswaran, J. Gray, R. Lorie, I. Traiger, "The Notion of Consistency and Predicate Locks in Database Systems" in *Comm. ACM 19(11): 624-633*, November 1976.

[Fla96]   M. Flanagan *A System for Flexible Concurrency Control in an Object Store,* Ph.D. thesis, Computer Science Department, University of Sydney, January 1996.

[GHK+94]   D. Georgakopoulos, M. Hornick, P. Krychniak, F. Manola, "Specification of Extended Transactions in a Programmable Transaction Environment" in *Proceedings International Conference on Data Engineering,* 1994.

[GR93]   J. Gray and A. Reuter, *Transaction Processing*, Morgan Kaufmann 1993.

[SG91]   S. Simmel and J. Godard "The Kala Basket" in *Proceedings OOPSLA* 1991.

[Mun94]   D. Munro "On the Integration of Concurrency, Distribution and Persistence" University of St Andrews Research Report CS/94/1.

[MCM+94]   D. Munro, R, Connor, R. Morrison, S. Scheuerl, D. Stemple "Concurrent Shadow Paging in the Flask Architecture" in *Proceedings POS 6*, 1994.

[SRM+96]   S. Scheuerl, R, Connor, R. Morrison, D. Stemple "The DataSafe Failure Recovery Mechanism in the Flask Architecture" in *Proceedings Australasian CS Conference* 1996.

[SM92]   D. Stemple, R. Morrison "Specifying Flexible Concurrency Control Schemes: An Abstract Operational Approach" in *Proceedings Australasian CS Conference* 1992.

[Wei89]   W. Weihl, "Local Atomicity Properties: Modular Concurrency Control for AbstractData Types" in *ACM TOPLAS 11(2): 249-282, April 1989.*

Ensuring efficiently the integrity of persistent object systems via abstract interpretation.

Véronique Benzaken, Xavier Schaefer,*
L.R.I. Bat 490
Université de Paris XI
91405 Orsay Cedex, France
e-mail: Veronique.Benzaken@lri.fr, Xavier.Schaefer@lri.fr

September 24, 1996

Abstract

In this paper, we propose an efficient and reliable method to deal with integrity constraints in a persistent object system. First we provide the application programmer with the ability to *express* integrity constraints but we also give him the possibility to use high level language constructs to help him in *writing* safe transactions.

The goal of our approach is to avoid the (run time) checking of constraints by proving formally that transactions preserve integrity constraints. We mainly use two abstract interpretation techniques to do that. Abstract interpretation is a *semantics-based* tool that yields some reliable information about the possible run-time behaviour of programs, with *fully automatic algorithms*. We present informally the methods that we use: a simple method, based on *path reachability*, and a more powerful and complex method that uses a *predicate transformer*. A predicate transformer is a function that, given a transaction and a formula describing its input data, yields a formula describing its output data.

We finally describe the current prototype that applies those different techniques. It provides in fact the O_2 compiler with an integrity constraint manager.

Keywords: abstract interpretation, reliable persistent stores, database programming languages, integrity constraints, program semantics and static analysis, predicate transformers, safety proofs.

1 Introduction

A great concern for persistent system users is that the information stored should represent the real world faithfully. The data should respect at any moment a set of conditions, called semantic integrity constraints, given by the user. Integrity constraints can be a very critical topic when designing and implementing a persistent object system. On one hand, integrity constraints are very useful, particularly in the field of persistent object systems that offer integrated database facilities (persistent store, database programming language...). On the other hand, a naive management of integrity constraints can burden the system, as constraints have to be checked after each update. We propose in this paper an efficient model for the implementation of integrity constraints managers in persistent object systems. This model consists in providing:

- The application programmer with new programming language constructs
- The compiler with the ability of statically determining whether a transaction preserves integrity constraints.

The application programmer must be able to express constraints in a global and declarative way (as stated in [BLR92, BD93, BD95]), but must also be able to write *easily* transactions that respect those constraints. That is the reason for introducing new language constructs. To this end we extend the usual boolean expressions in conditionals (if's,etc.) by allowing logical quantifiers (those generalised conditions can be translated in standard OQL queries). Without that last construct, the task of the application programmer would be difficult, as he would

---

*Also in Université de Paris I - Panthéon - Sorbonne. Xavier Schaefer is currently supported by a PhD Grant from Ministère de L'Enseignement Supérieur et de la Recherche.

have to write the appropriate tests with a low-level imperative language. This would result in disseminating the semantics of integrity throughout the code. The resulting transaction will be difficult to read and maintain.

The problem of statically determining transaction safety is not new and has been dealt with in different ways. A first approach in [GM79, CB80, Qia90] uses a database extension of Hoare's logic. However, their works are not fully formalised and no steps towards a mechanisation of safety proofs is clear. A second approach in [SS89] uses a complex Boyer-Moore theorem prover and is actually implemented. Their method is quite heavy and complicated, as it is in fact an expert system. Also, it is not known whether it is consistent as it uses axioms that have not been proven so. In fact, since [Qia93], the problem of integrity has been dealt with in the opposite way: instead of analysing complex transactions, [Qia93] studies the generation of safe and correct transactions from some logical specifications. [Qia93] justifies that new direction in the following way: "The generation of unnecessary constraint checking and enforcement code should be avoided. It should be noticed that such optimisation is out of reach for conventional program optimisation techniques, because conventional program optimisers do not have the ability to reason about integrity constraint." We show in this article that such is not the case. Conventional program optimisation techniques such as *abstract interpretation* can also deal with that problem. Our approach consists in a compiler that checks that transactions preserve integrity constraints. We present several techniques for doing so, that are all based on *abstract interpretation*, which is a method widely used in optimising compilers.

- First we use a simple compilation technique to avoid checking the constraints. That method takes into account the *inertia* of a database, that is, the data that is not altered by a transaction. For instance, a transaction that only changes the age and the spouse of a person cannot violate constraints which are not concerned with the ages or the spouses of persons. That method has already been presented in [BD93, BD95].
- We then define a much more powerful analysis that cannot be applied directly on the original database programming language. That language must first be translated into an intermediate language, that is more simple and elementary. An *abstract interpretation* using a *predicate transformer* is applied to this intermediate language. This approach produces some very precise information about the possible behaviour of transactions and can lead to some very good optimisations.

The integrity constraints manager combines those methods and we are confident that most safe transactions can be detected as such and the checking avoided. Our method has the advantage of being *fully automatic* and implementable (as opposed to [GM79, CB80, Qia90]), simple and *semantically founded* (as opposed to [SS89]).

The paper is structured as follows: we present our framework in Section 2, which is an extension of the O_2 data model. We then describe in Section 3 the simple method to avoid checking the constraints. We present in Section 4 a more powerful method based on predicate transformers. We finally describe the integrity constraints manager that is currently being implemented.

2   The data model: O_2 with integrity constraints.

Our framework consists in a very simple extension of the O_2 data model. The programmer can define, together with the usual classes and transactions, some *semantic integrity constraints* which are well formed formulas on a specific language. Most of our data model is compatible with the O_2 model. The only changes that have been made are those that are necessary, that is:

- The ability to describe integrity constraints together with a schema and transactions.
- The ability to write *easily* transactions that are safe.

We point out that using the O_2 system is not essential to our approach. We give in the following a simple O_2 schema, several transactions, and some integrity constraints on that schema. We will assume that the reader is familiar with the O_2 data model. To make the concepts clearer, we will simplify the schema and reduce the use of concepts that are not essential to our approach.

2.1   Schema definition

We use the standard O_2 data definition language. Let's start with the definition of a simple schema on Figure 1.

A Person has a name, a spouse, owns some money, has several children and several friends. We also define a persistent name People, as a set of Persons. We the sake of simplicity , we will not consider methods.

```
class Person inherit Object
   public type tuple ( name:    string,
                       spouse:  Person,
                       children:  set (Person),
                       money:  integer,
                       friends:  set (Person)
                     )
end;

name People:  set (Person);
```

Figure 1: Schema

2.2 Integrity constraints

That schema is quite simple but many constraints can already be stated:

1. There must be at least one Person in the set People.
2. The child of a Person, say x, cannot be x.
3. The spouse of a Person, say x, cannot be the child of x.
4. There is a Person who is friends with everyone else.
5. If a Person x is married to another Person y, then y is married to x.

All those constraints are given Figure 2.

```
C1:   exists x in People;
C2:   forall x in People,  !(x in x->children);
C3:   forall x in People, !(x->spouse in x->children);
C4:   exists x in People, forall y in People, (y in x->friends);
C5:   forall x in People, x->spouse->spouse=x || x->spouse=nil;
```

Figure 2: Constraints

We can briefly give a general syntax for constraints. It is simple and close to first order logic. We first define terms, that is, variables like p and q, constants like nil and more complex terms like p->spouse->spouse. atomic formulas can be defined with standard predicates as =, ! =...and complex formulas can be built with the usual connectives "&&" (AND), "||" (OR), "!" (NOT). Quantification is also necessary. So, if "F" is a formula, then "forall p in S, F" and "exists p in S, F" are also formulas. We call that *range restricted quantification*, because the range on which the variable p varies is the set S^1. The semantics, i.e. the truth or falsity of those constraints with respect to a specific database should be clear. As usual, a database can be seen as a structure, that is a domain together with a set of relationships between elements of that domain. In our case, the domain is the set of object identifiers and values and the relationships are those that are given by the schema: name, spouse, money, children and friends, which are all binary relationships.

2.3 Extending the transaction language

The language we use to specify transactions is very close to O_2C. In fact, a single construct has been added. Consider the following O_2C construct: [if (b) then i_1 else i_2]. b is a boolean expression, and i_1 and i_2 are instructions. In our language, that construct is replaced by [if (f) then i_1 else i_2], where f is a *first-order formula*. The only difference is that we allow *quantifiers* like forall or exists to occur in the test. That extension of the standard O_2C syntax might seem artificial and unnecessary to the reader, but consider constraint C4 and assume that the application programmer wants to write a safe transaction which , given two Persons p and q, removes q from p->friends. So as not to violate C4, we have to check that there is a Person x in People, such that (x!=p) and every other Person in People is in x->friends. With the standard O_2C syntax, that transaction would be written:

---

[1]a slight difference with usual quantification is that formulas of the kind (forall p in S) and (exists p in S) are allowed.

```
transaction body end_friendship(p:Person,q:Person) in application family
{ o2 boolean bx=false;
  for (x in People)
    { o2 boolean by=true;
      for (y in People)
        { if ((x==p) || !(y in x->friends))
          by=false;}
      if (by) bx=true;}
    if (bx) p->friends-=q;}
```

The programmer has to introduce artificial flags (bx and by) and write the right loops in order to perform the appropriate tests. In order to relieve the programmer from the cumbersome task of writing those tests, we allow him to write instead:

```
transaction body end_friendship(p:Person,q:Person) in application family
{ if (exists x forall y (x != p) && (y in x->friends))
    p->friends -= q;
}
```

The appropriate test is stated in a declarative way with a quantified boolean expression. We insist that such a construct is the necessary counterpart of the constraints, inside the transactions. The programmer needs to be able to take some appropriate precautions with respect to integrity constraints in the same global and declarative way. That higher level construct will anyway be translated into standard O_2C instructions in a straightforward manner. We advocate that such a construct increases the application programmer productivity.

We give in Figure 3 a few transactions that might cause some problems with respect to integrity constraints. This set of transactions will be used as a running example throughout the remainder of the paper.

```
transaction body remove_People(p:Person) in application family
{ if ( exists q in People,(q != p))
    People-=p;
}
```

```
transaction body add_child(p:Person,q:Person) in application family
{ if ((q != p) && (q != p->spouse))
    p->children += q;
}
```

```
transaction body end_friendship(p:Person,q:Person) in application family
{ if (exists x forall y (x != p) && (y in x->friends))
    p->friends -= q;
}
```

```
transaction body divorce(p:Person) in application family
{ if (p->spouse!=nil)
    p->spouse->spouse=nil;
p->spouse=nil;
}
```

Figure 3: Transactions

1. remove_People removes a Person p from the set People. So as not to violate constraint C1, we have to check that there is another Person q in People such that q!=p.

2. `add_child` adds a child `q` to the set of `children` of a person `p`. So as not to violate constraints 1 and 2, we have to beware that `p≠q` and that `p->spouse≠q`.

3. `end_friendship` states that `q` is not `p`'s friend anymore. So as not to violate constraint 3, we have to check that somebody else than p is friends with everyone else.

4. `divorce` separates a person `p` form its spouse. To respect constraint 4, we also have to separate `p->spouse` from `p`.

3 A simple analysis: path reachability

We present in this section a first method to check out some transactions. This method is an instance of the so-called *path reachability methods* used in abstract interpretation. It is simple, cheap, and in fact quite efficient. It should be run as a preliminary analysis, before undertaking the complex analysis we present in the next section. The latter analysis is much more expensive and often unnecessary. Therefore, it should only be applied to check out "hard" transactions.

The *path reachability* method is based on the assumption that most transactions only change a specific part of the database. Similarly, constraints are only concerned about a part of the database. When a transaction does not modify that part, then it cannot violate the corresponding constraint. This analysis can be formalised in terms of abstract interpretation. However, such a complex formalisation is unnecessary for such a simple method. This method has already been presented in [BLR92, BD93, BD95] for a specific system: Thémis. We slightly reformulate it here as it will be implemented in our context. We first describe informally our method. We define in the following the paths that are relevant to an integrity constraint C and to a transaction t, denoted respectively by Δ(C) and ∇(t). What we call a path is either a persistent name, like `People`, or an expression of the form `type->attribute`. A persistent name S is relevant to C if an insert or a delete[2] from S might change the truth value of C. Similarly, a path `t->a` is relevant to C if a modification of the attribute `a` of an object of type `t` might change the truth value of C. Also, a persistent name S is relevant to a transaction S if an object is inserted into or deleted from S. Similarly, a path `t->a` is relevant to a transaction S if the attribute `a` of an object of type `t` is modified.

The paths that are relevant to an integrity constraint C can be computed by induction on the structure of constraints. Intuitively, if a term `o->a` appears in C, then the path `type(o)->a` is relevant to C. Similarly, if a persistent name S appears in C, then the path S is relevant to C.

Definition 1 Let `term` be a term. We define δ(`term`) as follows.

term	δ(term)
t->a	δ(t) $\cup$ {type(t)->a}
x, x is a variable	$\emptyset$
S, S is a persistent name	{ S }

Definition 2 Let C be a formula. We define the paths that are relevant to C, Δ(C), as follows.

C	Δ(C)
!C	Δ(C)
C_1 && C_2	$\Delta(C_1)$ $\cup$ $\Delta(C_2)$
C_1 || C_2	$\Delta(C_1)$ $\cup$ $\Delta(C_2)$
forall x in S, C'	δ(S) $\cup$ Δ(C')
exists x in S, C'	δ(S) $\cup$ Δ(C')
(t_1==t_2)	$\delta(t_1)$ $\cup$ $\delta(t_2)$
(t_1 in t_2)	$\delta(t_1)$ $\cup$ $\delta(t_2)$

Definition 3 Let t be a transaction. We define the paths that are relevant to t, ∇(t), as follows.

---

[2] what we call persistent names are in fact repositories, that is, persistent names structured as sets.

t	∇(t)
t->a=expr	{ type(t)->a }
S+=expr, S is a persistent name	{ S }
S-=expr, S is a persistent name	{ S }
t_1 ; t_2	$\nabla(t_1) \cup \nabla(t_2)$
if (b) t_1 else t_2	$\nabla(t_1) \cup \nabla(t_2)$
forall (x in s) t_1	$\nabla(t_1)$

Theorem 1 Let t a transaction and C a constraint. t is safe with respect to C if Δ(C)$\cap\nabla$(t)=$\emptyset$.
Proof sketch: if Δ(C)$\cap\nabla$(t)=$\emptyset$, the transaction updates a part of the database that is of no concern to C. Its truth value is therefore not modified by t. As it is always assumed to be true before the execution of t, it remains so.

Example 1 We give Δ(C) for each constraint C. C.

constraint	Δ(constraint)
C1	{People}
C2	{People, Person->children}
C3	{People, Person->children, Person->spouse}
C4	{People, Person->friends}
C5	{People, Person->spouse}

We also give ∇(t) for each transaction t.

transaction	Δ(transaction)
remove_People	{People}
add_child	{Person->child}
end_friendship	{Person->friend}
divorce	{Person->spouse}

From those results, with theorem 1, we can conclude which transaction may violate which constraint.

transaction	constraints that might be violated
remove_People	C1, C2, C3, C4, C5
add_child	C2, C3
end_friendship	C4
divorce	C3, C5

The evaluation of the benefits of that method is quite difficult. It is more expensive to check C2 than to check C1. Also, if remove_people is the only transaction that is run, no improvement has occured. As an indicator, if we consider that the cost of checking each constraint is equal, and that transactions are all run the same number of times, then we have in fact divided by two the checking overhead. That shows that some very satisfactory results can be obtained with simple methods. However, there is still some room for a lot of improvement. Transaction remove_People can obviously not violate C2, C3 and C5. That is why we need a more powerful method, that takes into account more precisely what is done by a transaction.

4   A complex analysis: predicate transformers

We present in this section a powerful method to prove the safety of transactions with respect to integrity constraints. This method undertakes a painstaking analysis of the transaction that takes many details into account. It uses the concept of *predicate transformer* and finds its place in the general framework of abstract interpretation. A *predicate transformer* is simply a function that, given a program and a formula describing its input data, yields a formula describing its output data. The application of predicate transformers to our problem is straightforward. The input data of a transaction t is described by an integrity constraint C. We apply the predicate transformer to t and C and get another formula C+ describing the output data of t. the main result of this section is that t cannot violate C if C+$\Rightarrow$C (C is a consequence of C+).

The idea of using Dijkstra or Hoare's methods to deal with integrity is not new at all. The idea was first mentioned in [GM79], further developed in [CB80] and in [Qia90]. However, the results presented in those works do not suggest an effective method of proving transaction safety. Our work is very close to those mentioned, but uses tools that allows an easy implementation. If [GM79, CB80, Qia90] ensure that a safety proof can be obtained for any safe transaction (due to completeness), *no effective way of obtaining it is given.* The reason for that is that they use non-deterministic deductive means to yield a proof, and it is not clear which choices have to be made to get a proof. On the contrary, abstract interpretation is an *algorithm,* where no arbitrary choice has to be made. Not only do we have to describe *what to get,* but also *how to get it.* The analogy with first-order theorem proving is enlightening. There are many valid proof systems for first-order logic: Natural Deduction, Hilbert systems, Tableaux, Resolution... But only Tableaux and Resolution are suited to automation. Going from Hoare's logic to abstract interpretation is not a mere matter of cosmetics, but a question of applicability. It requires a different outlook on the problem straight from the start, by privileging effective algorithms rather than logical relationships.

4.1 The intermediate language

Our method cannot be applied directly to the O_2C language. We have to translate the O_2C code into an intermediate language that is more simple. We present in this section the intermediate language we use to undertake the analysis. We also explain why that intermediate language is necessary.

O_2 is an object oriented database system. However, object orientation is not relevant to integrity constraints. The only information that is really relevant is the way the elements of the *domain* (object identifiers, values, persistent names) are related to each other. Attributes are considered as binary relationships and we have to translate the transactions into a logical form that is much more easy to handle. Constraints also have to be translated into classical first-order logic. Such a decomposition is necessary to be able to define the predicate transformer simply and clearly. Let us see that on an example. Consider the following precondition.

$$(p\text{->}spouse\text{->}spouse\text{==}q)$$

We might want to know the effect the execution of an instruction can have on that precondition. Consider the following instruction:

$$r\text{->}spouse\text{=}s;$$

We will have to consider many cases:
- `(r==p)` or `(r!=p)`.
- `(r==p->spouse)` or `(r!=p->spouse)`.

Which is not very easy with a precondition like that. It can be done easily if we decompose `(p->spouse->spouse==q)` into `(p->spouse==u && u->spouse==q)`. We translate complex terms into a conjunction of simpler terms. The effect of the instruction is then straightforward. Its effect on `(p->spouse==u)` is
- `(p->spouse==s)` if `(r==p)`.
- `(p->spouse==q && r->spouse==s)` if `(r!=p)`.

The overall effect is `((r==p && p->spouse==s)||(r!=p && p->spouse==u && r->spouse==s))`. The same can be done to get the effect on `(u->spouse==q)`:
`((r==u && u->spouse==s)||(r!=u && u->spouse==q && r->spouse==s))`. The final result is the conjunction of both effects, which is quite a big formula. However, that formula can be obtained with a succession of simple steps. We give in the following the way to translate constraints and programs into their logical form. Let us begin with the constraints

- each formula `[forall x in S, F]` is translated into `[forall x, (x in S) ==> F]`.
- each formula `[exists x in S, F]` is translated into `[exists x, (x in S) && F]`.
- each term of the form `[t->a]` is translated into `[a(t)]`.
- each formula `[F(a(x))]` (i.e. that depends of the term `a(x)` is translated into :`[forall y, a(x,y) ==>F(y)]`

All those transformations are fully justified. Indeed, in logic $[\forall x \in S, P(x)]$ is just an abbreviation for $[\forall x, (x \in S) \Rightarrow P(x)]$, $[\exists x \in S, P(x)]$ is just an abbreviation for $[\exists x, (x \in S) \land P(x)]$. Attributes are defined as functions that are applied to objects, therefore `o->a` can be written `a(o)`. Finally, functions are just a special kind of relations, thus any function $y = a(x)$ of type $D \rightarrow D$ can be rewritten $a(x, y)$ of type $D \times D$. Those changes are therefore not essential, but help to decompose the structure of constraints. For `C1` the detailed translation is:

```
forall p in People !(p in p->children)
forall p (p in People) ==> !(p in p->children)
forall p (p in People) ==> !(p in children(p))
forall p forall x (children(p,x) && (p in People)) ==> !(p in x)
```

We then show how to translate transactions. We will restrict ourselves to the most common O_2C constructs. We first have to introduce the target language of the translation. It is very close to first order logic and is therefore relational. However, some of its constructs are tailored to simulate more complex O_2C instructions. The syntax of that intermediate language, where t is a tuple and r is a relation, is given Figure 4.

```
instruction ::= insert t into r
              | delete t from r
              | instruction ; instruction
              | { instruction }
              | if (b) instruction
              | forall o where b do instruction
              | forone o where b do instruction
```

Figure 4: Target Language.

In persistent object systems, we mainly deal with binary relations, some of which are in fact functions. We insist that all the attributes defined in our schema will be considered as binary relations: name of type Person→string, spouse of type Person→Person, money of type Person→integer, children and friends of type Person×Person. Nearly all those constructs are very classical. The two first instructions are the classical tuple insertion and deletion. Only the last one might not be clear. The instruction [forone o where b do instruction] executes instruction for the only element o that satisfies b. If there is more than one element, then an error occurs (which never happens when that language is used as a target language). We now define Figure 5 how to translate each instruction. We will denote by $\Delta(i)$ the translation of instruction (i).

instruction	Δ(instruction)
i$_1$; i$_2$	Δ(i$_1$) ; Δ(i$_2$)
{ i }	{Δ(i)}
if (b) i	if (b) Δ(i)
for (o in x) { i }	forall o where (o in x) { Δ(i) }

o->a=expr (*o is a tuple)	forone x where a(o,x) do
	  { delete (o,x) from a;
	    insert (o,expr) into a}

o->a+=p (o->a is a set)	insert (o,p) into a
o->a-=p (o->a is a set)	delete (o,p) from a
S+=p (S is a repository)	insert p into S
S-=p (S is a repository)	delete p from S

Figure 5: Translation of transactions.

A repository is just a persistent name structured as a set. For instance, People is a repository. The question of whether that translation preserves meaning is not relevant, as we have not previously defined the formal semantics of the O_2C language. In fact, it is what we are doing right now as that translation defines the logical semantics of O_2C instructions ! However, we can easily see that that semantics follows the intuitive meaning of O_2C instructions. Something that does not appear, for sake of brevity, is that the boolean expression (b) in the if must also be decomposed, in the same way as the constraints. We have given the translation of a few basic instructions that can be generalised to more complex ones. For instance, consider the instruction [o->a->b->c=e] if [o->a->b] is a tuple object, then we translate that by:

```
forone x where a(o,x)
```

```
forone y where b(x,y)
 forone z where c(y,z)
  do
     {delete (y,z) from c;
      insert (y,e) into c;}
```

We insist that such a translation is necessary as it decomposes the changes that are performed by a transaction into small atomic instructions that only handle binary links, one at a time. The intermediate language can be seen as a database assembly language for the more complex O_2C language.

4.2 Defining a predicate transformer

Once the translation of (extended) O_2C transactions is done, we can define a predicate transformer that yields a post-condition according to a pre-condition. The predicate transformer is a function ∇ that has for input an instruction i and a formula f. The predicate transformer is defined recursively. It works in two steps:

- Formula parse. That parse defines a post-condition for a pre-condition in terms of the sub-formulas of that pre-condition.
- Instruction parse. That parse defines post-conditions for each instructions where the input formula is atomic (or a literal).

However, the order in which the parses are undertaken is only essential in the case of atomic instructions (insert and delete). The only assumption that is made is that negations are moved inside the formulas so that only atomic formulas are negated[3]. The formula parse is defined Figure 6

formula	∇(instruction,formula)
f && g	∇(instruction,f) && ∇(instruction,g)
f || g	∇(instruction,f) || ∇(instruction,g)
forall x, f	forall x, ∇(instruction,f)
exists x, f	exists x, ∇(instruction,f)
(f)	(∇(instruction,f))

Figure 6: Formula parse.

∇ is therefore a &&-morphism and a \|\|-morphism. The two following formulas are a consequence of that, as forall is a generalised conjunction, and exists is a generalised disjunction. The transaction parse is defined only for literals, that is, atomic formulas or their negation. See Figure 7.

instruction	literal	∇(instruction,literal)
insert t into r	l	if l=!r(u) then (t==u && r(u))||(t!=u && !r(u) && r(t)) else l && r(t)
delete t from r	l	if l=r(u) then (t==u && !r(u))||(t!=u && r(u) && !r(t)) else l && !r(t)
i_1 ; i_2	l	$\nabla(i_2,\nabla(i_1,l))$
{ i }	l	$\nabla(i,l)$
if (b) i	l	∇(i, l && b) || (l && !b)

forone x
  where a(o,x)
  do i
	l	exists x ∇(i, a(o,x) && l)

Figure 7: Transaction parse.

---

[3]That can be done easily by using the following equivalences: (!(f && g) = !f \|\| !g), (!(f \|\| g) = !f && !g), (!forall x, f = exists x, !f), (!exists x, f = forall x !f).

We have now fully defined a predicate transformer for our purposes, except for instruction `forall`. In fact, the formal semantics of the database loop is not well defined, because the order in which the elements are taken is not known, and might have some profound consequences at run-time. We need to have a clear denotational semantics to be able to define an abstract interpretation. However, no satisfactory semantics has been defined up to now, so we have to manage without it. The reason for that is that two valid executions can lead to thoroughly different results. Usually, some very restrictive assumptions are made upon the use of loops. Roughly, they amount to use database loops only for batch processing, that is, a program that is run recurringly on a number of items where each loop is independent from the others. Instead of taking those restrictions, that have been defined in [Qia90], into account, which would be cumbersome and would not lead to very satisfactory results, we propose a more simple approach. Each transaction is sliced into parts that do not contain any loops or recursive calls. Each part must be proven safe to prove the safety of the transaction. That method is justified by the fact that any composition of safe instructions is itself a safe instruction. It is a pragmatic approach, but considering the way transactions are programmed, it produces in fact some very good results. Indeed, transactions are very often composed of small and independent updates that can be analysed separately.

Not only do we have to define a predicate transformer but we also have to prove that it is *correct*. The correctness requirement is very important and ensures that we can rely on the information that has been generated by the predicate transformer. In our case:

Theorem 2 Let B a database and B_+ the same database after an execution of transaction t. Let f be a formula. If f is true in B, then $\nabla(t,f)$ is true in B_+.

The proof of that theorem is done by induction both on formulas and on instructions and can be found in [BS95]. The direct consequence of that theorem is the possibility of using predicate transformers to prove transaction correctness.

Theorem 3 Let t a transaction and c an integrity constraint. Then t is safe with respect to c if $\nabla(t,c) \Rightarrow c$.
Proof : Let B be a database and B_+ the same database after an execution of t. We can assume that c is true before the execution. Because of theorem 2, if B satisfies c, then B_+ satisfies $\nabla(t,c)$. Therefore, B_+ satisfies $\nabla(t,c)$. If $\nabla(t,c) \Rightarrow c$ then Therefore, B_+ satisfies c and t cannot violate c.

We have partly solved the problem, as a proof remains to be done: that the constraint c is the logical consequence of $\nabla(t,c)$. The problem, in general, is undecidable. However, many proof techniques, like resolution or tableaux, exist and can be applied very efficiently. A very nice property of those proof techniques is that they are *complete*. If a proof exists, it will be found sooner or later. So, if a transaction t is safe with respect to c, we will be able to say so in a finite time. The problem occurs when the transaction is not safe, because a proof will be sought indefinitely. We therefore have to put a limit on the search space. We will have to conclude, for some safe transactions, that they might not be safe. We insist that, even if we had a decision procedure (which exists in many cases, see [Gri90]), it would certainly be too expensive to be undertaken efficiently (even the decision procedure for propositional logic is NP-complete and we have to use non-deterministic deductive means to improve the process). For our prototype, we have chosen the resolution method, which is the method that is most widely used for automatic theorem provers.

4.3 A simple example

We show how the predicate transformer analysis works for one of the examples we have given. We point out that the analysis can involve much information, even for simple cases. That is why we will just outline what happens for the first example. However, that information can be dealt with easily and efficiently by a computer. We want to prove that transaction `remove_People` cannot violate constraint C1 (which is indeed the case).

```
transaction body remove_People(p:Person) in application family
{ if (exists q in People, (q != p))
    People -= p;
}
C1:  exists p in People;
```

We first make the appropriate translation:

```
transaction body remove_People(p:Person) in application family
{ if (exists q, People(q) && (q != p))
    delete p from People;
}
C1:  exists x, People(x)
```

If `C1` is true before the execution of `remove_People`, which is always the case, then ∇(remove_People,C1) is true after its execution.
We give the first steps to compute ∇(remove_People,C1):

```
∇(remove_People,C1)
  =∇(remove_People,exists x  People(x))
  =exists x ∇(remove_People,People(x))
  =exists x ∇( { if...}, People(x))
  =exists x ∇( if..., People(x))
  =exists x ∇( delete...,People(x) && (exists q People(q) && (q != p)))
            || People(x) && !(exists q People(q) && (q != p)))
  =exists x exists q ∇( delete...,People(x) && People(q) && (q != p)))
            || People(x) && !(exists q People(q) && (q != p)))
  =exists x exists q ∇( delete...,People(x))
                  && ∇( delete...,People(q))
                  && ∇( delete...,(p!=q))
            || People(p) && !(exists q People(q) && (q != p)))
  =exists x exists q (p=x && !People(x))||(p!=x && People(x) && !People(p))
                  && (p=q && !People(q))||(p!=q && !People(p) && People(q))
                  && (p!=q) && !People(p))
            || People(x) && !(exists q People(q) && (q != p)))
```

Let us call that big formula F. What remains to be done is the proof that: (F ==> C1). We then use a classical first-order logic proof technique: resolution. This amounts to showing that (!(F ==>C1)) is *unsatisfiable*. For the sake of brevity, we do not give the proof produced by the resolution method. We have to start by putting F into conjunctive normal form. Which simplifies the structure of F but also increases its size, as we end up with a formula that has around 150 terms! We insist that during this part of the proof, we strictly apply standard proof techniques as can be found in [Fit90]. As mentioned earlier, such a proof, if it exists, will always be obtained by the resolution method in a finite time. That is a consequence of *resolution completeness*. The real problem occurs when the transaction violates the constraint, as the resolution algorithm will go on looking for a proof whereas none exists! As said earlier, we will have to put bounds on the search space for a proof. If no proof exists within that search space, we will have to conclude that no proof exists. That conclusion might of course be wrong, but it will just result in saying we must check the constraint whereas the checking is not necessary. So, to summarise, our method:

- provides a safety proof for safe transactions.
- does not terminate for unsafe transactions.

However, when implementing a method, we have to ensure that it always terminates. The integrity manager will in fact:

- provide a safety proof for *some* safe transactions.
- will stop without having reached a conclusion for *all* unsafe and *some* safe transactions.

The power of the integrity manager depends, not surprisingly, of the time and space we are willing to devote to each proof. We are confident that most safe transactions could be detected easily. Serious tests will be done when the prototype is completed.

5   Implementation

We present in this section the prototype that is currently being implemented. It is a concrete application of the theory we have presented to persistent object systems. Instead of creating from nothing a persistent object system with integrity constraints, we have decided to add an integrity management facility to an existing system: O_2. The integrity manager works with:

- an O_2 database schema together with a set of integrity constraints.
- a set of transactions written in the extended O_2C language.

We have already seen that we have to extend the standard O_2 syntax with a new construct: we allow, instead of boolean expressions, *quantified* boolean expressions. That provides us with a simple and efficient way of making the run-time tests that are necessary when writing *safe* transactions. The transactions in the application are written in extended O_2C. We show in Figure 8 how quantified boolean expressions are translated into O_2C. This translation deserves an explanation. The truth value of the expression that is translated is stored in the boolean bx that is declared previously. If M(x) has quantifiers, then the translation must be undertaken recursively.

expression	translation

exists x in S, M(x)	o2 boolean bx=false;
	  for (x in S)
	    { if (M(x)) bx=true;}

forall x in S, M(x)	o2 boolean bx=true;
	  for (x in S)
	    { if (!M(x)) bx=false;}

Figure 8: Translation of quantified boolean expressions.

As an example, let us consider the instruction already seen in transaction end_friendship:

```
if (exists x forall y (x != p) && (y in x->friends))
  p->friends -= q;
```

We first translate the first quantification:

```
{ o2 boolean bx=false;
 for (x in People)
   {
     if (forall y (x!=p) && (y in x->friends))
       bx=true;}
 if (bx) p->friends-=q;}
```

A quantification remains to be translated:

```
{ o2 boolean bx=false;
 for (x in People)
   { o2 boolean by=true;
    for (y in People)
     { if ((x==p) || !(y in x->friends))
       by=false;}
    if (by) bx=true;}
 if (bx) p->friends-=q;}
```

The integrity manager is in fact a pre-processor that takes the different elements of an application, checks that the transactions are safe and generates the corresponding O_2C files. For the sake of simplicity, the prototype does not consider methods. However, that restriction is not essential to our approach. The main objective of the prototype is to show that our method works well for simple, straight-line transaction. We will then generalise it to any transactions involving loops, recursive calls and message passing. The generalisation, as mentioned earlier, is a simple one. Each transaction is decomposed into simpler updates, each of which is proven safe. We show in Figure 9 the general structure of the integrity constraints manager. We explain in the following the role of each part of the database manager.

- First, the simple *path reachability* technique is used to check out in a simple way transactions that do not violate any constraints.
- After that, for transactions that have not been proven safe, the more sophisticated method of *predicate transformers* is applied in different steps:
  1. The transactions and constraints are decomposed.

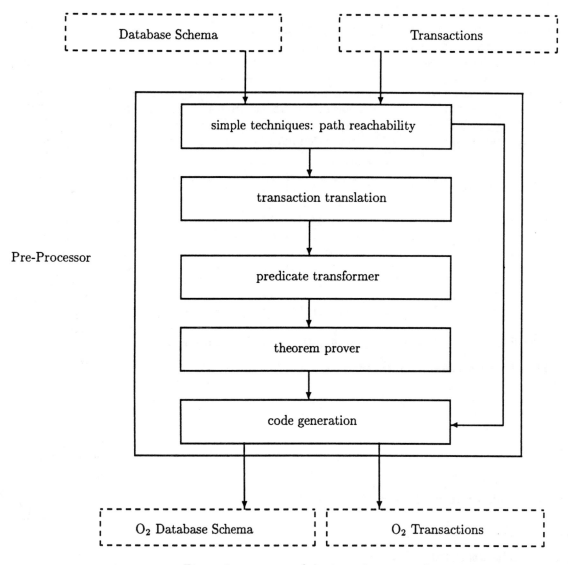

Figure 9: structure of the integrity constraint manager

2. For each transaction and each constraint, the predicate transformer is applied. Which transaction has to be checked for which constraint is determined by the path reachability analysis.

3. An automatic first-order theorem prover based on resolution is applied to the result provided by the predicate transformer.

4. The code generator finally takes into account the results of the analysis to generate the O_2 schema (if needed) and the O_2C transactions. Tests with quantified boolean expressions are translated and checking algorithms are automatically generated if the safety proof for a transaction has failed. Those can be found in [BD93, BD95].

6   Related works

The study of integrity constraints has been a topic of large interest [Sto75, Nic79, GM79, CB80, LT85, HI85, BM86, KSS87, HCN84, WSK83, BDM88, SS89]. Several works concern the optimisation of checking: [Nic79, HI85] for relational databases, [BM86] for deductive databases, and [BD95] for object-oriented databases. The subject of finding consistency proofs for transactions is not new: [GM79] gives some indications on how Hoare's logic could be used for that purpose. The invariance of integrity constraints is proven, by hand, for several examples. However, the ideas exposed are not formalised and no systematic procedure for obtaining such proofs is given. Besides, [Cla79] has spotlighted the deficiencies of Hoare's logic for languages with complex features such as aliasing, side effects... that are shared by most database programming languages. [CB80] attempt to give a logical method to assess database transaction semantics in general, with a particular interest for integrity constraints. Their work is closely related to [GM79], with a special interest in dynamic logic and aggregate operations. However, the problems about the formalisation and automatisation of the process remain. The work of [Qia90] is in the line of [GM79, CB80], and presents an axiom system for transaction analysis. However, the applicability of such an axiom system is unclear. As mentioned earlier, [Qia93] assert that conventional methods are not suited to automatic transaction safety verification and takes the opposite direction of *transaction synthesis*. [SS89] is, to our knowledge, the most in-depth application of the axiomatic method to our problem. It uses a very complex theorem prover that uses Boyer-Moore's computational logic, based on higher-order recursive functions. The complexity of their method makes the task heavy and difficult to follow. Their theorem prover uses a knowledge base where some properties of database constructs are kept. Some theorems are derived and the knowledge base grows. A complex strategy, with many heuristics, is used to improve the search process. Their method seems difficult to apply to a real system, as it requires very heavy proofs of theorems with hundreds of terms for only small transactions.

Our work differs from the other works on the subject of consistency proofs for transactions, in that we use the technique of *abstract interpretation* rather than *program verification*, which is used in [GM79, CB80, Qia90, SS89]. The goals of abstract interpretation are similar to those of program verification. The difference between the two approaches is that abstract interpretation is a *semantics-based* method, that yields an *approximate* description of a program's run-time behaviour, which is obtainable with *fully automatic algorithms*, whereas program verification uses *deductive* or *axiomatic* methods. By using abstract interpretation, we solve the problems that arise from [GM79, CB80, Qia90]. Having a semantic approach, rather than deductive, allows us to get an abstract description of program semantics with *algorithms*. No room is left for human intervention. As [GM79, CB80], our approach is based on first-order predicate logic, rather than higher order recursive functions, as in [SS89]. It is therefore difficult to compare the power of the two approaches. However, we point out that, our method being much *lighter*, should be more efficient and easy to handle. Moreover, whereas [SS89] seems to have reached the limits of the axiomatic semantics, conventional abstract interpretation techniques yield very good results. The reader interested in abstract interpretation can find a complete and recent overview of the domain in [JN95], and can of course consult the seminal work of [CC77]. Predicate transformers are exposed in [Dij76, DS90].

7   Conclusion

We have presented a general method to reduce statically the number of integrity constraints to check after the execution of a transaction. We have shown that, by using abstract interpretation techniques, we can obtain a simple safety proof for a transaction, with fully automatic means. First, a simple *path reachability* method is run. Then a more powerful method is run for the cases that remain to be proven safe. Assuming that the integrity constraint is true before the execution of the transaction, we show how to generate a first-order sentence that is true after the update. From that sentence, we prove that the constraint is true after the update. The use of abstract interpretation greatly reduces the use of deductive methods, which are non-deterministic and therefore inefficient. The method works well for complex straight-line updates, and can be extended to other kinds of updates. However, some problems remain:

- The use of first-order logic to express integrity constraints causes many problems: logical implication and equivalence are undecidable properties.
- The semantics of database loops is not formally defined, and therefore cannot be given a good abstract interpretation.

It seems that abstract interpretation reaches its limits when applied to integrity constraints management, because of the amount of information we have to collect to prove that a transaction is safe. However, we are confident that our approach will be used efficiently and detect safe transactions in most cases. The integrity constraint manager that is currently being implemented should give some further information about the applicability of our method.

Acknowledgements

We would like to thank Giorgio Ghelli and Atsushi Ohori who first recommended us study abstract interpretation techniques. We also would like to thank Serenella Cerrito and Giuseppe Castagna for reading an early version of this paper.

References

[BD93]   V. Benzaken and A. Doucet. Thémis: a database programming language with integrity constraints. In Shasha Beeri, Ohori, editor, *Proceedings of the 4th International Workshop on Database Programming Languages*, Workshop in Computing, pages 243–262, New York City, USA, September 1993. Springer-Verlag.

[BD95]   V. Benzaken and A. Doucet. Thémis: A Database Programming Language Handling Integrity Constraints. *VLDB Journal*, 4(3):493–518, 1995.

[BDM88]   F. Bry, H. Decker, and R. Manthey. A Uniform Approach to Constraint Satisfaction and Constraint Satisfiability in Deductive Databases. In Missikoff Schmidt, Ceri, editor, *Proceedings of the EDBT International Conference*, LNCS 303, pages 488–505, 1988.

[BDS95]   V. Benzaken, A. Doucet, and X. Schaefer. Integrity Constraint Checking Optimization based on Abstract Databases Generation and Program Analysis. *Journal de l'Ingénierie des Systèmes d'Information*, 1(3):9–29, 1995.

[BLR92]   V. Benzaken, C. Lécluse, and P. Richard. Enforcing Integrity Constraints in Database Programming Languages. In R. Morrison A. Albano, editor, *Proceedings of the 5th International Workshop on Persistent Object Systems*, Workshop in Computing, pages 282–299, Pisa, Italy, September 1-5 1992. Springer-Verlag.

[BM86]   F. Bry and R. Manthey. Checking Consistency of Database Constraints: A Logical Basis. In *Proceedings of the VLDB International Conference*, pages 13–20, August 1986.

[BS95]   V. Benzaken and X. Schaefer. Abstract interpretation and predicate transformers: an application to integrity constraints management. Technical report, L.R.I, Université de Paris XI, 1995.

[CB80]   M. A. Casanova and P. A. Bernstein. A formal system for reasonning about programs accessing a relational database. *ACM Transactions on Database Systems*, 2(3):386–414, July 80.

[CC77]   P. Cousot and R. Cousot. Abstract Interpretation: A Unified Lattice Model for Static Analysis of Programs by Construction or Approximation of Fixpoints. In *4th POPL, Los Angeles, CA*, pages 238–252, January 1977.

[Cla79]   E. M. Clarke. Programming languages constructs for which it is impossible to obtain good hoare axiom systems. *Journal of the ACM*, 26(1):129–147, January 79.

[Dij76]   E. W. Dijkstra. *A Discipline of Programming*. Prentice-Hall, 1976.

[DS90]   E. W. Dijkstra and C. S. Scholten. *Predicate Calculus and Program Semantics*. Texts and Monographs in Computer Science. Springer-Verlag, 1990.

[Fit90]   Melvin Fitting. *First-order logic and automated theorem proving*. Texts and monographs in computer science. Springer-Verlag, 1990.

[GM79]   G. Gardarin and M. Melkanoff. Proving the Consistency of Database Transactions. In *VLDB International Conference*, pages 291–298, Rio, Brasil, October 1979.

[Gri90]   S. Grigorieff. Décidabilité et complexité des théories logiques. In B. Courcelle, editor, *Logique et Informatique*, chapter 1, pages 7–99. INRIA-collection didactique, 1990.

[HCN84]   L. Henschen, W. Mc Cune, and S. Naqvi. Compiling constraint checking programs from first order formulas. In H. Gallaire, J. Minker, and J.M. Nicolas, editors, *Advances in Database Theory*, volume 2. Plenum, 1984.

[HI85]   A. Hsu and T. Imielinski. Integrity Checking for Multiple Updates. In *Proceedings of the ACM SIGMOD International Conference*, pages 152–168, 1985.

[JN95]   N. D. Jones and F. Nielson. Abstract interpretation. In S. Abramsky, D. M. Gabbay, and T. S. E. Maibaum, editors, *Semantic Modelling*, volume 4 of *Handbook of Logic in Computer Science*, chapter 5, pages 527–636. Oxford Science Publication, 1995.

[KSS87] R. Kowalski, F. Sadri, and P. Soper. Integrity Checking in Deductive Databases. In *Proceedings of the VLDB International Conference*, pages 61–70, 1987.

[LT85]   J. W. Lloyd and R. W. Topor. A basis for deductive database systems. *Journal of Logic Programming*, 2(2), 1985.

[Nic79] J.M. Nicolas. Logic for Improving Integrity Checking in Relational Databases. Technical report, ONERA-CERT, 1979.

[Qia90] Xiaolei Qian. An axiom system for database transactions. *Information Processing letters*, 36:183–189, November 1990.

[Qia93] Xiaolei Qian. The deductive synthesis of database transactions. *ACM Transactions on Database Systems*, 18(4):626–677, December 1993.

[SS89]   T. Sheard and D. Stemple. Automatic Verification of Database Transaction Safety. *ACM Transaction on Database Systems*, 14(3):322–368, September 1989.

[Sto75] M. Stonebraker. Implementation of Integrity Constraints and Views by Query Modification. In *ACM SIGMOD International Conference*, San Jose, California, May 1975.

[WSK83] W. Weber, W. Stugky, and J. Karzt. Integrity Checking in database systems. *Information Systems*, 8(2):125–136, 1983.

State Caching in the EROS Kernel

Implementing Efficient Orthogonal Persistence in a Pure Capability System

Jonathan S. Shapiro
David J. Farber
Jonathan M. Smith
University of Pennsylvania *

2 September, 1996

Abstract

EROS, the Extremely Reliable Operating System, addresses the issues of reliability and security by combining two ideas from earlier systems: capabilities and a persistent single-level store. Capabilities unify object naming with access control. Persistence extends this naming and access control uniformly across the memory hierarchy; main memory is viewed simply as a cache of the single-level store. The combination simplifies application design, allows programs to observe the "principle of least privilege," and enables active objects to be constructed securely.

Prior software capability implementations have suffered from poor performance. In EROS, cacheing techniques are used to implement authority checks efficiently and to preserve the state of active processes in a form optimized for the demands of the machine. The resulting system provides performance competative with conventional designs. This paper describes the EROS object model and the structures used to efficiently map this model onto one hardware implementation: the Intel 80x86 processor architecture.

1 Introduction

EROS, the Extremely Reliable Operating System, provides an environment for long-lived persistent application systems. The motivation for this effort is to facilitate research in user environments, reliable application design, scheduling, security, and (in the future) recoverable distribution in such systems. A primary design objective is to achieve a software mean time between failures (MTBF) measured in years.

Two essential differences between EROS and conventional systems are the use of *persistence* and *capabilities*. Persistence simplifies the construction of *active objects*, which have greater expressive power than the passive objects of conventional systems. A consistent snapshot of all system state, including processes, is periodically written to the disk by a lightweight, fault-tolerant checkpointing mechanism. This mechanism allows EROS to recover after transient failures in less than one minute, having lost a bounded amount of work. In addition, it dramatically improves the efficiency of disk write traffic.

Capabilities unify object naming with access rights. While access control lists (ACLs) provide equivalent power in conventional systems, capabilities offer several conceptual advantages over access control lists:

- Their authority can be delegated.

- They support the "principle of least privilege." Applications can be designed to hold no more authority than they require.

*This work was supported by the Hewlett-Packard Research Grants Program, the AT&T Foundation, CNRI as manager for NSF and ARPA under cooperative agreement #NCR-8919038, NSF #CDA-92-14924, and ARPA #MDA972-95-1-0013.

- They provide encapsulation: objects can undetectably act as proxies for most other objects without compromising security.

- They eliminate the need for the kernel to have any notion of user identity. A single system can therefore support multiple simultaneous administrative policies defined by mutually adversarial sources of human authority.

Prior software capability implementations have suffered from poor performance. In EROS, cacheing techniques are used to implement authority checks efficiently and to preserve the state of active processes in a form optimized for the demands of the machine. This design reduces kernel size and complexity, limits the scope of software errors, and facilitates their detection before committing their consequences to the disk. The resulting system provides performance competative with conventional designs.

This paper presents the EROS object architecture, and describes how the architecture is efficiently mapped on to the Intel processor architecture.

2   The Object Architecture

EROS is a fine-grain capability system. All stateful abstractions are composed from only two primitive, fixed-size object types. **Pages** are the basic unit of user data storage, and contain an architecture-defined amount of user data. **Cgroups** are the basic unit of capability storage, and hold 16 capabilities. Cgroups are protected by partitioning. Only the kernel is permitted to examine or modify the content of a cgroup. As a result, applications are unable to examine or forge capabilities.

Pages and cgroups are composed to construct objects such as memory segments and domains of authority.

2.1   Capabilities

Objects and services in EROS are named by capabilities, which consist of a (*type, object id, authority*) tuple. The semantic interpretation of an object in a given context is determined by the type field of the capability. Placing the type indicator in the capability rather than the object allows us to take advantage of knowing the underlying object representations to support user-level manipulation of composite objects, for example in fault handlers. While it is possible to fabricate combinations of capabilities that are nonsensical, doing so does not violate the integrity of either the kernel *or* the application.

In addition to naming objects, capabilities can also name the program obeyed by a domain or an operating system service. They therefore subsume both system calls and interprocess communication.

The major capability types supported by the EROS kernel are shown below. Types shown in **bold** are objects constructed from cgroups and pages. Types shown in *italic* are services implemented directly by the kernel. These are shown for completeness, but are not described by this paper.

page	cgroup	number	**segment**
domain	**start**	**resume**	sense
schedule	*misc*	*device*	

Pages and cgroups have already been described. The corresponding capabilities exist in read-write and read-only variants. Segment capabilities can also be read-write or read-only.

A **number** capability is a self-describing object containing a 96 bit unsigned constant that can be fetched by the application. They are primarily used in domains, as we will see shortly. A number capability whose value is zero is referred to as a **null capability**.

A **sense capability** is similar to a read-only cgroup capability, except that its read-only property is "sticky." The holder of a sense capability cannot obtain read-write access to any object that is transitively reachable through the sense capability.

2.2 Segments

Memory segments ("segments") are the basic data organization mechanism of EROS. They are constructed by assembling cgroups into a tree whose leaves are pages (Figure 1). [1]

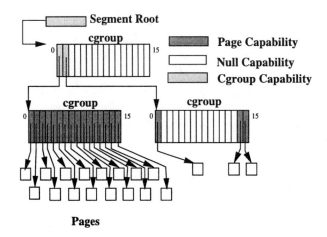

Figure 1: A 19 page segment

The segment structure is similar to page tables in conventional memory mapping architectures, and structurally similar to the file system indirection blocks of UNIX [Tho78]. EROS address spaces are implemented as segments. Data access rights are determined by starting at the segment root and walking down the tree to the page; if any capability on the path from the root of the tree to the page is read-only, then all accesses within the corresponding subsegment are read-only, even if read-write capabilities exist within the subsegment.

As in hardware address spaces, segments may have undefined subregions. This is used to describe unmapped portions of a contiguous area or unallocated portions of a program heap.

Unlike hardware address spaces, the height of an EROS segment tree is variable. The size of an EROS segment is 16^h pages, where $0 \leq h \leq 30$ is the height of the tree. EROS segments therefore range in size from 1 to 2^{120} pages. This is adequate for most currently envisioned databases, and can readily be extended. The biased log of the segment size (**BLSS**) is contained in its capability. BLSS is defined as

$$log_{16}(segsize\,in\,bytes) - 1$$

The bias comes from the fact that the value is almost always used in traversing cgroups while walking segment trees, where the index desired at a given cgroup is given by

$$(segment\,offset \gg BLSS)$$

2.2.1 Red Segments

The simple segment cgroups described above are known in EROS as **black segments**. A special sort of segment known as a **red segment** exists to construct more complex segment structures. Red segments provide for the identification of the segment's fault handler, and for segments of variable size, and for "background segments."

We mention red segments primarily to make it clear that EROS provides efficient support for copy-on-write and a mechanism for user-level handling of memory access exceptions, but will not address them further in this paper. For a more complete discussion, the reader is referred to the online EROS documentation [Sha96a, Sha96b].

---

[1] For this reason, following the conventions of KeyKOS [Har85], *cgroups* are called *nodes* in the bulk of the current EROS documentation. To avoid collision with the distributed systems community, we are abandoning this term in favor of "cgroup."

2.2.2 Segmode Capabilities

Given a cgroup capability, the holder may ask for a segment capability for the same cgroup. Cgroup capabilities and segment capabilities can be used interchangeably to identify a segment. Cgroup capabilities expose the structure of the segment to the holder, while segment capabilities keep the internal structure opaque. Typically, a segment will be constructed out of cgroups using cgroup capabilities, and a red or black segment capability is then fabricated for the root cgroup and handed to the user. Similarly, a page capability may be used for sufficiently small segments. The term **segmode capability** is used in contexts where any of these three types of capability is acceptable. The slots of a black segment cgroup contain segmode capabilities.

2.3 Domains

In reviewing the CAL/TSS project, Butler Lampson noted that *domains of authority* and *processes* should have been unified [Lam76]. Similar conclusions are suggested by Wulf's postmortem on HYDRA/C.mmp [Wul81]. EROS unifies domains of authority and processes into a single object known as a **domain** (Figure 2).

A domain is a cgroup (known as the **domain root**) which contains:

- A *schedule capability*. The EROS scheduler implements *processor capacity reserves* [Mer93]. **Schedule** capabilities convey the authority for a running domain to execute instructions under a particular scheduling reserve.

- A *keeper start capability* naming the domain (the keeper) responsible for handling execution faults incurred by this domain.

- A *segmode capability* naming the address space for the domain. The domain is said to obey the program embodied in its address space.

- A cgroup capability to the *capability registers cgroup*, which serves as the capability registers of the domain. The application may invoke a capability giving the index of the capability register that contains it.[2]

- A cgroup capability to the *general registers cgroup*. The general registers cgroup contains number capabilities holding those register values for the domain that could not be squeezed into the available slots of the domain root. On the 80x86 architecture, it is required only for domains that use the floating point unit.

- A *brand*, which is a capability used by the fabricator of the domain to identify the domains it constructed.

- A *status*, which is a number capability containing the current state of the domain (running, available, or waiting) and the current fault code and fault information (if any).

Each of these capabilities resides in a designated slot within the domain root. The remaining slots of the domain root are used to hold the register values for the domain.

Possession of a domain capability allows the holder to alter most of the slots of the domain. Domain capabilities thus convey authority over the *structure* of the domain. By contrast, **start capabilities** and **resume capabilities** convey the authority to invoke the *program* embodied in a domain. Because the program and its associated state are persistent, a start capability in effect names an active object.

In its role as a process, a domain can be in one of three states:

Available An *available* domain can be invoked by any holder of a start capability for that domain. Domains return to the available state when their program performs a **return** invocation.

Running Once invoked, a domain moves from the available state to the *running* state. A running domain is servicing an invocation. If a start capability is invoked while the domain is running, the invoker will block until the domain becomes available.

---

[2]The capability registers cgroup may be omitted for emulation domains, since these domains cannot invoke capabilities.

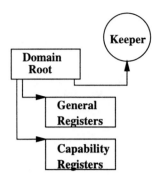

Figure 2: Domain with keeper

Waiting A domain that has invoked a capability and is waiting for a response moves from the running state to the *waiting* state. It remains in this state until a **resume capability** to the domain is invoked.

The vast majority of domains in an EROS system are *available* at any given time. If a domain is not *available* when a start capability is invoked, the invoker will block until the domain becomes *available*. If a domain is not *waiting* when a resume capability is invoked, the invocation procedes as though a null capability had been invoked.

2.4   Capability Invocation

EROS objects are manipulated by invoking capabilities. An invocation names the capability to be invoked (the index of the slot in the capability registers cgroup containing the capability), and a message to be sent to the invoked object. The message includes an *operation code* identifying the operation requested (in the reply, this is a *return code)*, up to 64K of contiguous data, and four capabilities (indices into the capability registers). In addition, the invocation specifies which capability registers should be overwritten by the replying invocation, where the reply data should go, and how many bytes of the reply should be accepted. Capability register zero is "hardwired" to the null capability, and is used in place of capabilities that should not be sent or received.

There are three types of invocation: *call, return,* and *send.* A **call** invocation blocks for a response. It places the invoker in the *waiting* state and the recipient in the running state. A **return** invocation is the inverse of the call invocation. The invoker is placed in the *available* state and the recipient in the *running* state. The **send** invocation sends a message without waiting for a reply; both invoker and recipient end up in the *running* state.

An unusual characteristic of the EROS invocation mechanism is that the kernel does *not* maintain a call stack. Instead, every domain has an associated **call count**. The *call* operation generates a resume capability containing the current call count of the domain. When a valid resume capability is invoked, the call count is incremented. If the call count of the domain and the call count of the resume capability do not match, the resume capability acts like a null capability. Among other uses, this allows a domain to act as a single entry point for a multithreaded service, as shown in Figure 3.

2.5   Threads

It is useful to distinguish between a running domain and the thread of control that occupies it. A **thread** associates a running domain with a particular processor group. Threads are the unit acted on by the EROS kernel scheduler. EROS threads are stateless, and are second class abstractions in the sense that they have no associated capability.

A thread occupies exactly one domain, and a domain occupied by a thread is in the *running* state. When a domain performs a *call* or *return* invocation, its thread migrates to the new domain. If the two domains operate under the same schedule capability this action does not require a rescheduling call, which significantly reduces the complexity of the IPC path. The result is similar to the migrating threads of Mach 4.0 [For93] or the shuttles of

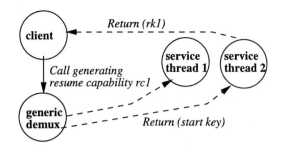

Figure 3: User level demultiplexing

the Spring [Ham95] system. Once we have a chance to tune the paths, we expect to achieve context switch times comparable to with L3 [Lie93b] and Mach 4.0.

A further reason to distinguish threads and domains is that the thread embodies the smallest part of a domain that must be kept in memory when the domain is not executing instructions. Domains such as login agents and detached user interfaces spend most of their time blocked in the kernel while waiting for an event to occur. Isolating the thread structure allows these domains to be paged out.

3   Mapping to the Machine

The simple object model provided by EROS is relatively easy to reason about and easy to render persistent, but it is not intrinsically efficient. The basic abstractions provided by EROS must be mapped onto the underlying hardware representation, and consistency must be maintained between the abstractions and the resulting representation. This mapping is the key to an efficient software capability implementation. The mapping must:

- Ensure that the object named by a valid capability is in memory when needed, and that an efficient mapping exists from the capability to the in-memory object.

- Ensure that only one interpretation of a cgroup (segment, domain constituent, etc.) is required during any given invocation.

- Construct and maintain a mapping from segment cgroups to the hardware address mapping mechanism.

- Provide a representation for domain state that facilitates efficient context switching.

- Ensure that the semantics of reads and writes to cgroup slots are preserved by these optimizations.

To perform this mapping, the EROS kernel implements structures that serve as architecture-specific caches of state whose definition is in cgroups.

3.1   Preparing Capabilities

Capabilities have two forms: unprepared (on-disk) and prepared. In its unprepared form (Figure 4), a capability contains the object identifier and version number of the object. Whenever a capability is dereferenced, it is first *prepared*. Preparing a capability has two effects:

- If necessary, the object named by the capability is brought into main memory.

- The version number of the capability (or in the case of a resume capability, the call count) is compared to the version number (call count) of the object. If they do not match, the capability conveys no authority and is converted to a null capability.[3]

---

[3]Incrementing the version number of the object invalidates outstanding capabilities, allowing objects to be securely reused.

93

r wp **Type**	**SubType**	**Info**
Version[31:0]		
OID[47:32]	**Version[47:32]**	
OID[31:0]		

Figure 4: An unprepared capability

Once prepared, the capability points to an object table entry, which in turn points to the object (Figure 5). Every capability has a *prepared* bit (**P**) that indicates the current form of the capability. The object named by a

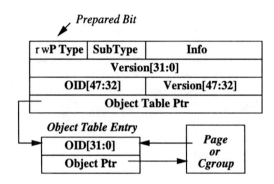

Figure 5: A prepared capability

prepared capability is guaranteed to remain in memory for the duration of the current invocation.

Before being written to disk, a capability is first converted back to the unprepared format. This ensures that kernel memory pointers are never written to the disk. All existing capabilities to an object can be invalidated by incrementing the object's version number. Doing so guarantees that all access to the corresponding cgroup or page has been rescinded.

3.2 Preparing Cgroups

A given cgroup can be interpreted in several ways:

1. As a raw cgroup,

2. As a domain root,

3. As the general registers of a domain,

4. As the capability registers of a domain,

5. As a node in a segment tree.

Only one of these interpretations is valid during any single capability invocation.[4] A cgroup that is interpreted as a domain root will not be interpreted as a segment during the same invocation.

As with capabilities, a cgroup must be prepared before it can be referenced in a particular context. If a hardware address mapping table depends on the capability values of a given cgroup, that cgroup must be prepared

---

[4]It is possible to construct a domain whose address space segment whose cgroup is in fact the domain root. Such a domain is *malformed,* and will not execute instructions.

as a segment cgroup. If a context structure (Section 3.3) depends on the capability values of a given cgroup, that cgroup is must be prepared as a domain root, general registers, or capability registers cgroup. The current interpretation of a cgroup is cached in the in-memory cgroup data structure, and serves to identify how the state of the cgroup's capabilities may be cached.

Every capability slot in a cgroup includes *write hazard* and *read hazard* bits (The "w" and "r" fields in figures 4 and 5). If a cgroup is prepared, some or all of its capabilities may be *hazarded*. A write hazard indicates that some machine-specific data structure depends on the current value of the capability, and must be invalidated before the capability slot can be written. A read hazard indicates that the current value of the capability is not up to date, and must be written back from the machine-specific data structure before the capability can be read. Read hazards typically apply to capabilities containing domain register values. All read hazards are also write hazards.

Like capabilities, cgroups are always written to the disk in unprepared form. Unlike capabilities, the interpretation of a cgroup may change over time. Before preparing a cgroup in a new way, the cgroup is first *deprepared* to its raw form. A side effect of depreparing the cgroup is to invalidate or flush all cached copies of the cgroup's state. This guarantees that:

- No stale cache state remains when the cgroup is written to the disk.

- A cgroup has exactly one semantic interpretation at a time.

- Malformed objects, such as a domain root whose address space capability points to the domain root cgroup, are detected.

3.3   The Context Cache

In conventional operating systems, processor state is saved to an interrupt stack. If the current thread of control is preempted, this state is then transferred to process structure whose layout is carefully tuned to the processor architecture.

The EROS domain layout is chosen for the convenience of the abstract machine. Number capabilities provide a space-efficient way to store register values in a cgroup, but this representation is not efficient for loading and saving registers during a context switch. Instead, the register values of a domain are loaded into an architecture specific **context** structure before the process is loaded onto the hardware. The cgroups of the associated domain are prepared as domain root, general registers, and capability registers, and the hazard bits of the associated slots are set to indicate that the values of the capabilities that make up the domain are cached.

When necessary, information is selectively flushed from the context structure back to the domain cgroups to clear these hazards. The context maintains a separate hazard mask indicating which parts of the context need to be reloaded before the context is ready to run.

It is rare for an invocation to require that the register values be flushed back to the domain. Once the register values are loaded into a context structure it is easier to fetch them from the context structure than from the domain. EROS maintains a cache of the context structures for recently activated domains, avoiding the overhead of unload and reload. The state of the active domains therefore remains in machine-specific form most of the time.

The $80x86$ processor automatically writes process state to the supervisor stack when an interrupt or system call occurs. To take advantage of this, the EROS kernel arranges for the supervisor stack pointer to point to the top of the context cache entry for the active context. The context structure is laid out in such a way that the values written to the supervisor stack by the processor are written directly to the appropriate locations in the context structure. Once the registers have been saved, the supervisor stack pointer is reloaded to point to an interrupt stack. Similar techniques are used in L3 [Lie93a] and Mach 4.0 [For93] to avoid copying state from the stack to the process structure.

3.4   Address Space Management

Address space management in the EROS kernel consists of:

- Constructing address mappings in response to page faults.

- Ensuring that any write to a segment cgroup is properly reflected in the hardware-specific data structures.

- Ensuring that mapping entries are properly invalidated when cgroups and pages are removed by aging.

Constructing the hardware mapping tables is a simple matter of walking the domain's segment tree starting at the address space capability to determine the validity and access rights of the mapping. If no mapping is found that satisfies the access type (read or write), a segment-designated fault handling domain – the segment keeper – is invoked.

Regardless of architecture, EROS tracks page dependencies by maintaining an inverse mapping from page frames to mapping table entries. Before a page is removed the page dependency table is traversed to invalidate the dependent mapping entries.

The 80x86 implements a two-level page table with authority verification at both levels. A mapping entry (at either level) is constructed by walking a segment tree, and depends on the values of the traversed cgroup slots. If any of these slots is later modified, the corresponding mapping entries must be invalidated. To guarantee this, the address of each traversed slot is associated with the address of the generated mapping entry in a *slot dependancy table*, and the slot is marked as write-hazarded. Before a write to such a slot can proceed, the hazard must be cleared by traversing the slot dependency table and invalidating all dependent mapping entries.

Segments typically range from three to five cgroups in height. If the slot dependency table is constructed in a naive fashion, every bottom-level mapping entry will therefore have between three and five dependency table entries depending on the height of the segment tree. In a tree structured mapping system, mapping entries in upper level mapping tables need their own additional dependency entries. The space overhead of this is quite large, and must be reduced.

First, we note that the dependency tables are not a *complete* mapping from slots and pages to mapping entries. It is sufficient for the dependency tables to capture the fraction of all mappings that are actually being referenced. The size of the dependency table is therefore a function of dynamic dependencies rather than static dependencies.

The 80x86 provides hierarchical authority checking. As a result, the segment slot dependencies can be built hierarchically as well (Figure 6). The reduced construction is correct because the upper level mapping entry

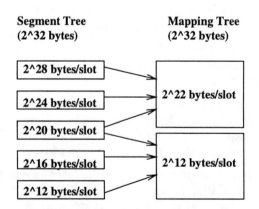

Segment Tree
(2^32 bytes)

Mapping Tree
(2^32 bytes)

2^28 bytes/slot

2^24 bytes/slot

2^20 bytes/slot

2^16 bytes/slot

2^12 bytes/slot

2^22 bytes/slot

2^12 bytes/slot

Figure 6: Segment mapping dependencies

permissions override the lower level permissions.

In addition, if we view the segment slots as projecting a shadow onto the page table entries that depend on them, it develops that the shadow of a given cgroup slot is contiguous in the mapping table. This can be leveraged by the slot dependency mechanism to transparently coalesce dependency entries into ranges. Together these optimizations substantially reduce the size of the slot dependency table.

4 Checkpoint

EROS implements persistence and exogenous fault recovery using a recoverable checkpoint mechanism. Before any object may be modified in memory, space is reserved for it in the log. On pageout, dirty objects are appended to the log. Object faults are satisfied first from the log and then from the object's home location (Figure 7).

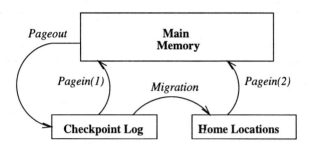

Figure 7: Flow of objects in the system

When a checkpoint is taken, computation is temporarily suspended and all dirty objects are marked, disabling further modification. Copy-on-write techniques enable several gigabytes to be marked in under 100 ms. Once the mark pass completes, computations is resumed and the dirty objects are asynchronously written to the log.

When the log writes have completed, a migrator is started to copy the objects back to their home locations. The checkpoint/migrate approach ensures that the system is always able to recover from the most recent successful checkpoint, even if a failure occurs while taking a checkpoint or performing a migration.

The EROS checkpoint mechanism is similar to that of KeyKOS [Lan92], but the use of a circular log makes it more adaptable to runtime load variations. In addition, a circular log structure allows the migrator to proceed incrementally [Gra93]. If there are heavy demands on memory, the migrator can move a small number of objects, write a new checkpoint directory, and update the checkpoint log header to reflect the new "most recent checkpoint" directory.

The circular log also allows us to continue reloading objects from the log until the space is reused, which improves disk arm locality. A recent examination of disk write traffic under Linux suggests that over half of the disk write traffic during a full rebuild of the EROS source tree is done to update file system metadata. Nearly all of these writes are eliminated in a recoverably persistent system. Better still, the checkpoint log allows migration to proceed in order of disk destination, which yields significant improvements in write bandwidth relative to conventional file systems.

5 Status and Conclusions

The system described in this paper is currently running, though the checkpoint mechanism is still being debugged. The design and implementation meet all of the principles set forth in the introduction. Even disk I/O delay bounds can be stated for the current implementation.

At present, the code is broken down approximately as follows:

Lines	Description
14,424	Machine-independent C++ code
17,254	Machine-specific C++ code
1,696	Machine-specific assembler

The system is not yet ready for distribution, but will be made available for use by interested researchers. To join the information list, please see the EROS home page at http://www.cis.upenn.edu/~eros

Stability

After a few weeks of shakedown, the kernel has proven surprisingly robust. To stress test the early system, we implemented kernel daemons to perform constraint checking and object invalidation, and ran these at 20 ms intervals. In addition, we and set the hardware clock to interrupt at approximately 0.5ms intervals. We then tried to run the system on a 20Mhz 386SX. Somewhat to our surprise, it runs, makes real progress on user domain execution, and does not miss an interrupt.

Performance

In the prototype's untuned IPC implementation, a one-way domain-to-domain invocation takes 3520 cycles (user to user) on a 133 Mhz Pentium (26.5 μS), as reported by the hardware cycle counter. Of these, roughly 100 cycles are taken by the hardware privilege crossing mechanism. Subsequent tuning has reduced this to 312 cycles (2.34 μS). We will not reach the lower limit of 250 cycles [Lie93a] reported by Liedtke for the 486DX50; the Pentium has a higher CPU to memory cycle ratio than the 486, and some cycles are required in our IPC path for validating the invoked capability and for the capability copy portion of the invocation.

Correctness

A key objective of the EROS effort is to sustain a mean time between sotware failures measured in years. A further objective, and in some ways a more important one, is to ensure that we *never* write an inconsistent checkpoint image to the disk. The worst problem in persistent systems is that *errors* are persistent too.

The careful tracking of dependencies and interpretation contexts allows us to ensure with high likelihood that states written to the disk are consistent. Verifiable consistency constraints can be derived from them, and are applied before the system commits a checkpoint image. If any consistency constraint is violated, the system restarts rather than committing a damaged checkpoint image.

These checks provide protection against some insidious errors, including many unreported memory errors. The state constraint tracking in effect provides a degree of redundant encoding, which makes localized memory errors in cgroups, the object table, and the in-memory object headers relatively detectable. The system even does an occasional checksum on *un*modified pages.

These measures are sufficient to protect the system overall, but they do not allow us to catch memory errors in dirty user pages. We expect that these will eventually become the dominant source of data corruption on current commodity hardware, and can be prevented only with hardware support.

Related Efforts

EROS is closely related to KeyKOS [Har85, Bom92], a system developed by Key Logic, Inc. to support reliable time sharing services among mutually suspicious users. The EROS microkernel design borrows heavily from their experiences. The implementation is completely new, and EROS departs from the KeyKOS architecture in two ways. First, we have abandoned the KeyKOS *meters* notion in favor of processor reserves. Second, KeyKOS had no notion of a thread. Threads were originally introduced in the EROS kernel to support precise scheduling of drivers, and to provide a locus at which scheduling policy might be attached independent of the domain for research purposes. Schedulable kernel drivers are proving to be a significant and useful facility, but it is not clear that they warrant the overhead of the thread abstraction.

With the addition of memory reserves (pinned objects), we believe that EROS could be used in many real-time applications. The overhead of the checkpoint mechanism should be both predictable and schedulable. Persistent active objects, however, raise a number of questions concerning scheduling, particularly in the area of priority inheritance. When the client/server relationship is transitive, or (as in EROS) does not observe a strict stack-oriented call/return discipline that preserves thread identity, the priority inheritance mechanisms proposed by Tokuda et. al. [Kit93] are inadequate. Further, it is not at all apparent that priority inheritance is an appropriate model for communications between conceptually independent active agents.

Future Directions

The current EROS system was constructed as a baseline for a future distributed system. The single-level store and careful dependency tracking lend themselves well to Lamport's vector time notions [Lam78] and his subsequent work on distributed snapshots [Cha85]. By combining the logging checkpoint approach with careful coloring strategies, we hope to be able to implement a recoverable distributed system with acceptable space and performance overhead.

Acknowledgements

Bryan Ford of the University of Utah has actively participated in the design discussions that led to this design, as have Norman Hardy, Charles Landau, and William Frantz of the Key KOS group.

Early readers caught a number of errors – some substantial – in this paper. Thanks to Mitchell P. Marcus, William Frantz, Colin McLean, Dennis Allison, and Ben Chen for their efforts in reviewing under severe time pressure.

References

[Bom92]   Allen C. Bomberger, A. Peri Frantz, William S. Frantz, Ann C. Hardy, Norman Hardy, Charles R. Landau, Jonathan S. Shapiro. "The KeyKOS NanoKernel Architecture," *Proceedings of the USENIX Workshop on Micro-Kernels and Other Kernel Architectures.* USENIX Association. April 1992. pp 95-112.

[Cha85]   K. Mani Chandy and Leslie Lamport. "Distributed Snapshots: Determining Global States of Distributed Systems," *ACM Transactions on Computer Systems.* Vol 3, No 1 pp. 63-75 (February 1985)

[For93]   Bryan Ford and Jay Lepreau, "Evolving Mach 3.0 to a Migrating Threads Model," *Proceedings of the Winter USENIX Conference,* January 1994.

[Gra93]   Jim Gray and Andreas Reuter. *Transaction Processing, Concepts and Technology.* Morgan Kaufmann. 1993.

[Ham95]   Graham Hamilton and Panos Kougiouris, *The Spring Nucleus: A microkernel for objects,* Sun Microsystems Laboratories, Inc.

[Har85]   Norman Hardy. "The KeyKOS Architecture" *Operating Systems Review.* Oct. 1985, pp 8-25.

[Kit93]   Takuro Kitayama, Tatsuo Nakajima, Hiroshi Arakawa, and Hideyuki Tokuda. "Integrated Management of Priority Inversion in Real-Time Mach." *IEEE Real-Time Systems Symposium.* December 1993

[Lam76]   Butler W. Lampson and Howerd E. Sutrgis. "Reflections on an Operating System Design." *Communications of the ACM* Vol 19, No 5, May 1976.

[Lam78]   Leslie Lamport. "Time, Clocks, and the Ordering of Events in a Distributed System," *Communications of the ACM.* Vol 21, No 7, pp. 558-565 (July 1978).

[Lan92]   Charles R. Landau. "The Checkpoint Mechanism in KeyKOS," *Proceedings of the Second International Workshop on Object Orientation in Operating Systems.* IEEE. September 1992. pp 86-91.

[Lie93a] Jochen Liedtke. "Improving IPC by Kernel Design," *Proceedings of the 14th ACP Symposium on Operating System Principles,* ACM, 1993

[Lie93b] Jochen Liedtke. "A Persistent System in Real Use – Experiences of the First 13 Years" *Proceedings of the 3rd International Workshop on Object-Orientation in Operating Systems,* Asheville, N.C. 1993

[Mer93]   Clifford W. Mercer, Stefan Savage, and Hideyuki Tokuda. "Processor Capacity Reserves: An Abstraction for Managing Processor Usage," *Proceedings of the Fourth Workshop on Workstation Operating Systems (WWOS-IV),* October 1993

[Tho78]   K. Thompson, "UNIX Implementation," *Bell System Technical Journal*, Vol 57, No 6, Part 2, pp. 1931-1946, July/August 1978

[Sha96a] Jonathan S. Shapiro. *A Programmer's Introduction to EROS*. Available via the EROS home page at `http://www.cis.upenn.edu/~eros`

[Sha96b] Jonathan S. Shapiro. *The EROS Object Reference Manual*. In progress. Draft available via the EROS home page at
`http://www.cis.upenn.edu/~eros`

[Wul81]   William A. Wulf, Roy Levin, and Samuel P. Harbison. *HYDRA/C.mmp: An Experimental Computer System* McGraw Hill, 1981.

Automating Systems Design in a Persistent Environment

S. Berman[†] and R. Figueira[*]

Department of Computer Science, University of Cape Town

sonia@cs.uct.ac.za[†]   ricardo@cs.uct.ac.za[*]

Abstract

A Design Workbench has been built for Napier88 [MBC+94] as part of the natural progression towards developing better product systems and improving software construction tools. Our system includes a Metamodeller (enabling users to specify the data and process models they prefer), a Model Builder which supports multiple co-existing models, a Target System Generator, and Change Absorption tools. Our experience using the Workbench has shown that it is easy to use, increases productivity, improves programming standards and facilitates code sharing. The Persistent Workshop [WPA+95] is an extensible, integrated set of tools that enable Napier88 systems to be built more easily and more effectively. Our system has been integrated in the Workshop, and has demonstrated the benefits of this structured programmer's environment, with objects migrating between multiple specialised workbenches.

This paper describes how the Workshop was extended to contain a new workbench for system design. It describes the metasystem, and shows how a design created using one set of models can be viewed and changed using other models. The change absorption facility is presented to illustrate how models can be altered without losing edits that have already been made to generated code.

Keywords: persistent environments, conceptual modelling, code generation, change management.

1   Introduction

Persistent programming languages claim to be better than conventional database systems at supporting complex data, as needed eg in computer-aided software engineering. This paper describes a complex application which substantiates this claim by showing how a sophisticated Systems Design Workbench can be built in Napier88 [MBC+94]. Our product is a useful toolkit for Napier88 programmers, which has been integrated into a structured software construction system called the Persistent Workbench [WPA+95].

Napier88 systems are typically constructed in the following way. Many textual specifications are developed by team members, on paper and in Unix directories. It is difficult to see which represent alternatives, which are successive refinements of an approach, how they relate to each other and where to find documentation on any one subsystem. It is also difficult for programmers to remain aware of structures and code produced by other team members, so software reuse is limited. Ensuring that all members use the same type definitions and the same interfaces to shared procedures requires some effort; it is harder still to ensure that components adhere to conventions so that the system is easy to understand and modify. Browsers support exploration of the stable store, but typically only give the name and type of objects; a hyperprogramming browser [KCC+92] can show associated source; but additional documentation is needed before software reuse can confidently be done. Information on types is not available, and specifications and documentation are not generally maintained on the store.

We discern three developing strands of provision for software construction in persistent languages: a bottom-up approach exemplified by hyperprogramming [KCC$^+$92]; a top-down approach (see for example [CT92, Wet94]); and a methodological approach (for example [ABC$^+$93]). These concentrate primarily on the implementation stage; we believe there is a need to complement them with good systems design aids. To be used in practice, it is essential that design tools be sufficiently flexible to allow everyone to use the models they prefer. Moreover, such a system needs to ensure that, once a target system has developed from a given model, it is possible to alter the model without abandoning the code already developed from it. Finally, it is essential that the systems design component can be integrated with a good program development environment. It order for a design toolkit to be used in practice, it must be quick and easy to use, offer significant short-term benefits and permit programmers to use their own favourite methodology [Mar88]. This paper shows how a persistent data repository makes it possible to create such a system

Section two describes the user's view of our system. The next section outlines the Workshop and how new workbenches can be added to this. Section 4 shows how multiple co-existing models can be supported. This leads us to describing the Metamodeller, which permits a specific model (eg OMT [RBP$^+$91], Entity-Relationship [Che76], etc.) to be defined. Section 6 outlines the data structures and methodology employed for change absorption and section 7 discusses our experience using the workbench. In the Conclusion we suggest some avenues for future research.

2   The Systems Design Workbench

This section introduces the Systems Design Workbench depicted in Figure 1; its advanced features are described in the remainder of the paper. The system inputs data and process models, verifies consistency, highlights incomplete information and generates target code on request. It can also use its dependency data to indicate the impact of a possible design change.

The main components of the system are the Data Modeller and Process Modeller, the Data Repository and the User Interface (UI). The repository resides on the persistent store and contains all procedures, types, models, programs, specifications, etc. designed by the user or produced by the workbench tools. The Data Modeller accepts, edits and checks designs, and automatically generates Napier types and bulk data objects based on this. Standard procedures for manipulating these types (*handlers*) can also be generated, eg to input or display an instance. Users input both process and data models from a file; textual input is preferred over graphical design because it is faster [Mar88]. Process models are designed, and skeleton code generated and organised in a hierarchy on the persistent store by the Process Modeller. The UI includes a graphical display feature, and a query facility which allows users to retrieve information on any aspect of the developing system.

3   The Persistent Workshop

The Workshop is a software architecture for building persistent systems. It uses an abstraction that sees a persistent programmer as a carpenter having tools and items that the tools work on. The Workshop developers built a single workbench, the "Programmer's Workbench", that helps in editing and managing

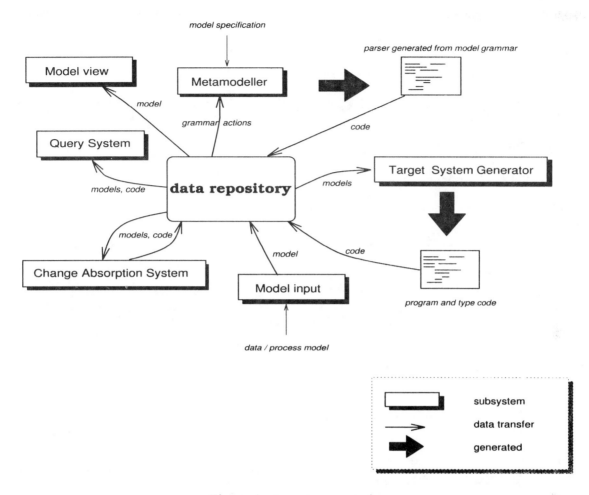

Figure 1: A system overview

persistent application systems. Its tools include editors, compilers, store visualisers, source code completers, pretty-printers and an application builder [SPW+95]. Our Design Workbench complements this, providing a set of tools useful to persistent system designers, and allowing items to move freely between the two workbenches. It is a vehicle for studying the interaction of multiple workbenches sharing tools and workitems, and the ease with which new systems can be incorporated into this technology. This section outlines the steps involved in adding the new workbench to the Workshop.

3.1 Workshop abstraction

The Workshop is a *workshop* with a number of *workbenches*. Each workbench contains a set of *work tools* and a number of *work items*. Tools interact through an established *communication space* on each workbench. They are the routines that alter the state of the workbench, by modifying, querying or creating work items. A set of Workshop rules specify the type, organization and behaviour of tools and work items. These rules include updating management information, the type of interface a tool must have and the structure of work items and tools.

3.2   Integrating the new workbench

The first step in integrating our system as a second workbench was to identify its tools and items. The individual components of the four main subsystems became the tools:

- data model input

- process model input

- type generation (from data model)

- handler generation (procedures to manipulate instances of these types)

- program generation (environments, data structures, procedure stubs and skeleton code)

- view data model

- view process model

- data repository querying

- share tool (copies a work item to another workbench)

More tools were added when the advanced features were implemented.

Different representations of programs etc. had been used by the two workbenches. To permit migration of items without loss of information, our data types had to be changed: data found in the other workbench (but often stored differently) was replaced by an object having the type used in the Programmer's Workbench. This typically meant that the revised type now contained values not used within our system; we benefitted from this additional information and the associated functionality provided by the other workbench.

Workbenches, tools, items and communication spaces have a defined structure that a workbench designer must conform to. Rewriting the code to fit the abstraction involved two types of transformation. The first involved coding an additional layer of procedures that take work items from the workbench and use them as input to the original procedures for each tool. They also insert, replace and remove work items on the workbench.

In the original system all design object manipulation was done through the repository. The second transformation changed the tools to fit the Workshop abstraction by passing work items as parameters. Procedures that queried or altered one of the data repository maps [ALP+91] are now passed a DesignWorkItem object which has the maps as fields. This DesignWorkItem type encapsulates all the parts of a system design: data and process models, types, handlers, bulk variables, constraints and programs. At first we attempted to use the individual design components (types, bulk variables, etc.) as separate work items; but with that approach it became difficult to determine which component came from which design.

3.3 Benefits

Integration in the Workshop produced a more structured implementation of our system; and having the tools conform to Workshop conventions made them independent of other programs; so the resulting system is easier to maintain. Integration amounts to changing the interface between system and user, and between tools. The new DesignWorkItem type we developed in this way made it easier to manipulate a design as a whole, and to keep different target systems separate.

Our workbench provides the first opportunity to study the interaction between workbenches in the workshop. The communication between workbenches includes the sharing of work items and tools and the interaction between tools on different workbenches. Tools, such as the "Share" tool that copies references to work items to another workbench, are shared between workbenches.

4 Supporting Multiple Co-existing Models

A single repository can be used to represent a variety of data- and process-models. Such a repository architecture permits alternative views of a design, and allows it to be viewed, edited and queried using different modelling languages at different times. This allows a group of designers to change between models to get different perspectives and designers can choose to work with the model they prefer. This section outlines the steps involved in extending the workbench to cater for known data models (based on surveys such as [HK87, PM88]), and to permit changing from one model to another while working on a single design. We then consider how new modelling constructs that may arise in future might be accommodated. Note that so far our work has focused on data modelling, with less emphasis on the process modelling aspect.

4.1 Data modelling

There are a number of conceptual data modelling abstractions: aggregation, generalization, classification, association, derivation and constraints. Since all current models use some subset of these abstractions, a repository that can represent all the above constructs should be able to represent any conceptual model. While building the repository, it became evident that more than one model could be accommodated by this single complex object. This was seen when integrating a new model into the system: the repository catered for all its constructs and did not need changing to accommodate the model.

The first step in supporting a new data model is to find a mapping from the model's conceptual constructs (such as aggregation or generalisation) to repository components. At the same time, a reverse mapping needs to be found so that the repository unambiguously represents the constructs. These mappings allow many data models to be represented in the repository where each conceptual construct (primitive) is uniquely represented.

4.2 Issues

Unfortunately, the differences between conceptual data models implies that conversion is not always seamless. Models differ in expressive power, since not all constructs are represented in every model.

For example, aggregation is only implemented at the attribute level in the ER [Che76] model, while IFO [AH87] allows aggregation of objects; and Daplex [Shi81] does not have explicit association.

For example, in the ER model a relationship `Delivery` between `Supplier` and `Part` can have two attributes `Date` and `Discount`. In order to represent this using Daplex, a `Delivery` entity needs to be created:

```
DECLARE Delivery() -> ENTITY
DECLARE Date(Delivery) -> STRING
DECLARE Discount(Delivery) -> INT
DECLARE Delivers(Supplier,Part) -> Delivery
```

To view the ER model from a Daplex perspective requires converting this relationship into an entity.

In future, new modelling constructs may be invented. A method is needed to represent such constructs in the repository. One possibility is to assume that any new modelling primitive can be represented as some combination of existing constructs. An alternative approach is to provide a minimal set of primitives, and define all existing and future models in terms of this set.

5   The Metamodeller

Support for multiple co-existing models can be generalized to allow arbitrary models to be incorporated in a single data repository. The designer firstly needs to specify the model's representation in the repository and its language syntax. The Systems Design Workbench allows users to specify their own models by supplying the model's input grammar. A compiler-compiler similar to Yacc [Joh75] was built, and the Metamodeller then based on this. It generates a parser for a given grammar (that is, a program to parse models input as text and update the repository accordingly). To facilitate the coding of "actions", procedures for inserting tokens into the repository exist in the store, so these simply need to be called with the correct parameters. A conceptual model designer thus merely needs to know of these action procedures in order to create her metamodel.

Model specifications must ensure the displaying and querying of designs is appropriate to the new model. The Design Workbench Query tool accepts SQL-type statements, given in terms of the user's conceptual model as defined to the metasystem. This metasystem specification is similar to SQL view definition, and indicates how the repository should be seen by a user of the new model. For example, a (simplified) ER view could be:

```
DEFINE VIEW ER
{Entities = (SELECT name,keys,kind,attributes FROM Objects);
 Relationships = (SELECT * FROM Links, Objects
                         WHERE Objects(refsTo) = Links(refsTo) );
 Attributes = (SELECT name,kind,belongsTo FROM Attributes) }
```

For this, the metamodelling user is given an outline of the relevant parts of the data repository. Effectively she works with a view of the repository, based on which she defines the view to be presented to users.

For graphical displays, persistent procedures are used to draw appropriate shapes for repository objects. To specify a particular convention required by a user-defined model, the default procedures must be known, and can be reset accordingly, eg

```
DEFINE DRAW ER
  { DrawObject = DrawBox;
  DrawLink = DrawDiamond;
  DrawAttribute = DrawOval }
```

Conceptual models that have been specified via the Metamodeller are ER, Daplex, OMT [RBP+91], DFD [YC75] and structure chart [Tri88] models; these have all been used in subsequent system designs. Work on query and viewing specifications for some of these is still in progress.

6 A Change Absorption System

Code maintenance and model modification require adequate handling of changes to the system. The simplest solution is to replace all design objects affected by a change. However, since certain design objects are *generated* and *then edited* by users, any previous code changes would be lost. This section outlines some of the issues in designing a change absorption system.

As an illustration, the following change may be made to part of a handler that outputs student information:

The code unit: `writeString("DOB: ")` could be changed to
`writeString("Date of Birth:   ")`

If any change to student causes straight-forward *re-generation* of its handlers, the above edit, which does not affect other parts of the system, would be lost. Change absorption can be used to control and propagate changes through a design (both models and code). Such a system needs to distinguish between those parts of the design that cannot be changed and those that can. One solution is to divide the handler programs into cells, and distinguish user-modifiable cells. For the example code unit above, the following decomposition is created:

```
writeString( "DOB:  " )
```

where only unboxed code is user-editable. The collection of cells still needs to be associated with the "DOB" attribute so that, if the attribute is deleted, the entire code unit disappears. We represent generated code by separate code units, differentiating system-created from user-created units. The latter represent text inserted between generated statements. A system unit is a collection of code cells, each flagged as user-replaceable or not. Initial work on change management has begun with the introduction of control over the generated system.

7 Discussion

The system was developed initially to support modelling with Entity-Relationship and Data Structure Diagrams. It was then used to design an improved version of itself, capable of supporting additional models, specifically OMT [RBP+91] and Daplex [Shi81]. This exercise highlighted the advantages of automated code generation, and of having textual input rather than GUI-based input. The re-implementation of the system to support different models involved a great deal of code reuse, and emphasised the advantages of a metasystem. The metasystem was then developed, and new models specified in a fraction of the time taken to implement OMT. Because of the versatility of the data repository, it followed almost automatically that the system was able to support multiple co-existing models and the ability for users of different models to work on the same design. At the same time, this revealed the relative advantages and disadvantages of these well-known models. The change absorption tools are currently nearing completion, and we expect to have some preliminary testing in place by the end of May.

Our tests involved the building of three different systems by seven programmers. In the light of this experience we obtained some answers to our initial questions:

- *Do programmers prefer using the Design Workshop, and why?* Yes they do, because of increased productivity and an absence of tedium.

- *Which parts of the Workshop are used most, and why?* The data model creation, and resulting code generation, were the most used. This is mainly because this aspect is the most fully developed; the ratio of text input to code generated is largest here.

- *How easy is is to use the Workshop?* We found that even second year students were easily able to learn and utilise the metamodelling and system design aspects.

- *Should generated code be kept entirely within the store, or copied to Unix files as well?* Programmers felt more confident working with generated Unix files when making changes: response time is faster, there is a greater feeling of control over the developing system, concurrent design is possible. Our change absorption facilities were not available then; this may make "living within the store" more attractive.

8 Conclusion

This paper described a Design Workbench for Napier88 which inputs data and process models and automatically generates the kernel of the target software system. All designed and implemented components are kept together on the persistent store, and can be queried or graphically viewed. The workbench supports multiple co-existing models and a metasystem allows user-defined models to be specified. Thus programmers can use their preferred models, even when working in teams on a single design. A change absorption facility ensures that changes to generated code are not lost when models are altered.

Our product permits applications to be developed more easily and quickly, and produces better systems, because code and documentation are generated automatically and according to prescribed conventions [ABP+94]. Its immediate benefits relieve programmers of tedious software construction tasks; its long-term advantages are improved quality, increased reliability, greater software reuse and easier accommodation of change. We hope that Napier88 programmers will be interested in obtaining a copy and using it in their own work.

We believe that this project has clearly demonstrated the benefits of persistent object systems for computer-aided design. It has demonstrated the utility, and therefore the need, for persistent programming languages such as Napier88 and shown how persistent systems can be exploited to provide better software engineering environments than are supported by conventional databases. There is scope for further extension, particularly in the areas of software visualisation and version management. Some work in this area is being done by [Lav94]. Persistence is a fundamental property of objects, and increased co-operation between POS and Software Engineering researchers will be highly beneficial.

References

[ABC+93] M. Atkinson, P. Bailey, C. Christie, K. Cropper, and P. Philbrow. Towards bulk type libraries for napier88. Technical report, Dept. of Computer Science, University of Glasgow, 1993.

[ABP+94] Malcolm Atkinson, Pete Bailey, Paul Philbrow, and Ray Welland. *An Organization for Napier88 Libraries*. Technical Report 94-77, FIDE, 1994.

[AH87] S. Abiteboul and R. Hull. IFO: A Formal Semantic Database Model. *ACM Transactions on Database Systems*, 12(4):525–565, December 1987.

[ALP+91] M. Atkinson, C. Lécluse, P. Philbrow, and P. Richard. Maps as Bulk Types for Data Base Programming Languages. Technical Report FIDE/91/24, FIDE ESPRIT BRA Project 3070, 1991.

[Che76] P.P.S. Chen. The entity-relationship model - Toward a unified view of data. *ACM Transactions on Database Systems 1*, 1:9–36, March 1976.

[CT92] R.L. Cooper and I. Tabkha. A Semantic Framework for the Design of Data Intensive Applications in a Persistent Programming Language. In *Proceedings of the Twenty-Fifth Hawaii International Conference on System Sciences*, volume II of *Software Technology*, pages 799–809, 1992.

[HK87] Richard Hull and Roger King. Semantic Database Modeling: Survey, Applications, and Research Issues. *ACM Computer Surveys*, 19(3):201–260, September 1987.

[Joh75] S. C. Johnson. Yacc - yet another compiler compiler. Technical Report 32, AT&T Bell Laboratories, Murray Hill, N.J., 1975.

[KCC+92] G. Kirby, R. Connor, Q. Cutts, and R. Morrison. Persistent hyper-programs. *Fifth International Workshop on Persistent Object Systems*, pages 86–106, 1992.

[Lav94] Darryn Lavery. The Design of Effective Software Visualizations for Persistent Programming Environments. Technical Report FIDE/95/116, Dept. of Computer Science, University of Glasgow, 1994.

[Mar88] C.F. Martin. Second-Generation CASE Tools: A Challenge to Vendors. *IEEE Software*, pages 44–49, March 1988.

[MBC$^+$94] R. Morrison, F. Brown, R.C.H. Connor, Q. Cutts, A. Dearle, G. Kirby, and D. Munro. The Napier88 Reference Manual (Release 2.0). Technical Report CS/93/15, University of St Andrews, 1994.

[PM88] Joan Peckham and Fred Maryanski. Semantic Data Models. *ACM Computer Surveys*, 20(3):153–189, September 1988.

[RBP$^+$91] J. Rumbaugh, M. Blaha, W. Premerlani, F. Eddy, and W. Lorensen. *Object-Oriented Modeling and Design*. Prentice-Hall International, 1991.

[Shi81] David W. Shipman. The Functional Data Model and the Data Language DAPLEX. *ACM Transactions on Database Systems*, 6(1):140–173, March 1981.

[SPW$^+$95] D.I.K Sjøberg, P.C Philbrow, C. Waite, and R. Welland. Build Management in Database Programming Language Environments. In *6th International Workshop on Database Programming Language Environments, Gubbio, Italy*, 1995.

[Tri88] L.L. Tripp. A survey of graphical notations for program design - an update. *ACM SigSoft Software Engineering Notes*, 12(4):39–44, 1988.

[Wet94] 1994 Wetzel, I. *Programming with STYLE: On the Systematic Development of Programming Environments*. PhD thesis, University of Hamburg, 1994.

[WPA$^+$95] C.A. Waite, P.C Philbrow, M.P. Atkinson, R.C. Welland, D.O. Lavery, S.D. Macneill, T. Printezis, and R.C. Cooper. Programmer's Persistent Workshop—Principles and User Guide. Technical Report FIDE/95/125, ESPRIT Basic Research Action, Project Number 6309—FIDE$_2$, 1995.

[YC75] E. Yourdon and L.L. Constantine. *Structured Design*. Yourdon Press, 1975.

Supporting Persistent Object Systems in a Single Address Space*

Kevin Elphinstone, Stephen Russell, Gernot Heiser[†]
School of Computer Science & Engineering,
The University of New South Wales, Sydney 2052, Australia

Jochen Liedtke
GMD SET-RS, Schloß Birlinghoven, 53757 Sankt Augustin, Germany

Abstract

Single address space systems (SASOS) provide a programming model that is well suited to supporting persistent object systems. In this paper we show that stability can be implemented in the Mungi SASOS without incurring overhead in excess of the inherent cost of shadow-paging. Our approach is based on the introduction of a limited form of aliasing into the SASOS model and makes heavy use of user-level page fault handlers to allow implementation outside the kernel. We also show how the demands of database systems for control over page residency and physical I/O can be accommodated. An approach to user-level implementation of distributed shared memory (DSM) coherency models is outlined.

1 Introduction

Single address space operating systems (SASOS) such as Angel [MSS+93], Opal [CLF+94] and Mungi [VRH93] are based on the idea that a single, large virtual address space holds all data in a (potentially distributed) computing system. It has been pointed out before [RSE+92] that this class of operating systems provides a natural solution to an old problem of persistent programming: How to save arbitrary data structures on secondary storage having to translating them first into a form that allows reconstruction in memory at a later time. In a SASOS this becomes a non-problem: Secondary store is solely a backing device for virtual memory (VM) paging, and data are guaranteed to always appear at the VM location at which they were originally created. Hence internal references continue to work without any need for translation.

The single-level store of a SASOS is, in principle, persistent in the sense that data allocated in memory can outlive the process that created them, and also survive an orderly system shutdown and restart. However, stability in case of an unplanned system shutdown, e.g. in the case of a power failure, is a much harder problem. Classical approaches to achieving stability are logging and shadow paging. It is obviously possible to implement such stability schemes in the kernel, as was done in Monads [HR93]. However, this dictates a specific stability model to applications, and makes it difficult to adapt to specific needs of applications. For example, some applications never require stability, and should not have to pay the runtime overhead, while other applications require stability at certain times, others again require it constantly. It is, therefore, desirable to give the application maximum control over the stability model. It is not, *a priori*, clear that this can be done in a SASOS without incurring overhead in the form of having to keep redundant memory copies or to perform extra copy operations.

Object-oriented database systems, such as ObjectStore [LLO+91] or O₂ [D+91], seem well-suited for implementation on top of a SASOS, as their data model fits the SASOS model very well. In fact, one of the main difficulties facing the implementation of these system is the need to construct and efficiently handle system-wide unique object identifiers. A SASOS provides these for free in the form of VM addresses. However, database management systems (DBMS) tend to be very demanding customers for an operating system: For efficiency reasons they need to control residency of data in memory, and they need control over backing store allocation in order to reduce disk seek times. Can such systems be accommodated in a SASOS, which is characterised by a single-level store and hence the absence of an I/O model, without breaking the SASOS paradigm?

---

*This work was supported by grants from the Australian Research Council (ARC) and the German Ministry for Education and Research (BMBF).
[†]E-mail: G.Heiser@unsw.edu.au, fax: +61 2 9395 5995, phone: +61 2 9395 5156

We will address these issues in the remainder of this paper. We will demonstrate that by introducing aliasing into the SASOS model we can, with the help of user-level pagers, implement shadow-paging efficiently in the Mungi system. We will also show that DBMS demands for control of physical memory (PM) and physical I/O can be met, without creating a need to integrate the DBMS, or parts of it, into the kernel.

2 Support for Persistent Object Systems in Mungi

2.1 Mungi Overview

In Mungi, virtual memory is allocated in contiguous, page-aligned segments called *objects*. Objects are also the unit of protection: Access rights are object-based. The system makes no assumptions about the internal structure of objects.

Access control is based on password capabilities, i.e. (base address, password) pairs. The access rights conferred to a holder by a capability are a combination of read, write, execute and delete. A capability conferring all these rights is called an *owner capability*. A system wide directory called the *object table* contains information about all objects, including their set of valid capabilities and corresponding access rights. Capabilities can be added or revoked by a holder of an owner capability.

When an object is first accessed by a thread, a page fault will occur as there exists no virtual to physical memory (VM→PM) mapping for the thread. The kernel will validate the access by matching the thread's list of capabilities with the set recorded for that object in the object table. If the access is valid, the kernel caches the validation information and invokes the appropriate page fault handler to set up a mapping for the accessed page.

In the following subsections we will present the extensions proposed to Mungi for supporting persistent object systems. These are all concerned with the relationship between physical and virtual memory. They are summarised in Fig. 1 and explained in the remainder of this section.

InstallPager (Capability obj, Capability pager);
Flush (Address adr, Int length)
Copy (Address from, Address to, Int length) Map (Address from, Address to, Int length, Mode m) Unmap (Address to, Int length)

Figure 1: Mungi system calls dealing with the relationship between virtual and physical memory.

2.2 User-level pagers

In Mungi, each object is associated with a *pager* which will be called by the system to handle page faults. When an object is first allocated, its pager is the system's default pager, which performs normal VM paging. A user-level pager (ULP) can be installed with the InstallPager system call. A null pager capability will re-install the default pager. Owner capability is required for changing an object's pager.

Pagers are invoked in three cases: access of a non-resident page (*residency fault*), write attempt to a read-only page (*write fault*), and a Flush call executed on a page (*flush event*).

The default pager handles a write fault by signalling a protection violation to the offending thread. Default handling of a residency fault results in allocating a physical frame to it, which is either zero-filled if the virtual page has not been allocated before, or reloaded from disk. Default pager action on a flush event is explained below.

2.3 Flushing dirty pages

The Flush system call causes invocation of the appropriate pager with a flush event. Both adr and length must be page-aligned, and all affected pages must be part of the same object.

The default pager handles flush events by writing the pages' contents to disk if they are dirty **and** ensures that the kernel's mappings of these pages to backing store are flushed as well. The kernel uses a stable logging scheme for storing these mappings on disk. No write will occur on a clean page.

2.4 Virtual memory mapping primitives

The mapping primitives Map and Unmap are based on similar calls in the L3 operating system [Lie93] (although semantics differ significantly from the L3 operations). Copy is related to these as it also affects mappings. Address and length parameters must be page aligned, and if a range of pages is specified, all pages within the range must be part of the same object. The mode can either be read-only or read/write.

2.4.1 Copy-on-write

The Copy system call performs page-wise memory copy. Page faults will be generated if the source or destination pages are not resident, or if the destination pages are R/O. The source and destination ranges must not overlap. Read capability on the source and R/W capability on the destination is required.

If the destination is handled by the default pager, the implementation uses copy-on-write. This not only avoids copying pages which never get modified, but also avoids zeroing a newly allocated page immediately before overwriting it. If the target of a Copy is flushed or aliased at a later time, the physical copy will be forced if it has not already been made. If the source is later unmapped, the destination inherits the source's physical mappings (including backing store) if the physical copy has not yet been made. Mapping of the source pages to backing store will not be changed by a Copy operation.

2.4.2 Map

Map(from,to,length,mode) creates an alias in the virtual address-space by mapping VM addresses [to,to+length-1] to the same physical frames as VM addresses [from,from+length-1]. The destination is implicitly unmapped prior to establishing the alias.

The two address ranges must not overlap, unless they are identical, in which case the call serves to modify the access mode (R/O or writable) without changing any VM→PM mappings. This call is a no-op on non-resident pages (i.e. will not fault them into PM).

R/W capability is required on the objects affected by a Map, even in the case of a R/O mapping. The operation will cause a page fault on the source pages if they are not resident. Fig. 2 shows the effect of a Map operation.

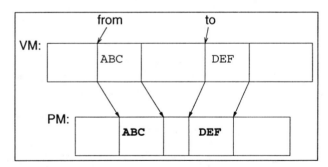 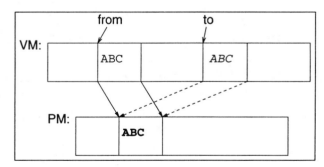

Figure 2: Address-space before (left) and after (right) execution of a Map(from,to,length,ro) **system call. Dashed arrows indicate R/O mappings, slanted text indicates R/O data.**

An alias established by a Map operation only exists as long as the pages are resident. This implies that the Map operation is essentially only of use to ULPs, as it needs to be reestablished on any residency fault. For the same reason, a Map operation whose destination pages are handled by the default pager makes no sense and is therefore invalid.

2.4.3 Unmap

The aliasing in Fig. 2 can be undone with the operation Unmap(to,length); however, Unmap can also be applied to pages which are not aliased. On return, to does not have any mapping to PM or backing store, as if newly allocated. Hence, if a page to be unmapped was an alias, the alias is simply removed; if another page was mapped to it, ie more than one level of aliasing, then both pages will become unmapped. Unmapping also removes any write protection from the specified address range. Unmapping a page which is neither resident nor backed on disk is a no-op. R/W capability is required for performing an Unmap operation.

For an object serviced by the default pager unmapping is semantically equivalent to zeroing all memory at addresses [to,to+length-1], as Mungi's default pager uses zero-on-read for uninitialised memory. Fig. 3 shows an example of an Unmap operation.

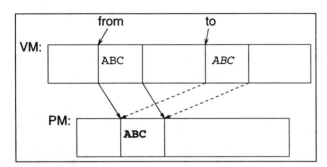 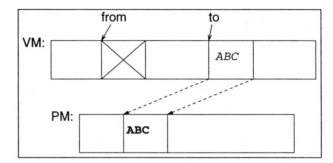

Figure 3: Address-space before (left) and after (right) execution of an Unmap(from,length) **system call. Crossed-out pages are unmapped.**

2.5 Recursive address spaces?

Systems like Grasshopper [DdB+94] and L4 [Lie95] use similar mapping operations, but use them in a hierarchical fashion to recursively construct address spaces. This does not fit the SASOS model, as there can only be one address-space, so mappings can only operate between different parts of the same address-space. However, pagers can be nested in our model: If a ULP handles a page fault by mapping another page onto the faulting one, this may trigger a fault on the source page, invoking its ULP. This will continue until a resident page is mapped to the faulting one, or the default pager is invoked.

3 Implementation of Shadow-Paging

If we ignore stability issues we can checkpoint an object simply by copying it. To roll back, the checkpoint is copied back onto the object. The copy-on-write semantics of the default pager for the Copy system call ensures that only dirty pages are actually copied.

A stable version of the checkpointing scheme can be built with the help of a user-level pager using explicit shadow-paging [Lor77] and an atomic update operation [Cha78]. For the purpose of using Challis' atomic update algorithm we use a two-page object st_page which is located at a well-known address (e.g. pointed to by the checkpointed object's entry in the object table). We can then do atomic updates to stored values as shown in Fig. 4. The basic idea of the algorithm is to alternate between two pages for writing data to disk, so that in case of a system failure during a write operation there is always a stable copy left. Pages are written with a timestamp at the beginning and the end. When reading them back, the timestamps are compared and a page is considered stable if its timestamps agree. If both pages are stable, the timestamp identifies the most recent copy.

To implement shadow paging for object O_0, we allocate two additional objects, O_1 and O_2, of the same size as O_0. O_1 and O_2 are both handled by the default pager. Note that the allocation of an object only allocates virtual memory. No physical memory is allocated until the object is actually accessed.

```
typedef struct St_map {              get_stable (Int &index, St_map &m) {
    Address a[2];                        if (st_page[0].d_0 == st_page[0].d_1)
    Bool pm[...];                            if (st_page[1].d_0 == st_page[1].d_1)
}                                                if (st_page[0].d_0 > st_page[1].d_0)
typedef struct St_page {                             index = 0;
    Date d_0;                                    else
    St_map m;                                        index = 1;
    Char fill[...];                          else
    Date d_1;                                    index = 0;
}                                        else
                                             index = 1;
St_page st_page[2];                      m = st_page[index].m;
put_stable (Int index, St_map m) {   }
    st_page[index].d_0 = timestamp();
    st_page[index].m = m;
    st_page[index].d_1 = st_page[index].d_0;
    Flush(st_page[index],ps);
}
```

Figure 4: Pseudocode implementation of Challis' algorithm.

The addresses of O_1 and O_2 are held in the stable object st_page, as is a bitmap which indicates for each page of O_0 to which of the two shadow objects it is mapped.

Fig. 5 shows the algorithm (ignoring locking). The variable st_index indicates which page of st_page holds the bitmap for the stable copy of O_0. The variable map holds the bitmap of the dirty copy of O_0, while dirty identifies pages which have been modified since the last checkpoint. WriteProtect has been used as an alias for a Map call which only serves to make an object read-only, and size parameters have been omitted for clarity. The procedures current and other query the page map while swap_current_other modifies it (by flipping the appropriate bit).

The Copy, Unmap and Flush system calls in the setup code serve to dissociate the physical backing store from O_0 and associate it with O_1. The copy-on-write semantics of the Copy operation ensure that this happens without actual copying. This sequence is not required if stable checkpointing is used from the time O_0 is allocated.

After setup, O_1 holds the stable copy of the object. On a write fault a new page is allocated and the corresponding bit in map is flipped to indicate the location of the dirty page, as shown in Fig. 6. On a checkpoint, all dirty pages are flushed and the present state recoded as the stable one. After the first checkpoint, some stable pages belong to O_1, others to O_2, depending on how often they have been modified.

While the mappings of VM pages to backing store for the backup pages referenced by O_1 and O_2 need to be persistent (ensured by Flush calls in Fig. 5), this is not the case for the mappings of O_0 or those of dirty pages in O_1 and O_2. As a consequence, no mappings need to be made persistent between checkpoints, hence no Flush calls need to be performed by the pager.

Objects O_1 and O_2 are in the protection domain of the pager, but not necessarily in the protection domain of the application. Hence, objects O_1 and O_2 can be hidden from the application; all data accesses by application programs go through O_0, thereby ensuring that all embedded references work correctly. The algorithm can easily be applied to consistently checkpoint a set of related objects, the stable object st_page then contains object references and bitmaps for all the involved objects.

4 Other Applications of the Model

4.1 Controlling page residency

Certain applications, like DBMS, require the ability to pin pages in memory for efficiency reasons. To support this, we create a special region, σ_0, in virtual memory to map all of PM. This region is "magical", i.e. the kernel knows about its special

```
St_map map;                                          pager(faulting_page) {
Bool st_index;                                           current_page = current (map, faulting_page);
Bool dirty[...];                                         other_page = other (map, faulting_page);
setup() {                                                if (write_fault)
    map = { {O₁, O₂}, 0};                                    /* create dirty page: */
    dirty = 0;                                               Copy(current_page, other_page);
    st_index = 0;                                            Map(other_page, faulting_page, rw);
    Copy(O₀, O₁); /* copy-on-write */                        swap_current_other(map);
    Unmap(O₀); /* leave mapping to pager */                  /* no Flush needed! */
    Flush(O₁); /* make sure backup is stable */             dirty[faulting_page] = TRUE;
    InstallPager(O₀, pager);                             elsif (not_resident) /* re-establish mapping: */
    put_stable(st_index, map);                              if (dirty[faulting_page])
    put_stable(!st_index, map);                                 Map(current_page, faulting_page, read_write);
}                                                           else
                                                                Map(current_page, faulting_page, read_only);
checkpoint() {                                           /* ignore flushes */
    WriteProtect(O₀);                                }
    Flush (O₁); /* only flushes dirty pages */  rollback() {
    Flush (O₂);                                      get_stable(st_index, map);
    st_index = !st_index;                           for (all pages p)
    put_stable(st_index, map);                          /* free dirty blocks: */
    dirty = 0;                                           Unmap(other (map, p));
    for (all pages p)                               dirty = 0;
        /* unmap old backups: */                }
        Unmap(other (map, p));
}
```

Figure 5: Stable checkpointing of object O_0.

relationship to PM. Any page in VM is resident *if and only if* it is aliased to a page in σ_0. No page fault will ever occur in σ_0; is is essentially a permuted frame table.

The system administrator has the option of allocating an object O_σ in σ_0. Such an object is thereby known to the kernel to be unpagable. By handing a R/W capability for O_σ to a DBMS, the system administrator thereby enables the DBMS to pin pages in PM by aliasing them to O_σ. In the example in Fig. 7, page q has been pinned by a

$$\text{Map(q, } O_\sigma.\text{page[n])}$$

system call. The page can be unpinned and the pinning slot reused to pin page p by executing

$$\text{Map(p, } O_\sigma.\text{page[n])}.$$

Simply doing

$$\text{Unmap(} O_\sigma.\text{page[n])}$$

unpins the page without pinning another one in its place.

The advantage of this scheme over introducing special system calls to pin and unpin pages is that it ties in neatly with our capability-based protection scheme. By handing out a capability to an object of a particular size, the system allows the holder of the capability to pin a strictly limited number of pages.

4.2 Physical Disk I/O

As the SASOS model presents the user with a single-level store, I/O is not part of the model but is hidden in the operating system. This has significant advantages in simplifying application code. However, there are cases where applications (like

116

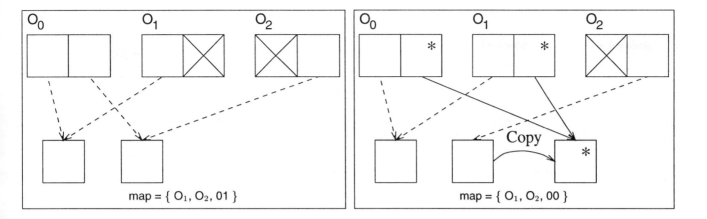

Figure 6: Copy-on-write operation in the stable checkpointing example. An asterisk indicates a dirty page, the current page map is shown at the bottom.

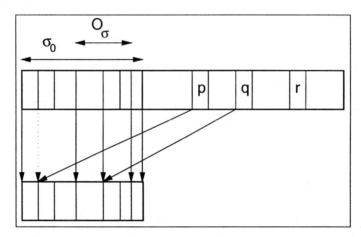

Figure 7: Locking pages in PM by aliasing to O_σ: Page p is resident and pageable, page q is pinned in memory (unpagable), page r is not resident. Page p's alias in σ_0 is only known to the kernel.

DBMS) require control over I/O operations for efficiency.

A certain amount of control over I/O is already available through ULPs and the Flush system call. However, in order to optimise seek times, some applications may want to have control over the actual allocation of pages on the disk.

We can support this in Mungi by mapping all of secondary storage into the virtual address space, as another special region σ_d. An object O_d is allocated covering all (or part) of σ_d, and R/W capability to that object is given to the application. The DBMS can then map virtual pages to specific disk blocks by mapping the appropriate pages of O_d to its memory objects.

To combine I/O control with control over page residency, the application needs to alias some pages of O_d twice—once to the data object and once to σ_d. To pin page p of object O, backed by disk block q, into physical frame r, the DBMS needs to execute

$$\text{Map } (O_d.\text{page}[q], O.\text{page}[p], ...);$$
$$\text{Map } (O_d.\text{page}[q], O_\sigma.\text{page}[r], ...).$$

To enable an application to optimise its physical I/O, it needs to be given information on the physical layout of the disk (number of tracks, cylinders, etc.) This information can be stored in a standard format at a well-known location, e.g. the first disk block.

Note that, in spite of the large amount of disk storage mapped into VM, this approach does not use up a significant fraction of VM: Mungi's total virtual address space is 2^{64} bytes or sixteen billion gigabytes.

4.3 Network I/O and distributed shared memory

Our last example does not directly deal with persistence but is included because it deals with distribution, which is certainly of great practical importance to persistent systems. We show how a distributed shared memory (DSM) coherency protocol can be implemented *at user level* in Mungi.

As above we map all of PM into VM, each node's PM is mapped to VM at a different location. Node n_i's memory is mapped to VM region σ_0^i, and the kernel on n_i ensures that no $\sigma_0^j, i \neq j$ is ever accessed by n_i. The kernel also needs to ensure that no thread with access to σ_0^i ever migrates.

Assume a thread executing on node n_0 triggers a residency fault on page p. When the appropriate pager is called, it requests the page from the network (via broadcast or other appropriate means). Assume the page happens to be resident on n_1, i.e. it has been mapped into σ_0^1. Node n_1 sends the contents of the page to n_0. Depending on the coherency model used, the pager on n_1 may first unmap or write-protect the page and its aliases (see Fig. 8).

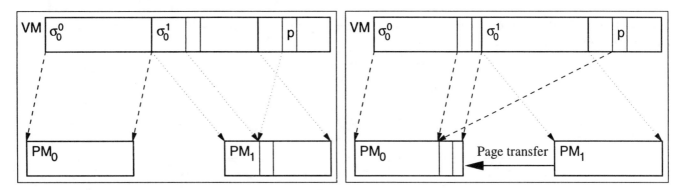

Figure 8: DSM paging: Page p is originally resident on node n_1 (left) but transferred to node n_0 (right). Broken arrows indicate VM→PM mappings of node n_0, while dotted arrows represent mappings of node n_1.

The default pager implements a default DSM protocol (e.g. multiple reader, single writer). This takes care of such cases as the user level DSM pager not presently residing in the node's memory or backing store.

Obviously, we have only sketched the DSM implementation, glossing over most of the details. In particular, a complete solution will need to integrate disk I/O with network I/O.

5   Conclusions

In this paper we have shown that stability based on shadow paging can be elegantly integrated into a SASOS, without the need to implement it in the kernel. We have demonstrated that shadow-paging can be implemented at the user level if we introduce virtual memory aliasing and use user-level page fault handlers. This can be achieved without performance overhead in the form of extra copying operations or redundant copies being kept on disk or in RAM.

We have shown that the same mechanisms can be used to support database systems by allowing them to pin pages in RAM and to control physical I/O. A user-level implementation of DSM coherency models was also outlined.

The question arises whether the resulting system is still a proper SASOS. The answer is "yes", as the basic SASOS paradigm is still valid: each user thread sees the same[1] data at a given address (if they see anything at all); there is still just a single address space. Furthermore, our mapping operations do not allow users to do anything they could not do by copying, but they ensure that it can be done efficiently.

We have not addressed stability issues with respect to distribution. However, having shown that we can employ the usual approach to solve the problem of stability on a single node, there is no reason to believe that schemes providing stability in other distributed systems cannot be used in ours.

---

[1] In a distributed system, the word "same" needs to be taken with a grain of salt, as some threads may see a somewhat newer copy than others. This is not different from any other distributed shared memory system.

References

[Cha78]   Michael F. Challis. Database consistency and integrity in a multi-user environment. In Ben Shneiderman, editor, *Databases: Improving Usability and Responsiveness*, pages 245–70. Academic Press, 1978.

[CLF+94]   Jeffrey S. Chase, Henry M. Levy, Michael J. Feeley, and Edward D. Lazowska. Sharing and protection in a single address space operating system. *ACM Transactions on Computer Systems*, 12:271–307, November 1994.

[D+91]   O. Deux et al. The O_2 system. *Communications of the ACM*, 34(10):34–48, October 1991.

[DdB+94]   Alan Dearle, Rex di Bona, James Farrow, Frans Henskens, Anders Lindström, and Francis Vaughan. Grasshopper: An orthogonally persistent operating system. *Computing Systems*, 7(3):289–312, 1994.

[HR93]   Frans A. Henskens and John Rosenberg. Distributed persistent stores. *Microprocessors and Microsystems*, 17:147–59, 1993.

[Lie93]   Jochen Liedtke. A persistent system in real use—experience of the first 13 years. In *Proceedings of the 3rd International Workshop on Object Orientation in Operating Systems*, pages 2–11, Asheville, NC, USA, December 1993. IEEE.

[Lie95]   Jochen Liedtke. On μ-kernel construction. In *Proceedings of the 15th ACM Symposium on OS Principles*, pages 237–250, Copper Mountain, CO, USA, December 1995.

[LLO+91]   Charles Lamb, Gordon Landis, Jack Orenstein, and Dan Weinreb. The ObjectStore database system. *Communications of the ACM*, 34(10):51–63, October 1991.

[Lor77]   Raymond A. Lorie. Physical integrity in a large segmented database. *ACM Transactions on Database Systems*, 2:91–104, 1977.

[MSS+93]   Kevin Murray, Ashley Saulsbury, Tom Stiemerling, Tim Wilkinson, Paul Kelly, and Peter Osmon. Design and implementation of an object-orientated 64-bit single address space microkernel. In *Proceedings of the 2nd USENIX Symposium on Microkernels and other Kernel Architectures*, pages 31–43, September 1993.

[RSE+92]   Stephen Russell, Alan Skea, Kevin Elphinstone, Gernot Heiser, Keith Burston, Ian Gorton, and Graham Hellestrand. Distribution + persistence = global virtual memory. In *Proceedings of the 2nd International Workshop on Object Orientation in Operating Systems*, pages 96–99, Dourdan, France, September 1992. IEEE.

[VRH93]   Jerry Vochteloo, Stephen Russell, and Gernot Heiser. Capability-based protection in the Mungi operating system. In *Proceedings of the 3rd International Workshop on Object Orientation in Operating Systems*, pages 108–15, Asheville, NC, USA, December 1993. IEEE.

A Rollback Technique for Implementing Persistence by Reachability

Scott Nettles

Computer and Information Science
University of Pennsylvania
Philadelphia, PA 19104
nettles@central.cis.upenn.edu

James O'Toole

Laboratory for Computer Science
Massachusetts Institute of Technology
Cambridge, MA 02139
james@lcs.mit.edu

Abstract

Orthogonal persistence based on reachability provides a safe and convenient model of object persistence, but can have a substantial runtime cost. In systems that provide separate transitory and persistent stores, newly persistent objects must be identified and relocated at transaction commit time. We have implemented a transaction system that supports orthogonal persistence in a garbage collected heap. In our system, replicating collection provides efficient concurrent garbage collection of the heap. Replicating garbage collection is also used to transport newly persistent objects, and a "rollback" method is used to reduce commit operation latencies and improve asymptotic performance.

In this paper, we describe our previous implementation of transactions and explain how a large transitory heap contributes to the cost of the commit operation. We explain the rollback method and show that it eliminates the additional costs attributable to the transitory heap. Performance measurements show that the rollback processing is small part of the total cost of transaction commit processing.

1 Introduction

Systems that allow arbitrary data structures to be stored persistently are becoming increasingly important. Such systems form the basis of both persistent programming languages and object-oriented databases. We believe that these technologies are likely to find widespread application in future Internet applications. An important design choice in persistent programming languages is deciding how objects will become persistent. Although many systems rely on explicit programmer actions to make particular objects persistent, we believe that orthogonal persistence [ACC82] based on reachability is the more desirable choice for reasons of safety and convenience. We have built a system that provides this form of orthogonal persistence and in this paper we present an optimization to its implementation.

This research was sponsored by the Avionics Lab, Wright Research and Development Center, Aeronautical Systems Division (AFSC), U. S. Air Force, Wright-Patterson AFB, OH 45433-6543 under Contract F33615-90-C-1465, Arpa Order No. 7597, by the Air Force Systems Command and the Defense Advanced Research Projects Agency (DARPA) under Contract F19628-91-C-0168, and by the Department of the Army under Contract DABT63-92-C-0012.

The views and conclusions contained in this document are those of the authors and should not be interpreted as representing the official policies, either expressed or implied, of the Defense Advanced Research Projects Agency or the U.S. Government.

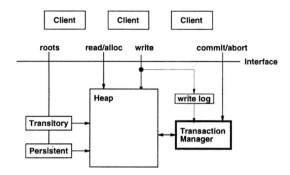

Figure 1: **The Transactional Heap Interface**

In a system with orthogonal persistence, the persistence of an object is orthogonal to its other properties, in particular its type. One common form of orthogonal persistence is persistence by reachability, in which an object is persistent if it is reachable from a special persistent root via pointers. The persistent root is a distinguished object that is always persistent. We have used copying garbage collection techniques to implement orthogonal persistence as part of a general purpose multi-threaded transaction system. Garbage collectors use reachability criteria to decide which objects must be retained, and so it seems natural to reuse garbage collection techniques to implement orthogonal persistence.

We have previously shown [ONG93] that a new garbage collection technique, replicating collection, can be used to provide an efficient concurrent garbage collector for our persistent storage system. In that system, we found that the performance of transaction commit operations was poor if the transitory heap, which contains the non-persistent objects, was large. By using a variation of replicating garbage collection to re-implement transaction commit operations, we have been able to significantly improve on this aspect of system performance.

The new implementation of transaction commit is more complicated because it requires a "rollback" step to allow the client application to continue executing after a transaction commit while using persistent objects whose final relocation from the transitory heap to the persistent heap has been postponed. However, this method has an important performance advantage, since it eliminates the dependence of transaction commit performance on the size of the transitory heap.

All of the sections that follow assume some familiarity with copying garbage collection techniques. First, we present our basic implementation and the performance problem it introduces. We then present our solution to this problem and describe its implementation. Finally, we present performance measurements that attempt to quantify the benefit achieved using the new implementation.

2   The Design Context

Figure 1 shows the basic interface of our system. The system supports read, write, allocate, abort and commit operations. Objects that are reachable from the persistent root at commit are guaranteed to survive program failures. Objects that are only reachable from the transitory root are lost upon program failure. A concurrent replicating garbage collector provides storage reclamation of both transitory and persistent objects. To support abort, persistence, and generational and replicating collection the location and old value of each write operation is recorded in a write log. The commit operation must maintain the orthogonal persistence property that all objects that have become reachable from the persistent root as a result of committed modifications must become persistent. Its implementation is the focus of the remainder of this section. For more details about our system see O'Toole et al. [ONG93] and Nettles [Net95].

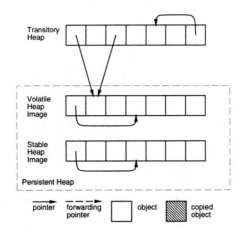

Figure 2: **A Committed State**

Figure 2 shows a detailed view of the key components of our system when it is in a committed state. Permanent objects are stored in the persistent heap; all other objects are stored in the transitory heap. The persistent heap is composed of two images: the stable image, which is stored on disk and which holds the committed image of the heap, and the volatile image, which is found in main memory and which holds any uncommitted data. The client reads and writes the volatile image. In a committed state all objects reachable from the persistent root must be found in the persistent heap. Thus in a committed state no pointers may point from the persistent heap into the transitory heap. Pointers may point from the transitory heap into the volatile image.

Figure 3 shows the system when uncommitted data is present. Assignments have created pointers from the volatile image into the transitory heap. Commit must guarantee that any object that is now reachable from the persistent root is in the volatile image and that the stable image is atomically updated to reflect all changes to the volatile image. The only changes to the stable image are those explicitly requested by the system. Other details about of how the stable image is updated are irrelevant to this discussion.

We assume that all pointers from the volatile image into the transitory heap refer to objects that are now reachable from the persistent root. (This is a conservative assumption.) The system traverses its write log to identify such pointers and uses them as the roots of a copying garbage collection. This collection moves all objects that are reachable from these roots into the volatile image. Figure 4 shows the state of the system after the collection has been done and the

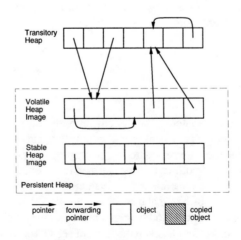

Figure 3: **Before Commit**

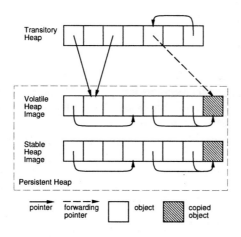

Figure 4: **Before Scan**

stable image updated. The cost of updating the persistent heap is proportional to the number of writes and the amount of data that must transferred to the volatile and stable images.

However, the work of commit is not complete. Figure 4 shows that pointers remain in the transitory heap that refer to objects that have been moved into the volatile image. An obvious way to ensure that all such pointers are updated is to scan the entire transitory heap. The forwarding pointers left by the copying collection allow these pointers to be identified and updated. Figure 5 shows the result of such a scan. Another option is to immediately garbage collect the transitory heap; during the collection these references will be redirected to the copies in the volatile image.

Both of these methods add a cost to commit that is proportional to the total size of the transitory heap. Unfortunately, we do not know a more efficient way to identify the pointers in the transitory heap that will require updating at the time of transaction commit. The kinds of remembered set techniques used to track pointers in generational garbage collectors are not applicable, because any object can become persistent and it would not be practical to track all pointers using remembered sets. In fact, the difficulty that a programmer would have in correctly predicting where these pointers are is one of the primary reasons that orthogonal persistence is so useful. It seems inevitable that the cost of updating these pointers will depend on the size of the transitory heap, yet we would like the cost of a single transaction to be independent of the total amount of transitory data. We want the latency of an individual commit operation to depend only on the number of write operations performed and the amount of data that must transferred to the volatile and stable images as a result of those write operations.

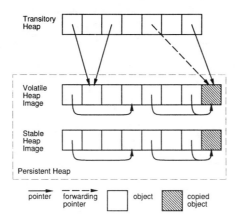

Figure 5: **After Scan**

3 Proposed Solution: Rollback

A way to eliminate the need to examine the entire transitory heap after committing the transaction would be to have the client continue using the original copies of the newly persistent objects, which remain in the transitory heap. To preserve the correctness of the commit operation, we must ensure that the stable image contains the the committed data. However, there is no fundamental requirement that the stable and volatile images be identical, nor that the transitory heap be updated. Of course, if we delay updating the transitory heap pointers, then we must also avoid updating the pointers in the volatile image. Thus, we have the outline of a proposed solution:

1. Do the commit up to the point of the scan, but retain enough information to reverse the effects of this step.

2. Update the stable image using the volatile image.

3. Rollback the effects of the first step.

One problem with this plan is that copying collectors usually destroy the original version of the object that they are copying by overwriting it with a forwarding pointer. Even if we can undo this damage during the rollback step, we must also ensure that subsequent commit operations modify the stable image in a manner consistent with the placement of newly persistent data in the stable image that was committed in earlier commit operations. Therefore, we must retain complete placement information in the volatile image about objects that have been made persistent but that the client is using in the transitory heap.

To identify and transport newly persistent objects, we have used replicating garbage collection. Replicating collection was originally developed for incremental and concurrent garbage collection [NO93b, ON94]. Replicating collection allows the client to continue using the original objects in the transitory heap and preserves the required placement information so that it can be used by subsequent commit operations.

The key idea of replicating collection is to perform the basic copy operation non-destructively. Non-destructive copying requires that the object not be overwritten by the forwarding pointer. The existence of more than one potentially valid copy of a mutable object implies the possibility that the copies might become inconsistent. Our implementation deals with this consistency issue in the following way:

- The client reads and writes the original version of the object.

- All write operations are recorded in an update log.

- When convenient, the system reads the log and applies the writes to the new version of the object.

- Clients are permitted to switch to the new version of the object only if all log entries have been processed.

This method enables the system to replicate objects but bring the replicas "into service" with the client at a later time.

We are using this log-based replicating collection method to implement the transaction commit operation. After the replicating collection is completed, the changes to the volatile image are written to the stable image. Then the rollback step is carried out by scanning the same update log and restoring the old values of all the modified locations in the volatile image. Each "rolled-back" location is saved on an auxiliary list called RB. Each element of RB points to a location in the persistent heap that points to an object in the transitory heap that has been replicated in the persistent heap. Figure 6 shows the state of the system after this step.

After the commit operation has been completed, the client continues to use the original objects in the transitory heap. Although the replicating collection is non-destructive, it does leave forwarding pointers to the objects it copied, it simply does not overwrite the original object with them. Subsequent commit operations do not recopy these objects because they are already marked with forwarding pointers that indicate that the object has been moved into the persistent heap. The write logging performed by the client ensures that the replicas are kept up to date by the replicating collector.

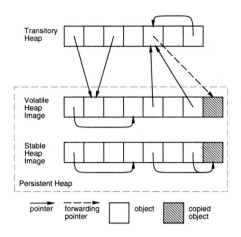

Transitory Heap

Volatile Heap Image

Stable Heap Image

Persistent Heap

pointer | forwarding pointer | object | copied object

Figure 6: **After Rollback**

Later, when the system eventually garbage collects the transitory heap, all of the pointers in the transitory heap are updated just as in Figure 5. At that time, the pointers in the volatile image that were reset to their original values are also be updated.

4 Implementation Details

We implemented the rollback optimization by modifying our previous transactional persistent system [ONG93]. The implementation did not require significant new algorithms because the system already contained the mechanisms needed to support replicating collection. However, for the rollback step of this optimization and associated bookkeeping, we found that the following changes to our implementation were needed:

- When the commit operation has updated the stable image, the log is processed to create the RB list (see above).

- The write log processing code that supports replicating garbage collection was extended to create transaction log entries when it reapplies write operations to replicas of persistent objects.

- After a transitory heap garbage collection is completed, the entries on the RB list are used to redirect the persistent heap pointers to point at the persistent replicas of object made persistent since the last transitory heap collection. These changes are also recorded in the write log so that the persistent garbage collector will be aware of them.

- Because the rollback step leaves forwarding pointers connecting newly persistent objects in the transitory heap to their persistent heap replicas, and these persistent replicas can be replicated again by the persistent garbage collector, it is possible to have chains of forwarding pointers of length two. We changed our code for following forwarding pointers to deal with this possibility.

- We modified the persistent garbage collector to use the RB list to identify additional pointers into the persistent heap. These are forwarding pointers installed on newly persistent objects in the transitory heap, and would otherwise be ignored by the persistent GC. Similarly, when the persistent garbage collection is completed and must flip, the RB list must be used to locate these forwarding pointers and update them to point at the persistent to-space copies of the objects.

CPU time	Concurrent		Stop&Copy	
	secs	%	secs	%
Commit	1.08	71.0	0.84	54.0
Rollback	0.04	2.3	0.03	1.9

Table 1: **CPU Times**

Elapsed time	Concurrent		Stop&Copy	
	secs	%	secs	%
Commit	2.16	77.0	1.50	47.0
Rollback	0.04	1.3	0.03	0.9

Table 2: **Elapsed Times**

5 Performance Measurements

We expect the rollback method to eliminate the strong dependence of transaction commit latency on the size of the transitory heap, but we do not currently have experimental evidence to support this belief. Our current measurements are of the elapsed time and cpu execution time of commit operations and the rollback operation (a component of the total commit operation). These measurements are shown for both the Concurrent and the Stop&Copy cases.

Table 1 shows the CPU time measurements. The times shown in seconds is the amount of time required for the Commit and Rollback steps. The accompanying percentages express that time as a percentage of the total time of one iteration of the benchmark. The benchmark used for these preliminary measurements is the OO1 Engineering Database benchmark [Cat91], modified to maintain constant live persistent heap size as described in our previous work [ONG93]. The main point of these measurements is that they demonstrate that the rollback step is very inexpensive compared to the commit operation as a whole.

Table 2 shows the elapsed time measurements of the same experiments. By comparing the elapsed time results to the CPU time results, we confirm that while commit processing requires I/O to make newly persistent objects stable, the rollback step does not require any I/O.

6 Related Work

We proposed the rollback optimization described here in a previous workshop [NO93a], but had not completed the design or started the implementation. In contrast with that work, this paper offers details of the actual implementation together with experimental measurements. The rollback optimization was implemented and measured by Scott Nettles [Net95].

The presentation of this optimization has been closely tied to the implementation of our system. Because of the ease of implementing orthogonal persistence using copying collection, we expect this issue to arise in other systems. For example, Kolodner [Kol92] discusses this problem in the context of his Argus design, but does not offer a satisfactory solution. We are unaware of any other solution.

How best to update pointers that cross between two heaps is a common problem for distributed and generational garbage collectors [Bis77, LH83, PS92]. Unfortunately, none of this work is applicable to the transaction commit problem because transaction commit happens when chosen by the client, and the set of objects that must be made newly persistent is defined by reachability from the persistent root at that time. In contrast, generational collectors and other similar systems that track pointers are able to identify the relevant pointers well in advance of when they must be updated. This allows the pointers to be recorded incrementally in auxiliary data structures and updated efficiently during a garbage collection.

7 Conclusion

In this paper we have illustrated a subtle performance problem with the implementation of orthogonal persistence and shown how replicating collection and a novel rollback technique can be used to eliminate the problem. Our solution uses the update logs that are central to our previous implementation to keep track of pointers that must be updated when using the rollback method. The preliminary measurements show that the technique is feasible and efficient. We expect more comprehensive measurements to show that the rollback technique avoids the direct dependence in transaction commit latency on transitory heap size.

References

[ACC82] M. P. Atkinson, K. J. Chisolm, and W. P. Cockshott. PS-Algol: an Algol with a persistent heap. *SIGPLAN Notices*, 17(7):24–31, July 1982.

[Bis77] Peter B. Bishop. *Computer Systems with a Very Large Address Space and Garbage Collection*. PhD thesis, Massachusetts Institute of Technology Laboratory for Computer Science, May 1977. Technical report MIT/LCS/TR-178.

[Cat91] R. G. G. Cattell. An engineering database benchmark. In Jim Gray, editor, *The Benchmark Handbook for Database and Transaction Processing Systems*, pages 247–281. Morgan-Kaufmann, 1991.

[Kol92] Eliot K. Kolodner.. Atomic Incremental Garbage Collection and Recovery for a Large Stable Heap. Technical Report MIT/LCS/TR-534, Massachusetts Institute of Technology, February 1992.

[LH83] Henry Lieberman and Carl Hewitt. A Real-Time Garbage Collector Based on the Lifetimes of Objects. *Communications of the ACM*, 26(6):419–429, June 1983.

[Net95] Scott M. Nettles. Safe and Efficient Persistent Heaps. Technical Report CMU-CS-95-225, Carnegie Mellon University, 1995.

[NO93a] Scott M. Nettles and James W. O'Toole. Implementing Orthogonal Persistence: A Simple Optimization Based on Replicating Collection. In *Proceedings of the SIGOPS International Workshop on Object-Orientation in Operating Systems*, December 1993.

[NO93b] Scott M. Nettles and James W. O'Toole. Real-Time Replication Garbage Collection. In *SIGPLAN Symposium on Programming Language Design and Implementation*. ACM, June 1993.

[ON94] James W. O'Toole and Scott M. Nettles. Concurrent Replicating Garbage Collection. In *Proceedings of the ACM Conference on Lisp and Functional Programming*, 1994.

[ONG93] James W. O'Toole, Scott M. Nettles, and David K. Gifford. Concurrent Compacting Garbage Collection of a Persistent Heap. In *Proceedings of the 14th ACM Symposium on Operating Systems Principles*. ACM, SIGPLAN, December 1993.

[PS92] David Plainfosse and Marc Shapiro. Experience with Fault Tolerant Garbage Collection in a Distributed Lisp System. In Yves Bekkers and Jacques Cohen, editors, *International Workshop on Memory Management*, number 637 in Lecture Notes in Computer Science, pages 116–133, St. Malo, France, September 1992. Springer-Verlag.

Fragment Reconstruction:
A New Cache Coherence Scheme for Split Caching Storage Systems
(Looking at the Doughnut and not the Hole)

Liuba Shrira, Barbara Liskov, Miguel Castro and Atul Adya

Laboratory for Computer Science
MIT
Cambridge, MA 02139

Abstract

Fragment reconstruction is a cache coherence protocol for transactional storage systems based on global caching in a network of workstations. It supports fine-grained sharing and works in the presence of object-based concurrency control algorithm. When transactions commit new versions of objects, stale cached copies of these objects get invalidated. Therefore, pages in a client's cache may become *fragments*, i.e. contain "holes" corresponding to invalid objects. When such a page is used in the global cache, the coherence protocol fills in the holes using modifications stored in a recoverable cache at the server.

Fragment reconstruction is the first coherence protocol that supports fine-grained sharing and global caching in transactional storage systems. Because it is integrated with the recoverable modification cache, it works correctly even in the presence of client failures, and can take advantage of lazy update propagation and update absorption, which is beneficial when pages are updated repeatedly. This paper describes the fragment reconstruction protocol and presents its correctness invariant wich insures that only correctly reconstructed fragments are propagated to the database.

1 Introduction

The distributed applications of tomorrow will need to provide reliable service to a large number of users and manipulate complex user-defined data objects. Therefore, these applications will require large-scale distributed storage systems that provide scalable performance, high reliability, and support user-defined objects.

Global caching techniques [MWTP94, FMP+96] are a promising approach in scalable storage systems, that avoids the increasingly formidable disk access bottleneck, a major performance impediment as systems scale to support many users. Global caching avoids disk access by taking advantage of emerging high speed local area networks to provide remote access to huge primary memories available in workstations. However, current global caching techniques only work for file systems [MWTP94] and virtual memory systems [FMP+96], and do not provide support for transactions and fine-grained sharing (i.e., sharing of objects that are smaller than pages).

In this paper we describe a new cache coherence protocol *fragment reconstruction* that supports fine-grained sharing and global caching in a transactional storage system architecture called *split*

This research was supported in part by the Advanced Research Projects Agency of the Department of Defense, monitored by the Office of Naval Research under contract N00014-91-J-4136. M. Castro is supported by a PRAXIS XXI fellowship.

caching. In split caching, clients exploit network speed and large aggregate client memory by fetching pages from other clients' caches to avoid disk reads. Servers cache only new versions of recently modified objects, using a large recoverable cache called the *mcache*, to perform disk updates more efficiently [OS94b, Ghe95]. When objects are moved from the mcache to the database on disk, it is necessary to first perform an *installation read* to obtain the containing pages; these pages are read from client caches to avoid reading them from disk.

Fragment reconstruction coherence protocol supports fine-grained sharing in split caching. The protocol works in the presence of object-based concurrency control techniques (e.g., adaptive call-back locking [CFZ94] or the optimistic approach used in Thor [AGLM95]); such techniques are desirable because they avoid conflicts due to false sharing. In such systems, when a transaction commits new versions of some objects, this may cause pages in other client caches to become *fragments*, i.e. pages containing stale copies of the objects modified by those transactions. Research indicates that bringing such pages up to date by *propagating* the new object versions at commit time is not efficient [CFLS91]. Therefore, we instead invalidate those stale copies, and use fragment reconstruction to bring those pages up to date using the fragment and the information in the mcache. Because the coherence protocol is integrated with the recoverable mcache, we can take advantage of lazy update propagation and update absorption, which is beneficial when pages are updated repeatedly. Importantly, the protocol works even in the presence of client failures.

Our work has been done in the context of Thor [LAC+96]. Thor supports fine-grained sharing and uses an mcache architecture to optimize updates. However, Thor clients maintain an object cache, whereas split caching architecture uses a page cache; and Thor servers have a page cache, unlike servers in the split caching architecture that only maintain the mcache. We describe a revised Thor design that incorporates fragment reconstruction and split caching. Although the design is based on Thor's optimistic concurrency control mechanism, it can be easily adapted to a system with a different concurrency control mechanism, such as adaptive call-back locking.

The paper is organized as follows. We introduce the basic Thor architecture in Section 2, describe the split caching and fragment reconstruction protocol in Section 3, and sketch a correctness proof for the protocol in Section 4. We discuss related research in Section 5 and our conclusions in Section 6.

2 Thor Architecture

We are carrying out our studies in the context of the Thor object-oriented database system [LAC+96]. Thor has a distributed client/server architecture. Persistent objects are stored on disk at the servers. Application code runs at clients. Applications interact with Thor within atomic transactions that read and write persistent objects. Below, we give a brief overview of the Thor architecture, focusing on the parts that are important for our work. In particular, we describe the client–server protocol and the organization of disk storage management.

2.1 Client/Server Protocol

Each client has a front-end cache that is used to store recently accessed objects. If the application requests an object that is not present in the client cache, the client sends a fetch request to the server. The server responds with a copy of the requested object. Clients cache objects across transaction boundaries.

Thor uses a new optimistic concurrency control and cache consistency protocol based on loosely synchronized clocks and invalidation messages [AGLM95]. When the application requests a transaction commit, the new values of the objects modified by the transaction are sent from the client cache to the server along with other concurrency control information. The server validates the transaction, using a two-phase commit protocol if a transaction accesses multiple servers. The server stores information about prepared and committed transactions in a stable write-ahead transaction log; it notifies a client that a transaction has succeeded only after the modifications have been recorded in this log. If the transaction commits, the client starts executing another transaction; if it aborts, the client run-time system first restores the cached copies of modified objects to the state they had before the transaction started (or discards those objects if it is not possible to restore their old states).

When a transaction commits successfully, the updates performed by that transaction become immediately visible and will affect future fetches. Earlier fetches could not reflect the changes and therefore client caches may contain obsolete information. Transactions that use the obsolete information will abort. To reduce the probability of such aborts, servers notify clients about obsolete information by sending them *invalidation messages*. When a client receives such a message, it removes the obsolete information from its cache and aborts the current transaction if it used the obsolete information. Invalidation messages allow such aborts to happen quickly, avoiding wasted work, and offload detection of the aborts from the server to the client.

The Thor transactional consistency protocol has a number of interesting features: it uses timestamps to obtain a global ordering for transactions, and also to discard concurrency control information without causing aborts; it uses page granularity directories that keep track of cached pages and, in addition, keep track of objects on those pages that have been modified recently; it piggybacks cache invalidation information on messages already being exchanged between servers and clients. Simulation studies show that this scheme outperforms the best pessimistic scheme (adaptive callback locking [CFZ94]) on almost all workloads [Gru96].

2.2 Server Organization

The servers have disk for storing persistent objects, a stable transaction log and some memory. The disk is organized as a collection of large pages that contain many objects, and that are the items read and written to disk. The stable log holds commit information and object modifications for committed transactions. The server memory is partitioned into a page cache and a modified object cache (the *mcache*). The page cache holds pages that have been recently accessed by clients. The mcache holds recently modified objects that have not yet been written to disk. As transactions commit, modifications are streamed to the log and also inserted in the mcache.

To satisfy a fetch request, the server first looks in the mcache, since if an object has been modified recently, its newest version is stored there. If the object is not found in the mcache, the server looks in the page cache. If the object is not in the cache, the server reads the object's page from disk, stores it in the cache, and replies to the client when the disk read completes.

The mcache-based server architecture improves the efficiency of disk updates for small objects [OS94b, Ghe95]. It avoids the cost of synchronous commit time *installation reads* that obtain pages from disk in order to install the modifications on their containing pages. Installation reads performed at commit time can reduce the scalability of the server significantly [OS94b, WD95]. Instead, installation reads are performed asynchronously by a background thread that moves modified objects from the mcache to the disk using a read-modify-write cycle. First, the modified page is read from disk. Then the system installs the modifications in the page and writes the result to disk. Once modifications have been written to disk, they are removed from the mcache and the transaction log, thus freeing up space for future transactions. If the server crashes, the mcache is reconstructed at recovery by scanning the log.

The mcache architecture reduces the number of disk update operations. It stores modifications in a very compact form, since only the modified objects are stored. This allows the system to delay writing modifications to the database longer than if the pages containing the objects were stored. Therefore, it increases *write absorption*: the mcache can accumulate many modifications to a page before an object in that page is installed on disk. This reduces the number of disk installation reads and also reduces the number of disk writes since the system can write all these modifications in a single disk operation while preserving the clustering that enables efficient disk reads.

Performance studies show that for most workloads the mcache architecture outperforms other architectures [OS94b, Ghe95], including conventional architectures in which the server stores modified pages, and the clients ship entire pages to the server at commit.

3 Fine-grained Sharing in Split Caching

This section describes the split caching architecture and presents the new fragment reconstruction coherence protocol that suports fine-grained sharing in split caching. The split caching architecture is based on Thor. As in Thor, clients send the new versions of modified objects to the server when transactions commit. The server stores them in the transaction log and the mcache. However, unlike Thor, a server does not have a page cache; it only has the mcache. Furthermore, clients fetch and evict pages instead of objects. The split caching architecture extends Thor by allowing clients to fetch pages from the caches of other clients; and by allowing servers to avoid installation reads by taking advantage of pages in client caches.

The split caching architecture assumes that clients can communicate faster with each other than they can access the disk. This is true for modern local area networks and disks. It also assumes that the users of client machines are willing to cooperate. Clients are workstations with reasonably large primary memory. This is a reasonable assumption for two reasons: clients must have enough primary memory to cache their working set otherwise they will not perform well. Increase in primary memory is supported by current trends in workstation technology. Servers also have primary memory, but the aggregate memory at the clients is significantly larger than the server memory.

Split caching architecture is based on the following three observations.

1. Earlier research has shown that when there is a large number of clients with caches, and when they are sharing a large database whose size is much larger than the server memory, the server cache is relatively ineffective [MH92].

2. Work on the mcache has shown that for most workloads, performance improves as memory is shifted from the server cache to the mcache [Ghe95].

3. Fine-grained concurrency control is much better than coarse-grained concurrency control because it avoids the problem of false sharing.

The first two points motivate split caching. Since the server page cache is ineffective, servers only have an mcache. Clients cache pages and these are used for fetches and installation reads, thus avoiding disk reads at the server.

131

The third point motivates the need for the fragment reconstruction coherence protocol. When transactions commit it is possible that they modify objects that reside in pages in other client's caches. At that point we could bring those pages up to date by sending the new states of the modified objects to those clients. Earlier research has shown that such propagation is not always a good idea. For example, it is wasted work if that client is not going to use the modified object. Therefore, we do not propagate the objects to the clients. Instead, the server just informs the relevant clients to mark the old versions of objects as invalid. We use a new coherence protocol, *fragment reconstruction*, to determine whether it is possible to rebuild a page from the client cache and the mcache. A client page is used to satisfy a fetch or an installation read only if the page can be reconstructed.

The details of our approach are described in the following sections. We describe the caching architecture, discuss cache management at clients, describe the cache coherence protocol, and then discuss some possible optimizations.

3.1 Split Caching

As discussed earlier, split caching relies solely on the client caches to avoid disk reads, and uses the server cache solely to optimize disk updates. The entire server memory is dedicated to the mcache. In addition, the server maintains directories in which it records information about which pages are cached at which clients.

Split caching uses client caches for two purposes. First, to avoid disk accesses at the server due to client fetches. When there is a miss in a client cache, the client requests the page of the missing object from the server. The server checks its directories to determine whether the page is present in the cache of another client. If so the server redirects the fetch to this client, which sends the page directly to the first client. In addition, the server forwards all updates in the mcache for that page to the first client, which uses them to update the page. If the page cannot be obtained from a client cache, the server reads it from disk in the usual way, and sends the page and updates to the page in the mcache to the requesting client. In response to a fetch, the client gets a description of what data to expect (a page and updates or just a page or just updates) followed by the data itself, and applies the updates as required. In the case when the page comes from the server disk, this organization enables a very efficient path from the server disk directly onto the network and into the client cache. This avoids page copying through the server memory and can be beneficial in reducing the server load and improving server scalability.

Second, client caches help the server in reducing disk accesses due to installation reads. When a modification has to be moved from the mcache to the data disk, the server checks the client directories to determine whether that modified page exists in some client cache. If so, the server fetches the page from the client (else it simply reads the page from disk), updates the page with the modifications stored for it in the mcache, writes the page to disk, and removes the modifications from the mcache.

3.2 Fragments

As discussed earlier in this section, when a client receives an invalidation message for an object x, it marks x as invalid (if the current transaction has used x, the transaction is aborted). These invalid objects in a client's page are termed *holes* and a page with holes is called a *fragment*. Support for fine-grain sharing by performing invalidations at the object level allows the client to avoid extra aborts; if the client is required to invalidate the page on which x was located, it may have to abort unnecessarily (if the client had used other objects on that page). This approach also avoids discarding frequently used objects that happen to reside on the page. As a result, this scheme allows eviction to be based on general algorithms such as LRU, although the algorithms might also take into account page "population" (e.g., a page that is very fragmented might be a more desirable victim than one that is full).

3.3 Integrating Cache Coherence and Modified Object Cache

To ensure correctness, the cache coherence protocol has to be coordinated with the mcache. The system must ensure that applying updates to a fragment obtained from a client results in an up-to-date copy of the corresponding page. This condition may be violated if the fragment is missing updates that have already been installed on disk and are no longer in the mcache. Our cache coherence protocol, *fragment reconstruction*, guarantees that such situations do not occur, i.e., whenever a page is reconstructed using a fragment and the mcache, the protocol ensures that the page is up-to-date.

As mentioned, the server maintains directories that record information about what pages are cached at each client. For each page it records a status: *complete*, *reconstructible*, or *unreconstructible*. A complete page at a client has the latest versions of all its objects. A reconstructible page may contain old versions of some objects, but new versions of these objects are stored in the mcache. An unreconstructible page may contain old versions of some objects for which the mcache does not contain new versions.

Now we discuss how the system works. When the server responds to a fetch request from client A, it redirects the request to another client B only if B's directory information indicates that B's page is either complete or reconstructible. In either case, the server asks B to send the page to client A. If the page is marked as reconstructible, it also sends the updates in the mcache for that page to client A (this client must wait for the updates from the server and the fragment from client B, before it can proceed). In either case, the server then marks the page as complete in the directory for client A. Figure 1 shows the case where client B has a fragment cached for page P.

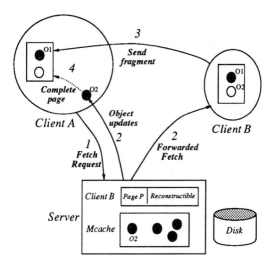

Figure 1: Redirecting an object fetch

If the requested page has uncommitted modifications, client B does not send them to client A; it

133

sends only the latest *committed* versions of objects. To do this a client makes a copy of an object the first time it is modified in a transaction. These copies are discarded when the transaction commits or possibly when there is cache management. If client B receives a request for a page and it does not have the copy of the committed state for one of the objects in the page, it replies to the server saying that the page is unavailable. The server will then obtain the page from disk or another client and send it to A.

Client B may be unable to satisfy the fetch request if it has discarded the page P. In this case, it replies to the server, which marks the page as absent from client B's cache. To improve performance, clients can inform the server when they evict a page by piggybacking that information on the next message sent to the server.

When the server commits a transaction for a client, this has no impact of the statuses of pages stored at that client, but it can affect statuses of pages at other clients, since they may become out-of-date for some objects. The server checks to see whether any complete pages at other clients have been affected by the transaction, i.e., whether the transaction has modified objects in a complete page at some other client. All such pages are marked reconstructible.

Fetching pages from clients for avoiding installation disk reads is done in a similar manner. When the server wants to install object modifications for page P from the mcache, it fetches page P from a client A if the directories indicate A has a complete or reconstructible version of the page. After installing the modifications, the server removes the changes from the mcache and checks its directories to see if any client has reconstructible copies of page P. Directory entries for page P for all such clients are marked as unreconstructible. As a result, such pages will not be used in future fetches or installation reads. Marking of these cached pages as unreconstructible is necessary because after discarding the modifications from the mcache the server can no longer bring the pages up to date using the mcache. Figure 2 depicts the case where A caches a reconstructible fragment of page P.

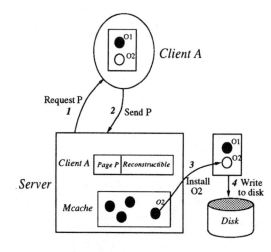

Figure 2: Installation read avoidance

3.4 Optimizations

Now we discuss some optimizations to the protocol. Our first optimization avoids pages from becoming unreconstructible; unreconstructible pages are not desirable because they can no longer be used in the global cache and only benefit the client caching them. When a server decides to install object updates, instead of just asking a client A for the fragment, it can send the mcache updates for the page to A. The client installs the modifications to the page and sends back the complete page to the server. The server then marks the page as complete at that client. This technique prevents a page from becoming unreconstructible at client A. Note that this optimization is similar to update propagation but is not exactly the same. The server sends the mcache updates relatively rarely, e.g., the updates may be sent after many updates to the same page have been absorbed in the mcache. Note that the server need not update all the cached copies for the page; it just needs to ensure that there exists at least one reconstructible page in the system.

Suppose that a client has a page fragment and needs an object that is missing from the page. The client does not need to receive the whole page from another client. If the client informs the server that it has the page, and the server determines that the page is reconstructible, the server can simply send the updates in the mcache to the client and mark the page as complete. This optimization avoids a network roundtrip delay of getting the page from another client.

Finally, it is possible to distinguish "degrees" of fragmentation. Suppose that a client A fetches page P from a server (with some updates from the mcache); the server marks this page complete for client A. The server now receives an update for object x on page P from another client and marks P as reconstructible for client A. If client A now asks for page P, the server should send object x only (rather than all the updates for P in the mcache). This optimization can be implemented by maintaining extra information in the directory entries for each client. The server numbers the committing transactions, furthermore for each entry in a client's directory, it stores the number of the latest transaction whose modifications are reflected in the client's cached copy. We rejected such a scheme in favor of the one described here because our scheme is simpler and requires less storage at servers. Furthermore, the extra information will probably not have much impact on system performance: it may reduce the message size for fetch replies but does not reduce the number of messages in the system.

4 Correctness of Fragment Reconstruction

Demonstrating the correctness of the fragment reconstruction protocol is a good way to understand the protocol itself, and is an interesting topic in its own right. We now discuss this issue informally (a detailed proof appears in [Shr96]). Our basic approach is to establish an equivalence between the recoverable states of two systems: the *basic* Thor system configured (for simplicity) with a zero-size page cache at the server and the *extended* Thor system using fragment reconstruction. We show that each system satisfies its own simple invariant, and that the extended invariant implies the basic invariant. As a result, we show that any sequence of committed transactions will produce the same recoverable states in both the basic and extended systems, so the two systems "appear the same" to any sequence of application transactions. It follows that the extended system is a correct optimization of the basic system.

In the basic Thor system, the mcache-based database update protocol guarantees the *basic invariant* that at any point in a system execution sequence that contains a given set of committed transactions, all committed updates have either been propagated to the database on disk or reside in the (recoverable) mcache. It is easy to see that the mcache-based database update protocol that 1) obtains a page P from the database, 2) installs all updates to page P from the mcache, 3) writes the updated page P to the database, and 4) removes updates to page P from the mcache, maintains the basic invariant.

135

The extended Thor system uses pages from the client caches and modifications in the mcache to update the database disk. The *extended invariant* for the extended system needs to guarantee that if the cache of client A provides a page to avoid an installation read then this page and the mcache combined include all the committed updates. Since a system satisfying the extended invariant also satisfies the basic invariant, the extended invariant insures that when a system with fragment reconstruction uses the cached copy of the page to update the disk, this has the same effect as reading the page from disk.

The extended invariant presented below constrains how the page status information recorded in the server page directories reflects the committed updates contained in the mcache and in pages cached at the clients. It highlights the point that when a cached page P is forwarded to another client or server, a clean copy of a page is provided by the fragment reconstruction protocol. A clean copy contains updates of committed transactions, and holes corresponding to invalidations caused by commits of transactions of other clients, but does not contain updates of aborted transactions and also does not contain updates of uncommitted transactions.

The Extended Invariant:

If a page p cached at client A is marked as complete in the directory, then either the client A has discarded page p (or some object on page p) and this information has not yet been recorded in the directory, or client A has a clean version of page p that contains all the committed updates to page p and no uncommitted updates.

If a page p cached at client A is marked as reconstructible in the directory, then either client A has discarded page p (or some object in p) and this information has not yet been recorded in the directory, or client A has a clean version of page p that when combined with the committed updates to page p residing in the mcache contains all the committed updates to page p and no uncommitted updates.

For simplicity, assume that client caches maintain clean copies of modified pages that do not include modifications of the current transaction. (The implementation optimizes cache space and only maintains clean copies of modified objects; it reconstructs a clean page when asked to forward the page to another client or return it to the server.) The optimistic concurrency control protocol in [AGLM95] insures that when a client aborts a transaction all uncommitted effects in the client cache are undone. By examining the coherence protocol actions it is easy to see that the extended invariant is preserved by the directory update operations resulting from client and server fetches, transaction commits, and database updates.

5 Related Work

Our work on the fragment reconstruction coherence protocol builds on techniques for supporting fine-grained sharing and techniques for providing global caching. To put our work in perspective, we consider related work on global caching in file systems and transactional storage systems, and work on avoiding false sharing problems in distributed shared memory systems.

Work in the xFS file system [MWTP94] explores global caching in a scalable serverless storage architecture. The xFS coherence protocol improves on earlier file-level coherence protocols by supporting disk block level sharing. In contrast, the fragment reconstruction protocol supports sharing of fine-grained objects.

Franklin et al. [FCL92] studies global caching in a client/server database. Clients interact with each other via servers. Servers redirect fetch requests between clients. The study evaluates several global memory management algorithms. This work is similar to ours in that it considers a transactional database. The difference is that Franklin et al. consider coarse-grained page-based concurrency control and do not address the problem of false sharing. Another difference is that their system uses locking while our system uses optimistic concurrency control.

A coherence scheme similar to fragment reconstruction is described in [DR92]. In this scheme, the database server manages a cache of recent updates. Before a client accesses an object, it contacts a server to retrieve the updates needed to bring the cached copy of the object up to date. This scheme does not support global caching, i.e., clients can not fetch pages from other clients. In addition, it is is based on locking, whereas fragment reconstruction is based on optimistic concurrency control and invalidations.

Work in distributed shared memory systems has addressed the problems caused by false sharing. These systems allow concurrent accesses to shared pages by supplying synchronization primitives to support weaker consistency models, e.g., release consistency [LLG+90] in Munin, lazy release consistency [KCZ92] in TreadMarks, and multiple writer protocols [CBZ94] in both Munin and Trademarks. This work differs from our work because it does not consider transactional updates to persistent data.

The distributed shared memory coherence work by Feeley et al. [MJVH94] is similar to ours because it considers transactional updates. This approach assumes a single-server, main-memory-based transactional store. Transactions use distributed locking. To keep caches coherent, at transaction commit time, clients propagate the commit log containing fine-grained updates to other clients. This approach does not consider global caching. The coherence protocol by Feeley et al. needs to propagate updates to cached pages at commit time to tolerate client failures. In contrast, our mcache-based coherence protocol propagates updates lazily and benefits from update absorption; furthermore it works correctly even in the presence of client failures.

Our work builds on the hybrid caching work [OS94a] that proposes sending pages from clients to the server cache at commit time in order to avoid installation reads; our scheme extends this work by investigating fetching and reconstructing pages at installation time.

6 Conclusions

This paper presents the new transactional fragment reconstruction coherence protocol integrated with Thor's mcache. The fragment reconstruction protocol supports fine-grained sharing in split caching object storage architecture. It is the first fine-grained coherence protocol that supports global caching in a transactional storage system.

The fragment reconstruction coherence protocol is attractive because it is simple. In addition, it is applicable to object storage architectures different from Thor. In particular, fragment reconstruction could be used in a more traditional caching architecture where servers cache pages. It could also be used with different concurrency control mechanisms although the concurrency control mechanism affects how coherence works, e.g., a system that uses locking [CFZ94] might have to send a page with holes in response to a fetch (since some of its objects are locked right now).

The paper presents the correctness invariant for fragment reconstruction protocol that guarantees that the protocol preserves the correctness of the concurrency control and recovery protocols in Thor. This is important, since it ensures that as far as application transactions can tell, the system with fragment reconstruction is a correct optimization of the current Thor system.

Earlier work shows that support for fine-grain sharing avoids the performance penalties of false sharing and that global caching is effective in improving the scalability of a storage system. Fragment reconstruction and split caching integrate these two techniques in a new context, a transactional storage system, and should retain the performance benefits of both techniques. We are currently implementing split caching and fragment reconstruction in Thor and exploring how fragment reconstruction interacts with mcache management.

References

[AGLM95] A. Adya, R. Gruber, B. Liskov, and U. Maheshwari. Efficient optimistic concurrency control using loosely synchronized clocks. In *International Conference on Management of Data*. Association for Computing Machinery SIGMOD, June 1995.

[CBZ94]   John B. Carter, John K. Bennett, and Willy Zwaenepoel. Techniques for reducing consistency-related communication in distributed shared memory systems. *To appear in ACM Transactions on Computer Systems*, August 1994.

[CFLS91] Michael J. Carey, Michael J. Franklin, Miron Livny, and Eugene J. Shekita. Data caching tradeoffs in client-server dbms architectures. In *Proceedings of the ACM SIGMOD International Conference on Management of Data*, pages 357–366, 1991.

[CFZ94]   M. Carey, M. Franklin, and M. Zaharioudakis. Fine-Grained Sharing in a Page Server OODBMS. In *Proceedings of SIGMOD 1994*, 1994.

[DR92]   A. Delis and N. Roussopoulos. Performance and scalability of client-server database architecture. In *Proceedings of the 18th Conference on Very-Large Databases*, 1992.

[FCL92]   M. Franklin, M. Carey, and M. Livny. Global memory management in client-server dbms architectures. In *Proceedings of 18th VLDB Conf.*, 1992.

[FMP+96] M. Feeley, W. Morgan, F. Pighin, A. Karlin, H. Levy, and C. Thekkath. Implementing global memory management in a workstation cluster. In *SOSP*, 1996.

[Ghe95]   S. Ghemawat. *The Modified Object Buffer: A Storage Management Technique for Object-Oriented Databases*. PhD thesis, Massachusetts Institute of Technology, 1995.

[Gru96]   R. Gruber. *Optimism vs. Locking: A Study of Concurrency Control for Client-Server Object-Oriented Databases*. PhD thesis, Massachusetts Institute of Technology, 1996.

[KCZ92]   P. Keleher, A. Cox, and W. Zwaenepoel. Lazy Release Consistency for Software Distributed Shared Memory. In *ISCA*, May 1992.

[LAC+96] B. Liskov, A. Adya, M. Castro, M. Day, S. Ghemawat, R. Gruber, U. Maheshwari, A. Myers, and L. Shrira. Safe and efficient sharing of persistent objects in thor. In *Proceedings of the 1994 ACM SIGMOD*, 1996.

[LLG+90] D. Lenoski, J. Laudon, K. Gharachorloo, A. Gupta, and J. Henessy. The directory based cache coherence protocol for the dash multiprocessor. In *Proceedings of the 17th Annual International Symposium on Computer Architecture*, 1990.

[MH92]   D. Muntz and P. Honeyman. Multi-level caching in distributed file systems or your cache ain't nothin' but trash. In *Winter Usenix Technical Conference*, 1992.

[MJVH94] M.Feeley, J.Chase, V.Narasayya, and H.Levy. Integrating coherency and recoverability in distributed systems. In *Usenix Symposium on Operating System Design and Implementation*, 1994.

[MWTP94] M.D.Dahlin, R.Y. Wang, T.E.Anderson, and D.A. Patterson. Cooperative caching:using remote client memory to improve file system performance. In *Proceedings of Operating Systems Design and Implementation*, 1994.

[OS94a]   James O'Toole and Liuba Shrira. Hybrid Caching for Scalable Object Systems (Think Globally, Act Locally. In *Proceedings of the 6th Workshop on Persistent Object Systems*, Tarascon, France, September 1994. ACM.

[OS94b]   James O'Toole and Liuba Shrira. Opportunistic Log: Efficient Installation Reads in a Reliable Object Server. In *Proceedings of OSDI*, 1994.

[Shr96]   L. Shrira. A Correctness Proof for Fragment Reconstruction. In *MIT/LCS Programming Methodology Group Memo*, 1996.

[WD95]   Seth J. White and David J. DeWitt. Implementing crash recovery in quickstore: a performance study. In *ACM SIGMOD International Conference on Management of Data*, pages 187–198, 1995.

PMOS: A Complete and Coarse-Grained Incremental Garbage Collector for Persistent Object Stores

J. Eliot B. Moss[1], David S. Munro[2], and Richard L. Hudson[1]

Department of Computer Science[1]
University of Massachusetts
Amherst, MA 01003-4610, USA
{moss,hudson}@cs.umass.edu

Department of Computer Science[2]
University of St. Andrews
St. Andrews, Fife, KY16 9SS, UK
dave@dcs.st-and.ac.uk

Abstract. Traditional garbage collection techniques designed for language systems operating over transient data do not readily migrate to a persistent context. The size, complexity, and permanence characteristics of a persistent object store mean that an automatic storage reclamation system, in addition to ensuring that all unreachable and only unreachable data is reclaimed, must also maintain store consistency while limiting I/O overhead when collecting secondary-memory data.

Research has shown that careful selection of which area of a store to collect can significantly increase the amount of reclaimed storage while reducing the I/O costs. Many garbage collectors for existing stores, however, either are off-line or rely on reclaiming space in a predefined order. This paper presents a new incremental garbage collection algorithm specifically designed for reclaiming persistent object storage. The collector extends the Mature Object Space algorithm to ensure incrementality in a persistent context, to achieve recoverability, and to impose minimum constraints on the order of collection of areas of the persistent address space.

Keywords: persistence, garbage collection, memory management, mature object space, train algorithm

Introduction

The principal intention of automatic storage reclamation is to relieve the programmer of the burdensome and often error-prone task of indicating which memory can be reused. It can also help reorganize data in an effort to improve performance. To achieve this a collector must distinguish reachable from unreachable objects and reclaim the storage occupied by garbage. An important aspect of any collector is that it is *complete*: it will, after a finite number of invocations, reclaim all unreachable storage.

In a persistent store, automatic reclamation still needs to meet the criteria above. Indeed, lack of completeness will be a more acute problem than in transient systems since failure to reclaim all garbage leads to permanent space loss. Although many garbage collectors for main-memory programming languages and systems have been designed, built, and measured (see Wilson's survey [Wilson, 1992] for a good introduction), the collection of garbage for a persistent store raises additional concerns:

- The sheer size of many persistent stores suggests that semi-space techniques will be unworkable because they approximately double space requirements. Likewise, "stop-the-world" style collection would result in prohibitively long pauses.

- Because pointers in these stores refer to objects in secondary memory, updates resulting from object movement in copying and compacting collectors can incur high I/O costs.

- Persistent stores exhibit some notion of stability whereby a consistent state can always be reconstructed after a crash. Most existing collector algorithms are not inherently atomic and are thus unsuitable in this context.

We present here a new garbage collection algorithm for persistent object stores, called PMOS, tailored to address the issues above. The PMOS collector is an extension of the Mature Object Space (MOS) algorithm [Hudson & Moss, 1992] (colloquially known as "the train algorithm") which is an incremental main-memory copying collector specifically designed to collect large, older generations of a generational scheme in a non-disruptive manner. There are a number of essential features of MOS that make it an attractive starting point:

- The collector limits the amount of data moved during each incremental invocation.

- It naturally supports compaction and clustering.

- It can be implemented on stock hardware and does not require special operating systems support such as pinning or external pager control.

- It has been implemented, proved to be complete, and to achieve the stated objective of bounded time for any single collection [Seligmann & Grarup, 1995].

The PMOS collector partitions the persistent address space into distinct areas and retains many of the same features and mechanisms of MOS, but with two important extensions:

- Unlike MOS, the algorithm does not impose any constraints on the order of collection of the areas. Work by Cook, Wolf, and Zorn [Cook *et al.*, 1994a, Cook *et al.*, 1994b] suggests that a flexible selection policy allowing a collector to choose which partition to collect can significantly reduce I/O and increase the amount of space reclaimed. One of the design goals for PMOS was to free the algorithm from imposing any collection order thus allowing the implementor to provide a policy appropriate to the application.

- Results from the MaStA I/O cost model work [Scheuerl *et al.*, 1995, Munro *et al.*, 1995] suggest that no single recovery mechanism gives the best performance under different workloads and configurations. Hence one of the aims of the PMOS design was to provide atomicity to the MOS collector without binding it to a particular recovery mechanism.

Related Work

There are two bodies of prior related work in garbage collecting databases and object stores. The first, older, body is concerned primarily with designing garbage collection schemes that will work in the concurrent and atomic world of databases (i.e., in the presence of concurrency, concurrency control, and crash recovery). See, for example, [Detlefs, 1990, Kolodner, 1987, Kolodner *et al.*, 1989, Kolodner, 1990]. The second, more recent, body is more concerned with policies and performance [Cook *et al.*, 1994a, Cook *et al.*, 1994b]. Our scheme differs from the first group in that it uses *partitions* (we call them blocks or cars) and uses them to collect in a coarse-grained incremental way, but at least somewhat obeying the existing object clustering pattern. Granted, the earlier schemes outlined above work on a page by page basis, but our partitions may be larger than a page and might vary in size, as convenient. Also, these earlier schemes tend to impose a specific order of collecting pages (breadth first copying). The essential difference is that this earlier body of work was concerned with devising *correct* algorithms, in the face of concurrency and/or failures. We consider the correctness issue to be solved and are more concerned with issues of *performance* (but also portability, clean interfaces, etc.). Further, the correctness of recovery and concurrency control with our algorithm is simple to argue, whereas some previous schemes had more subtle, integrated algorithms.

The more recent body of work uses partitions, and is concerned with performance, but uses algorithms that do not guarantee completeness. Our scheme offers completeness, and allows (even requires in some sense) objects to be reclustered as they are collected. The work of Cook, Wolf, and Zorn has done a useful job in starting the investigation of suitable *policies* for selecting an order in which to collect partitions. To our knowledge, Bishop introduced the notion of partitioned gc [Bishop, 1977].

There are numerous papers on concurrent and/or distributed garbage collection, and undoubtedly more on persistent store or object base collection as well, but the references discussed above are representative of the prior and current art in object base garbage collection algorithms and performance.

Review of the Mature Object Space Algorithm

While generational schemes help reduce the length of time the average collection takes, the oldest generations tend to be large, and in any case, collecting them involves collecting all generations at once. The result is that while such collections are infrequent, they are unpleasantly slow when they do happen. Mature Object Space was designed to overcome this problem.

The basic idea of MOS is to divide the oldest generation into a number of fixed size blocks, and to collect just one block at a time.[1] The hard part is to guarantee that all garbage is collected eventually. Completeness is achieved by organizing the collections in a way explained by using a metaphor: *trains* made up of *cars*.

Each block of MOS is a car, and each car belongs to a train. The cars of a train are ordered by age, with the oldest car at the "front" of the train. New cars are added to the "rear" or end of the train. It is assumed there are at least two trains (it

---

[1]The technique can handle objects larger than a block as well; see [Hudson & Moss, 1992] for details.

is a policy issue as to the number of trains), and that the trains are also ordered from oldest to newest (in terms of the time the trains were created).

The goal of the MOS algorithm is to copy reachable data out of the oldest train into other trains, and then to discard the oldest train when it contains no reachable data. In this way, cycles of garbage larger than a single car can be reclaimed, *if* we can get them into a single train. At each collection, we copy all reachable data out of the oldest car of the oldest train. However, we are careful as to where we copy the data:

1. Data locally reachable [2] *from global variables, the program stack and registers, or from younger generations*, is copied to any other train, adding a car to that train if needed. The youngest train might be a good destination for the objects moved.

2. Data locally reachable *from other trains* is copied to those trains, adding a car if needed. If an object is reachable from more than one other train, it may be copied to any train from which it is reachable (one might pick the youngest train to put off copying the data again soon).

3. Data locally reachable *from other cars of this train* is copied to the youngest car of this train, adding a new car as needed.

4. Remaining data is *unreachable* and is reclaimed immediately.

Note that the above steps are performed *in order*. Steps 1, 2, and 3 can be performed efficiently if we keep per-car remembered sets. One more rule we need is the following:

0. If no object in the oldest train is reachable from outside the train, reclaim the *entire train*. If necessary, create another train (to insure that there are always at least two trains).

The precondition of this rule can be determined by keeping a count of the number of references from outside the oldest train to objects inside it. This count is the sum of such counts for each car, and can be maintained fairly simply by keeping the count for each car and adjusting the total count after each collection.

Changes Needed to Support Object Store Collection

The MOS algorithm seems appropriate for garbage collecting object bases: it works a block at a time (what we called a *coarse-grained incremental* approach based on *partitions*), and it guarantees all garbage will be collected eventually (it is complete). However, as pointed out above, MOS is not suitable for object store garbage collection as it stands, principally because of the forced collection order and the I/O costs induced by pointer updates.

The MOS algorithm records only pointers from newer cars (and references from outside MOS) to older cars. Since only the oldest car is ever collected, this works out nicely in two ways. First, (only) the oldest car's remembered set information includes all references from outside that car. Thus, the knowledge required by the algorithm is available when needed. Second, pointers *from* the oldest car appear in *no* remembered set, and thus other cars' remembered sets never need to have items *removed*, only added.

In order to collect cars in any order (which is not particular to object base garbage collection but can also be used for main memory garbage collection), complete remset information is needed for *every* car, and some way of updating that information is required as cars are collected. Maintaining complete remset information for cars does not pose conceptual problems, but it does raise performance issues. For simplicity and performance when collecting, it would be preferable if a car's remset be stored with the car. However, keeping that remset accurate means fetching, updating, and writing back that remset any time a pointer to any object in the car is created or destroyed.

We propose to solve the problem in the following way. When a car is read in, its *outgoing* references (references to objects in other cars) are summarized. When a modified car is about to written back, its outgoing references are summarized again, and the differences recorded, namely references destroyed and references created. Note that collecting a car causes all of its outgoing references to be destroyed, and new references to be created (from other cars) from copied surviving objects. The remset changes are noted along with the car changes, and a table of changes not yet applied is maintained, called a Δref set. When a car is read in, any changes that are pending for that car's remset can then be applied. This process is illustrated in Figure 1.

---

[2] To be precise, we say an object Y in the oldest car is locally reachable from a source object X if there is a direct pointer from X to Y, or there is a chain of pointers X, Y1, Y2, ..., Y where X has a pointer to Y1, Y1 has a pointer to Y2, etc., and all the Yi objects are in the oldest car.

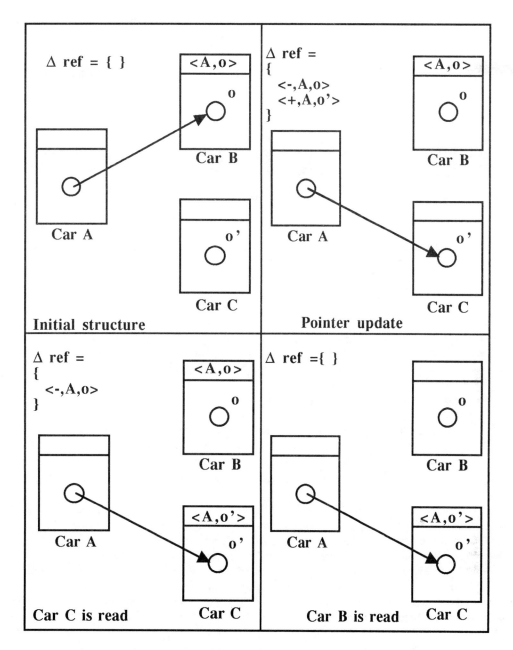

Figure 1: Illustration of algorithm handling creation/deletion of references

Initially, an object in Car A refers to object o in Car B. The pointer is modified to refer to object o' in Car C, which results in two entries in the Δref set, one indicating that a reference from Car A to object o has been dropped, and one indicating that a reference from Car A to object o' has been added. (Object "names" such o and o' are considered to include the identity of the car currently containing the object.) Note that the remsets for Car B and Car C are *not* updated yet. When Car C is read in, we update its remset and remove the + entry from the Δref set. Likewise, when Car B is read, we delete the remset item and the − entry in the Δref set. The point is that pointer changes require immediate access only to the car being modified and the Δref set, and actual remset additions and deletions can be deferred to a later time. The Δref set would probably be maintained in primary memory, and only moved to disk as a last resort. Presumably there would be background actions scheduled to read cars so as to purge the Δref set. It is now well known that such scheduled I/O is quite advantageous compared with synchronous I/O.

A similar process is followed for dealing with movement of objects from one place to another, using a Δ*loc set*, as shown in Figure 2. Here object o in Car B is moved to Car C when Car B is collected. The new object address is n, and

143

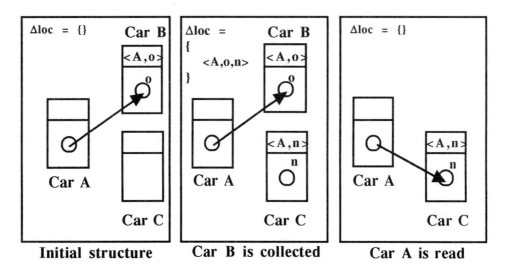

Figure 2: Illustration of algorithm handling movement of objects

we create an entry in the Δloc set indicating that Car A has a reference to object o which has now moved to location n. When Car A is next read in, the Δloc entry is applied, updating the pointer and "consuming" the Δloc entry. The principle behind the Δloc set is the same as for the Δref set: to allow updates to modify only locally available information, and to defer the remaining work to a later time.

The Δref and Δloc sets can be thought of as a special kind of log, and indeed, one could implement recovery of the Δref and Δloc information that way. However, it may be more convenient to use an underlying logging mechanism and to view the Δref and Δloc sets as just additional database data. In this way we achieve independence of any specific recovery mechanism. Likewise, when updating a car, we need only lock (or apply other appropriate concurrency control) that car, even even just the accessed subparts of the car. We do need to apply concurrency control to the data structures used for the Δref and Δloc sets as well, but their set semantics will allow high-concurrency semantics-based techniques to be applied, if necessary, to achieve the best performance.

The completeness of the original MOS algorithm substantially depends on the order in which the cars are collected. This comes about through the rule that places objects reachable from other trains into (one of) those trains. If cars are allowed to be collected in any order, completeness may be lost. For example, objects might just shuffle back and forth between two trains if the objects refer back and forth, and a cycle of such garbage objects may never be collected. The proposed solution is to maintain a notion of order (or age) of the trains, and allow objects to be copied from one train to another only in one direction. This is adequate for insuring completeness, if combined with a rule that every train has every car collected eventually. Note that this does not affect the choice of which car to collect, but may affect the degree of progress made in collecting any particular car.

The Persistent MOS Algorithm

We now present the PMOS algorithm itself. We will offer detailed pseudo-code in an online technical report, since space precludes presenting it here. For present purposes, we offer a description in English, at a somewhat greater level of detail than the overview given above.

Data Structures

The PMOS algorithms' data structures include a *store*, *trains*, *cars*, *objects*, *remsets*, a Δ*loc* set, a Δ*ref* set, and *buffers*.

Stores: A store *s* consists primarily of a set of *trains*, used to group cars as in the original MOS algorithm, a set of *cars*, which contain the objects of the store and associated information for the algorithm (and each of which is associated with a train), and a set of *root objects*, designated by their *locations* in the store. An object location is a unique name for an object within the store. We assume that we can determine an object's car from its location, and thus access the object, but locations need not have any particular form (i.e., they may be physical addresses, object identifiers, etc.). A store also has an associated Δloc set and Δref set, and a set of buffers.

Trains: Trains are numbered 1, 2, 3, ..., with new trains assigned numbers higher than any existing train. We assume that we can readily determine the train of any car, and of any object; in practice this probably requires maintaining various tables and keeping them resident in main memory insofar as possible. Each train also has associated with it an *external reference count*, summarizing the number of references from outside the train to objects stored in cars of the train; this includes root references (members of the containing store's root object set). Each train also has a set of zero or one *old root references*, and zero or one *old cross-train references*, whose use is explained later.

Cars: Every car has an associated identifier, unique among the cars of a store. We assume we can find and retrieve a car and its associated information given the car's identifier. A simple way to assign car identifiers is from a persistent global counter, but any scheme insuring uniqueness will work. We assume that it is possible to examine the objects in a car and determine the references they contain to objects in other cars. These are termed *outgoing references*. While a car may contain (objects having) multiple references to the same object, each reference occurs only once in the outgoing references set. We note that any given object is contained in only one car at a time.

Objects: An object is identified by its unique location (or "name"). We are not much concerned with the internal structure of objects, except that we assume we can find and update outgoing pointers from any given object, and so we ignore details of object format, copying their contents, etc.

Remsets: Every car has an associated remembered set, containing information about *incoming references*. Each entry in a remset identifies the object that is the target of the reference and the car containing the source of the reference. If a car has multiple references to the same object, they are summarized by a single remset entry.

Δloc *sets:* A Δloc set records information about objects that have moved, so that references to those objects can be updated at some later time. The algorithms maintain a single Δloc set for the entire store, summarizing all object references that need updating. We use separate entries for each car needing updating to avoid the problem of knowing when to discard object relocation information if all we recorded was the old and new address of each object.

Δref *sets:* A Δref set records information about cross-car references that have been created or deleted. (A pointer change is treated as a deletion plus a creation.) This information is used to update the remset of a target car at some later time. The algorithms maintain a single Δref set summarizing all remset updates that are pending.

Buffers: A buffer holds a main memory version of a car, so it has all the data structures that the car has. Additionally, each buffer has an *old outgoing reference set*, which summarizes the car's outgoing pointers as they were when the car was read in (an empty set for a newly created car). Note that buffers are lost in case of a system failure.

For the moment we will assume that each car's remset can be stored with the car, and that the Δloc set and Δref set fit in main memory. We will discuss later how we can relax these assumptions.

Algorithms

We describe how PMOS performs a number of operations on the store, each in turn. For brevity we omit a number of simple and obvious operations, such as initializing new stores, trains, and cars.

Adding a root: This must add the root to the store's root set and increment the external reference count of the train containing the new root object.

Removing a root: We remove the root from the store's root set and decrement the external reference count of the train containing the deleted root object.

Reading in a car: We create a buffer, read in the car, summarize and save the car's outgoing reference set, and then update in the buffer the car's references and remset (separate algorithms below).

Updating a car's references: This consists of locating any Δloc entries for this car and applying them to each object reference in the buffer, and in the saved outgoing reference set. The applied Δloc entries are deleted from the Δloc set.

Updating a car's remset entries: For each Δref entry indicating that a new remset entry needs to be added, add the entry and delete the Δref item. Likewise, for each Δref entry indicating that an existing remset entry should be deleted, delete the entry from the remset and delete the Δref item from the $\Delta refset$.

Writing a buffer back to the store (updating a car): Scan the buffer and build a new outgoing reference set. Compare it with the saved outgoing reference set. For old items that no longer appear, add a Δref item indicating that this car no longer refers to the target object. Similarly, for new items that did not previously appear, add a Δref item indicating that this car now refers to the target object. Then we write the car to persistent storage.

Garbage collecting a buffer: For objects locally reachable from roots, move them to any car in a higher numbered (younger/newer) train. For objects locally reachable *from higher numbered trains*, move them to any car of a referring train. For objects locally reachable from other cars of the current train, or only from lower numbered (older) trains, move the objects to another car of the current train. The preceding steps must be applied in order; see below for details of adjustments to data structures when objects move. All other objects are unreachable and can be discarded. We use the saved outgoing reference set to generate new Δref entries to indicate that the references from this car are now gone. The car and buffer can now be deleted. Note that garbage collecting does require having present all the cars to which we are moving objects. With additional data structures, we could define a holding set for objects "in transit" and avoid this requirement, but we are not certain is is a good idea, because it may place too high a demand on primary memory; yet it may be worthy of further investigation.

Moving an object from one car to another: Let us call the original location of the object its *source car* and its new location the *destination car*. We allocate space in the destination car and copy the object's contents. For each remset entry of the source car pertaining to the moved object, we delete the remset entry from the source car and add a corresponding entry to the destination car. If the cars are in different trains, we need to decrement the source train's external reference count appropriately, and increment the destination train's external reference count. Whether a particular remset entry causes a decrement (increment) depends on whether the source (destination) train also contains the car referring to the object being moved. For each remset entry we must also add an item to the Δloc set.

Additionally, we must also insure that we update any references from resident buffers to the moved object, that we update the root set if the object being moved is a root, and that we update the Δloc set if there remain pending entries from a previous move of the object.

Collecting a whole train: If a train's external reference count goes to zero, we can collect the entire train. However, we must make sure that any resident cars of the train are entirely up to date, since in-memory modifications may have created pointers, etc.

Insuring progress: The algorithms described above do not absolutely insure progress. As with the original MOS algorithm, a running program can change pointers in between collections and prevent the algorithm from removing objects from a given train. We give a series of necessary changes here, to avoid cluttering the descriptions of the algorithms offered above.

What is needed is to record for each train, one external reference. It may be an *old root reference* or an *old cross-train reference* (from a higher numbered train only). Whenever we create a new root (cross-train) reference to a given train, we save it as the "old" reference if we do not already have an "old" reference saved. When we collect a car in the train, if there are no current root or cross-train references that allow us to move objects from the car, then we check the train's "old" root and cross-train references. If either mentions an object in the current car, we move that object (as for a regular root or cross-train reference). If there *are* references that allow us to move at least one object out of the current train, we clear out the train's old root and cross-train references, since their only purpose is to guarantee progress and we made progress.

Correctness Argument

Now that we have described the algorithm, we sketch a correctness argument, in several stages:

1. **Remset Invariant:** That remsets, once updated from Δref, reflect exactly all cross-car references.

2. **Location Invariant:** Object references, once updated from Δloc, correctly reflect the object graph.

3. **Train Count Invariant:** Train counts accurately reflect the number of cross-train plus root references. In particular, if a train's count is zero, then no objects in it are reachable.

4. **Safety:** That no object reachable from a root is ever collected.

5. **Completeness:** That if every car is collected eventually, then all garbage is collected eventually.

Remset Accuracy

The invariant is easy to establish initially. There are four changes to the world that we must consider:

1. Adding a cross car reference: This is handled by the algorithm for writing a modified car back to the store. It detects a new reference and adds it to the Δref set. If the target car is resident, we will update the remset before writing the car back; if the car is not resident, it will be read in eventually and the remset update applied by the car reading algorithm at that time.

2. Deleting a cross car reference: This is handled analogously to adding a reference, using a $-$ entry rather than a $+$ entry in the Δref set.

146

3. Moving an object that is a target of cross-car references: In this case the objet moving algorithm populates the new object's car's remset from the remset of the old car, and the old remset entries are discarded, which correctly accounts for the change.

4. Moving an object that contains cross-car references: When we write back the car containing the new object, we will detect the new references and add any necessary new remset entries. The car collecting algorithm takes care of noting that the old remset entries need to be deleted.

Reference Accuracy

The invariant is trivially established initially. The only thing that can affect it is movement of objects, which inserts entries into Δloc based on the old object's car's remset entries (which we just argued are correct). For a non-resident referring car these entries are applied when the car is next read in. We have several options as to how to update any references that are currently resident (immediate, deferred, etc.), but we assume they are taken care of some time before the resident cars are written back. Things still work if an object should move multiple times before a referring car is read in, because the object moving routine also takes care of updating pending Δloc entries.

Train Count Accuracy

Again, the invariant is easy to establish initially. The root manipulating algorithms adjust the count in the obvious way, and the car writing algorithm adjusts counts in exactly those places that references are seen to be created or destroyed (and those references are from one train to another).

Safety

There are two ways in which objects are discarded: from single car collections and from the dropping of entire trains. Given that train counts are correct as just argued, dropping a train whose count is 0 is correct, since a 0 count means the train has no root objects and there are no references from other trains to objects in it. Hence there is no path from any root object to any object in the train. (Note that we must take care that any resident cars do not have unrecorded references to objects in the train; hence, we may need to "synchronize" our knowledge of the contents of resident cars.)

Correctness of car collection is also fairly straightforward. We move, and thus preserve, all objects in that car reachable from roots (and "relocate" those roots). We also move all objects reachable from outside the car. Hence, anything left is not reachable from outside the car and is garbage.

Completeness I: Progress Evacuating the Lowest Train

One way in which the algorithms could fail to collect all garbage eventually is if they do not make progress. While we require that each car be collected eventually, and (as we shall see later) the algorithm is complete as described so far, this is true only provided that the mutator (running program) does not move pointers and roots around in between car collections. The MOS algorithm has the same problem, noted and fixed by Grarup [Seligmann & Grarup, 1995]. Here is a description of the problem via an example. Suppose we have a cycle of objects lying in two cars, and one of the objects is a root. If we collect both cars, we would expect to remove all the objects to another train, but consider the following sequence of actions. We collect the car not containing the root (the objects stay in the current train since they are reachable from the car with the root). The mutator moves the root to the car we just collected. We now have a picture like before, which can perpetuate indefinitely.

The solution is to remember an "old root" and treat it as indeed a root. This old root reference it guarantees that if the mutator creates a root, and hence some object was reachable by the mutator at that time, we will move the object out of the train later. If the object becomes garbage, then it is not a root when it is moved, and in any case, it is not added to the new train's old root set (not the least because, since the object is garbage, the mutator cannot access it to designate it a root). Thus the old root technique will not cause garbage to be retained forever.

Similar to moving roots around, the mutator could move around pointers from some other train. The old cross-train reference solves this problem in the same way that the old root reference does for roots. There is one difference, though: we need worry only about references from higher numbered trains, since we cannot move an object to a lower numbered train.

We arrive at the following progress argument. Consider the set of cars of the lowest numbered train at some time t. Eventually, we will collect each of those cars. Either the train's count has gone to 0, and the entire train has been collected

147

(progress) or the count is not 0. If the count is not 0, and the train had an "old" reference (root or cross-train) at t, then we will have move at least the "old" object to another train, reducing the number of objects in the lowest numbered train. If the train had no "old" object at t and did not gain any, then we will have encountered each of the root and cross-train references in the original count, and thus will have made progress. If there was no "old" reference, we gained one, and now have none, then we made progress, since the "old" references are cleared out only when we make progress. Finally, if we have an "old" reference, when we process the car referred to, we will make progress. Thus, from any point in time, there will always be a future time when the lowest numbered train will have its count go to 0 or we will remove an object from it. The one additional thing we need is for the mutator not to allocate new objects in the lowest numbered train—then we can guarantee that the lowest numbered train will always shrink.

Completeness II: Progress Reclaiming Garbage

Suppose a particular object o becomes unreachable from any root. We argue that it will eventually be reclaimed. First, if o was mentioned as an "old" object from a time when it was still reachable, we will move o once; thereafter, it can never be an "old" object again (because the mutator cannot refer to it, since it is unreachable). Now consider the case in which no object refers to o. If o is "old", it can be moved once, but after that it will be collected in a local collection. Thus, trees and DAGs of garbage will disappear from their roots down, since each object will eventually not have any references to it.

That leaves only cycles of garbage for consideration. First, we know that eventually each car containing the cycle will be collected, and thus any "old" references from the time before the cycle was garbage will be processed. Once that has happened, consider an object of the cycle that is in the highest numbered train containing any object of the cycle. None of the cycle objects can be moved to any higher numbered train than that, and, by the progress argument, lower numbered trains are eventually evacuated, so in the worst case the cycle will eventually lie entirely in the lowest numbered train. There will be no "old" references to any of the cycle's objects, and so once all reachable objects are removed from this train, the train's count will be 0 and the cycle will be reclaimed.

Recovery Issues

We assume that there is some underlying serializable transaction system. in this view, a transaction updates cars, and as a "side-effect" creates Δref and Δloc entries. Note that collecting a car can be viewed as a transaction, too. The main point is that just as the changes to cars need to be recorded atomically, so also must we record changes to the Δloc and Δref sets. While we may wish to apply "special" (i.e., semantics based concurrency control) techniques to take advantage of the maximum possible concurrency, there is no need to develop specialized algorithms to permit garbage collection. It *is* possible that garbage collecting will introduce additional concurrency control conflicts, because of its need to update cars that receive additional objects. However, with suitably sophisticated semantics based concurrency control, we can avoid most such conflicts while introducing only a moderate amount of additional implementation complexity.

Extensions

The PMOS algorithm as described assume that remsets never overflow cars and that the Δloc and Δref sets can be maintained in primary memory. How can we relax these restrictions?

Large Δref and Δloc sets

It is not too difficult to handle large Δref or Δloc sets. One technique is to store them in a suitably sorted secondary memory structure (e.g., a B-tree), with a caching mechanism to hold recently accessed chunks in primary memory. This induces extra overhead in some cases. Note that we can keep recent updates in a primary memory buffer before adding them to the secondary memory structure, and thus batch our updates to that structure.

An alternative strategy is to schedule affected cars to be read in, so that we can apply the pending updates and remove them from the Δloc and Δref sets. This approach seems promising in that the costs of scheduled I/O are likely to be substantially less than the synchronous reads introduced by the secondary memory data structure approach.

Large remsets

Large remsets may be more difficult to handle well. One needs to handle an overflow immediately. In such "emergency" situations a memory resident overflow table sounds like a good alternative. One could also add to the affected car a pointer to a remset overflow area stored elsewhere in secondary storage. In any case, the car will probably need to be marked as having overflowed. A combination of main memory and secondary memory overflow tables can probably be tuned to work well, given more knowledge than we currently have as to the distribution of the number of remset entries needed by each car. Note that it is not a good idea to attempt the "popular object" ideas of the MOS algorithm: the MOS algorithm's collection order can discard and rebuild remsets, whereas PMOS really needs them maintained at all times. Finally, it may be reasonable to consider *splitting* a car into two cars, each of which may then have a smaller remset. This will not work if the large number of references are all to one particular object. In that case we really must employ an overflow mechanism.

Conclusions

We have presented a new database / persistent store garbage collection algorithm, PMOS (Persistent Mature Object Space), and sketched arguments as to its correctness. PMOS is incremental (at the level of blocks of memory) and is guaranteed to collect all garbage eventually, provided only that each block is eventually collected individually. While PMOS is based on copying techniques, it does not require semi-spaces: it only needs enough space to copy the block being collected, and then that block will be freed. The design of PMOS is such that one can use any serializable concurrency control and recovery scheme to support it in a resilient multi-user environment. No prior schemes had these attributes of incrementality, completeness, and independence of specific transaction mechanisms. We look forward to implementing PMOS and evaluating its performance in practice.

References

[Bekkers & Cohen, 1992] Yves Bekkers and Jacques Cohen, Eds. *International Workshop on Memory Management* (St. Malo, France, September 1992), no. 637 in Lecture Notes in Computer Science, Springer-Verlag.

[Bishop, 1977] Peter B. Bishop. *Computer Systems with a Very Large Address Space and Garbage Collection*. PhD thesis, Massachusetts Institute of Technology, Cambridge, MA, May 1977.

[Cook et al., 1994a] Jonathan E. Cook, Artur W. Klauser, Alexander L. Wolf, and Benjamin G. Zorn. Effectively controlling garbage collection rates in object databases. Tech. Rep. CU-CS-758-94, Department of Computer Science, University of Colorado, Boulder, CO, October 1994.

[Cook et al., 1994b] Jonathan E. Cook, Alexander L. Wolf, and Benjamin G. Zorn. Partition selection policies in object database garbage collection. In *Proceedings of the 1994 ACM SIGMOD International Conference on Management of Data (SIGMOD '94)* (Minneapolis, MN, May 1994), pp. 371–382.

[Detlefs, 1990] David L. Detlefs. Concurrent, atomic garbage collection. Tech. Rep. CMU-CS-90-177, Carnegie Mellon University, Pittsburgh, Pennsylvania, October 1990.

[Hudson & Moss, 1992] Richard L. Hudson and J. Eliot B. Moss. Incremental collection of mature objects. In [Bekkers & Cohen, 1992], pp. 388–403.

[Kolodner, 1990] Elliot Kolodner. Atomic incremental garbage collection and recovery for a large stable heap. In *Proceedings of the Fourth International Workshop on Persistent Object Systems* (Martha's Vineyard, Massachusetts, September 1990), Alan Dearle, Gail M. Shaw, and Stanley B. Zdonik, Eds., Published as *Implementing Persistent Object Bases: Principles and Practice*, Morgan Kaufmann, 1990, pp. 185–198.

[Kolodner et al., 1989] Elliot Kolodner, Barbara Liskov, and William Weihl. Atomic garbage collection: Managing a stable heap. In *Proceedings of the 1989 ACM SIGMOD International Conference on Management of Data* (Portland, Oregon, June 1989), *ACM SIGMOD Record 18*, 2 (May 1989), pp. 15–25.

[Kolodner, 1987] Elliot K. Kolodner. Recovery using virtual memory. Tech. Rep. MIT/LCS/TR-404, Laboratory for Computer Science, MIT, Cambridge, Massachusetts, July 1987.

[Munro et al., 1995] David S. Munro, Richard C. H. Connor, Ron Morrison, J. Eliot B. Moss, and Stephan J. G. Scheuerl. Validating the MaStA I/O cost model for DB crash recovery mechanisms. Position paper for workshop on database performance at OOPSLA '95, October 1995.

[Scheuerl et al., 1995] Stephan J. G. Scheuerl, Richard C. H. Connor, Ron Morrison, J. Eliot B. Moss, and David S. Munro. Validation experiments for the MaStA I/O cost model. In *Second International Workshop on Advances in Databases and Information Systems (ADBIS '95), Volume 1* (Moscow, Russia, June 1995), pp. 165–175.

[Seligmann & Grarup, 1995] Jacob Seligmann and Steffen Grarup. Incremental mature garbage collection using the train algorithm. In *Proceedings of the European Conference on Object-Oriented Programming (ECOOP '95)* (Aarhus, Denmark, August 1995), no. 952 in LNCS, Spring-Verlag, pp. 235–252.

[Wilson, 1992] Paul R. Wilson. Uniprocessor garbage collection techniques. In [Bekkers & Cohen, 1992].

MULTIGRANULARITY LOCKING WITH THE USE OF SEMANTIC KNOWLEDGE IN A LAYERED OBJECT SERVER[1]

G. Amato[‡], S. Biscari[±], G. Mainetto[±], F. Rabitti[±]

[±]CNUCE–CNR
Via S. Maria, 36 – Pisa – Italy

[‡]IEI–CNR
Via S. Maria, 46 – Pisa – Italy

Abstract

Object-oriented database programming languages use a data model which, by its nature, leads to a hierarchical organisation of persistent data. Multigranularity Locking (MGL) is the concurrency control protocol that allows a better organisation of concurrent accesses to such a hierarchy of data items.

Modern Object–Oriented Database Management Systems adopt a client–server architecture, where the server component is often an object server. The application of software engineering criteria in the design of an object server leads to a system structured in interpretation layers. In a layered object server, the semantic knowledge needed to decide how the nodes of the MGL data item hierarchy should be locked is distributed among all the system layers. A suitable technique to co-ordinate such decisions is thus needed.

This paper presents some guidelines on the design of the hierarchical organisation of data items for use by an Object–Oriented Database Management System supporting the MGL protocol, along with an original concurrency control technique called Expandable MGL which provides all the system layers with the ability to lock those granules that each layer considers to be the most appropriate on the basis of its partial knowledge of a transaction's behaviour.

Keywords: Concurrency Control, Multigranularity Locking Protocol, Object Server, Persistent Object Store, Object–Oriented Databases

1. INTRODUCTION

Research on *Object–Oriented Database Management Systems* (*ODMSs*) is currently trying to overcome the performance limits of first generation systems. Several new techniques for a better engineering of *ODMS* specific mechanisms are under investigation. As far as concurrency control is concerned, an appealing and promising area of investigation is the design of new mechanisms that are able to exploit the several different sources of semantic knowledge present in an *ODMS*.

This paper focuses on the source of (operational) semantic knowledge represented by the implementation of the object–oriented database programming language (*OODBPL*) supported by the *ODMS*. Our view is that an *ODMS* should be integrated with the run–time support of an *OODBPL* and thus it should also be integrated to the virtual computer defined by the language implementation. This virtual computer is actually a hierarchy of virtual computers which is successively transformed by layers of software into radically different virtual computers, until the hardware computer has been achieved. The key point of this paper is that each layer of the hierarchy can have some layer–specific semantic knowledge that is useful for concurrency control. This knowledge varies according to the level of abstraction provided by the layer. It ranges from high level semantic knowledge used by the optimiser of an *OODBPL* compiler, down to low level semantic knowledge about the implementation details of indexes owned by that low layer which abstracts over associative accesses. Thus, it would be highly desirable if an *ODMS* could use a unifying concurrency control mechanism that exploited all the layer–specific semantic knowledge present in the system.

ODMSs use a data model which, by its nature, leads to a hierarchical organisation of persistent data. Each object belongs to a set of objects, i.e. to a class, each class can be a subset of several superclasses, and so on. Such a natural hierarchy of data items can be exploited in the framework provided by the Multigranularity Locking (*MGL*) protocol because this protocol was expressly designed for data organised into hierarchies. In fact, some *ODMSs*, such as ORION and O_2, have already investigated the use of this protocol. We believe that *MGL* may be the concurrency control mechanism that would allow the exploitation of all the semantic knowledge present in a layered *ODMS*.

[1] This work has been partly supported by grants from the EU under ESPRIT BRA Project No 6309 FIDE2 (Fully Integrated Data Environment) and from the CNR under bilateral Italy–USA SIENOSP Project.

If we consider the *MGL* protocol as being plunged into a layered system, then the *MGL*'s hierarchy of data items could be shared among all system layers and used as a means to exchange locking decisions. To this aim, two elements are necessary: a well-structured organisation of the hierarchy of data items and the use of a technique for co-ordinating the locking decisions taken by the various layers.

This paper first presents a set of useful guidelines for designing the hierarchical organisation of data items for the *MGL* protocol. Then it describes a technique, called *Expandable MGL* (*EMGL*), which allows the capability to request locks on the nodes of a shared global data item hierarchy to be distributed among all the system layers. We show the application of these ideas to the *Physically Independent Object Server* (*PIOS*), which is a research prototype aimed at exploring new development directions in *ODMSs*, primarily the effectiveness of *physical independence* in *ODMSs*. However, these ideas should be applicable to other *DMSs*[2] that support a rich data model and that are structured as layered systems.

The rest of the paper is organised as follows. In the remainder of this section, we introduce the terminology and some basic concepts about layered systems and the *MGL* protocol. In Section 2, we describe in detail the new techniques that we propose and their motivations. Section 3 outlines the layered architecture of *PIOS* and the type of semantic knowledge owned by each layer that could be exploited in the *MGL* protocol. In Section 4, we provide the results of some simple performance tests that we have performed in *PIOS*. Conclusions are drawn in Section 5.

1.1 Object Server as a Layered Subsystem

The design of every processing system leads to a layered architecture, made of the implementation of several languages placed on different levels of abstraction [Das84]. Each level of the architecture coincides with the language defined for it. Each language controls and manages a set of resources of its level. The hierarchical relationship among levels of abstraction is made explicit by the development of the system, since the implementation of an upper level language consists of programs that use the constructs provided by some lower level languages. This emulation continues until the hardware or firmware machine language has been reached.

The design of programming languages is a particular case of the design of computer architectures. [Pra84] states that when a programming language is implemented, the run–time data structures and algorithms used in program execution define a virtual computer. As above, a level corresponds to a language. Each layer of the architecture is an implementation of a higher level programming language in terms of a lower level one. The layer performs a mapping between a higher level language and a lower level language. The layer implements the data structures and statements of the higher language by means of the data structures and statements of the lower language. The typical example of a layered architecture defined by a language implementation is the one represented from the following virtual computers: PASCAL, PCODE, operating system, firmware and hardware. Notice that the information hiding principle suggests that each layer should not be aware of the implementation strategy adopted for the languages of lower layers.

The application of these ideas to the design of *OODBPLs* has led to layered client–server architectures [JT+91]. A first set of layers implements the client that can be the translator of either an *OODBPL* or a set–oriented query language. A second set of layers constitutes the server component which manages the shared database of persistent objects on behalf of its clients. Servers are classified on the basis of the unit of transfer with clients. They can either be object servers or page servers. If the server is an object server then the architectural organisation of layers and languages is quite clear because the layers of the server above all implement the language represented by the operators of the object data model and the layers of the client implement the *OODBPL* by using the language implemented by the server.

PIOS is an object server with a three–level architecture [ABR93] [AB+95]. On the top of the highest level, another layer should be provided, which implements an external *OODBPL*. The two upper levels correspond to languages of two object data models, the *logical data model* and the *physical* one. Programs written in these languages contain sequences of data model operations embedded within transaction operations. The *PIOS* logical data model is a classical object–oriented data model in which a single logical object can simultaneously belong to several logical classes that are in an inheritance relationship [AB+89]. On the other hand, every physical object of the *PIOS* physical data model belongs to exactly one physical class because the logical inheritance relationship has been flattened out.

The third level of the architecture is the *storage* level. It corresponds to the functionality for storing and retrieving persistent objects supplied by the concurrent Persistent Object Store [MC+94]. The storage level hides operating system details and it provides the upper layers with a heap of persistent objects and with primitives for accessing them expressed in a transactional context.

---

[2] We use the acronym DMS instead of the more traditional DBMS.

	IS	IX	S	SIX	X
IS	√	√	√	√	No
IX	√	√	No	No	No
S	√	No	√	No	No
SIX	√	No	No	No	No
X	No	No	No	No	No

Table 1: Compatibility matrix of Multiple Granularity Locking protocol

1.2 Multiple Granularity Locking Protocol

The *MGL* protocol is a widely used protocol that allows the performances of a *DMS* to be tuned. The key element of the protocol is the possibility to strike a balance between the locking overhead of an executing transaction and the amount of concurrency that such a transaction allows in the system.

This is done by exploiting the natural hierarchical relationship among database data items of different *size* or *granularity*. This hierarchical relationship is a *containment* relationship that relates data items of coarser granularity (e.g. relations, classes) to those of finer granularity (e.g. records, objects). The data items of different size are called *granules*. The scheduler of a *DMS* uses the data structure called *Lock Instance Graph* (*LIG*) to manage the locks on granules. The *LIG* stores locking information about the actual data items of the database, i.e. it is used, for example, to remember if the "Persons" relation has been locked or not. In the first proposal of the *MGL* protocol [GL+75], the *LIG* was a tree.

Transactions can lock granules *explicitly*, which in turn lock descendants *implicitly*. Two *modes* of locks are defined: an *exclusive* (X) lock excludes any other transaction from accessing (reading and writing) the granule; a *shared* (S) lock permits other transactions to concurrently read the granule but prevents any updates.

If the scheduler has to grant a lock on a given granule to a certain transaction, then it would have to check if any other transaction has explicitly locked any ancestor of the granule. This is clearly inefficient. To solve this problem, a third kind of lock mode called *intention* lock was then introduced [Gra78]. All the ancestors of a node must be locked in intention mode before an explicit lock can be placed on the node. In particular, nonleaf nodes can be locked in three different intention modes. A nonleaf node is locked in *intention–shared* (IS) mode to specify that some descendant nodes will be explicitly locked in S mode. Similarly, an *intention–exclusive* (IX) lock on a node means that some descendant nodes will be X locked. A *shared and intention–exclusive* (SIX) lock on a given node implies that the whole subtree rooted at that node is being locked in S mode and that explicit X locking will be done in some nodes of the subtree. **Table 1** shows the compatibility relationships amongst the different modes of locking (a check mark √ indicates compatibility).

The above description is an informal presentation of the *MGL* protocol rules. Notice that a transaction acquires locks in root–to–leaf order. The complete protocol includes another rule that governs lock release (leaf–to–root order or all at once). Furthermore, *MGL* protocol has been generalised to work for direct acyclic graphs (DAGs) of resources rather than simple trees [Gra78].

The capabilities offered by the *MGL* protocol are highlighted when the workload of the transaction processing system consists of a combination of short transactions with a few accesses and transactions, such as audit transactions, that last for a long time by accessing a large number of data items. Short transactions, which incur a negligible locking overhead, can allow a high level of concurrency by choosing to lock at a fine granularity. Long transactions, which in any case allow a low degree of concurrency, can reduce their locking overhead by choosing to lock at a coarse granularity.

For simplicity, in the rest of the paper we will frequently use the *Lock Type Graph* (*LTG*) to reason about *MGL* protocol. A *LTG* synthetically represents the locking information of a *LIG* because it stores the containment relationship among the data type constructors of the database's data items (see **Figure 1**).

2. THE *EXPANDABLE MGL* TECHNIQUE

In this section we present the *Expandable MGL* technique, a technique that gives each layer of a *DMS* the capability of requesting locks on granules belonging to different portions of a shared global data item hierarchy. This organisation of *DMS*'s concurrency control functionality derives from the consideration that each layer can choose the granule to lock on the basis of its partial but specific knowledge of the overall behaviour of the transaction.

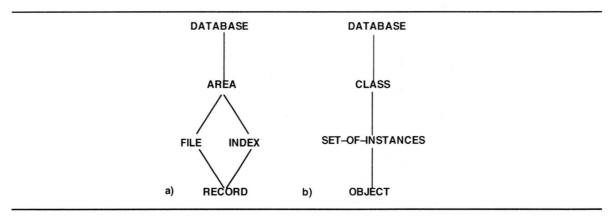

Figure 1: Relational and OO Lock Type Graphs

To take full advantage of the technique, the *LTG* of the *DMS* should be carefully designed. Thus we now describe some guidelines on modelling the hierarchical organisation of data items. We apply these guidelines to *PIOS* and we show how the resulting *LTG* differs from other *LTG* proposed in the literature.

2.1 Multigranularity Locking in *ODMSs*

The first proposal for using the *MGL* protocol appeared in the context of relational *DMSs* [GL+75]. In this context, the relevant entities for the protocol are tuples and sets of tuples, i.e. relations. **Figure 1a** shows the traditional *LTG* described in [Gra78] and reported in BHG87. In the figure, a file is the storage counterpart of a relation, and record stands for tuple.

In the *OODB* context, *MGL* protocol has been developed in ORION, an *ODMS* that supports multiple inheritance [GK88], and proposed in O$_2$ [CF90]. The reason for using the *MGL* protocol in an *ODMS* is that the object–oriented data model provides a natural hierarchical organisation of data items in granules of different sizes: each object is a member of the set representing the extension of a class; a class can be a subclass of one or several superclasses, which implies that there is a subset relationship among the extension of a subclass and the extensions of its superclasses. In this context, when most of the objects belonging to the extension of a class have to be accessed, it makes sense to set one lock for the whole class extension, rather than one lock for each individual object of the extension.

In [GK88] the hierarchies representing the inheritance relationship and the *instance_of* relationship are inserted into the traditional *LTG*. **Figure 1b** (taken from [BHG87]) shows the resulting *LTG*. Given an ORION database schema, a *LIG* will be a *rooted direct acyclic graph* (*RDAG*) that directly connects the database root node to base class nodes (roots in the inheritance hierarchy). Subclasses of base classes are represented as subnodes of base class nodes, and so on, thus representing all the inheritance hierarchy. Class nodes are connected to nodes that represent their extensions and extensions to objects, thus characterising the *instance_of* relationship. A *LIG* is not a tree: it is an *RDAG* because in ORION there is multiple inheritance.

Note that the *LTG* in **Figure 1b** distinguishes common properties of classes, such as class variables and class definitions, from class extensions (sets of instances). Unfortunately, these two different aspects of the notion of class are related in the hierarchy. For example, if a class is locked in X mode because a transaction is changing the value of a class variable, then the set of instances of the class will be implicitly locked too. To overcome this difficulty, [GK88] proposes to add new ones to the standard lock modes, with their own new semantics, and to modify the semantics of standard lock modes when they regard classes. On the other hand, our approach is to operate on the organisation of the *LTG*.

2.2 Design of the Lock Type Graph

A trivial choice of the *LTG* may lead to modest performance and thus it may reduce any benefits of adopting a complex protocol such as the *MGL*. To understand the origins of these potential shortcomings, we will try to adapt the *LTG* proposed in [Gra78] and used in relational *DMSs* to a simple *ODMS* such as *PIOS*. We assume that physical class attributes are not present, such physical classes are flat (i.e., without inheritance), and that it is impossible to modify a physical class definition during the operational period of *ODMS*'s activity.

In this hypothesis, the database will be the topmost granule of a containment relationship that has physical classes and indices in intermediate positions, and physical objects as the smallest granules (**Figure 2**). The parents of physical

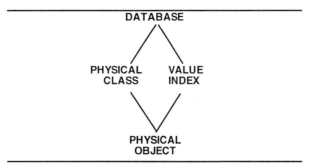

Figure 2: A trivial Lock Type Graph

objects are physical classes and indices, since a physical object is contained in the extension of a physical class and it can also be accessible through an index, provided that a value index for that physical class has been defined[3].

The corresponding *LIG*s are simple and easy to understand, but a deeper analysis reveals their inadequacy as illustrated by the following example. Let us suppose that at a certain moment in the system there are two running transactions T1 and T2. T1 counts the number of objects in a physical non–indexed class C. T2 updates the state of a physical object that belongs to the same physical class C accessed by T1. T1 does not need to access any object state: it just has to access the data structure that represents the physical class. On the contrary, T2 does not access any physical class since it accesses the physical object state directly by means of its identity.

T1 and T2 should thus be able to be executed in parallel because there is no logical conflict between them. On the other hand the trivial *LTG* generates a conflicting situation. According to the *MGL* protocol, T1 should set one single shared lock S on the physical class C, and T2 should lock the same physical class C in IX mode, since it has to lock in X mode a physical object that belongs C. S lock is not compatible with IX lock on the same granule C and so the two transactions cannot run in parallel. Similar examples could be provided for indices.

This drawback is due to the meaning of the physical class granule. A physical class in the trivial *LTG* has a double meaning since it is used for representing a set of individuals (the extension of the physical class intended as the set of identities of physical objects), and the set of values that the individuals take (the extension of the physical class intended as the set of *states* of physical objects). An *LTG* with two types of granules for the two concepts should enhance the throughput of the *ODMS*. If an *ODMS* is able to separate the two concepts, then it could allow parallel executions of: a transaction t1 that inserts a new individual into a set and a transaction t2 that only updates the value of another individual belonging to the same set, a transaction that removes an individual from a set and a transaction that only accesses the value of another individual belonging to the same set, a transaction that queries about the cardinality of a set of individuals and a transaction that modifies the value associated with an individual of the same set, and so on. In terms of *LTG* this separation means that the granules representing sets of individuals and the sets of values of individuals should not be related.

We notice that a layered *DMS* can arrange for a greater throughput of transactions if it organises granules according to criteria that strictly depend on the semantics of the statements (operations) of the various languages involved. Each layer knows how the statements of its language are implemented and the effects of the execution of statements on the data items of the database. For a given language at a certain level, the general pragmatic criteria we believe should be followed are that:

- a distinct node should be provided for each distinct type of database data items accessible during the execution of a statement of the language;

- a parent node should be introduced in the hierarchy only when the language provides a (set of) statement(s) that manipulates a collection of database data items as a whole.

The second criterium is the outcome of the need to support queries in a *DMS*.

Following these two general criteria, the previous *LTG* becomes the one shown in **Figure 3**. The previous Physical Class granule has been split into two granules. The first one, still called Physical Class, represents the physical class data item that implements the extension of a physical class, i.e. a set of object identities; it is no longer a parent of the Physical Object State granule. The second granule is called Bag_of Physical Object State[4] and is the unique parent node of all physical object states of a physical class. The index granule has been positioned in a different place with respect to the trivial *LTG*. A value index plays the same role as a physical class in the *LTG*. The reason is that a value index is defined on some

---

[3] For simplicity we will limit our attention to value indices.

[4] We refer to the notion of "bag" since two different objects can have the same state.

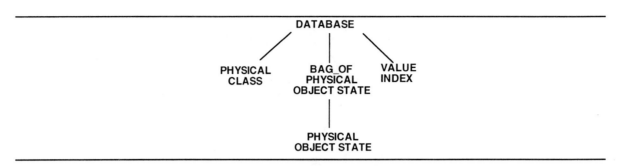

Figure 3: A more intelligent Lock Type Graph

descriptive attributes of a physical class and thus it can be considered as an "associative" physical class that maps a value to a set of identities. As with physical classes, a value index will contain all the identities of the physical objects of the physical class on which it has been defined.

With this solution, the previous transactions T1 and T2 can run in parallel without any interference. T1, the transaction that counts, only asks for a shared lock on a Physical Class granule and an intention–share lock on the Database. T2, the transaction that updates, asks for an exclusive lock on a Physical Object State granule, and intention–exclusive locks on Bag_of Physical Object State and Database granules. In this case, there is only one shared entity, the Database, between the two transactions, and IS and IX lock modes do not conflict.

2.3 The *Expandable MGL* technique

Given a level and a language that manages some data items of the database, the layer that implements the language manipulates the data items at that level of abstraction. These data items can be used by the implementation of some higher level data items and can use in their implementation some data items belonging to lower levels. In a complex system organised into levels of different abstractions, only the system component that makes an abstraction mechanism knows the details about the data items used in the implementation. Each layer can exploit only the semantic knowledge about its own data items, but it is not aware of the implementation details of some components of its own data items. Thus, in the general case, there are situations in which the decisions about concurrency control can be taken by one layer and these decisions will be valid for all lower levels, and there are situations in which the knowledge is imprecise and thus the decision has to be made by the lower layers.

We will illustrate the situation with a simple example. Let us consider a trivial *DMS* consisting of two levels and two languages. The higher language is a query language that allows one to express a query represented by an universally quantified simple predicate defined on an attribute of an object belonging to one collection (i.e., a set of object identifiers). The lower level language, which is part of the run-time support of the query language, provides operations for manipulating the following data items: value indexes, collections and objects. For our pourposes, there are two particularly interesting types of operations provided from the lower level: one is the index operation that, given the value of an attribute and a relational operator, returns the set of object identifiers that satisfy such predicate; one is the set of operations that allows to visit all the objects of a collection, that is scan operations (open scan, fetch next object identifier, etc.).

When a simple query is submitted to the query processor, this layer will generate an execution plan of the query based on the following strategy: if there is an index defined on the collection specified in the query and if this index concerns the attribute specified in the query, then use the index; otherwise scan the collection looking for the objects that satisfy the condition. Here is the point. There are two different situations. In one situation, the query processor only has the knowledge that it will invoke the index manager, but it cannot infer any particular information on the way an index is used. Hence, for the sake of concurrency control, it should leave the locking decisions about indexes to the index manager. In the other situation, it knows that the query execution will have to access all the objects of a collection and thus the query processor has all the semantic knowledge needed to take a locking decision: set just one lock on the entire collection.

The previous example suggests that the following general properties should characterise the layers of a complex system:

- The higher layers can assume locking decisions on coarse granules;
- The lower layers can assume locking decisions on fine granules.

The first type of decision allows the locking overhead to be reduced. The second type the parallelism to be increased (**Figure 4**).

156

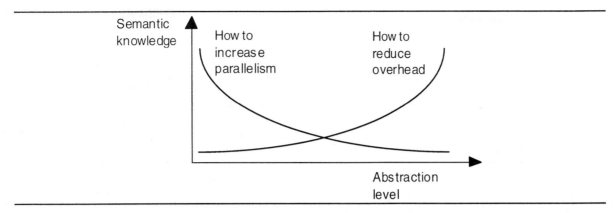

Figure 4: Semantic knowledge for MGL in a layered system

It is worth noting that if a system only shows the first property, then there may be a low overhead in the management of concurrency control and a small degree of parallelism among transactions since coarse granules can potentially raise several conflicts. Instead, if a system only presents the second property, then it could achieve a greater degree of parallelism at the price of a greater locking overhead.

Our approach aims at providing a unifying framework that exploits both types of semantic knowledge. The idea is to allow each layer to require locks on granules corresponding to its level of semantic knowledge and to use the *LTG* as a means for exchanging lock information among layers. If a higher layer infers from its own semantic knowledge that it cannot take a final decision on a coarse granule, then it can delegate to lower layers of the system the task of exploiting the semantic knowledge on finer granules. However, if a higher layer holds all the knowledge necessary to take a definitive decision on a coarse granule, then it can inhibit lower layer requests on some finer granules.

This is obtained by modifying the standard way in which a system layer manages the *LIG*. As far as the *LIG* is concerned, we introduce the idea of *expandability of leaves*: a granule, that is viewed as a leaf from a higher layer, can be expanded from a lower layer with a subtree of finer granules (**Figure 5**). The *MGL* protocol allows an intermediate layer to lock what it sees as a leaf granule in IS or IX mode as well. These apparently unnatural lock modes are utilised to communicate among layers. When a higher layer wants to permit a lower layer to expand a granule, it will set an intention lock on the granule concerned. We call this technique *Expandable MGL*.

Let us consider an example that illustrates this technique. There are two running transactions T3 and T4. T3 is going to insert a new physical object in an indexed physical class. T4 is willing to update the state of a physical object belonging to the same indexed physical class.

Let us firstly analyse the case in which the *EMGL* technique was not used. T3 during its execution has to lock in X mode a Physical Class granule representing the extension of the physical class and a Value Index granule representing the index defined on the physical class. T4 must lock in X mode a Physical Object State granule and the Value Index granule. T3 and T4 cannot run in parallel since they ask for an incompatible lock on the same Value Index granule. This happens because some higher layer of the system had no detailed semantic knowledge of the index data structure and it decided to lock the whole index.

The use of the *EMGL* technique and expandability of leaves can ensure parallel executions. Both T3 and T4 ask for a

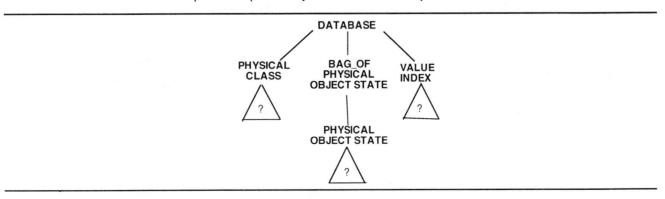

Figure 5: Expandability of leaves

Level	VM	Language	DB data items	Layer
0	EXTERNAL	*PIOS* query, i.e. implicit RO trans	Logical classes	Compiler
1	LOGICAL	Logical trans	Logical classes and logical objects	Compiler
2	PHYSICAL	Physical trans	Physical classes and objs, value and navigation idx	Interpreter
3	STORAGE	FLASK trans	FLASK objects	Library

Figure 6: Layered architecture of *PIOS*

IX lock on the same Value Index granule, and the index manager adopts its own ad-hoc policy for expanding this granule. If for instance T3 and T4 work on different pages of the B-Tree data structure, then they can run in parallel without interference.

These ideas have been applied to high levels of *PIOS*. Inheritance relationships, which are features of the logical data model, have been added to the *LTG* of **Figure 3** by inserting a first intermediate node between the Physical Class and the Database, and a second intermediate node between the Bag_of Physical Object State and the Database. The two new intermediate nodes have no other relationship with any other nodes. The first new intermediate node represents the extensional constraint of inheritance, which establishes that a set of identities of a subclass is a subset of the set of identities represented by its superclasses. The second new intermediate node is useful for modelling the fact that queries on the objects of a class also refer to the objects of its subclasses.

3. THE CONTEXT OF THE EXPERIMENT: *PIOS*

The *Physically Independent Object Server* (*PIOS*) is a research prototype that aims to explore new development directions in *ODMSs*. The main research direction pursued in the development of *PIOS* is the verification of the effectiveness of *physical independence* in *ODMSs*. To support physical independence *PIOS* makes use of a multi–level architecture founded on three languages, i.e. on three different levels [ABR93] [AB+95].

The two topmost levels correspond to the languages of two object data models, the *logical data model* and the *physical* one. The *PIOS* logical data model is a classical object–oriented data model in which a single logical object can simultaneously belong to several logical classes that are in an inheritance relationship [AB+89]. On the other hand, every physical object of *PIOS* physical data model belongs to exactly one physical class because the logical inheritance relationship has been flattened out. To flatten inheritance, *PIOS* database designers can choose from several different physical organisations of a given logical schema and they can define *value and navigation indices* on physical classes [ZR93] to enhance the overall system performance.

The third level of the architecture is the *storage* level. This corresponds to the functionalities for storing and retrieving persistent objects supplied by a concurrent Persistent Object Store [MC+94]. The storage level hides the operating system details and provides the upper layers with a heap of persistent objects and with primitives for accessing them expressed in a transactional context.

A further level, placed on the top of the previous hierarchy of virtual machines, is defined from the so–called *external languages* of *PIOS*. These are software layers such as the compiler of an external language, the front–end of *PIOS* query language processor, a browser, etc.

The previously summarised layered architecture of *PIOS* is outlined in **Figure 6**. For each level, the Figure shows its language, the database data items managed from the language and how the language is implemented.

At run–time *PIOS* as a whole represents the server component of a client-server *ODMS*. Internally, *PIOS* is in turn structured according to a client-server architecture in which several *Logical/Physical Translators* are the clients of a single *PHysical Object Server* (*PHOS*). Each *Translator* is a process that acts on behalf of an external *Client* process. Peer *Client–Translator* processes can run on different machines connected through an interconnection structure that is usually a local area network. Each *Translator* interacts with a *PHOS* by means of the interprocess communication facilities provided by the operating system.

3.1 Translators of external languages

These software layers access the persistent objects and classes stored in the *PIOS* database only by means of the logical data model operators, both those that allow navigational accesses and those that ensure set–oriented accesses. The navigational operators of the *PIOS* logical data model can be integrated with the run–time support of object-oriented database

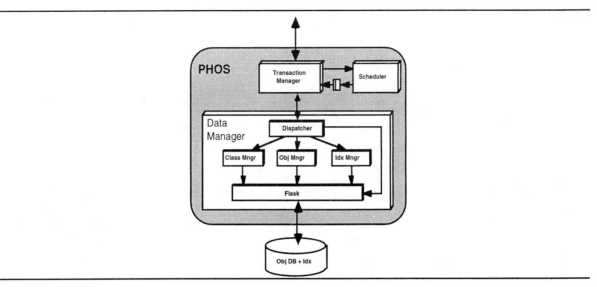

Figure 7: PHOS architecture

programming languages, such as the extension of the Common LISP used in ORION [KB+89], the extension of Smalltalk used in GemStone [BOS91], or Galileo [ACO85]. Logical set–oriented operators are combined to form sentences of *PIOS* query language [RBD94].

The translator of an external language can provide *PIOS* with a logical–level semantic knowledge about a transaction behaviour that is useful for reducing the locking overhead. For example, if a simple query needs to be made which just projects some attributes of all the objects belonging to a logical class, then the current *PIOS* query language processor only requires one lock for the logical class instead of a set of locks, one for each logical object. Semantic knowledge can also be used for supporting a Conservative Two Phase Locking. [AGM93], for instance, illustrates a technique for a static analysis of transactions defined using a strongly and statically typed object-oriented language, which automatically infers a safe approximation of the readset and writeset of the transactions. This allows one to implement a conservative policy, i.e. to lock in advance all the data the transaction is going to access.

3.2 Translator of logical transaction language

The purpose of each *Logical/Physical Translator* is the dynamic mapping of logical access operations (to logical "virtual" objects) into physical access operations (to physical "database" objects). The translation concerns both navigational and set–oriented accesses, but the translation and optimisation of logical queries are of paramount importance for the overall performance of *PIOS*.

The *Logical/Physical Translator* is the layer of the system that owns the semantic knowledge about logical–physical correspondences of objects and classes. Furthermore, as shown in **Figure 6**, this is the layer that makes use of the statistical information on physical object states for query optimisation purposes. Statistical information is also quite important for deciding the granularity of items to lock during a query evaluation: for example, if a query performs a navigation from the set of physical objects of physical class A to the set of physical objects of physical class B, then it is possible to predict the percentage of physical objects belonging to B extension that will be accessed during the query evaluation. The locking overheads of setting one lock for a whole physical class and that of setting locks for the physical objects of a physical class have been inserted in the cost model developed for *PIOS* query language [RBD94].

The *Logical/Physical Translator* is the *PIOS* layer that has the intermediate knowledge needed to connect the high level logical knowledge about a transaction behaviour to the lower level physical one. Thus it plays a central and important role in *PIOS*: it is the layer responsible for generating some lock primitives of the *MGL* protocol. In particular, it generates those lock primitives that concern the granules of the *LTG* in which the physical data items are organised.

3.3 Translator of physical transaction language

PHOS provides the upper layers with both the operations of the *PIOS* physical data model and the operations for interacting with navigation and value indices. *PHOS* is a process that integrates the functionalities of a Transaction Manager, a Scheduler and a Data Manager (**Figure 7**). *PHOS* is also responsible for generating statistical information about the state of the database.

159

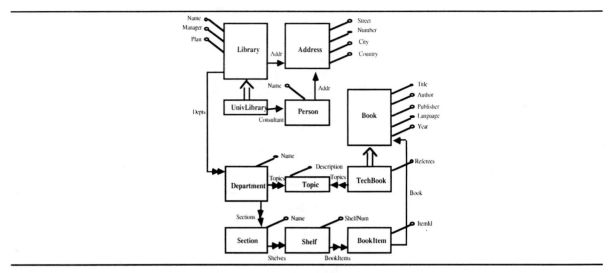

Figure 8: Sample database schema

PHOS is the layer of the system that owns semantic knowledge about physical–storage correspondences of objects and classes. This knowledge is concentrated in the components of the *Data Manager* that directly deal with the storage level to map physical level operations (*Class*, *Object* and *Index Managers* in **Figure** 7).

The Persistent Object Store library called FLASK [MC+94] represents the storage level. FLASK offers some basic facilities for manipulating persistent objects, along with useful help in recovery and in implementing concurrency control. The key feature of FLASK is the *Concurrent Shadow Paging* mechanism that ensures database consistency after system and transaction failures. The FLASK programming interface contains operations, indexed by a transaction identifier, to create, delete, update, and access persistent objects of a generic format. The interface provides primitives for beginning, committing and aborting transactions.

Clearly, the lowest level components of the *PIOS* architecture have a specific semantic knowledge close to implementation details of the storage level. This knowledge is as important as that owned by higher layers and it should be integrated with the others in a unique framework. A classical example of *PIOS* is the index locking: a *Translator* has the knowledge to decide whether it is convenient to lock an index in its entirety, and if not, then it should delegate the *Index Manager* of *PHOS* to manage the locking policy.

4. PERFORMANCE SAMPLES

This section presents some performance figures regarding a *PIOS* version that fully exploits the *EMGL* technique. To appreciate the performance improvements achieved, we show the performance results obtained running exactly the same experiment on two different versions of *PIOS*. In the former version, called *Old PIOS*, the lock requests are solely generated by a unique centralised component, i.e. the *Logical/Physical Translator*, which is only aware of the existence of indices and physical classes and consequently it orders the lock of the entire corresponding granule when it has to be accessed. In the latter version, called *New PIOS*, the lock management policy is distributed among the various layers of the architecture. In particular, the *Index* and *Physical Class Managers* decide on the generation of lock requests for the internal granules of indices and classes when the *Logical/Physical Translator* is unable to decide for the entire data structure.

The logical object–oriented database schema is depicted in **Figure 8**. The two inheritance relationships in the figure have been resolved with the fragmentation of logical objects belonging to Library–UnivLibrary and Book–TechBook pairs of classes into two physical objects, one for each logical class of each pair. In the physical database schema, there are four value indices defined on the physical classes corresponding to Topic, Book, Library and TechBook logical classes.

The test transactions are generated so that there are both navigational and set–oriented accesses to the database. Each *PIOS* transaction in the tests executes just one logical *PIOS* operation. The operations are randomly chosen from the insertion of a new logical object in a randomly chosen logical class, the update of an old logical object of a randomly chosen logical class, and the query on a randomly chosen logical class. Note that the choice of just one *PIOS* operation for every *PIOS* transaction is not a heavy restriction: each logical *PIOS* operation can even be translated into hundreds of physical operations, and several transaction conflicts are possible.

The experiments always run on the same fixed database initially populated with 2M objects. Indices are loaded with 64K keys. Each node in the index contains at most 200 keys and the B-Trees have three levels. In the B-Trees there are around 600 leaf nodes and 7 non leaf nodes. The experiments run on a completely dedicated Sun Spark 4[5], a single processor machine with 24 MBytes of RAM and 1 GByte of disk.

Old PIOS and *New PIOS* execute two kinds of experiments that use the multi-programming (*MPL*[6]), i.e. the number of transactions that have begun execution, as a means to generate different degrees of data and resource contentions. An experiment consists of 15 tests performed with *MPL* ranging between 1 and 15. Each test is performed while keeping constant the *MPL*. It is the routine that generates transactions that keeps constant the *MPL* by launching a new test transaction as soon as a previously executing transaction reaches its end. At the end of an interval of time sufficient to obtain stable results (10 minutes), the average value of the measures is given as the final result of each test. Each test on both versions is repeatedly (7 times) executed with exactly the same stream of transactions. The final result of a test is obtained by firstly discarding both the worst and the best measures and then by computing the average of the remaining (5) measures.

The outcome of the first experiment is shown in **Figure 9a**. It provides the quotient between the average number of running transactions and the number of active transactions, i.e. the *MPL*. The difference between the two numbers is represented by those transactions that are blocked because of conflicts. During a test, the measure is computed from the *PIOS* scheduler that at short fixed time intervals verifies the number of running transactions at a given moment and that outputs the average number when the test finishes.

Figure 9b shows the result of the second experiment, that gives the throughput in transactions per second. The result of each test is the quotient between the number of transactions that have successfully committed and the time of duration of the test (10x60 secs). The throughput of the new version of *PIOS* is greater because in the average there are fewer blocked and aborted transactions.

The results of the two experiments clearly demonstrate that *EMGL* performs better than standard *MGL* under the same circumstances. We believe that if the experiments had continued with a greater *MPL*, then the differences shown from the two curves would have been more noticeable. The reason is that highly concurrent algorithms are absolutely necessary to deal with contentions in heavily used data structures. In the tests, the data structures adopted to implement the indices and the physical classes represent bottlenecks for concurrent transactions. *Old PIOS* uses the trivial policy of locking the entire index when a physical object belonging to an indexed physical class is updated and the entire physical class when a new physical object is inserted into a physical class. The risk of reducing parallelism is clear because the transaction locks all indexed physical objects and all the objects of a physical class. *EMGL* allows one to adopt ad-hoc policies in each structure representing a leaf in the lock type graph, as physical classes or indices, that result in finer granularity locking and hence in a better performance.

5. CONCLUSIONS

In this paper we have presented some guidelines on the design of the hierarchical organisation of data items for use by an *ODMS* supporting the *MGL* protocol, and a technique for concurrency control that provides all the system layers with the ability to lock those granules that each layer considers the most appropriate on the basis of its partial knowledge of a transaction's behaviour. We have shown the application of these techniques to *PIOS*, an object server that uses the *Concurrent Shadow Paging* mechanism provided by the FLASK persistent object store, and some simple experimental results.

The techniques we propose to adopt seem to be well–suited for the high levels of a complex system, though they appear to be less adequate for the low levels. We believe that the complementary situation holds for multi–level transaction [Wei91], and in the new future we will investigate the possibility of combining the two approaches into a single framework. Another future work will be a closer examination of the measurements provided by the proposed techniques.

6. REFERENCES

[ABR93]

Aloia N., S. Barneva and F. Rabitti, "Supporting physical independence in object databases", *Database Technology*, Vol. 4, No. 4, pp. 265–286.

---

[5] The improvements in software components are highlighted by the ancient hardware!

[6] The *MPL* is the number of active transactions, i.e. transactions that have started but have not yet become committed or aborted. Thus, active transactions are either running or blocked transactions.

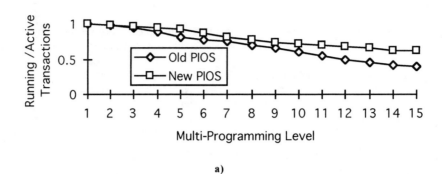

a)

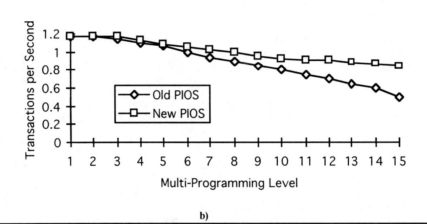

b)

Figure 9: Results of the two experiments

[AB+89]

Atkinson M.P., F. Bancilhon, D. DeWitt, K. Dittrich, D. Maier and S. Zdonik, "The Object–Oriented Database System Manifesto", *Proc. Int. Conf. DOOD* , Kyoto, Japan, pp. 40–57, 1989.

[AB+95]

Amato G., S. Biscari, G. Mainetto and F. Rabitti,"Overview of *PIOS*: a Physically Independent Object Server", in *Fully Integrated Data Environments,* M.P. Atkinson (ed.), 1995. to be published by Springer Verlag.

[ACO85]

Albano A., L. Cardelli and R. Orsini, "Galileo: A strongly typed interactive conceptual language", *ACM Transactions on Database Systems, Vol. 10, N. 2,* pp. 230-260.

[AGM93]

Amato G., F. Giannotti, G. Mainetto,"Data sharing analysis for a database programming language via Abstract Interpretation", *19th International Conference on Very Large Data Base,* Dublin, Ireland, 24-27 August 1993, pp. 405-415.

[BHG87]

Bernstein P., V. Hadzilacos and N. Goodman, *Concurrency Control and Recovery in Database System*, Addison–Wesley, Reading, MA, 1987.

[BOS91]

Butterworth P., A. Otis, J. Stein, "The Gemstone Object Database Management System", *Communication of ACM, Vol. 34, N. 10*, pp. 64–77.

[CF90]

Cart M. and J. Ferriè, "Integrating Concurrency Control into an Object–Oriented Database System", *Proc. Int. Conf. EDBT* , Venice, Italy, pp. 363–377, 1990.

[Das84]

Dasgupta S., *The Design and Description of Computer Architectures*, Wiley, Chichester, UK, 1984.

[GK88]

Garza J. F. and W. Kim, "Transaction Management in an Object–Oriented Database System", *Proc. ACM SIGMOD Intl. Conf. on Management of Data*, Chicago, Illinois, pp. 37–45, 1988.

[GL+75]

Gray J., R. Lorie, G. Putzolu and I. Traiger, "Granularity of locks and degrees of consistency in a shared database", *IBM Res. Rep. RJ1654,* IBM Research Laboratory, San Jose, CA, 1975, also in *Modeling in Database Management Systems*, Nijssen (ed.), North Holland, 1976.

[Gra78]

Gray J., "Notes on Database Operating Systems", *IBM Res. Rep. RJ2188*, IBM Research Laboratory, San Jose, CA also in *Operating Systems – An Advanced Course*, R. Boyer, R. M. Graham and G. Siegmüller (eds.), Springer Verlag, LNCS 60, 1978.

[JT+91]

Joseph J. V., S.M. Thatte, C.W. Thompson and D.L. Wells, "Object-Oriented Databases: Design and Implementation", *Proc. of IEEE*, Vol. 79, No.1, pp. 42-63,1991.

[KB+89]

Kim W., N. Ballou, H. T. Chou, J. F. Garza and D. Woelk, "Features of the ORION Object-Oriented Database." In *Object-Oriented Concepts, Databases, and Applications*, edited by Won Kim and Frederick H. Lochovsky, ACM Press Frontier Series, 1989, pp. 251-282.

[Kim90]

Kim W., *Introduction to Object-Oriented Databases*, The MIT Press, Cambridge, Mass., 1990.

[MC+94]

Munro D.S., R. C. H. Connor, R. Morrison, S. Scheuerl and D.W. Stemple, "Concurrent Shadow Paging in the Flask Archiecture", *Proc. of Sixth Int. Workshop on Persistent Object Systems*, Tarascon, France, September 6-9, 1994, Workshops in Computing, Springer, pp. 16-42.

[Pra84]

Pratt T.W., *Programming Languages: Design and Implementation*, Prentice Hall, Englewood Cliffs, NJ, USA,1984.

[RBD94]

Rabitti F., L. Benedetti and F. Demi, "Query Processing in *PIOS*", *Proc. of Sixth International Workshop on Persistent Object Systems,*Tarascon, France, September 6-9, 1994, Workshops in Computing, Springer, pp. 415-440.

[Wei91]

Weikum G., "Principles and Realization Strategies of Multilevel Transaction Management", *ACM Transactions on Database Systems, Vol. 16, No. 1,* pp. 132–180.

[ZR93]

Zezula P. and F. Rabitti, "Object Store with Navigation Accelerator", *Information Systems, Vol. 18, No. 7*, 1993, pp. 429-460.

Semantic Cardinality Estimation for Queries over Objects [†]

Marian H. Nodine, Mitch Cherniack, Mark H. Nodine

Computer Science Department
Box 1910 Brown University
Providence, RI 02912
{mhn,mfc}@cs.brown.edu

Motorola
5918 West Courtyard Drive
Austin, TX 78730
r31609@email.mot.com

Abstract

In this paper, we address the problem of estimating cardinalities of queries over sets of objects. We base our estimates on a knowledge of subset relationships between sets (e.g., **Students** form a subset of **People**). Previous work on cardinality estimation has assumed that every subset is a representative sample of the set it is taken from. We maintain (offline) information for the cases where the subset is not a uniform representative, and use this information to improve the accuracy of our cardinality estimates.

We present cardinality estimation techniques for *image sets* and *select sets*. Image sets are created by applying a function to an existing set. Select sets contain the elements that satisfy some predicate in an existing set. Empirically we show that we can obtain estimates within a factor of four for reasonable image sets on our test database while maintaining offline statistics requiring space linear in the number of named sets in the database and the number of attributes defined per type. We also present an approach for estimating cardinalities of select sets. Our approach is orthogonal to statistical sampling approaches that give a more accurate estimation of the distribution of values an attribute can take in a set, but do not deal with semantically meaningful subsets whose attributes may not have the same distribution.

1 Introduction

The development of advanced databases such as nested relational databases, complex object bases and object-oriented databases has been motivated by the limited modeling capabilities of other database paradigms. Expressive modeling power is partially achieved by extensible data types and type relationships such as subtyping. Unfortunately, this expressiveness directly impacts the use of heuristics in query optimization. In this paper, we show how information about meaningful data subsets (such as those which are the extents of subtypes) can be used to guide the optimization of an object-oriented query.

Persistent object systems by their nature maintain information about sets and their subsets. For example, given a type hierarchy we know that the extent of some type T is a superset of the extents of each subtype of T. Subtype extents are a special case of *semantically meaningful subsets*. A semantically meaningful subset is **not** a representative sample of its supersets but differs by some characteristic in a statistically significant way. For example, the set of **Students** by nature is distinct from the general set of **People** with respect to age. Other semantically meaningful subsets are formed as a result of queries.

In an advanced database, sometimes the only way to decide whether a transformation would improve the execution time of a query is to compare estimated costs for the original and transformed queries. In this paper, we examine cardinality estimation, which is a prerequisite to accurate cost estimation. We describe techniques to use set and subset information to improve the accuracy of cardinality estimation. We keep information on sets and subsets in an *extent table*. This information includes, for each known extent (and possibly other subsets), its

---

[†]Partial support for this work was provided by the Advanced Research Projects Agency under contract N00014-91-J-4052 ARPA order 8225, and contract DAAB-07-91-C-Q518 under subcontract F41100.

cardinality and its smallest known superset. Also, for each attribute, the extent table includes information used to estimate the number of distinct values that attribute takes in the set.

The extent table helps by allowing us to track natural, non-representative subsets. We can estimate the cardinality of a query result by determining the smallest set that contains the result (the result's *smallest known superset*, or SKS) and using its cardinality information to extrapolate the result set cardinality. If the result's SKS is not much bigger than the result, this should lead to very accurate cardinality estimates.

Also, this approach allows us to maintain better domain information for an attribute. One problem in estimating selectivities is determining the logical domain over which users are going to choose the values to select against. For instance, when determining the selectivity of all the **Students** that have name n, the two potential domains for n are (1) the set of student names and (2) the set of character strings. Neither is a satisfactory approximation. In our scheme we approximate the logical domain of n as the domain of the "name" attribute of **Students**' most general supertype, **People**.

This paper is organized as follows. We present our data model and assumptions in Section 2. We describe our algorithms for maintaining extent information in Section 3. In Section 4, we present our cardinality estimation techniques for mapping[1] and selection queries. Section 5 shows experimental results validating our estimation techniques for mapping query size estimation. We discuss related work in Section 6 and conclude in Section 7.

2 Data Model, Definitions, and Basic Assumptions

2.1 Data Model

We assume an object-like model for the data in our database. This model incorporates features of the nested relational and complex object data models.[2] Every entity in our model is an object. Objects in our model are one of the following:

- *Base objects* are **Boolean**, **String** or **Integer** values.[3]

- *Complex objects* belong to user-defined complex types. These types name sets of *attribute selectors* which when invoked return associated objects.

- *Pair objects* [e, e'] where e and e' are base, complex or pair objects.

- *Function and predicate objects* are invocable with single arguments. We denote arbitrary functions (predicates) with variable names f and g (p and q). Specific functions and predicates are referred to by their bodies, italicizing implicitly lambda-bound variables.

- *Sets* are homogeneous collections of base, complex, or pair objects. We denote sets using capital letters A and B. We use the standard notation $|A|$ to denote the cardinality of a set. We use lower-case letters and primes a, a' to denote elements of the set.

In this paper, we use a sample schema with the types **Person**, **Address** and **City**. **Person** has attributes **firstname**, **lastname**, **address**, **gender**, **age**, **spouse** and **numRoommates**. **Address** has attributes **number**, **street** and **city**. **City** has attributes **name**, **state**, **zip** and **mayor**. We assume that attribute selectors are *unary*, and invoked using dot notation (as in **p.address**). Attribute selectors can be composed to form *path expressions*, as in **p.address.street**. Vector notation (as in $\mathbf{x}.\vec{f}$) denotes an arbitrary path expression.

Our model accounts for two set constructions:

- *Type Extents* are assumed for all base and complex object types. Type extents for base types (named **Integers**, **Booleans** and **Strings**) include constants used in the database. Type extents for complex types include all constructed objects of that type. For a given type extent, if the type's parent is **Object**, it is a *root type extent*. If the type has as its ancestor some root type, the extent is a *subtype extent*. Subtype extents include references to the smallest known superset.

---

[1] Here, mapping applies a function to the elements of a set, and subsumes relational projection.

[2] In fact, this model incorporates object-oriented features with the exception that we do not deal with object mutability.

[3] Currently, we do not support **Real** values in base objects because a bounded set of reals still has an infinite number of values, so our methods for maintaining type extents for **Integers** fail with **Reals**.

Function / Predicate	Example Denotation	Meaning
identity	x	$\lambda\,(x)\,x$
constant	c (c a constant)	$\lambda\,(x)\,c$
path expression	$x.\vec{f}$	$\lambda\,(x)\,x.\vec{f}$
path expression = value	$x.\vec{f} = c$ (c a constant)	$\lambda\,(x)\,x.\vec{f} = c$
path expression $\in$ Set	$x.\vec{f} \in S$ (S a set)	$\lambda(x,y)\,x.\vec{f} \in S$
path expression$_1$ = path expression$_2$	$x.\vec{f} = x.\vec{g}$	$\lambda(x,y)\,x.\vec{f} = x.\vec{g}$
path expression$_1$ $\in$ path expression$_2$	$x.\vec{f} \in x.\vec{g}$	$\lambda(x,y)\,x.\vec{f} \in x.\vec{g}$

Table 1: Allowable bodies of function and predicate arguments to mapping and selection queries.

- *Query Sets* in this paper are restricted to *image sets* and *select sets*.[4] An image set $\tilde{\pi}_f(A)$ is formed by applying the unary function f to each element in the set A, giving the set $\{f(a)|a \in A\}$. If f is a path expression, we also refer to the set $\tilde{\pi}_f(A)$ with the notation $A.\vec{f}$. A select set $\tilde{\sigma}_p(A)$ is formed by filtering out the elements that satisfy the predicate p from the set A, giving the set $\{a|a \in A \wedge p(a)\}$ Table 1 lists the forms of functions and predicates allowed in queries.

2.2 Definitions: Selectivity and Projectivity

The *projectivity* of a function over the elements of a set is the ratio of the size of its range to the size of its domain. Formally:

Definition 2.1 (Projectivity) *For any function f and non-empty set A,* $proj\,(f, A) = \frac{|\tilde{\pi}_f(A)|}{|A|}$.

The *selectivity* of a predicate on a set is the ratio of the number of selected elements of the set to the size of the set. Formally:

Definition 2.2 (Selectivity) *For any predicate p over elements of nonempty set A,* $sel\,(p, A) = \frac{|\tilde{\sigma}_p(A)|}{|A|}$.

2.3 Basic Assumptions: Uniform Ratio and Uniform Distribution

Barring other information, we make a few assumptions about the data in the database. The first is the *uniform ratio assumption*, which is used in cases where we have no information contradicting the assumption that B is a representative subset of A.

Assumption 1 (Uniform Ratio Assumption) *For a given subset B of set A, where A and B are of the same type with attribute f, $proj\,(f, A) \approx proj\,(f, B)$*

The second assumption is the *uniform distribution assumption*:

Assumption 2 (Uniform Distribution Assumption) *For a given set A and path expression $\vec{f}$, and any two values c_1 and c_2 from the image set $\tilde{\pi}_f(A)$, $sel\,(a.\vec{f} = c_1, A) \approx sel\,(a.\vec{f} = c_2, A)$*

The uniform ratio assumption is used when alternative distribution information is not available. It also allows us to transform a selectivity expression into a second one that is approximately equal, but is selecting from an image set. For example, by the uniform distribution assumption, we know for a given constant c in the image set $A.\vec{f}$ that $|\{a \in A \mid a.\vec{f} = c\}| \cdot |A.\vec{f}| \approx |A|$. Because $A.\vec{f}$ is a set, we also know that $|\{a' \in A.\vec{f} \mid a' = c\}| = 1$. Therefore, we can compute the ratio

$$\frac{|\{a \in A \mid a.\vec{f} = c\}|}{|A|} \approx \frac{|\{a' \in A.\vec{f} \mid a' = c\}|}{|A.\vec{f}|},$$

i.e., $sel\,(a' = c, A.\vec{f}) = sel\,(a.\vec{f} = c, A)$. Note that for $c \notin A.\vec{f}$ this last equality also holds trivially, because both selection operations return the empty set. We use this type of transformation in our deductions of selectivities in Section 4.

---

[4]Other query sets have been addressed using this approach, and are written up in [NCN95].

166

Index	Name	Size	Projectivity	SKS	Comments
0	Objects	14477	-	0	The set of all objects
1	Strings	1501	-	0	The set of string literals
2	Ints	1001	-	0	The set of all integer constants used
3	Addresses	3500	-	0	Type extent of `Address`
4	Cities	52	-	0	Type extent of `City`
5	People	9959	-	0	Type extent of `Person`
6	Students	4009	-	5	Type extent of `Student`
7	Grads	1056	-	6	Named Set
8	UGrads	2953	-	6	Named Set
9	Faculty	503	-	5	Named Set
...					
11	Addresses.city	-	0.015	4	Image set
13	Cities.state	-	0.288	1	Image set
20	People.address	-	0.351	3	Image set
25	Students.address	-	0.578	20	Image set
...					
35	UGrads.address	-	0.505	25	Image set
...					

Table 2: An Example Level$_1$ Extent Table

3   Extent Tables

In this section, we consider the statistical and semantic information that we maintain about selected sets in the database for use in estimating cardinalities. This information is maintained in an *extent table*. Our concern is to keep enough information in the extent table to allow for reasonable estimates without making it unwieldy to maintain. To this end, we consider what sets to keep in the table, what information to keep for each set, and how to infer statistical and semantic information for sets not in the table.

The crucial information kept in the extent table concerns the sizes and smallest known supersets of sets and the *projectivity* of functions. Every type extent represented in the extent table has an associated *size* field, while image sets ($\tilde{\pi}_f(A)$) have associated projectivity fields ($proj\ (f, A)$). We maintain projectivities for image sets because they are likely to remain fairly stable with respect to set insertions and deletions, while image set sizes may need to be updated more frequently.

3.1   The Sets Kept in the Table

Extent tables can vary in complexity according to how many and which sets are represented. Every extent table at a minimum has entries for all base, root, and subtype extents as well as all image sets $A.\vec{f}$ where A is a root type extent and $\vec{f}$ is a path expression of length 1. A *minimal extent table* only has this information, and is the smallest one that can be used to estimate cardinalities for all image and select sets. Additional image sets may be kept in the table. We classify the complexities of non-minimal extent tables as follows:

- A *Full Level$_i$ Extent Table* (for $i \geq 1$) includes entries for all image sets, $A.\vec{f}$, where $\vec{f}$ is of length $n \leq i$ and A is a type extent. Table 2 shows a portion of a full level$_1$ extent table based on our example schema. Note that a minimal table would only include the sets indexed from 0–20.

- An *Adaptive Level$_i$ Extent Table* subsumes the minimal extent table and also includes selected image sets for paths of length $n \leq i$. Adaptive level$_i$ extent tables keep track of the subset of the information in the full level$_i$ extent table that cannot be derived accurately from superset information, i.e., minimal extent information plus information on non-representative subsets.

Algorithm 3.1 (Extent Table Maintenance)
```
algorithm update_table (A.f:name of an image set, n:actual size of image set)
    if A.f is not in the extent table then
        use techniques of Section 4.1 to estimate its size, m
        if the estimate is not reasonable,
            add entry for A.f to extent table with projectivity of n/|A| (estimated |A|).
    else
        pretend that A.f is not in the table and use techniques of Section 4.1 to
            estimate its size, m
        if the estimate is reasonable, remove entry for A.f from table
        else update entry for A.f so that projectivity is n/|A| (estimated |A|).
```

Figure 1: Extent Table Maintenance Algorithm

Algorithm 3.2 (SKS)
```
algorithm SKS (s: string) : string // (s is of the form S.m_1. ... .m_n)
    if for some i, Table[i].name = s return (Table[Table[i].sks].name)
    else return (SKS (S.m_1. ... .m_{n-1})||'.'||m_n)
```

Figure 2: Unary Smallest Known Superset (SKS) Algorithm.

3.2 Adaptive Extent Table Maintenance

We propose a simple algorithm to maintain relevant image set information in an adaptive extent table.[5] We envision the algorithm being executed every time normal database activity such as querying or indexing reveals the actual cardinality of an image set. Thus, the maintenance of the extent table should not generate additional database accesses.

The high-level idea behind the algorithm is simple; we want to add all non-representative sample sets to the extent table as we recognize them, and similarly remove all representative sample sets from the extent table. We remove representative sets to save space, because their cardinalities can be derived easily from other information in the extent table.

The pseudocode for an extent table maintenance algorithm is given in Figure 3.1. Here, we assume the designer can specify his own algorithm for deciding whether or not an estimate is a "reasonable approximation".[6] In Section 5 we show empirically that the adaptive maintenance technique can be used to compute reasonable estimates for all sets without demanding an unreasonably large extent table.

3.3 Inference of Supersets

Even with reasonably complex and complete extent tables, cardinalities and projectivities will need to be estimated in some cases. The algorithm for estimating projectivities and cardinalities is described in Section 4.1. In this section we present algorithms for finding the name of the smallest known superset (SKS) for any image set (Figure 2) and the name of the smallest known common superset (SKCS) of any two image sets (Figure 3). Note that both algorithms take set names as inputs and return set names as outputs. This works because the naming scheme for image sets and extents facilitates the search for the SKS and SKCS. Note also that we use the *index* column of the extent table in standard array-like fashion. Therefore, `Table[5]` refers to the entry describing the extent set `People` while `Table[20].ratio` refers to the ratio, *proj* (`address`, `People`). The last line uses string concatenation (||) to form the result.

---

[5] Cardinalities of type extents might be maintained rigorously by updating the extent table at times of insertions, removals, object creations, removals and assignments of constant values. Off-line sampling could used to estimate cardinalities.

[6] Reasonableness means that its error falls within some bounds specified by some input standard error metric.

Algorithm 3.3 (SKCS)

```
algorithm SUBSET? (s₁, s₂:  string) :  Bool
    -- return true if s₁ names a set which is a subset of s₂
        if (s₁ = s₂) return true
        else if (s₁ = ''Objects'') return false
        else return SUBSET? (SKS (s₁), s₂)

algorithm SKCS (s₁, s₂:  string) :  string
    -- finds the smallest known common superset of s₁ and s₂
        if SUBSET? (s₁, s₂) then return s₁
        else if SUBSET? (s₂, s₁) then return s₂
        else return SKCS (SKS (s₁), SKS (s₂))
```

Figure 3: Smallest Known Common Superset (SKCS) Algorithm for Pairs of Sets

The correctness of the SKS algorithm (Figure 2) comes from the observation that the SKS of any image set, $A.f_1. \cdots .f_n$ is the image set formed by applying attribute selector f_n to the set that is the SKS of $A.f_1. \cdots .f_{n-1}$. For example, the SKS of `Students.address.city` is `People.address.city` which in turn has an SKS which is `Addresses.city`. For all type extents or image sets formed from path expressions in the table, this algorithm will find the SKS directly.

The SKCS algorithm is shown in Figure 3, along with the SUBSET? algorithm, which takes the names of two sets as input and returns true if the first names a set which is a subset of the second. The SKCS algorithm computes the smallest known common superset of its input sets. The correctness of this algorithm follows from both the correctness of the SKS algorithm and the partial ordering of the subset relation on sets with `Objects` as the superset of all sets. According to this algorithm

$$\begin{aligned}\text{SKCS(UGrads.address, Faculty.address)} &= \text{SKCS(Students.address, People.address)}\\&= \text{People.address.}\end{aligned}$$

4 Estimating Cardinalities

4.1 Image Sets and Projectivities

Our estimation technique estimates the cardinality of an image set $\tilde{\pi}_f(A)$ by first estimating the projectivity $proj(f, A)$. Projectivity is either looked up directly in the extent table (for image sets of non-representative subsets) or computed using the uniform ratio assumption (for representative subsets). The cardinality of the result of a mapping query that takes the image of function f on set A is $|A| \cdot proj(f, A)$.

In Figure 4 we present an algorithm for estimating the projectivity of any function of the form $x.\mathbf{f}_1. \cdots .\mathbf{f}_n$. The projectivity of the identity function x is 1. For path expressions of length > 1, we look the projectivity up directly if it is in the table, or compute the projectivity from the most accurate information found in the extent table if it is not. The final else clause uses the uniform ratio assumption because no information to the contrary is available. Note that where the uniform ratio assumption does not in fact hold, the result will be incorrect, but the extent table will also be updated with correct information during the processing of the affected query.

Algorithm 4.1 is guaranteed to terminate so long as we have at least a minimal extent table. However, the result will be more accurate when more information is available.

The call of `est_proj(address.city,Students)` in the level₁ extent table of Table 2 proceeds as follows:

$$\begin{aligned}&\text{est\_proj(address.city, Students)}\\&= \text{est\_proj(address, Students)} \cdot \text{est\_proj(city, Students.address)}\\&= \text{est\_proj(address, Students)} \cdot \text{est\_proj(city, Persons.address)}\end{aligned}$$

Algorithm 4.1 (Projectivity)

```
algorithm est_proj (f₁. ... .fₙ:  String, A: String)
    (f₁. ... .fₙ is a path expression, A is the name of a set)
        if A.f₁. ... .fₙ is in the extent table then
            return the projectivity entry in the extent table
        else if ∃k < n such that A.f₁.....fk is in the extent table then
            choose the largest such k and
            return (est_proj (f₁.....fk, A)) · (est_proj (fk+1.....fn, A.f₁. ... .fk)).
        else return (est_proj (f₁.....fn, SKS(A)))
```

Figure 4: Projectivity Estimation Algorithm.

$$= \text{est\_proj(address, Students)} \cdot \text{est\_proj(city, Addresses)}$$
$$= 0.00867$$

Thus, the cardinality of `Students.address.city` is estimated at $|Students| \cdot 0.00867 = 34.75803$.

4.2 Select Sets and Selectivities

Select queries have the form $\tilde{\sigma}_p(A)$ over finite set A, where p is a predicate of one of the forms given in Figure 1. The cardinality of the result of the select query is $|A| \cdot sel(p, A)$. Though this section deals only with simple predicates, other papers (e.g., [SAC+79]) provide techniques for computing selectivities of simple predicates to estimate selectivities for more complex predicates.

Our primary contribution with respect to selectivity is to the extent table information to obtain better bounds on the domain of the attributes of the elements in a set, giving a better estimate for selectivity. We use the extent table information in two ways:

1. To get a better estimate on the number of values an attribute can take on a set using the techniques in the previous section to estimate the projectivity of the attribute.

2. To get a better estimate on the number of values that can be logically chosen to select against by looking up the projectivity of the attribute in the enclosing root type extent.

For two given sets A and B, with elements $a \in A$ and $b \in B$, let $SKCS(A, B)$ be the smallest known common superset of the two sets (which may be the extent of the underlying type). We can derive the following formulae for use in estimating selectivity[7]:

$$|A \cap B| \approx \frac{|A| \cdot |B|}{|\text{SKCS}(A, B)|}$$
$$sel(a \in B, A) \approx \frac{|B|}{|SKCS(A, B)|}$$
$$sel(a = b, A \times B) \approx \frac{1}{|SKCS(A, B)|}$$

4.3 Predicate selectivities

Table 3 summarizes the different forms of predicates defined in Table 1, and shows the formulae for estimating their selectivity. In this table, a is an element of the argument set A, c is some constant not computed from a taken from some set C, and C is some set not computed from elements of A. The first column in the table shows the form of the predicate, the second column the selectivity, the third column an approximately equal selectivity derived

---

[7]The complete derivations can be found in [NCN95].

Predicate form	Selectivity	Equivalent Selectivity	Estimation Formula
$a.\vec{f} = c$	$sel(a.\vec{f} = c, A)$	$sel(a' = c, A.\vec{f})$	$\dfrac{1}{|SKCS(A.\vec{f},C)|}$
$a.\vec{f} \in C$	$sel(a.\vec{f} \in C, A)$	$sel(a' \in C, A.\vec{f})$	$\dfrac{|C|}{|SKCS(A.\vec{f},C)|}$
$a.\vec{f} = a.\vec{g}$	$sel(a.\vec{f} = a.\vec{g}, A)$	$sel(a' = a'', A.\vec{f} \times A.\vec{g})$	$\dfrac{1}{|SKCS(A.\vec{f},A.\vec{g})|}$
$a.\vec{f} \in a.\vec{g}$	$sel(a.\vec{f} \in a.\vec{g}, A)$	$sel(a' \in a'', A.\vec{f} \times A.\vec{g})$	$\dfrac{|A.\vec{g}|}{|SKCS(A.\vec{f},A.\vec{g})|}$

Table 3: Selectivity estimation formulae.

using the uniform distribution assumption, and the fourth column the resulting estimation formula using one of the equations from the previous section. Experiments with the derived formulas, reported in detail in [NCN95] show the promise of this approach.

5 Empirical Results

In order to evaluate the effectiveness of our estimates we implemented Perl scripts to create a sample database and to run mapping queries over it.[8] Our sample database contained 3500 households containing roughly 10000 people from 52 cities. Some of the data were uniform: names, street names, and zip codes. Others were not uniform: ages, states, city names (since the same city can be associated with several zip codes), and the number of residents per household. While we realize that this is a toy database, we observe that the data has many of the characteristics that make size estimation difficult.

Figure 5 shows the accuracy of our estimates for mapping queries. In this experiment, we ran mapping queries using all of the possible 118 path expressions of length ≤ 4 from our database. For each extent table discipline, we give the proportion of queries whose cardinalities were looked up directly, and estimated exactly, to within factors of 1.5, 2, and 4, and worse than a factor of 4. Because the queries were evenly distributed over the data, the "looked up" proportion indicates the relative size of the extent table.

The different extent table disciplines we used were the minimal extent table, $level_1$–$level_3$ with both the full extent table and with replacement when estimates differed by factors of 4, 2, and 1.5, and the full $level_4$ extent table. At $level_4$, all the queries were looked up directly in the extent table, since our queries had lengths 4 or less. As expected, for each level extent table, the accuracy of the estimates improves as the replacement factor μ decreases, with the full extent table providing the most accuracy. Also, as expected, $level_i$ tables in general did better than $level_{i-1}$ tables that used the same replacement factor.

Even with a minimal extent table, we were able to estimate more than half the queries within a factor of 4. As expected, increasing the sizes of a full extent table improves the quality of the results, with a dramatic improvement occurring between $level_2$ and $level_3$. In general, we found that we were able to estimate accurately path expressions of length n with an extent table of length $n-2$. Unfortunately, the size of the full $level_2$ extent table is quite high: approximately three times the size of the minimal extent table. We can get most of the accuracy improvement possible from a full $level_n$ table using an adaptive $level_n$ extent table, while keeping significantly less information. As a guide to deciding an appropriate discipline, the horizontal white line in the figure indicates twice the size of the minimal extent table.

6 Related Work

Most of the literature on cost models deals with relational or extended relational databases. System R [SAC$^+$79] estimates selectivities for relational select, project and join operations using available indices. Where indices are not present, they use an arbitrary constant fraction. We instead use projectivities (which we can always approximate) to estimate selectivities of arbitrary path expressions. Also, they tend to overestimate select set size

---

[8] We have, in fact, run selection queries over the test database as will, with similarly encouraging results.

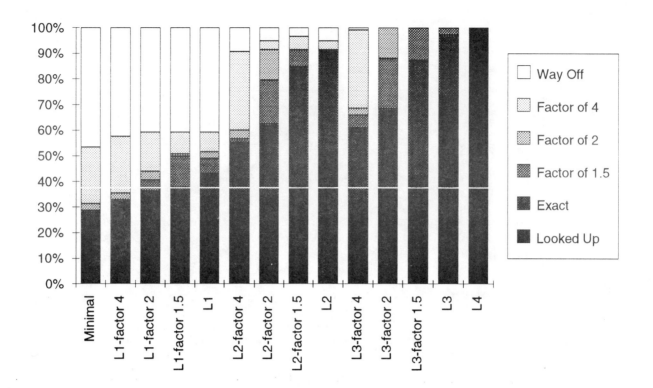

Figure 5: Accuracy of estimates for mapping queries with different extent table disciplines.

because they assume a constant specified by the user is in the set of actual database values for the expression that they compare with the constant. Our approach more accurately assumes that the constant is taken over some logical underlying domain.

Statistical sampling and related techniques are frequently proposed for approximating selectivity and projectivity where the uniform distribution assumption is violated. Such approaches include Hou et.al. [HOD91], Lipton et.al. [LNS90], Haas and Swami [HS92], and Haas et.al [HNSS95]. Histogram techniques [PC84] are also used to improve selectivity estimates. Initial results combining statistical sampling techniques with our semantic estimation techniques is promising.

As an alternative to sampling, Sun et.al. use a regression model to approximate the underlying distribution of the data [SLRD93]. Antisampling techniques [Row85] are based on the premise that it is better to maintain a profile of all the information in the database, and deduce properties of the subsets of that data that are specified by a query from the information in the that profile. They assume that a subset is representative of its superset, and thus maintains the same data distributions.

With respect to optimization of queries over objects, little work has been done on cost and size modeling. At the query level, we only know of the work by Kemper and Moerkotte [KM90], which uses access support relations to derive sizes and cost of path expressions.

7 Conclusions

This paper addresses the problem of estimating cardinalities in persistent object bases. We observed that persistent object bases maintain natural set-subset relationships among the type extents of the types in the type hierarchy. We use this (and other) subset information to make more accurate cardinality estimations for query results. In this paper, we make the following contributions:

- We use *semantic* information to the schema manager (specifically inclusion relationships between sets) to infer cardinality estimates on the basis of known sizes of related sets.

- We propose a method for *adaptively* maintaining the information required for estimation in an extent table. We show empirically that an extent table need not be large but only intelligently maintained to allow for accurate cardinality estimation. In particular, keeping entries only for non-representative sample sets can be efficient and effective for estimating both image and select set cardinalities.

- We propose a more accurate method for estimating selectivities within the context of the uniform distribution assumption. This method uses image set cardinalities for root type extents to approximate the size of the domain over which users specify the values to select against.

Two areas of current and future work include better methods for estimating selectivities, and expanding this work to other complex object query operations. [NCN95] presents results for join and grouping queries.

References

[HNSS95] Peter J. Haas, Jeffrey Naughton, S. Sechadri, and Lynne Stokes. Sampling-based estimation of the number of distinct values of an attribute. In *Proceedings of the 21st VLDB Conference*, pages 311–322, 1995.

[HOD91] W.-C. Hou, G. Ozsoyoglu, and E. Dogdu. Error-constrained count query evaluation in a relational database. In *Proceedings of the ACM SIGMOD International Conference on Management of Data*, pages 279–287. ACM, 1991.

[HS92] Peter J. Haas and Arun N. Swami. Sequential sampling procedures for query size estimation. In *Proceedings of the ACM SIGMOD International Conference on Management of Data*, pages 341–350, 1992.

[KM90] Alfons Kemper and Guido Moerkotte. Access support in object bases. In *Proceedings of the ACM SIGMOD International Conference on Management of Data*, pages 364–374, 1990.

[LNS90] R. J. Lipton, J. F. Naughton, and D. A. Schneider. Practical selectivity estimation through adaptive sampling. In *Proceedings of the ACM SIGMOD International Conference on Management of Data*, pages 1–11, 1990.

[NCN95] Marian H. Nodine, Mitch Cherniack, and Mark H. Nodine. Semantic cardinality estimation for object-oriented queries. Technical Report CS-95-35, Brown University Department of Computer Science, December 1995.

[PC84] Gregory Piatesky-Shapiro and Charles Cornell. Accurate estimation of the number of tuples satisfying a condition. In *Proceedings of the ACM SIGMOD International Conference on Management of Data*, pages 256–276. ACM Press, 1984.

[Row85] Neil C. Rowe. Antisampling for estimation: An overview. *IEEE Transactions on Software Engineering*, SE-11(10):1081–1091, October 1985.

[SAC+79] P. Griffiths Selinger, M.M. Astrahan, D. D. Chamberlin, R. A. Lorie, and T. G. Price. Access path selection in a relational database management system. In *Proceedings of the ACM SIGMOD International Conference on Management of Data*, pages 23–34, 1979.

[SLRD93] Wei Sun, Yibei Ling, Naphtali Rishe, and Yi Deng. An instant and accurate size estimation method for joins and selection in a retrieval-intensive environment. In *Proceedings of the ACM SIGMOD International Conference on Management of Data*, pages 79–88. ACM, 1993.

Residency check elimination for object-oriented persistent languages

Antony L. Hosking*
hosking@cs.purdue.edu
Department of Computer Sciences
Purdue University
West Lafayette, IN 47907-1398, USA

Abstract

We explore the ramifications of object residency assumptions and their impact on residency checking for several subroutine dispatch scenarios: procedural, static object-oriented, and dynamic (virtual) object-oriented. We obtain dynamic counts of the residency checks necessary for execution of several benchmark persistent programs under each of these scenarios. The results reveal that significant reductions in the number of residency checks can be achieved through application of residency rules derived from the dispatch scenario under which a program executes, as well as additional constraints specific to the language in which it is implemented.

Keywords: residency checks, optimization, object-orientation, static/dynamic dispatch

1 Introduction

Persistent programming languages view permanent storage as a stable extension of volatile memory, in which objects may be dynamically allocated, but which persists from one invocation to the next. A persistent programming language and object store together preserve *object identity*: every object has a unique identifier (in essence an address, possibly abstract, in the store), objects can refer to other objects, forming graph structures, and they can be modified, with such modifications being visible in future accesses using the same unique object identifier. Access to persistent objects is *transparent* (at least from the programmer's perspective), without requiring explicit calls to read and write them. Rather, the language implementation and run-time system contrive to make objects resident in memory on demand, much as non-resident pages are automatically made resident by a paged virtual memory system.

Treating persistence as orthogonal to type [ABC+83] has important ramifications for the design of persistent programming languages, since it encourages the view that a language can be extended to support persistence with minimal disturbance of its existing syntax and store semantics. The notion of persistent storage as a stable extension of the dynamic allocation heap allows a uniform and transparent treatment of both transient and persistent data, with persistence being orthogonal to the way in which data is defined, allocated, and manipulated. This characterization of persistence allows us to identify the fundamental mechanisms that any transparent persistent system must support. Notable among these is the need for some kind of *residency check* to trigger retrieval of non-resident objects.

To be widely accepted, orthogonal persistence must exhibit sufficiently good performance to justify its inclusion as an important feature of any good programming language. We offer evidence that orthogonal persistence can be added to an object-oriented language without compromising performance. Our focus is on avoiding residency checks on objects when their residency can be guaranteed by the context in which their references are used. We consider several scenarios under which residency checks can be eliminated, and characterize the execution of a suite of benchmark persistent programs for each scenario in terms of the number of residency checks incurred by the benchmark. The scenarios represent a spectrum of styles of execution: procedural (i.e., non-object-oriented); object-oriented with static binding of methods to call sites; and object-oriented with dynamic method dispatch.

The remainder of the paper is organized as follows. We begin by reviewing object faulting and residency checking, followed by a description of the execution scenarios we consider. A discussion of the experimental framework follows, including description of the prototype persistent Smalltalk implementation used for the experiments, the benchmark programs and metrics used for evaluation, and presentation of results. Finally, we offer brief conclusions.

---

*See also: http://www.cs.purdue.edu/people/hosking. This work was supported by Sun Microsystems, Inc.

2 Object faulting and residency checking

As in traditional database systems, a persistent system caches frequently-accessed data in memory for efficient manipulation. Because (even virtual) memory may be a relatively scarce resource, it is reasonable to suppose that there will be much more persistent data than can be cached at once. Thus, the persistent system must arrange to make resident just those objects needed by the program for execution. Without knowing in advance which data is needed, the system must load objects on demand, from the persistent object store into memory. An *object fault* is an attempt to use a non-resident object. It relies on *residency checks*, which can be implemented explicitly in software, or performed implicitly in hardware and giving rise to some kind of hardware trap for non-resident objects. A wide range of object faulting schemes have been devised,[1] each having different representations for references to persistent objects. Some approaches drive all faulting with memory protection traps and make object faulting entirely transparent to compiled code; these have only one representation: virtual memory pointers to apparently resident objects. However, there is evidence to suggest that such totally transparent schemes do not always offer the best performance [HMS92, HM93a, HM93b, HBM93, Hos95, HM95]. Thus, multiple representations arise for references to resident objects (which can be used without causing an object fault), versus references to non-resident objects, along with explicit residency checks to distinguish them.

Efficient implementation of residency checks is one key to implementing a high-performance persistent programming language. The mechanism must be sufficiently lightweight as to represent only marginal overhead to frequently-executed operations on fine-grained objects. Nevertheless, even marginal overhead will have a cumulatively significant impact on overall performance. Thus, any opportunity should be exploited to elide residency checks where they are not strictly necessary [HM90, HM91, MH94]. Such optimizations rely on data flow analysis and code transformations (e.g., hoisting or combining residency checks) and the imposition of special rules about the residency of particular objects. Example rules and their ramifications include:

Pinning: *Objects once resident are guaranteed to remain resident so long as they are directly referenced from the machine registers and activation stacks (i.e., local variables).*

> Thus, repeated residency checks on the same object referenced by a local variable can be merged into one check the first time the object is accessed through the variable.

Target residency: *The first argument of an object-oriented method call (i.e., the target object) will (somehow) automatically be made resident at the time of the call and remain so throughout.*

> Thus, methods need not contain checks on the residency of their target object.

Coresidency: *Whenever object a is resident so also must object b be resident. This constraint is written $a \rightarrow b$.*

> Thus, if a contains a reference to b, then b can be accessed directly from a (i.e., the reference from a to b can be traversed) without a residency check. Since a is resident as the source of the reference to b the coresidency constraint means that b will also be resident. For swizzling purposes, the reference from a to b is always represented as a direct memory pointer. Note that coresidency is asymmetric: $a \rightarrow b \not\Rightarrow b \rightarrow a$.

Pinning can be assumed to apply in all situations, since it enables all other residency check optimizations – in its absence no local variable can be guaranteed to refer to a resident object despite prior residency checks on that reference. The effect of the *target residency* and *coresidency* rules on the number of residency checks executed by a program is the topic of this paper. We consider several rule scenarios and measure the number of residency checks required under each scenario for execution of a suite of object-oriented persistent benchmark programs.

3 Execution scenarios

The residency rules to be applied at run-time dictate statically where residency checks are needed and where they can be elided. Our experiments include results for the following general execution scenarios:

Procedural: Execution in a non-object-oriented procedural language proceeds through the invocation of statically determined procedures. Ignoring possibilities for optimization of residency checks based on local/global data flow analysis, every dereference requires a residency check.

---

[1][ACC82, BC86, KK83, Kae86, CM84, RMS88, SMR89, BBB+88, Ric89, RC90, Ric90, SCD90, WD92, HMB90, Hos91, HM93a, LLOW91, SKW92, WK92]

Static OO: Object-oriented programs execute through the invocation of methods on objects. A method typically accesses the encapsulated state of its target object. Thus, applying the *pinning* and *target residency* rules eliminates all residency checks on the target object of a method. Instead, a residency check on the target must be performed at the time the method is invoked, unless the method invocation is directed at the caller's own target object, in which case no check is needed. For non-virtual (i.e., statically bound) methods the method code is invoked directly so the target residency check must be performed explicitly prior to the call.

Dynamic OO: A defining feature of object-oriented languages is their support for inclusion polymorphism through mechanisms such as subclassing, subtyping and inheritance. Such polymorphism means that a given call site may involve target objects of any number of different but compatible types/classes. For virtual (i.e., dynamically dispatched) methods, the particular method code to be invoked is determined dynamically based on the type/class of the target object. Once again, we assume both *pinning* and *target residency*, but it is now possible to fold the target residency check into the dynamic method dispatch mechanism. The precise approach depends on the nature of the mechanism, but in general there is no additional overhead due to residency checking. Rather, the inherent indirection of dynamic dispatch is subverted, so that method invocations on non-resident objects are directed first to proxy faulting routines that make the target object resident, before forwarding the call to the appropriate resident object method. Again, no target object residency checks are necessary in the called method.

Note that although optimizations [Cha92, HU94, CG94, Fer95, DGC95, GDGC95, DMM96] may convert many indirect calls to direct calls, so increasing the number of explicit checks required, it is also likely that similarly aggressive optimizations can discover and eliminate redundant residency checks through intra- and inter-procedural data flow analysis.

In addition to these general scenarios regarding target object residency, a given program may benefit from *coresidency* rules that allow further elimination of residency checks. Such rules depend on the particular execution patterns of a given program. We consider the effect of specific coresidency rules below in the context of the prototype persistent system used in the experiments.

4 Experiments

We have instrumented the execution of several benchmark persistent programs executing in our prototype persistent Smalltalk system [Hos95] to obtain dynamic counts of residency checks performed under each of the above scenarios. We also consider the effect of additional coresidency constraints arising from specific knowledge of Smalltalk's bytecode instruction set and execution semantics.

4.1 A prototype implementation: Persistent Smalltalk

The prototype is an implementation of Smalltalk [GR83], extended for persistence. It has two components: a *virtual machine* and a *virtual image*.

The virtual machine implements the bytecode instruction set to which Smalltalk source code is compiled, along with certain *primitive methods* whose functionality is built directly into the virtual machine. These typically provide low-level access to the underlying hardware and operating system on which the virtual machine is implemented. For example, low-level floating point and integer arithmetic, indexed access to the fields of array objects, and object allocation, are all supported as primitives. A primitive method is invoked in exactly the same way as an ordinary method expressed as a sequence of Smalltalk expressions, but its implementation is not a compiled method. Rather, the virtual machine performs the primitive directly, without the need for a separate Smalltalk activation record. Since the primitives are coded by hand in the virtual machine, we are also able to hand-optimize the primitives to remove redundant checks. The compiler in a compiled persistent language might discover the same optimizations automatically through intra-procedural data flow analysis.

The virtual image is derived from Xerox PARC's Smalltalk-80 image, version 2.1, with minor modifications. It implements (in Smalltalk) all the functionality of a Smalltalk development environment, including editors, browsers, a debugger, the bytecode compiler, class libraries, etc. – all are first-class objects in the Smalltalk sense. Bootstrapping a (non-persistent) Smalltalk environment entails loading the entire virtual image into memory for execution by the virtual machine.

The persistent implementation of Smalltalk places the virtual image in the persistent store, and the environment is bootstrapped by loading just that subset of the objects in the image sufficient for resumption of execution by the virtual machine.

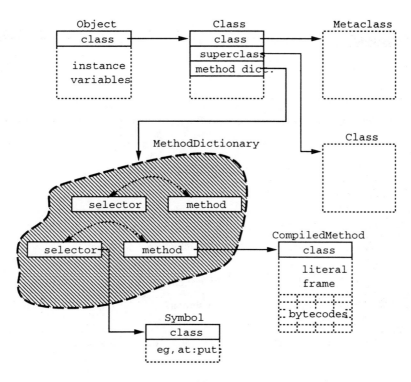

Figure 1: Objects, classes, inheritance, and method dispatch

We retain the original bytecode instruction set and make only minor modifications to the virtual image. Rather, our efforts focus on the virtual machine, which is carefully augmented with residency checks to fault objects into memory as they are needed by the executing image. The precise location of residency checks depends on the particular execution scenario.

4.1.1 Smalltalk method dispatch

A Smalltalk *object* (see Figure 1) is an encapsulation of some private state and a set of operations called its *interface*. The private state consists of a number of data fields, called *instance variables*, directly accessible only from the code implementing the object's operations. Every object is an *instance* of some *class* object, which implements the common behavior of all its instances; a class object is itself an instance of its *metaclass*. Classes are arranged in a hierarchy, such that a *subclass* will *inherit* instance behavior from its *superclass*. Thus, an instance of the subclass will behave as an instance of the superclass, except where the subclass overrides or extends that behavior.

Computation in Smalltalk proceeds through the sending of *messages* to objects. A message consists of a *message selector* (e.g., at:put:) and a number of arguments, and represents a request to an object to carry out one of its operations. The effect of sending a message is to invoke one of the *methods* of the object receiving the message (the *receiver*). Invoking a method may be thought of as a procedure call, with the receiver being the first argument to the procedure, preceding the arguments specified in the message. The particular method to execute is determined dynamically, using the message selector and the class of the receiver. Each class object contains a reference to a *method dictionary*, associating message selectors with *compiled methods*. A compiled method consists of the virtual machine bytecode instructions that implement the method, along with a *literal frame*, containing the shared variables,[2] constants, and message selectors referred to by the method's bytecodes.

Determining which method to execute in response to the sending of a message proceeds as follows. If the method dictionary of the receiver's class contains the message selector, then its associated method is invoked. Otherwise, the search continues in the superclass of the object, and so on, up the class hierarchy. If there is no matching selector in any of the method dictionaries in the hierarchy then a run-time error occurs.

---

[2] A shared variable is an object that encapsulates a reference to another object. If the contents of the variable are changed, then the change is visible to all other compiled methods holding references to that shared variable.

As described so far, the method lookup process is very expensive, especially since a given message may be implemented by a method in a class that is high up in the superclass hierarchy, far removed from the class of the receiver. A *method lookup cache* reduces this lookup cost significantly. A valid entry in the cache contains object references for a selector, a class, and a compiled method. Message sends first consult the method lookup cache, by hashing the object references of the selector and the receiver's class to index an entry in the cache. If the selector and class of the cache entry match those of the message, then the cached compiled method is invoked directly. Otherwise, the full method lookup locates the compiled method and loads the cache entry with the selector, class and method, before invoking the method.

4.1.2 The bytecode instruction set

We retain the standard Smalltalk-80 bytecode instruction set [GR83], which is partitioned by functionality as follows:

Stack bytecodes move object references between the evaluation stack of the current activation and:

1. the named instance variables of the receiver for that activation
2. the temporary variables local to that activation
3. the shared variables of the literal frame of the active method

Jump bytecodes change the instruction pointer of the current activation

Send bytecodes invoke compiled or primitive methods

Return bytecodes terminate execution of the current activation, and return control to the calling activation

4.2 Benchmarks

The performance evaluation draws on the OO1 object operations benchmarks [CS92] to compare the alternative execution scenarios. The operations are retrieval-oriented and operate on substantial data structures, although the benchmarks themselves are simple, and so easily understood. Their execution patterns include phases of intensive computation so that memory residence is important.

4.2.1 Benchmark database

The OO1 benchmark database consists of a collection of 20,000 *part* objects, indexed by part numbers in the range 1 through 20,000, with exactly three *connections* from each part to other parts. The connections are randomly selected to produce some locality of reference: 90% of the connections are to the "closest" 1% of parts, with the remainder being made to any randomly chosen part. Closeness is defined as parts with the numerically closest part numbers. We implement the part database and the benchmarks entirely in Smalltalk, including the B-tree used to index the parts.

The part objects are 68 bytes in size (including the object header). The three outgoing connections are stored directly in the part objects. The string fields associated with each part and connection are represented by references to separate Smalltalk objects of 24 bytes each. Similarly, a part's incoming connections are represented as a separate Smalltalk Array object containing references to the parts that are the source of each incoming connection. The B-tree index for the 20,000 parts consumes around 165KB.

4.2.2 Benchmark operations

The OO1 benchmarks comprise three separate operations:

Lookup fetches 1,000 randomly chosen parts from the database. A null procedure is invoked for each part, taking as its arguments the *x*, *y*, and *type* fields of the part (to ensure the part is actually made resident).

Traversal fetches all parts connected to a randomly chosen part, or to any part connected to it, up to seven hops (for a total of 3,280 parts, with possible duplicates). Similar to the Lookup benchmark, a null procedure is invoked for each part, taking as its arguments the *x*, *y*, and *type* fields of the part. OO1 also specifies a *reverse* Traversal operation, Reverse, which swaps "from" and "to" directions. Reverse is of minimal practical use because the random nature of connections means that the number of "from" connections varies among the parts – while every part has three *outgoing* connections, the number of *incoming* connections varies randomly. Thus, different iterations of the Reverse vary randomly in the number of objects they traverse, and so the amount of work they perform.

Insert allocates 100 new parts in the database, each with three connections to randomly selected parts as described in Section 4.2.1 (i.e., applying the same rules for locality of reference). The index structure must be updated, and the entire set of changes committed to disk.

Although this operation is a reasonable measure of update overhead, it is hampered by a lack of control over the number and distribution of the locations modified, and its mixing of updates to parts and the index. A more easily controlled benchmark is the following:

Update [WD92] operates in the same way as the Traversal measure, but instead of calling a null procedure it performs a simple update to each part object encountered, with some fixed probability. The update consists of incrementing the x and y scalar integer fields of the part. All changes must be reflected back to the persistent store. Here, the probability of update can vary from one run to the next to change the frequency and density of updates.

These benchmarks are intended to be representative of the data operations in many engineering applications. The Lookup benchmark emphasizes selective retrieval of objects based on their attributes, while the Traversal benchmark illuminates the cost of raw pointer traversal. The Update variant measures the costs of modifying objects and making those changes permanent. Additionally, the Insert benchmark measures both update overhead and the cost of creating new persistent objects.

4.3   Metrics

We obtain dynamic counts of the number of residency checks necessary for the execution of the benchmark operations using an instrumented version of the Smalltalk virtual machine. A benchmark *run* consists of ten iterations of the benchmark operation. Because each successive iteration accesses a *different* set of random parts, we characterize each benchmark in terms of the mean number of residency checks for the 10 iterations of the run, and calculate 90% confidence intervals to bound the variation among random iterations. Using different counters for each possible scenario enables the results for all scenarios to be gathered with just one run of each benchmark. Thus, each scenario sees the same run of random iterations.

4.4   Results

The initial statement of results ignores residency check counts attributable to Smalltalk's idiosyncratic treatment of classes, activation records, compiled methods, and process stacks as (orthogonally persistent) objects in their own right. Thus, the counts do not reflect residency checks needed when ascending the class hierarchy during method lookup for dynamic method dispatch, nor residency checks on processes and stacks during process management, and checks on activation records during returns. We do this so as to obtain the closest possible analogy to more traditional languages such as C, C^{++} and Modula-3, in which dynamic method dispatch is implemented as an indirect call through a method table associated with the target object, and which do not treat processes, activations, and classes/types as first-class objects. The intricacies of residency checks for such complications are discussed later.

The results appear in Table 1, with columns for each of the execution scenarios, and rows for each benchmark. The number of residency checks required for execution of the benchmark under each execution scenario appears along with the fraction of checks that can be elided in light of the scenario's residency rules. We also indicate the percentage of method invocations that result in primitive method executions. Recall that primitive methods are hand-optimized to minimize the number of residency checks necessary for their execution based on the access patterns of the primitive. Also, only primitives can directly access objects other than the target object; non-primitives must instead invoke a method on non-target objects. Thus, *target residency* optimizations are likely to be more effective when the ratio of primitives to non-primitives is low, since fewer non-target accesses will occur.

It is clear that the *target residency* rule significantly reduces the number of checks necessary under the object-oriented execution scenarios. The statically dispatched scenario, for which method invocations on objects other than the caller's target require a check, is able to eliminate 24–75% of checks, depending on the benchmark. The remaining checks are necessary

Benchmark	Execution scenario								Primitives versus non-primitives
	Procedural		Static OO		Dynamic OO				
	Checks	elided	Checks		elided	Checks		elided	
Lookup	44661± 29	0%	22330±	15	50%	1002±	0	97%	83%
Traversal	13158± 0	0%	3275±	8	75%	1±	0	99%	0%
Reverse	28106±8238	0%	13234±3884		52%	5880±1725		79%	33%
Update									
0%	12855± 0	0%	9738±	8	24%	1694±	0	86%	56%
5%	13481± 77	0%	9738±	8	27%	1694±	0	87%	56%
10%	14104± 101	0%	9738±	8	30%	1694±	0	87%	56%
15%	14753± 114	0%	9738±	8	33%	1694±	0	88%	56%
20%	15437± 110	0%	9738±	8	36%	1694±	0	89%	56%
50%	19311± 96	0%	9738±	8	49%	1694±	0	91%	56%
100%	25975± 0	0%	9738±	8	52%	1694±	0	93%	56%
Insert	30557± 423	0%	20026± 393		34%	2203± 122		92%	82%

(interval confidence is 90%)

Table 1: Residency checks by execution scenario and benchmark

because of invocations on objects other than the caller's target, and primitive accesses to objects other than the primitive callee's target.

The dynamic scenario eliminates the need for all checks on method invocation since target residency checking is folded into the indirect, dynamic method dispatch. As a result, this scenario requires 86–99% fewer residency checks than for procedural execution. The remaining checks are necessary as a result of primitive access to objects other than the target. In fact, it turns out that for these benchmarks the remaining checks are solely on arguments to primitives. The variation in the ratio of primitive to non-primitive checks illustrates this directly – where the primitive fraction is low (as in Traversal), a higher fraction of the checks are elided.[3]

4.5 Smalltalk complications

As mentioned earlier, there are additional complications for a persistent Smalltalk implementation, arising out of Smalltalk's treatment of control objects such as processes, activation stacks, and classes as first-class objects that can themselves persist. We add *coresidency* rules to eliminate checks on these objects as follows:

Class coresidency: An object's class is always coresident with each of its instances. Thus, the send bytecodes need not perform a residency check on the target object's class when probing the method lookup cache.

Sender coresidency: For any stack frame object, the stack frame representing its sender (i.e., calling) activation is always coresident. Applying this rule transitively results in all activations in a process stack being coresident – when an active stack frame is made resident (usually because its process is being resumed), its caller, its caller's caller, and so on up the process stack, are made resident along with it. Since the return bytecodes directly manipulate the active stack frame and the (calling) activation to which control is being returned, sender coresidency eliminates the need for a residency check on the caller in the return bytecodes.

Method coresidency: Methods are always coresident with their activation's stack frame, since an activation can only execute if its corresponding compiled method is resident. Thus, return bytecodes need not check the residency of the method in which execution resumes.

Literal coresidency: Literals are always coresident with the methods that refer to them. They include the selectors, constants and shared variables directly manipulated by the bytecodes of the method. Send bytecodes directly access literal selectors and certain stack bytecodes directly access shared variables. Thus, these bytecodes need not check the residency of the literals they manipulate.

---

[3]Multi-methods, as in Cecil [Cha95], in which method dispatch occurs on more than one argument of the method, would submit to folding of residency checks on all qualified arguments into the indirection of dispatch.

These special coresidency rules for Smalltalk force preloading of objects critical to the forward progress of computation, so that *all bytecode instructions of the persistent virtual machine execute without residency checks*. The persistent virtual machine must still check the residency of objects whose residency is not guaranteed by these rules. For example, full method lookup requires checks as it ascends the class hierarchy, to ensure that the superclasses and their method dictionaries are resident. Similarly, primitive methods must perform residency checks on objects they access directly (excluding the receiver, guaranteed resident by the *target residency* rule).

5 Conclusions

We examined the impact of several execution scenarios on the residency checks necessary for execution of several instrumented benchmark programs. The results indicate that the object-oriented execution paradigm enables a significant reduction in residency checks through the simple application of the target object residency rule. In addition, coresidency constraints specific to the persistent Smalltalk prototype allow a further reduction in the number of checks required, so that the bytecode instructions of the persistent Smalltalk virtual machine are able to execute without any residency checks at all. It would be interesting to consider the application of similar techniques for persistence to other dynamic object-oriented languages, such as Java [Sun95a, Sun95b].

A particularly promising avenue of further research is how optimization can both hinder (e.g., through aggressive elimination of dynamic method dispatch) and promote (e.g., through exploitation of coresidency rules specific to the application program, as well as discovery of residency invariants through data flow analysis) the elimination of residency checks.

References

[ABC+83] M. P. Atkinson, P. J. Bailey, K. J. Chisholm, P. W. Cockshott, and R. Morrison. An approach to persistent programming. *The Computer Journal*, 26(4):360–365, November 1983.

[ACC82] Malcolm Atkinson, Ken Chisolm, and Paul Cockshott. PS-Algol: an Algol with a persistent heap. *ACM SIGPLAN Notices*, 17(7):24–31, July 1982.

[BBB+88] Francois Bancilhon, Gilles Barbedette, Véronique Benzaken, Claude Delobel, Sophie Gamerman, Christophe Lécluse, Patrick Pfeffer, Philippe Richard, and Fernando Velez. The design and implementation of O_2, an object-oriented database system. In Dittrich [Dit88], pages 1–22.

[BC86] A. L. Brown and W. P. Cockshott. The CPOMS persistent object management system. Technical Report Persistent Programming Research Project 13, University of St. Andrews, Scotland, 1986.

[CG94] Brad Calder and Dirk Grunwald. Reducing indirect function call overhead in C++ programs. In *Conference Record of the ACM Symposium on Principles of Programming Languages*, pages 397–408, Portland, Oregon, January 1994.

[Cha92] Craig Chambers. *The design and implementation of the SELF compiler, an optimizing compiler for object-oriented programming languages*. PhD thesis, Stanford University, 1992.

[Cha95] Craig Chambers. The CECIL language: specification and rationale. Version 2.0. http://www.cs.washington.edu/research/projects/cecil/www/Papers/cecil-spec.html, December 1995.

[CM84] George Copeland and David Maier. Making Smalltalk a database system. In *Proceedings of the ACM International Conference on Management of Data*, pages 316–325, Boston, Massachusetts, June 1984.

[CS92] R. G. G. Cattell and J. Skeen. Object operations benchmark. *ACM Transactions on Database Systems*, 17(1):1–31, March 1992.

[DGC95] Jeffrey Dean, David Grove, and Craig Chambers. Optimization of object-oriented programs using static class hierarchy analysis. In *Proceedings of the European Conference on Object-Oriented Programming*, Aarhus, Denmark, August 1995.

[Dit88] K. R. Dittrich, editor. *Proceedings of the International Workshop on Object Oriented Database Systems*, volume 334 of *Lecture Notes in Computer Science*, Bad Münster am Stein-Ebernburg, Germany, September 1988. *Advances in Object-Oriented Database Systems*, Springer-Verlag, 1988.

[DMM96]   Amer Diwan, J. Eliot B. Moss, and Kathryn S. McKinley. Simple and effective analysis of statically-typed object-oriented programs. In *Proceedings of the ACM Conference on Object-Oriented Programming Systems, Languages, and Applications*, San Jose, California, October 1996.

[DSZ90]   Alan Dearle, Gail M. Shaw, and Stanley B. Zdonik, editors. *Proceedings of the International Workshop on Persistent Object Systems*, Martha's Vineyard, Massachusetts, September 1990. *Implementing Persistent Object Bases: Principles and Practice*, Morgan Kaufmann, 1990.

[Fer95]   Mary F. Fernandez. Simple and effective link-time optimization of Modula-3 programs. In *Proceedings of the ACM Conference on Programming Language Design and Implementation*, pages 103–115, La Jolla, California, June 1995.

[GDGC95]   David Grove, Jeffrey Dean, Charles Garrett, and Craig Chambers. Profile-guided receiver class prediction. In *Proceedings of the ACM Conference on Object-Oriented Programming Systems, Languages, and Applications*, pages 108–123, Austin, Texas, October 1995.

[GR83]   Adele Goldberg and David Robson. *Smalltalk-80: The Language and its Implementation*. Addison-Wesley, 1983.

[HBM93]   Antony L. Hosking, Eric Brown, and J. Eliot B. Moss. Update logging for persistent programming languages: A comparative performance evaluation. In *Proceedings of the International Conference on Very Large Data Bases*, pages 429–440, Dublin, Ireland, August 1993. Morgan Kaufmann.

[HM90]   Antony L. Hosking and J. Eliot B. Moss. Towards compile-time optimisations for persistence. In Dearle et al. [DSZ90], pages 17–27.

[HM91]   Antony L. Hosking and J. Eliot B. Moss. Compiler support for persistent programming. Technical Report 91-25, Department of Computer Science, University of Massachusetts at Amherst, March 1991.

[HM93a]   Antony L. Hosking and J. Eliot B. Moss. Object fault handling for persistent programming languages: A performance evaluation. In *Proceedings of the ACM Conference on Object-Oriented Programming Systems, Languages, and Applications*, pages 288–303, Washington, DC, October 1993.

[HM93b]   Antony L. Hosking and J. Eliot B. Moss. Protection traps and alternatives for memory management of an object-oriented language. In *Proceedings of the ACM Symposium on Operating Systems Principles*, pages 106–119, Asheville, North Carolina, December 1993.

[HM95]   Antony L. Hosking and J. Eliot B. Moss. Lightweight write detection and checkpointing for fine-grained persistence. Technical Report 95-084, Department of Computer Sciences, Purdue University, December 1995.

[HMB90]   Antony L. Hosking, J. Eliot B. Moss, and Cynthia Bliss. Design of an object faulting persistent Smalltalk. Technical Report 90-45, Department of Computer Science, University of Massachusetts at Amherst, May 1990.

[HMS92]   Antony L. Hosking, J. Eliot B. Moss, and Darko Stefanović. A comparative performance evaluation of write barrier implementations. In *Proceedings of the ACM Conference on Object-Oriented Programming Systems, Languages, and Applications*, pages 92–109, Vancouver, Canada, October 1992.

[Hos91]   Antony L. Hosking. Main memory management for persistence, October 1991. Position paper presented at the OOPSLA'91 Workshop on Garbage Collection.

[Hos95]   Antony L. Hosking. *Lightweight Support for Fine-Grained Persistence on Stock Hardware*. PhD thesis, University of Massachusetts at Amherst, February 1995. Available as Department of Computer Science Technical Report 95-02.

[HU94]   Urs Hölzle and David Ungar. Optimizing dynamically-dispatched calls with run-time type feedback. In *Proceedings of the ACM Conference on Programming Language Design and Implementation*, pages 326–336, Orlando, Florida, June 1994.

[Kae86]   Ted Kaehler. Virtual memory on a narrow machine for an object-oriented language. In *Proceedings of the ACM Conference on Object-Oriented Programming Systems, Languages, and Applications*, pages 87–106, Portland, Oregon, September 1986.

[KK83]   Ted Kaehler and Glenn Krasner. LOOM—large object-oriented memory for Smalltalk-80 systems. In Glenn Krasner, editor, *Smalltalk-80: Bits of History, Words of Advice*, chapter 14, pages 251–270. Addison-Wesley, 1983.

[LLOW91]   Charles Lamb, Gordon Landis, Jack Orenstein, and Dan Weinreb. The ObjectStore database system. *Communications of the ACM*, 34(10):50–63, October 1991.

[MH94]   J. Eliot B. Moss and Antony L. Hosking. Expressing object residency optimizations using pointer type annotations. In Malcolm Atkinson, David Maier, and Véronique Benzaken, editors, *Proceedings of the International Workshop on Persistent Object Systems*, Workshops in Computing, pages 3–15, Tarascon, France, September 1994. Springer-Verlag, 1995.

[RC90]   Joel E. Richardson and Michael J. Carey. Persistence in the E language: Issues and implementation. *Software: Practice and Experience*, 19(12):1115–1150, December 1990.

[Ric89]   Joel Edward Richardson. *E: A Persistent Systems Implementation Language*. PhD thesis, University of Wisconsin – Madison, August 1989. Available as Computer Sciences Technical Report 868.

[Ric90]   Joel E. Richardson. Compiled item faulting: A new technique for managing I/O in a persistent language. In Dearle et al. [DSZ90], pages 3–16.

[RMS88]   Steve Riegel, Fred Mellender, and Andrew Straw. Integration of database management with an object-oriented programming language. In Dittrich [Dit88], pages 317–322.

[SCD90]   D. Schuh, M. Carey, and D. DeWitt. Persistence in E revisited—implementation experiences. In Dearle et al. [DSZ90], pages 345–359.

[SKW92]   Vivek Singhal, Sheetal V. Kakkad, and Paul R. Wilson. Texas, an efficient, portable persistent store. In Antonio Albano and Ronald Morrison, editors, *Proceedings of the International Workshop on Persistent Object Systems*, Workshops in Computing, pages 11–33, San Miniato, Italy, September 1992. Springer-Verlag, 1992.

[SMR89]   Andrew Straw, Fred Mellender, and Steve Riegel. Object management in a persistent Smalltalk system. *Software: Practice and Experience*, 19(8):719–737, August 1989.

[Sun95a] The Java language specification. Technical white paper, Sun Microsystems Computer Corporation, August 1995. Release 1.0 Beta.

[Sun95b] The Java virtual machine specification. Technical white paper, Sun Microsystems Computer Corporation, October 1995. Version 1.0 Beta.

[WD92]   Seth J. White and David J. DeWitt. A performance study of alternative object faulting and pointer swizzling strategies. In *Proceedings of the International Conference on Very Large Data Bases*, pages 419–431, Vancouver, Canada, August 1992. Morgan Kaufmann.

[WK92]   Paul R. Wilson and Sheetal V. Kakkad. Pointer swizzling at page fault time: Efficiently and compatibly supporting huge address spaces on standard hardware. In *Proceedings of the 1992 International Workshop on Object Orientation in Operating Systems*, pages 364–377, Paris, France, September 1992. IEEE.

Indexing Type Hierarchies with Multikey Structures

Thomas A. Mueck   Martin L. Polaschek

Abteilung für Data Engineering
Universität Wien
{mueck, polaschek}@ifs.univie.ac.at

Abstract

Multikey index structures for type hierarchies are a recently investigated alternative to traditional B^+-tree based index structures. The most important prerequisite for the efficient use of multikey structures in this context is an appropriate linearization of the type hierarchy.

We present the relevant problem description, in particular the definition of an optimal hierarchy linearization, and an algorithm mapping type hierarchies to totally ordered attribute domains. The mapping is done in such a way that each subhierachy is represented by an interval of the resulting domain. This procedure is straightforward for single inheritance hierarchies but less obvious in case of multiple inheritance. Based on an example, it is argued that this kind of hierarchy-to-domain mapping yields a significant query performance enhancement in a multikey type index.

1 Introduction

Multikey index structures have been discussed as an alternative to traditional, B^+-tree based search structures in the context of type hierarchy indexing (see [RK95], [KRVV93], [KM94] and [MP95]).

The key idea is to incorporate the type hierarchy structure of a given database scheme into a standard multikey index implementation in such a way that the hierarchy is mapped to one of the multikey index domains (called *type domain* in the sequel). The result is a so called *multikey type index* with $n + 1$ keys corresponding to the n indexed object properties and to one additional property representing type membership. The principle is shown in Figure 1. This paper deals with the necessary setup of the type domain. Considering for example the ODMG-93

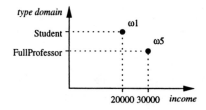

Figure 1: Data space of a multikey type index for one indexed property (*income*)

Object Database Standard [Cat94], query specifications always refer to collections of objects. Consequently, also the extents of object types are represented by collections. In the context of this paper the following simple database schema given in ODMG-93 notation will be used.

```
interface Person: ... { extent persons; attribute Integer id_card_no;
  attribute String name; attribute Integer income; };
interface Student: Person { extent students };
interface FacultyMember: Person { extent facultyMembers; };
interface Instructor: FacultyMember, Student { extent instructors; };
```

```
interface AssistantProfessor: FacultyMember { extent assistantProfessors; };
interface AssociateProfessor: FacultyMember { extent associateProfessors; };
interface FullProfessor: FacultyMember { extent fullProfessors; };
```

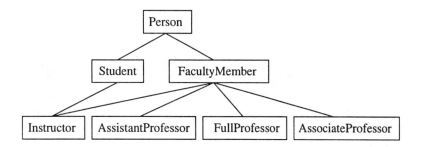

Figure 2: Type hierarchy of the example schema

Let queries Q_1, Q_2 and Q_3 (to be used in the following section) be defined for this schema as

Q_1: `select x from x in persons where x.income < 10000`

Q_2: `select x from x in facultyMembers where x.income <= 30000 and x.income > 20000`

Q_3: `select x from x in associateProfessors where x.income < 45000`

Keeping in mind the definition of extents, query Q_2 retrieves instances of `FacultyMember` as well as instances of its subtypes that fulfill this predicate. Consequently, this query contains an implicit predicate on the object type, i.e, $x.type \leq$ `FacultyMember`, where $\leq$ denotes the partial order relation of the type hierarchy. Using a multikey type index, these implicit predicates can be mapped to ranges of the type domain.

An obvious prerequisite for this mapping is a linearization of the type hierarchy (see Figure 1). However, since there are $|T|!$ linearizations for a particular type set T, one may ask if one linearization should be preferred to another. In the sequel, we show that some linearizations of a given T are better than others with respect to the resulting query performance.

Related work on type hierarchy indexing includes two proposals based on standard B$^+$-tree technology: the straightforward solution of maintaining one B$^+$-tree per indexed type (called *single class index* in [KKD89]) and an approach on replication of OIDs (called *Class Division* in [RK95]). Other proposals extend B$^+$-trees, e.g., the *Class Hierarchy Index* [KKD89] maintaining a common B$^+$-tree for all types and an additional leaf node organization scheme. Single type B$^+$-trees nested according to the inheritance hierarchy are introduced in [LOL92] as *H-trees*. *CG-trees* [KM94] and *hcC-trees* [SS94] extend B$^+$-trees with multiple lists to organize OIDs according to type membership.

The paper is structured as follows: Section 2 contains a detailed problem statement, i.e., a rationale for optimal hierarchy linearizations. The mapping algorithm used to find optimal linearizations is presented in Section 3. An application example, i.e., the implementation of a multikey type index with the help of an appropriate hierarchy linearization is given in Section 4. At the end of the paper, there are conclusions and references.

2 Hierarchy Mapping - The Problem Statement

Reconsidering the multikey indexing schema shown in the previous section and the necessary hierarchy mapping, we have to find an appropriate linearization for T. Figure 3 shows that different total orders yield different range query performance results.

The reason is that in a query like Q_2, `facultyMember` refers to the extent of `FacultyMember` (see Section 1), thus implicitly qualifying a range of the type domain. Consequently, assuming an arbitrary linearization, this range may also contain types which are not part of the subhierarchy of `FacultyMember`. Assuming that the resource consumption of a range query is positively correlated with the size of the respective range, we aim at minimal ranges for all extents, i.e., at a linearization in such a way that exactly one interval contains all types which are part of one subhierarchy. Looking at the geometrical interpretation of the multikey type index, such a

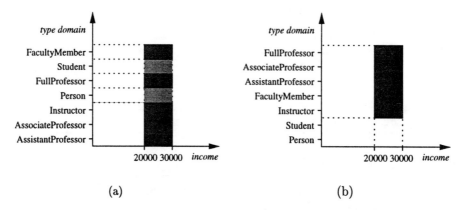

(a)   (b)

Figure 3: Subspaces qualified by Q_2 for different linearizations

linearization yields for each possible type in a query a subspace which does not contain any object identifiers not belonging to the query result (see Figure 4 containing the queries given in Section 1). Consequently, a type domain setup (linearization) resulting in minimal query subspace volumes is called *optimal*.

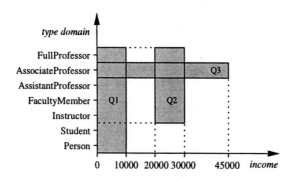

Figure 4: Regions of example queries

Definition 1 (Optimal linearization) *Let $(T, \leq)$ be a type hierarchy and $T_{\leq t}$ be the subhierarchy rooted at t (i.e., the interval $]\infty, t]$ in $(T, \leq)$). A linearization (total order) $\sqsubseteq$ is called* optimal *for $(T, \leq)$, if*

$$\forall t, u \in T : t \sqsubseteq u \vee u \sqsubseteq t \quad and \tag{1}$$

$$\forall t \in T : \exists u, v \in T_{\leq t} \text{ in such a way that } [u, v]_{(T, \sqsubseteq)} = T_{\leq t} \tag{2}$$

In other words, $\sqsubseteq$ is optimal for $(T, \leq)$, if $\sqsubseteq$ is a total order (1), and for each subhierarchy $T_{\leq t}$ of $(T, \leq)$, there is a closed interval $[u, v]$ in $(T, \sqsubseteq)$, containing the same elements (i.e., types) as $T_{\leq t}$ (2). Returning to our running example, Figure 3(b) contains an optimal linearization for the given hierarchy.

A closer look at the definition of an optimal linearization yields immediately two existence conditions ($super(t)$ denoting the set of direct supertypes of t):

- An optimal linearization exists if each type has at most one supertype, i.e. single inheritance ($\forall t \in T : |super(t)| \leq 1$ is sufficient).

- An optimal linearization does not exist if any type has more than two supertypes ($\forall t \in T : |super(t)| \leq 2$ is necessary).

186

In the case of single inheritance the computation of the optimal linearization is straightforward. For example, a standard depth-first traversal of the hierarchy will do. The respective traversals have been proposed in [RK95] and [MP95]. In the second case, Figure 5 illustrates that the second existence condition is only necessary. For both

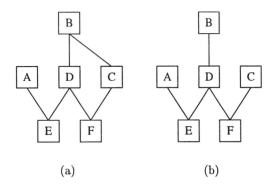

(a)   (b)

Figure 5: Type hierarchies (a) with and (b) without optimal linearization

hierarchies depicted in this figure, the condition holds. However, an optimal linearization exists only for hierarchy (a). From a practical point of view the second condition is less stringent than it might appear. Even in multiple inheritance environments, the existence of more than two supertypes for any type is not very frequent.

In the following section, we present an algorithm which finds all optimal linearizations for a given hierarchy $(T, \leq)$.

3   The Mapping Algorithm

The core part of the proposed algorithm is a recursive function *order*. Another integral part of this algorithm is a *structured set* S' constructed during the systematic traversal of $(T, \leq)$. Elements of S' are either atoms (i.e., type identifiers) or *structured lists*. Elements of structured lists are in turn again structured sets. The recursive definition of this data structure allows for arbitrary nestings. In the sequel, two special cases are used: *flat sets*, i.e., structured sets containing merely atoms, and *flat lists*, i.e., structured lists containing merely flat sets.

The following notational conventions for variables hold: flat sets are denoted by $A, B, C, \ldots$, structured sets by $\boldsymbol{A}, \boldsymbol{B}, \boldsymbol{C}, \ldots$, flat list by $\mathcal{A}, \mathcal{B}, \mathcal{C}, \ldots$ and atoms by $a, b, c, \ldots$. There are no variables used for structured lists.

After termination of the algorithm, a simple postprocessing step on $\boldsymbol{T'}$ yields all optimal linearizations (see example hierarchy below). Figure 7 depicts the high-level code of function *order*. The actual execution of *order* is illustrated by an example given below. Prior to the execution example we will define the exact meaning of all operators used in *order*. The following operations and symbols are used:

- $\{\}$, $()$ and $\emptyset$ denote the set constructor, the list constructor, and the empty set, respectively.

- Set operators defined on flat sets are union ($\cup$), difference ($\setminus$), cardinality ($||$), intersection ($\cap$) and set membership $\in$.

- The operators $\cup$, $\setminus$ and $\in$ are also defined for the top level of structured sets.

- $|\boldsymbol{A}|$ denotes the number of flat sets contained in $\boldsymbol{A}$, denoted by $A_1, A_2, \ldots, A_{|\boldsymbol{A}|}$.

     1. $D \leftarrow \emptyset$
     2. $\boldsymbol{T'} \leftarrow \text{order}(T, \leq)$

Figure 6: Wrapper for function *order*

187

```
        begin order(S, ≤)
3.          if |S| < 3 then
4.              S' ← S
            else
5.              M ← max(S \ D, ≤)
6.              L ← ⋃_{m∈M} {(S_{≤m})}
7.              D ← D ∪ M
8.              S' ← S \ ⋃_{m∈M} S_{≤m}
9.              while ∃A ∈ L do
10.                 L ← L \ {A}
11.                 if ∃B ∈ L : ⋃A_i ∩ ⋃B_j ≠ ∅ then
12.                     L ← L \ {B} ∪ {A ∘ B}
13.                 else
14.                     while ∃x ∈ max(⋃A_i \ D, ≤) : |{i|A_i ∩ S_{≤x} ≠ ∅}| > 1 do
15.                         A ← A * S_{≤x}
16.                         D ← D ∪ {x}
17.                     end
18.                     S' ← S' ∪ {(order(A_1, ≤), order(A_2, ≤), · · · , order(A_{|A|}, ≤))}
                    end
19.             end
            end
20.         return S'
        end order
```

Figure 7: Recursive construction of all optimal linearizations

- *max* yields a subset of a partially ordered set A in such a way that all elements in the subset are maximal elements of A and none of them are minimal elements of A, i.e.,

$$\max(A, \leq) \mapsto \{a \in A | \nexists a' \in A : a < a' \land \exists a'' \in A : a'' < a\}$$

- ∘ concatenates two *overlapping* flat list, i.e., flat lists with common types in their respective sets. More precisely, two flat lists A and B overlap if and only if $\bigcup A_i \cap \bigcup B_i \neq \emptyset$. All sets in such a list have to be nonempty and pairwise disjoint.

  It should be noted that ∘ is defined if and only if $!\exists(i,j) : A_i \cap B_j \neq \emptyset, i \in \{1, |A|\}, j \in \{1, |B|\}$. Informally, each of the two sets containing the common types has to be at one end of its enclosing list to enable concatenation. If this holds, there are 4 cases (empty sets are removed from the concatenation result):

i	j	$A \circ B$
$|A|$	1	$(A_1, \cdots, A_{|A|-1}, A_{|A|} \setminus B_1, A_{|A|} \cap B_1, B_1 \setminus A_{|A|}, B_2, \cdots, B_{|B|})$
$|A|$	$|B|$	$(A_1, \cdots, A_{|A|-1}, A_{|A|} \setminus B_{|B|}, A_{|A|} \cap B_{|B|}, B_{|B|} \setminus A_{|A|}, B_{|B|-1}, \cdots, B_1)$
1	1	$(A_{|A|}, \cdots, A_2, A_1 \setminus B_1, A_1 \cap B_1, B_1 \setminus A_1, B_2, \cdots, B_{|B|})$
1	$|B|$	$(A_{|A|}, \cdots, A_2, A_1 \setminus B_{|B|}, A_1 \cap B_{|B|}, B_{|B|} \setminus A_1, B_{|B|-1}, \cdots, B_1)$

Example: ({B},{C,D},{E,F})∘({F,G},{H}) yields ({B},{C,D},{E},{F},{G},{H}),
whereas ({B},{C,D},{E,F})∘({D,G},{H}) is undefined, since {C,D}∩{D,G}≠ ∅ and {C,D} is not placed at either end of its enclosing list.

- ∗ represents refinement. $A * B$ is defined if and only if A denotes a flat list of pairwise disjoint and nonempty sets, B denotes a flat set, $!\exists(i,j) : i < j$ and

$$\forall k, 1 \leq k \leq |A| : \begin{cases} A_k \cap B = \emptyset & \text{for } k < i \\ A_k \cap B \neq \emptyset & \text{for } k = i \\ A_k \subset B & \text{for } i < k < j \\ A_k \cap B \neq \emptyset & \text{for } k = j \\ A_k \cap B = \emptyset & \text{for } k > j \end{cases}$$

If $A * B$ is defined, the result is given by (again, empty sets are removed from the result):

$$A * B \mapsto (A_1, \cdots, A_{i-1}, A_i \setminus B, A_i \cap B, A_{i+1}, \cdots, A_{j-1}, A_j \cap B, A_j \setminus B, A_{j+1}, \cdots, A_{|A|})$$

Example: $(\{B\},\{C,D,E\},\{F,G\},\{H\})*\{D,E,F\}$ yields $(\{B\},\{C\},\{D,E\},\{F\},\{G\},\{H\})$.
$(\{B\},\{C,D,E\},\{F,G\},\{H\})*\{D,E,G,H\}$ is undefined, since $\{C,D,E\}\cap\{D,E,G,H\}\neq\emptyset$ and $\{H\}\cap\{D,E,G,H\}\neq\emptyset$ and $\{F,G\}\not\subset\{D,E,G,H\}$.

In a final step, we illustrate the execution of the algorithm by a simple example. Assuming $T = \{A,B,C,D,E,F,G\}$ with $\leq$ given in Figure 8.

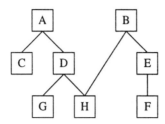

Figure 8: $\leq$ for the following example execution

The following tables provide snapshot information for selected variables and expressions. In each table, the first column refers to the line numbers given in Figure 7. In particular, the values in each table row correspond to the values of the traced expressions *after* the execution of the referenced line of code. Undefined expressions are denoted by "–". For notational convenience, the innermost set brackets are omitted, list elements are separated by white spaces, e.g., $\{(ABCD\ EF)\ (G)\}$ instead of $\{((\{A,B,C,D\},\{E,F\}),(\{G\}))\}$.

Set D is initialized as an empty set in step 1. Its purpose is to hold already processed type identifiers. The wrapping procedure concludes with the initial call to function *order* with T. For sets with more than 2 elements, an initialization phase takes place.

Call: order(ABCDEFGH)

	D	L	S'	M	
8	AB	{(ACDGH)(BEFH)}	$\emptyset$	AB	

After initialization, L contains the subhierarchies of the maximal elements of S in separate lists. In the following illustrations, all processed types (i.e., types in D) are shaded.

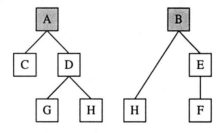

	D	L	S'	A	
9	AB	{(ACDGH)(BEFH)}	$\emptyset$	(BEFH)	
10	AB	{(ACDGH)}	$\emptyset$	(BEFH)	

	D	L	S'	A	B
11	AB	{(ACDGH)}	$\emptyset$	(BEFH)	(ACDGH)
12	AB	{(BEF H ACDG)}	$\emptyset$	(BEFH)	(ACDGH)

After a first concatenation operation, the situation is as follows (the dotted line connects buddies in a list):

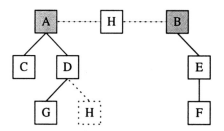

Although type H is no longer an element of {A,C,D,G}, its relation to D is of continuing relevance (this is expressed by the dotted H-labeled rectangle).

	D	L	S'	A	
9	AB	{(BEF H ACDG)}	$\emptyset$	(BEF H ACDG)	
10	AB	$\emptyset$	$\emptyset$	(BEF H ACDG)	

Subsequently, a refinement attempt is made for each list in L which cannot be concatenated further. Refinement candidates are the maximal elements of $\bigcup A_i \setminus D$, in this case D and E for ({BEF}{H}{ACDG}). The subhierarchy of D is {DGH} having a nonempty intersection with both, {H} and {ACDG}. It is thus a possible operand for $*$, ({BEF}{H}{ACDG})$*${DGH} gives ({BEF}{H}{GH}{AC}).

	D	L	S'	A	max(...)	x	$S_{\leq x}$
13	AB	$\emptyset$	$\emptyset$	(BEF H ACDG)	DE	–	–
14	AB	$\emptyset$	$\emptyset$	(BEF H ACDG)	DE	D	DGH
15	AB	$\emptyset$	$\emptyset$	(BEF H DG AC)	DE	D	DGH
16	ABD	$\emptyset$	$\emptyset$	(BEF H DG AC)	E	D	DGH

After refinement, A contains the sets {BEF}, {H}, {DG} and {AC} which are processed by subsequent invocations of the recursive function.

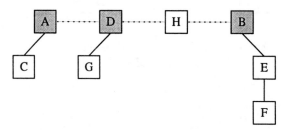

After termination of all four recursive decents, the resulting situation is given in the following table:

	D	L	S'	A	
18	ABDE	$\emptyset$	{(({B(EF)} H DG AC)}	({B(EF)} H DG AC)	

Result: {(({B(EF)} H DG AC)}

At this stage, *order* has produced the final result. A simple postprocessing traversal yields the $2 \cdot 2! \cdot 2 \cdot 2! \cdot 2! = 32$ optimal linearizations for T, e.g., (B,E,F,H,D,G,A,C), (B,F,E,H,D,G,A,C), (E,F,B,H,D,G,A,C), etc.

Applying the algorithm to the example hierarchy of Figure 2 results in {Person, ({FacultyMember, AssistantProfessor, FullProfessor, AssociateProfessor} {Instructor} {Student})} thus giving $2! \cdot 2 \cdot 4! = 96$ optimal linearizations.

4 Multikey Type Indices

In this section we show the actual application of the previous results, i.e., the implementation of a *multikey type index* with the help of optimal linearizations of $(T, \leq)$.

The central idea behind all multi-attribute search data structures is the interpretation of n-tuples as elements of an n-dimensional geometrical space. Based on this interpretation of tuple sets, several well-known formal properties of geometrical spaces are at hand.

All tuples actually stored have to be enclosed by an n-dimensional hyperrectangle defined by *finite* and totally ordered attribute domains (called *data space* in the sequel). The data space has to be successively partitioned into smaller hyperrectangles as the number of tuples increases. The following implementation example is based on standard gridfiles. Despite of their known deficiences the choice of this data structure is due to its conceptual simplicity. It should be noted that any more elaborate data structure could be used as well.

4.1 The Gridfile

The subspace partitioning (or "split") strategy as used in the original grid file approach can be outlined as follows. Each partitioning operation subdivides the initial data space into two buddy spaces resembling (smaller) n-dimensional hyperrectangles. More precisely, let *HR* denote the resulting set of smaller hyperrectangles corresponding to allocated storage segments. In any case, the union of all *hr* belonging to a particular *HR* has to equal the initial data space, since any possible n-tuple has to be stored in a storage segment if actually inserted into the search structure. Additionally, $hr_1 \cap hr_2 = \{\} \forall hr_1, hr_2 \in HR$ has to hold for any legal partitioning in a grid file.

In the initial approach ([NHS84]), the physical organization of the subspace boundary values is straightforward. In particular, n linear scales (hence the name of this particular data structure) in main memory, basically linked lists, are used to store boundary values. An additional directory data structure, conceptually an n-dimensional array, contains storage segment identifiers. In each scale entry, an array subscript value is used to bind a boundary value to the corresponding $(n-1)$-dimensional slice of the directory.

In Figure 9, the scales and the directory of a 2-dimensional grid file are shown. The figure contains two categories of geometrical objects. There are hyperrectangles defined by combinations of n scale subintervals (called *grid regions* and identified by integers in the figure). Further on, one or more grid regions form a hyperrectangle which corresponds to a storage unit, i.e. a storage segment. Such hyperrectangles (identified by upper case letters in the figure) are called *block regions*.

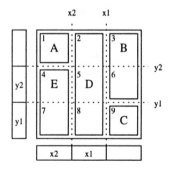

Figure 9: Grid file scales and directory

4.2 Using Gridfiles for Type Indexing

Any multidimensional search data structure used to implement database indices has to contain two parts, namely one storage structure for boundary values (i.e. the partitioning information) and a second storage structure for tuples containing the object identifiers, the types, and the actual values of the indexed attributes. In the sequel, the terms *boundary structure* and *value structure* will be used to refer to these parts. The key values component contains the values of the indexed attributes and is followed by a list of object identifiers referring to objects with appropriate attribute values. The type identifier is handled like any other attribute value, i.e., part of the key values component. Recalling the type hierarchy example from Section 1, a grid file structure could be used to implement an index on attribute `income`. Figure 10 depicts the boundary structure and the value structure for this example. Reconsidering

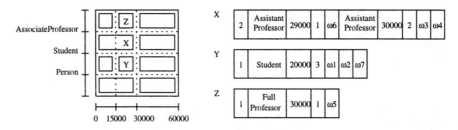

Figure 10: Grid file structure for the example hierarchy and the linearization of Figure 3(b)

Q_2, the query execution is supported by this index in the following way (with respect to attribute `income`). In a first step, the boundary structure is used to determine relevant parts of the corresponding value structure, X and Z in the example. In a subsequent step, these parts of the value structure are used to retrieve a set of object identifiers, ω_3, ω_4, ω_5, and ω_6 in this example. An important advantage of this kind of indexing framework is that *exactly the same* search structure technology could be applied to maintain *one* index structure for *both* relevant attributes of `Person`, namely `income` and `name` in the above example. Considering for example

Q_4: `select x from x in facultyMembers where x.income < 50000 and x.name < "Doe"`

the execution needs associative access to attribute `income` as well as to `name`. In single key approaches, the OODBMS is forced to maintain two distinct search data structures thus spending considerably more storage space for index maintenance and considerably more index scan time.

5   Conclusions and Work In Progress

We present a rationale for optimal type hierarchy linearizations in the context of multikey type indices, an algorithm used to find such linearizations and finally an application example using a common multikey search structure. Optimal linearizations yield query efficiency improvements since the corresponding query subspaces are minimal if and only if the hierarchy linearization is optimal.

A very interesting challenge is posed by hierarchies for which an optimal linearization in the definition of this paper does not exist. In these cases, there are in principle two possibilities: allowing for redundancy (i.e., duplicating types in the type domain) or allowing for a controlled suboptimal setup of the type domain.

References

[Cat94]   Roderick Geoffrey Galton Cattell, editor. *The Object Database Standard: ODMG-93 (Release 1.1)*. The Morgan Kaufmann Series in Data Management Systems. Morgan Kaufmann Publishers, San Mateo, California, 1994.

[KKD89]   Won Kim, Kyung-Chang Kim, and Alfred Dale. Indexing techniques for object-oriented databases. In Won Kim and Frederick H. Lochovsky, editors, *Object-Oriented Concepts, Databases, and Applications*, pages 371–394. Addison-Wesley, Reading, Massachusetts, 1989.

[KM94]   Christoph Kilger and Guido Moerkotte. Indexing multiple sets. In VLDB'94 [VLD94], pages 180–191.

[KRVV93]   Paris C. Kanellakis, Sridhar Ramaswamy, Darren E. Vengroff, and Jeffrey S. Vitter. Indexing for data models with constraints and classes (extended abstract). In Hector Garcia-Molina and H.V. Jagadish, editors, *Proceedings of the Twelfth ACM SIGACT-SIGMOD-SIGART Symposium on Principles of Database Systems*, pages 233–243, Washington, DC, May 1993. ACM Press.

[LOL92]   Chee Chin Low, Beng Chin Ooi, and Hongjun Lu. H–trees: A dynamic associative search index for OODB. In Michael Stonebraker, editor, *Proceedings of the 1992 ACM SIGMOD International Conference on Management of Data*, volume 21 of *SIGMOD Record*, pages 134–143, San Diego, California, June 1992. ACM Press.

[MP95]   Thomas A. Mueck and Martin L. Polaschek. A new approach to associative access in OODB. In Norman Revell and A Min Tjoa, editors, *Workshop Proceedings Database and Expert Systems Applications (DEXA)*, pages 1–10, London, UK, September 1995.

[NHS84]   Jürg Nievergelt, H. Hinterberger, and K. C. Sevcik. The grid file: An adaptable, symmetric multikey file structure. *ACM Transactions on Database Systems*, 9(1):38–71, March 1984.

[RK95]   Sridhar Ramaswamy and Paris C. Kanellakis. OODB indexing by class-division. In Michael Carey and Donovan Schneider, editors, *Proceedings of the 1995 ACM SIGMOD International Conference on Management of Data*, volume 24 of *SIGMOD Record*, pages 139–150, San Jose, CA, June 1995. ACM Press.

[SS94]   B. Sreenath and S. Seshadri. The hcC-tree: An efficient index structure for object oriented databases. In VLDB'94 [VLD94], pages 203–213.

[VLD94]   *Proceedings Twentieth International Conference on Very Large Databases*, Santiago, Chile, September 1994. Morgan Kaufmann Publishers.

Schema Evolution in Persistent Object Systems

Ashok Malhotra[1]
Steven J. Munroe[2]

[1]IBM Thomas J. Watson Research Center
P.O. Box 704, Yorktown Heights, NY 10598 USA
malhotra @ vnet.ibm.com, 914-784-6182

[2]IBM Application Business Systems
Highway 52 & Northwest 37th Street
Rochester, MN 55901 USA
sjmunroe @ rchvmx.vnet.ibm.com, 507-253-6182

Abstract

This paper discusses special facilities to support schema evolution in NOM, a persistent object system for the IBM AS/400*. NOM is designed to exploit the Single Level Store and other architectural features of the AS/400. Among others, NOM supports the following features to support schema evolution:

- Two-level method tables
- Two-level instance variable tables
- Class versions
- Changing method implementations on the fly

The final section of the paper includes a comprehensive list of schema evolution operations and a discussion of how the above features assist these operations.

1 Introduction

Schema evolution is an old and important problem in persistent data systems. Clearly, schema evolution is a necessity for long-lived data-intensive systems, the theme of this conference, because requirements change over time as do operating environments. These changes as well as perceived defects motivate changes. There has been a great deal of research in schema evolution for conventional database systems. See Sockut and Iyer [Soc93] for a comprehensive bibliography. Schema evolution, while never simple, is less complicated for simple data models. Most relational databases allow you only to add a table or add a column to a table [ANS86]. For more complex models, such as the Entity-relationship or the Object Oriented model, more operations need to be supported. Opdyke [Opd90] and Bannerjee et al. [Ban87], discuss the kinds of changes that need to be supported for object systems.

Changing a schema typically requires a number of operations, some complex, which must be carried out in a certain order. The real issue is to provide smooth migration from the old schema to the new schema with as little pain as possible. Essentially, schema migration involves:

- Making changes to the schema
- Converting (migrating) existing objects to conform to the new schema
- Converting (migrating) existing applications to use the new schema

We discuss a number of facilities to support schema migration. Some of these have been incorporated into products, some are in the process of being implemented, other have been designed but not yet implemented. Our

---

* The following terms, denoted by an asterisk (*) in this document are trademarks of the IBM Corporation in the United States and other countries:

- AS/400
- C/400
- System/38

194

purpose here is to describe the ideas behind these techniques and discuss how well they meet our goal of making schema evolution as painless as possible.

To simplify exposition, we speak as if all the facilities are incorporated into a single persistent object system implemented on the AS/400, called NOM[1]. NOM is designed to exploit the Single Level Store and take advantage of other architectural features of the AS/400* [Mal92]. To set the scene, we start with a brief discussion of the AS/400 architecture. This is followed by a discussion of how the requirements of Persistent Object Systems can be mapped onto the facilities offered by the architecture. After this, we discuss the design of the underlying structures that hold the class and behavior information and the design of class versions. This includes discussion about the special facilities that were added to the system to facilitate schema evolution. Finally, we take a typical list of schema evolution operations and discuss how the facilities included in NOM support these schema evolution operations.

2 AS/400*

The AS/400*, like its predecessor, the IBM System/38* [IBM86], is a capability based machine that provides a Single Level Store with 6-byte addresses that allows byte sequences to be accessed as virtual references. The 6-byte address is divided into *segment address* and *segment offset*. Only the offset portion is affected by address arithmetic while the segment address remains unchanged. The segment address extended with the two-byte IPL[2] count becomes the non-reusable *segment identifier*. Segment addresses can be reused but not within the same IPL.

To allow storage of pointers with others types of data while still maintaining capability integrity, the AS/400 implements a memory tagging scheme. Each quadword (16 bytes aligned on a 16 byte boundary) of storage has an extra bit called the tag[3]. Pointers contain the 8-byte segment identifier along with other information including a type code. Pointers are aligned on 16-byte boundaries and when stored as a pointer have their tag bits on. Instructions that use or copy pointers check alignment and tag bits. If an instruction changes data in a pointer the hardware turns the tag bit off and invalidates the pointer.

The AS/400 also provides an object-based, microcoded high-level machine interface [Sch89]. Object classes are provided to support fundamental operating system and database functionality. Each system object class consists of an interface and an implementation with only the former being visible to a client. An authorized client is allowed to perform only the operations permitted by the interface of the class.

One of the object classes provided by the system is called a space object. Space objects occupy a virtual memory segment and essentially provide a block of space that can be used to store data and pointers. NOM uses space objects to implement user defined objects. Some of the other interesting object classes that the AS/400 system provides are the Dump Space, Journal Port and Journal Space classes [IBM90a] that are provided to support recovery.

Objects are identified by their extended address represented as immutable pointers. Authority is checked the first time a pointer is used. An attempt to increment a pointer beyond the object (segment) boundary is detected by the system and an exception is raised. As discussed above, the identifiers are never reused. Any attempt to access a deleted object results in an exception. Dangling pointers are, thus, always detected. All addressing and storage on AS/400 is inherently persistent. Objects exist until explicitly deleted by the user or, if created with certain attributes, deleted by the operating system.

The AS/400 integrated lock manager supports several types of locks. Lock information is stored in a hardware-assisted hash table and the system manages lock contention and lock queues. The Single Level Store and integrated lock manager make implementing shared persistent objects straightforward. New objects can be created by asking the operating system for a space object. A pointer containing a virtual address can be used as the object identifier and the space object can be locked as required using the lock manager. The design of such a persistent object system is, however, complicated by the desire to support class evolution, minimize recompilation when classes change and by security and protection issues.

3 NOM

Although NOM is designed to support persistent objects in several languages, its current implementation supports only C++ objects.

---

[1] NOM stands for New Object Model, i.e. an extension of the object model incorporated in the System/38*, the predecessor to the AS/400.
[2] Initial Program Load -- performed every time the machine is restarted.
[3] The implementation on the System/38* and AS/400* models varies with the width of the mainstore bus, but the concept is the same.

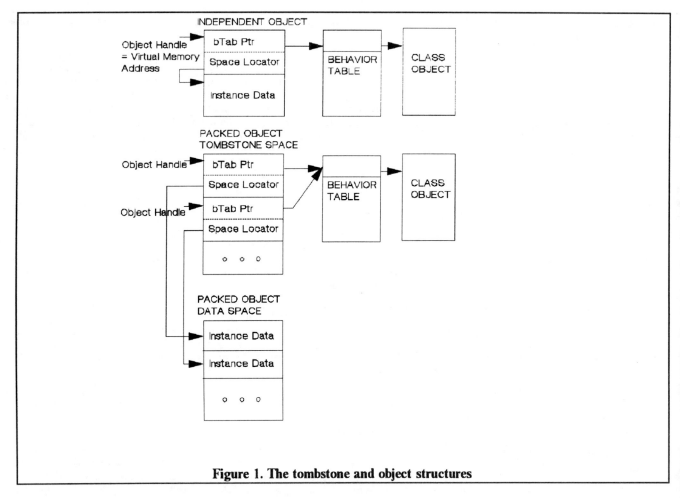

Figure 1. The tombstone and object structures

3.1 Mapping User Defined Objects to Space Objects

As mentioned, NOM maps user defined objects onto space objects. Space objects can be dynamically extended up to 16 megabytes in size. Authority information is stored in the first page of each object and checked on use. Object identifiers are never reused and access beyond the boundaries of the space object is not permitted. The problem with space objects is that they are designed to store large amounts of information. Each space object uses up one segment identifier and 16 megabytes of virtual memory address space. Thus, it seemed logical to use space objects for large user objects and pack many small user objects into a single space object. The problem with this approach is that the system will not recognize packed objects as system objects. Thus, all the objects packed into a space object will have to share the same authority profile. Moreover, there will be no system support for preventing a pointer to be incremented beyond the boundary of a packed object.

In NOM, the object identifier is a pointer that includes the virtual address of the object *tombstone*. A tombstone consists of two pointers. The first points to a behavior table (bTab) whose structure will be discussed in the next section. The second pointer points to the start of the object's data: a block of storage that contains the instance variables. For large objects, the tombstone and the object are in the same space object. For packed objects, the object data is in one space object and their tombstones in another space object. When an object is accessed only the tombstone is locked. The data space is locked only when adding or deleting a packed object. The structure for large and packed objects is shown in Figure 1.

If a packed object is deleted it is desirable to be able to reuse the space it occupied. At the same time, pointers to the deleted object should not be able to access the new object(s) that occupy the released space. This is accomplished by not deleting the tombstone but marking it with a special pattern (brand) to identify a deleted object. The space occupied by the object can then be consolidated with other empty space or pointed to by another tombstone.

3.2 Instance Behavior

In most C++ implementations [Ell90] for classes with single inheritance, the virtual function table (vft) is a single table containing function pointers for every virtual function defined for the class[4] For efficiency, the compiler

196

translates method calls into vft offsets which are used at runtime to locate the method implementation code and call it.

With this implementation, a client program using a set of classes has to recompile every time a method is added to a non-leaf class because the offsets of all the methods below it change in the vft. This is a serious problem that is exacerbated in persistent object systems because objects and classes live longer and are easily shared and so are likely to have more code using them.

To alleviate this problem, as well as to allow instance variables to be added without requiring recompilation of client code (discussed later), NOM uses a two-stage table. This is shown in Figure 2. The first stage table, the behavior table, starts with a header that includes a pointer to the class object and for single inheritance has as many slots as levels in the inheritance hierarchy. Each slot contains two entries: an offset to the instance variable block in the object representing that class and a pointer to a second stage or method table. Each second stage table, the method table (mTab), contains, for each method defined at that level, the method identifier (a unique integer) and a function pointer to the method implementation. The compiler uses the method name to generate a [method-id, offset-1, offset-2] triple for each method call. This method triple in combination with the behavior tables is used to dispatch the method at runtime.

The method-id needs to be a unique integer to confirm the match between the triple generated at compile time and the information in the mTab at run time. In NOM it is constructed by hashing together the class name, the method name and the method signature. This has the advantage that the method-id does not change if the method name and the signature remain the same.

The two-stage table approach can be extended to handle multiple inheritance essentially by having parallel two-stage tables for alternate paths between the root and the leaf nodes. With this arrangement, the method-id is checked at the given offsets for the first method table. If the method-id does not match and another table is available the method-id is checked at the given offsets for the next table. This continues till the method-id matches or the class runs out of method tables and a "do not understand" message is presented.

With the two-stage table arrangement, methods can be added to any class in the inheritance hierarchy without requiring a recompilation of existing client code. This is possible because method identifier and method pointer pairs can be added at the end of any second stage table and the method triple generated by the compiler will still find the right method. Similarly, deleting a method does not require recompilation of client code as long as its slot is left empty in the second stage table. This eliminates recompilation for the most common class changes but not for all. For example, adding a class in the middle of the hierarchy requires recompiling all code that includes methods for classes below the new class because the first offsets for all these methods will change. Moving a method up in the hierarchy requires less change. The moved method is added to the end of the second stage table of the class it is moved to. If the old slot for the method is left unoccupied, only code that uses the moved method will need to be recompiled.

All recompilation due to adding and deleting methods can be eliminated by going to, a Smalltalk style, name-based method resolution. This searches up the class hierarchy to find, by name, where each method is implemented. In the worst case this is very slow, but Smalltalk implementations use a caching scheme that works very well [Con84]. With a 2K cache, Berkeley Smalltalk resolves 95% of method calls in what we calculated to be 5 to 6 machine instructions.

Thus, the NOM method resolution is a trade-off between the extreme efficiency of the C++ design which takes 2 instructions but requires frequent recompilation and the flexibility of the Smalltalk style which takes 5 to 6 instructions most of the time. The NOM method resolution takes 3 instructions for the comparable single inheritance case.

Class versions and schema evolution, however, seriously complicate name-based method resolution because different versions of a class can have methods with the same name but with different implementations. As we have discussed, the NOM method resolution supports schema evolution and class versions. It also minimizes recompilation in the face of changes to the class with only a modest additional overhead.

3.3 Instance Variable Tables

If instance variables are accessed by direct offset, then method code for the class as well as all its subclasses has to be recompiled every time an instance variable is added. An alternate design is to use an offset table in the class [Ell90] and look up the offsets at run time.

Again, NOM takes an approach that provides additional flexibility at some additional runtime overhead. Although objects are stored contiguously, they are viewed as being broken into blocks of instance variables, each block containing the instance variables introduced at a single level in the inheritance hierarchy. As discussed above, the behavior table contains offsets to the start of every instance variable block. The compiler translates every variable reference to a block number and an offset from the start of the block. If new instance variables are added at

---

[4] For multiple inheritance the situation is more complicated but, in effect, the vft is a single table for each complete path from root to leaf.

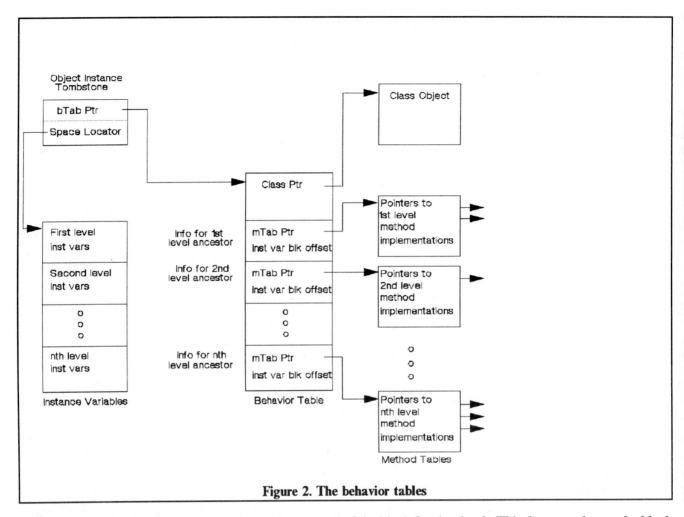

Figure 2. The behavior tables

any level in the class hierarchy they are located at the end of the block for that level. This does not change the block number and offsets for existing instance variables. Thus, this arrangement allows instance variables to be added to classes without method code having to be recompiled. More radical changes to instance variables would require recompilation. For example, changing the datatype of an instance variable in the middle of a block so it takes more space would change the offsets of instance variables that follow it in the block.

Having the blocks of instance variables handled this way also permits an easy implementation of multiple inheritance. This kind of multiple inheritance, called "virtual inheritance" in C++, requires that only one copy of the instance variables of an ancestor class exist even if that class is inherited from by multiple paths. The simplest example of this is B and C inheriting from A and D inheriting from both B and C. There may only be one copy of the class A instance variables in an instance of class D.

The way C++ and most other object-oriented languages handle single inheritance is to lay out the instance variables in the order of inheritance with the highest class's instance variables first, followed by the next class, etc.. This permits a subclass instance to be treated (or cast) as a higher class by simply ignoring instance variables beyond those required for the class. But this easy approach fails with multiple inheritance since there is no way to lay out the instance variables of a class which inherits multiply such that all its superclasses' instance variables are laid out as some contiguous section of the object.

C++ solves this problem by replacing the instance variables which have multiple paths with a pointer to a shared block of instance variables. But NOM already has the power of this pointer in its behavior tables. Each class can independently lay out its instance variable blocks in any order. This doesn't effect its ability to mimic (be cast as) a superclass at all.

4 Class Versions

If you wish to add an instance variable to a particular class or change the datatype of an instance variable, NOM allows you to create a new version of the class. Several versions of the same class can coexist, with object instances present for each version. Object instances of older versions can be transformed as necessary. Client code that does not explicitly work with the changed data should continue to run unchanged.

The new version starts with all the variables and methods of the previous version -- a kind of class delegation. Variables and methods can then be changed, added and deleted as required. A version number attribute in the class object is incremented every time the schema is changed. Clients that import schema information from the server can check this number to make they have the latest incarnation of the schema.

As an example, recall the time when the U.S. Postal Service added four digits to the five-digit zip code. The manager of an employee database might well decide that it was not worth the trouble to go out and find the new four digits for current employees, but it was important to record this data for new employees. Assume that the zipCode instance variable in the Employee class was char[5]. To make the change, a new version of the Employee class with a char[9] instance variable, zipCode, would be defined. All methods using the zipCode instance variable would be recompiled to deal with this longer field. A *transform* method would be written to convert instances of the old version to the new version by adding four blanks to the end of the old zipCode. The definition of the new version of class Employee would also result in new versions of all its subclasses. When a new employee is hired, the Employee object created would automatically be of the new type.

If zip code data were directly used by applications, then all applications that did so would have to be recompiled. They would then work with objects of the new version and would not work with objects of the old version. Better would be to have method interfaces hide the length of the instance variable. Different implementations of the methods for old and new versions would allow applications to run without recompilation with instances of old as well as new versions of the class.

Figure 3 shows a class object and the version structure. Object instances of the first version would point to the behavior table of the version 1 of the Employee class instances of the second version would point to the behavior table of the version 2. If the length of the zipCode variable increased, the offsets of all variables following it in the block would change. All methods using these variables would have to be recompiled. For methods that have to be recompiled the method tables in version 1 and 2 would point to different implementations. For methods that did not need to be recompiled the method tables in versions 1 and 2 would point to the same implementation.

Let us assume that an employee is moving on to a different project. The client program responsible for changing object instances to reflect movement to new projects will invoke the changeProject method. The compiled code will contain the method triple for the changeProject method. This will find the same method implementation in the method tables of both the old and new versions of the class. In the same way the code for the changeProject method refers to the currentProject instance variable by two offsets. This code will also work for both object instances as the offsets to the instance variable are unchanged.

The printLabel method would also have the same compiled method triple but it would find different method implementations in the method tables of the old and new versions.

An argument against class versions says that since the most common evolutionary steps are adding instance variables and methods, this can be done via subclassing. No new concept such as versions is required. Consider the above example implemented with subclasses. We need to change an instance variable in the Employee class. We do this by creating a subclass called EmployeeNew with the additional four characters in the zipCode variable. The getZipCode and setZipCode methods were defined as virtual and are now redefined for the new subclass. Now we want to create an instance of the changed class but an instance of EmployeeNew cannot be created without changing "Employee" to "EmployeeNew" in the client code that creates Employees. With class versions the system recognizes that Employee now has a new version and automatically creates an instance of the latest version. Thus, no change is required to the client code. Not even recompilation as we discussed earlier.

To create a new version, the definition processor creates a new behavior table and installs it as a new version of the class by making the Next Version pointer in the previous last version point to the new behavior table and the new behavior table point to the class object. The last version pointer in the class is set to point to the new behavior table and the version number is set in the new behavior table. The contents of the new behavior table are now constructed by copying from the last version and making additions as necessary. The first stage tables for all versions are identical expect for the pointers to the second stage method tables. This is because instance variables can only be added to the end of the last block. If instance variables are removed their space is still maintained in the object instance so as not to change the offsets of succeeding variables. The second stage tables are all identical to the last version except for the last level which may have additional [method signature, pointer] pairs.

4.1 Changing Versions

As discussed above, a special "transform" or "morph" method is used to change an object instance from one class version to another. Essentially, this allocates a new tombstone for the object which is a copy of its old tombstone i.e. it points to the old behavior as well as to the old object data. Space is now allocated for the new object data i.e. at the new size and the old tombstone is made to point to the new empty data space as well as the new behavior. A special copy constructor can now be run that uses the new tombstone as the source and the old tombstone as the target. This recursively calls copy constructors for its parent classes to copy their slice of data and initializes any

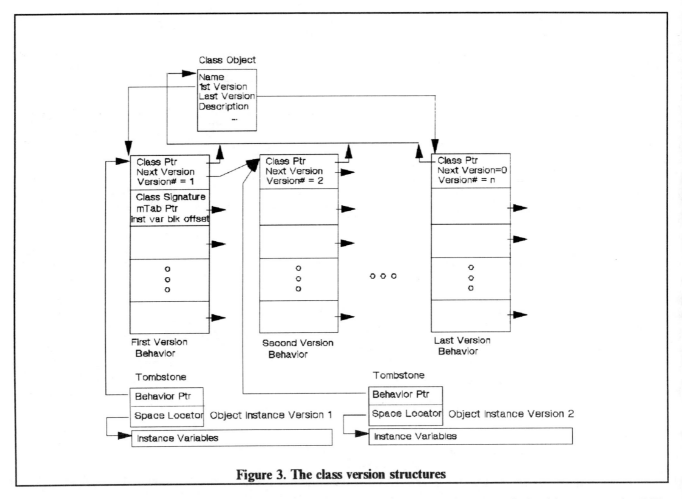

Figure 3. The class version structures

new fields. After this, the storage for the old data and the new tombstone can be released. In this manner, the OID, which is the address of its tombstone, is maintained and the object data changed to the new version.

The new tombstone is temporary and only exists for the duration of the morph operation. Also, morph operations are always performed under exclusive locks. It is impossible to guarantee object coherence for shared update from the time the behavior pointer is changed and until the morph process completes.

4.2 Changing Method Implementations

With standard compilers and binding technology the methods (and the vfts) are bound into the application and activated for each process that runs the application. If an application encounters a object instance that requires methods that it is not bound to, it will fail. So before the application can use the changed method it must be re-compiled and re-bound to the new method.

The problem is the procedure pointers that are stored in the virtual function table. Procedure pointers produced by a standard C compiler are only valid within a single process (or bound program) and can not be passed between processes, or stored in a (shared persistent) class object. Also, if class information is stored in Dynamic Link Libraries, these usually cannot be modified while they are being used and require rebinding for the changes to take effect.

The NOM solution is similar to that sketched out in [Mor85] which treats procedures as persistent objects and uses these facilities to create an advanced project support environment. On the AS/400*, the C/400* [IBM90b] Extended Program Model supports the Call External interface. Call External allows method calls via system pointers to program objects written in C/400* and other languages. System pointers can be stored in (shared persistent) space objects and support (process independent) calls with very low overhead. The method tables store system pointers to the method implementations. When a method is changed it needs to be installed in the class. This stores its system pointer in the method table. After this is done, the changed code executes when the method is called.

Such dynamic method binding can be used to change a method implementation at any time. The system is designed so applications do not lock the method tables. In this normal case, several applications can use the method tables for method routing and the Definition Processor can concurrently change the method implementations causing them to become visible immediately. This can result in parts of the application running with different method implementations. If the application does not want method implementations to be changed while it is running it needs to explicitly lock the class object using the Lock Shared Read Only (LSRO) [IBM90a] lock. This allows others to read but not update the method tables.

The Definition Processor can also use different locks to control the semantics of changing method implementations. For the most dynamic case it uses the Lock Exclusive Allow Read (LEAR) locks which allow it to modify and others to read. If it does not want the changes to affect running applications and be visible only when the applications terminate it should ask for a Lock Exclusive No Read (LENR) on the class objects. This will not be granted if any application is using the class object.

5 Supporting Change

As we have discussed, NOM system includes a number of facilities that assist in schema evolution:
- Two-level method tables
- Two-level instance variable tables
- Class versions
- Ability to transform an object from one class to another
- Changing method implementations without relinking
- Checking whether application is bound to right version of schema

Opdyke [Opd90] catalogs twenty six low level "refactorings" in object oriented systems. To come up with our list of essential schema change operations below, we have eliminated some of his refactorings such as "Inline method" and "Add method body" and combined some of his other categories. Also, since Opdyke was concerned only with behavior preserving changes, we have added some operations that change behavior such as "Add Method".

Many of the schema change operations listed below do not require the special facilities we discussed earlier. They do require a system that orchestrates the steps in a change and makes the changes in a running system in an orderly manner. The Definition Processor referred to earlier is a part of such a system. We will not discuss the details of this system here.

- Change class name
- Change variable name
- Change method name
- Change variable type
- Change variable access control
- Change method return type
- Change method arguments
- Change method implementation

- Instance variable to pointer
- Variable reference to function call
- Statement list to function

- Change superclass
- Move variable to superclass
- Move method to superclass
- Move variable to subclass
- Move method to subclass

- Add method
- Add instance variable
- Add subclass
- Remove method
- Remove instance variable

5.1 Change Class Name

This is a relatively simple kind of change. The new name must be unique in the class lattice. Source code must be changed to use the the new name instead of the old name and recompiled and relinked. No objects have to be transformed.

5.2 Change Variable Name, Change Method Name

This, again, is a relatively simple kind of change. The new name must be unique in the variable/method names of the class as well as the names in the classes that inherit from it. Source code must be changed to use the the new name instead of the old name and recompiled and relinked. No objects have to be transformed.

5.3 Change Variable Type

This was the case discussed earlier. Essentially, a new version of the class is created and the type of the variable is changed. Methods are then added and/or changed as required. Application code will now create objects of the new version. Objects of old versions will continue to run with their methods as they did before. Objects of old versions can be changed to the latest version as and when desired.

5.4 Change variable access control

No changes are required if the variable access is broadened, i.e. from private to protected or protected to public. If variable access is narrowed, then some variable references may need to be replaced by method calls. This requires introducing a new method and changing variable references to method calls. No objects need be transformed.

In this and other cases where it is not necessary to create a new version, it may still be desirable to create a new version if multiple interface changes are involved. Suppose the application is in the middle of calling a chain of methods of a class you just changed? If you are changing one method and that method is an exact semantic replacement for the original method then there is no problem. But what if you need to change 2 or more methods and the change involves a refactoring of the function (function moves from method M1 to method M2)? M1.v1 calling M2.v1 is OK. M1.v2 calling M2.v2 is OK. But M1.v1 calling M2.v2 that might be a problem. In this case it is better to version the behavior and wait until the application return from M1 and calls M1 again before morphing the instance to v2. This insures consistent semantics of the methods (M1.v1 and M2.v1 OR M1.v2 and M2.v2),

5.5 Change method return type, Change method arguments

This is very similar to removing a method and adding a different method except that there is no need to check the uniqueness of the new method name. The uniqueness of the arguments must, however, be checked against methods with the same name. Other methods have to be changed to use the new method instead of the old method, recompiled and relinked. No objects need be transformed.

5.6 Change method implementation

As discussed earlier, this is simple. The new method has to be written, compiled and installed and takes effect immediately.

5.7 Instance variable to pointer

This is exactly equivalent to changing the type of a variable.

5.8 Variable reference to function call

This may arise because variable access has changed -- see above. Existing objects do not have to be transformed.

5.9 Statement list to function

Let us assume this happens within a class. A new method needs to be introduced and implementations of other methods need to change to use the new method. No change to applications. No change to existing objects.

5.10 Change superclass

This is the case that cause the greatest disruption. The order of attributes in the class changes, changing the instance variable tables. The order of the methods changes, changing the behavior and the method tables. New versions may have to be created for several classes and, eventually, existing objects have to be transformed.

There is a special case that we can handle with less disruption: the insertion of a new superclass between the old superclass and the target class. In this case the target class logically moves down one in the behavior table. However we can use the multiple inheritance mechanism to build a behavior that includes the target class at both the new level and the old level. Both behavior tables (at the appropriate levels) would point to the common (target) method table and use the same data relocation offset. This would allow old and new clients to coexist which using single implementation of the target. This very useful when the superclass change is really a refactoring of the superclass into two.

5.11 Move variable to superclass

This changes the order of attributes and thus changes the instance variable changes. A new version has to be created for the class and, eventually, existing objects have to be transformed.

5.12 Move method to superclass

If you add the method to the superclass and remove the method from the class leaving its slot empty then no changes are required to existing objects. Applications need to be recompiled because the table offsets for the method have changed.

5.13 Move variable to subclass, Move method to subclass

Essentially similar to moving a variable or method to a superclass. There are times when it to useful morph an instance to one of its subclasses (i.e. pet to dog, dog to Springer Spaniel ...). The morph method described earlier can be used to do this. Thus, the same technique works for changing an instance from one version to another as well as changing from a class to its subclass.

5.14 Add Method

Methods can be added to a class without changing versions or recompiling existing client code. For the class itself, the lowest level second stage method table needs to be extended with another method-id, method pointer pair. For subclasses, the method-id, method pointer pair needs to be added to higher level second stage method tables. All of this can be done dynamically while applications are running. As discussed above, locks or other mechanisms can be used to control the semantics of when the change becomes visible to applications. No recompilation of client or method code if required.

5.15 Add Instance Variable

Adding an instance variable requires creating a new version. As discussed above, this can also be done dynamically. As soon as the new version is installed, the class creates new instances of the new version. Instances of previous versions can coexist and can be transformed to the new version as required. No recompilation of client or method code is required.

5.16 Add Subclass

Adding methods and subclasses is schema extension rather than schema modification and should be very simple. Adding a subclass requires adding information to the metadata that stores the class lattice. A new class object has to be created for the subclass and behavior tables created by copying the tables it inherits and adding information for the instance variables and methods added for the subclass. All of this can be done dynamically without affecting running applications or existing code.

5.17 Removing Methods and Instance Variables

As discussed above, methods and instance variables can be removed without impacting client and method code if the slots for the removed instance variables and methods are left empty. Removing, renaming or changing public methods and variables is not recommended as it impacts client code. Removing, renaming or changing protected behavior is less damaging as it only impacts the subclasses but should be discouraged. Removing, renaming or changing private behavior impacts only the methods of the class and is least disruptive.

Removing protected methods/instances creates dependances (subclass X V1.2 requires superclass Y V2.5 or newer) that have to be managed. So do adding public and protected methods and variables used by subclasses.

6 Conclusion

This paper has discussed special facilities to support schema evolution in NOM, a persistent object system for the

IBM AS/400*. It has discussed a comprehensive list of schema evolution operations and described how the facilities incorporated in NOM assist in implementing these operations.

Bibliography

[ANS86] Amer. Natl. Standards Institute, *Database Language SQL,* New York, NY, X3.135-1986, 1986.

[Ban87] J. Banerjee, Won Kim, H-J Kim, and H. Korth, *Semantics and Implementation of Schema Evolution in Object-Oriented Databases* Proc. ACM Sigmod Conference, San Francisco, May 1987.

[Con84] T.J. Conroy and E. Pelegri-Llopart, *An Assessment of Method-Lookup Caches for Smalltalk-80 Implementations,* in G. Krasner (ed.) *Smalltalk-80: Bits of History, Words of Advice* Addison-Wesley, 1984, pp. 239-248.

[Ell90] M.A. Ellis and B. Stroustrup, *The Annotated* C++ *Reference Manual* Addison-Wesley, 1990.

[IBM86] IBM Corporation, *IBM System/38 Functional Concepts Manual,* Order number GA21-9330-5, Nov. 1986.

[IBM90a] IBM Corporation, *AS/400 Machine Interface Functional Reference,* Order number SC21-8226-00, Sept. 1990.

[IBM90b] IBM Corporation, *AS/400 System/C 400, Programming RPQ P01102, Users Guide and Reference,* Order number SC09-1317-5, Sept. 1990.

[Mal92] A. Malhotra and S.J. Munroe, *Support for Persistent Objects: Two Architectures,* Proc. 25th Hawaii Intl. Conf. on System Sciences, 1992, pp. 737-746.

[Mor85] R. Morrison, A. Dearle, P.J. Bailey, A.L. Brown, amd M.A. Atkinson, *The Persistent Store as an Enabling Technology for Integrated Project Support Environments* Proc. 8th. Intl. Conf. on Software Engg, Imperial College, London, Aug 1985, pp. 166-172.

[Opd90] W. Opdyke, and R. Johnson, *Refactoring: An Aid in Designing Application Frameworks and Evolvong Object-Oriented Systems* Proc. Symposium on OO Prog. Emphasizing Practical Application (SOOPA), Sept 1990

[Sch89] D.L. Schleicher and R.L. Taylor, *System Overview of the Application System/400,* IBM Systems Journal, Vol 28, No 3, 1989.

[Soc93] G.H. Sockut, and B.R. Iyer, *Reorganizing Databases Concurrently with Usage: A Survey,"* Tech. Report 03.488, IBM Santa Teresa Lab., San Jose, CA, June 1993

A Storage Server for the Efficient Support of Complex Objects

Silvia Nittel*
Data Mining Laboratory
Computer Science Department
University of California, Los Angeles
silvia@cs.ucla.edu

Klaus R. Dittrich
Database Technology Research Group
Institut für Informatik
Universität Zürich
dittrich@ifi.unizh.ch

Abstract

Complex objects are a major advance achieved in modern database systems (DBS) to provide powerful data modelling capabilities. A complex object is highly structured, containing many dependent or independent subobjects. Most of today's DBS are based on the traditional two-level DBS architecture consisting of a storage and a logical data model level. In these systems, the structural aspect of a complex object is managed on the data model level, but lacks specific support from the storage level which could enhance overall DBS performance. In this paper, we present the concepts and implementation of the KIOSK storage object server designed to efficiently load complex objects from secondary storage. KIOSK introduces the notion of *complex storage objects* which facilitates modelling the structural aspect of complex objects at the *storage level*. KIOSK provides operators to load a complex storage object in its entirety from disk in one access and additionally allows clients to retrieve dynamically-defined portions of a complex storage object. Benchmark results presented suggest that using complex storage objects accelerates the processing of complex objects in a DBMS by a reasonable factor due to minimized load and store time.

1 Motivation

Complex objects have been introduced in non-standard database management systems to allow the easy modelling of complexly structured real-world entities that exist e.g. in engineering applications like CAD/CAM or VLSI, or computer-aided software construction. A *complex object* is an object that is composed of component objects each of which is itself an independent or dependent object, i.e. an object that just exists on behalf of the complex object. A component object may be a complex object itself. Since a DBMS is cognizant of a complex object's structure, it is responsible for its integrity, and in addition, provides support for the access and manipulation of a complex object and its subobjects, their reorganization, and associative queries over several complex objects.

In recent years, it has become clear that complex objects are only feasible if the DBMS provides adequate performance for the tasks mentioned above. Much work has been done on improving non-standard DBMS performance: efficient conversion of complex objects via pointer swizzling strategies [15, 10], query optimization, and new DBMS architectures like single-level stores [13, 17, 20, 21]. However, the influence of storage techniques and storage system support on the efficient processing of complex objects in a traditional DBMS architecture has been underestimated.

---

*This work was done while with the Database Technology Research Group, Institut für Informatik, Universität Zürich, Switzerland.

The storage system in a classical DBMS architecture [14] depicted in Figure 1 comprises the lower three levels of a DBMS and performs the page I/O to external storage devices, manages a page buffer, and realizes *storage objects* on top of pages. Storage objects are provided to the higher-level DBMS components; in these components, the logical objects of the data model are mapped onto storage objects for permanent storage. For efficient storage and access, the storage system has to support the specifics of the data model. For non-standard data models, this means that especially object types consisting of attribute types like sets, lists, arrays or bags, and complex objects as well as their access operations have to be supported.

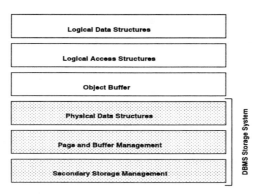

Figure 1: Classical DBMS Architecture

Looking at existing work, some proposals have been made for complex object storage support [1, 6, 8, 9, 12, 19, 22]. Some of them provide storage objects that are composed of different field types, e.g. fixed-sized fields, variable-sized fields, long fields, set-valued fields etc.). This approach was mainly employed by monolithic non-standard DBMS's [8, 12, 22]. Due to the large variety of different object types in non-standard data models, most of the proposals [1, 6, 9, 19] provide simple, unstructured storage objects, thereby making the storage component highly reusable while still providing the most efficient storage support with respect to the overall variety of operations on complex objects [12].

Nevertheless, support offered today is too limited. For example, if a complex object is loaded in its entirety, the knowledge about the *structure* of the complex object is available in the storage system, but can only be interpreted on the data model level. Thus, to analyze which storage objects are needed, the storage object representing the top-level single object, i.e. complex object root, is loaded first, and the information about other referenced objects is read. Typically, these are represented by their object identifier (OID) which is stored in the byte sequence of the storage object. By means of the OID, it is looked up in the data dictionary which storage object represents the referenced object. This storage object is now requested from the storage system. This procedure is necessary for each storage object that has to be loaded, and thus, is very inefficient. This effect is also true for the access of a complex object's parts and is even multiplied if associative queries over several complex objects are performed. Furthermore, in the aforementioned systems, storage objects can only be accessed in two granularities: as a single storage object, or as a cluster containing a larger set of storage objects. Assuming that a complex storage object is stored in a cluster, this interface offers too limited support for typical complex object accesses, e.g. access of varying complex objects parts, navigation through the complex object etc. which require retrieval of varying storage object sets.

In our work on the KIDS[1] Object Server (KIOSK), we have addressed storage support for access and manipulation of complex objects. In KIOSK, storage objects may contain *references* to each other. With

---

[1] "*Kernel-Based Implementation of Database Systems*"

the exception of Mneme [16] and EOS version 2.2 [4], we are not aware of other storage systems that provide references in storage objects. What distinguishes KIOSK from these systems is the extended use of references, and the introduction of *complex storage objects*. In KIOSK, storage objects referring to each other form *complex storage objects*. Through the use of complex storage objects it is possible to make the *structure* of complex objects known to the storage level. Similar to the data model level, KIOSK provides *operators on complex storage objects* allowing to access these objects based on their *structure*. Thus, it is possible to retrieve a *complete complex storage object* or *its parts* in one access from the storage system. Furthermore, KIOSK allows clients to navigate in complex storage objects and dynamically define which parts of a complex storage object should be loaded. This enables higher-level DBMS components to directly retrieve the storage object set for any kind of access operation on a complex object from the storage system. We claim that storage support as described above results in significant performance gains for the processing of complex objects.

The remainder of this paper is organized as follows. Section 2 presents the concepts of the KIOSK storage model in detail and presents the concept of complex storage objects and their operators. Section 3 discusses KIOSK implementation issues. In section 4, we present the organization of the OO7 benchmark for our performance tests, and the results of the benchmark. Section 5 covers related work in the area of storage techniques for non-standard DBMS for traditional DBMS architectures, and Section 6 presents our conclusions.

2   KIOSK Overview

The development of KIOSK was done as part of the KIDS project [7]. KIDS provides basic building blocks, tools, generators and methods for the construction of DBMS's. KIOSK is the reusable storage system within KIDS. The primary goals of KIOSK have been the support of a large variety of non-standard data models, complete reusability of its functionality, and high performance storage support.

2.1   The KIOSK Storage Object Model

In the following paragraphs, we present a short description of the representative concepts and operators of KIOSK. First, we introduce the basic concepts including storage objects, complex storage objects, and containers. Second, we present the main access and manipulation operators for complex storage objects. A detailed representation of the KIOSK interface can be found in [18].

2.1.1   Storage Objects

In KIOSK, a *storage object* is the smallest container for the storage of data. A KIOSK storage object consists of an *identifier*, an uninterpreted *byte sequence* and *references* to other storage objects. Figure 2 depicts a KIOSK storage object.

Storage objects are identified by a system-assigned identifier which has to meet several requirements: uniqueness during the storage object's lifetime and beyond, and provision of fast storage object access. To provide fast access, a storage object in KIOSK is identified by a *physical identifier* (physOID), i.e. the identifier corresponds to the physical address of the storage object. It consists of the storage area identification (14 bit), the page number (32 bit), and the slot number (10 bit) within the storage page that points to the object location within the storage page. The physical identifier thus can be directly used to locate the storage object, and the object is loaded by one secondary storage access. To keep the storage location reusable, the identifier contains an additional randomly-generated number (8 bit) that is assigned when the identifier is generated and is incremented each time the address is reused for a new storage object.

The *byte sequence* of a storage object is used for the storage of data in a byte format. The byte sequence can grow to virtually unlimited size, and its content is not interpreted by KIOSK.

References are used to represent relations between storage objects. A storage object can contain a virtually arbitrary number of references that are listed in an array and are accessible by their position in the array. A reference is represented by the identifier of the referenced storage object. KIOSK also allows the existence of "empty" references, i.e. references that contain a null value. Thus, if a reference does not contain a valid value for some time, but will be reused later on, the storage place can be reserved. Storage objects are allowed to reference other storage objects without any restriction. Therefore, a storage object can reference a given storage object several times and can also reference itself. In KIOSK, we did not want to restrict the use of references in order to allow the user a broad variety of applying references for different purposes.

In KIOSK, an identifier is known beyond the boundaries of the storage object's database, references are valid across all databases. Thus, referenced storage objects can be spread over several databases. As identifiers are unique and not reused in KIOSK, a reference is always valid. We define "validity" by the assertion that a reference always points to the original storage object that is referenced, and no other storage object. If a storage object is deleted access to the storage object via references produces an error message. Furthermore, as a storage object may contain a large number of references, the storage required for references becomes an important capacity issue. To reduce the storage space consumed by references, references are encoded before they are actually stored, reducing the storage requirements by a factor of 3.

Depending on the size of a storage object, KIOSK internally differentiates between *small* and *large* storage objects. Small storage objects can be stored within one storage page, while large storage objects are stored onto several pages. Large storage objects can grow to virtually unlimited size (several MByte). Internally, a large object consists of two parts: the storage object header which contains information about the storage object's physical organization and the storage object's data which is stored on several pages. When a large storage object is accessed, only the storage object header is actually loaded from disk. Further data is loaded on demand, i.e. when the specific byte range or references are requested. For the internal management of these storage objects, we have adapted the storage technique of EOS [2].

2.1.2 Complex Storage Objects

References are used to construct networks of storage objects that can span several databases. We define a *complex storage object* as an initial storage object and all storage objects that are reached by constructing the transitive closure of the initial storage object. The initial storage object is defined as the *root object*. In KIOSK, any storage object can play the role of a root object, thus complex storage objects are dynamically created by accessing the transitive closure of a storage object. KIOSK does not provide a special constructor for complex storage objects, i.e. the concept of a complex storage object as a definable

Figure 2: Format of a KIOSK Storage Object

unit does not explicitly exist at the KIOSK interface.

Complex storage objects are used to map the *structure* of complex objects known in the data model of the DBMS onto the *storage level*. Knowing the structure of complex objects at the storage level enables KIOSK to support operators that provide efficient access of complete or partial complex storage objects and their structural reorganization at the storage level. Additionally, the use of complex storage objects provides for the efficient storage representation of *overlapping complex objects*. If a subobject (or subobject hierarchy) is shared between several complex objects, it is represented as a single storage object (or complex storage object), and each storage object that shares this subobject contains a references to it. The shared storage object automatically takes part in all access and reorganization operations for every complex storage objects it is a part of.

The use of references is not restricted to complex objects. For example, references can be used for the efficient storage of set-valued attributes like sets, lists, arrays, and bags. Therefore, an element of such an attribute is stored in a single storage object while a root storage object contains the references to all storage objects. The operators presented in the following sections allow to access all elements or specific subsets of set-valued attributes with one access.

2.1.3 Container

Complex storage objects provide means for the representation of relations and dependencies between storage objects; however, a storage object's membership in a complex storage object has no effect on the physical placement of the storage object. For grouping storage objects *physically*, KIOSK supports the concept of *containers*. Storage objects that are placed in one container are stored on physically contiguous pages in secondary storage, thereby providing efficient access and loading time.

Containers in KIOSK can be nested, i.e. a container can be an element of another container. A container is placed into another container at its creation time, and a certain new amount of contiguous pages next to the parent container's pages is allocated. Thus, nested containers allow a fine-grained sub grouping of storage objects that are mostly processed together and provide efficient access to the complete storage object set as well as to subsets.

By providing complex storage objects and containers, KIOSK offers a richer set of constructs with which storage objects can be grouped and accessed compared to other existing storage systems. In KIOSK, storage objects can be stored as single units, they can be a part of one or several complex storage objects, and additionally, can be assigned to containers. As the grouping of storage objects into complex storage objects and containers are orthogonal, KIOSK provides several efficient access methods to storage object groups within the same storage layout.

2.2 Operators for Complex Storage Objects

Storage objects are identified by their physical identifier (physOID). After a storage object is loaded into main memory, an *object descriptor* is used to identify the storage object. An object descriptor is a direct pointer to the storage object in the KIOSK buffer and therefore allows accelerated access to the storage object. Furthermore, by providing the object decriptor KIOSK guarantees that the storage object is fixed in the KIOSK buffer during processing. Additionally, the object descriptor automatically holds an appropriate object lock, so that conflicts with other users are avoided.

In database applications, it is often not efficient to load a single storage object from secondary storage. More often, it is the case that a set of storage objects is needed to satisfy a query. This is especially true for the processing of complex objects, where all storage objects that represent a complex object are needed or more often certain subsets that are used to process a section of a complex object. These subsets vary significantly from query to query.

Performance improvements are achieved if these objects can be loaded with one access from secondary storage. Current storage systems just provide a limited approach to speed-up access time by storing all storage object composing a single complex object in the same cluster and loading the cluster in one access. Using a container does not help if just parts of a complex object are accessed. In this case, the needed storage objects have to be loaded separately; otherwise if the entire cluster is loaded, more storage objects are brought into main memory than are actually needed.

Based on the concept of complex storage objects, KIOSK supports specialized access methods for loading in one access operation exactly the storage objects of a complex storage object that are actually needed. These operators are presented in the following subsections.

2.2.1 *Accessing Complex Storage Objects in their Entirety*

Operations on complex objects often process the *complete complex object*, i.e. the root object and all of its subobjects and their subobjects etc. as needed. KIOSK provides the operator *KioskRetrieveComplexObjectAll()* that loads all storage objects that belong to a complex storage object within one operation. The operator is applied to the root object of a complex storage object. As any storage object can have the role of a root object, and can represent the root of a subobject hierarchy, this operator also allows to load any subobject hierarchy in its entirety with one access.

In order to provide fast access to the storage objects composing a complex storage object, *KioskRetrieveComplexObjectAll()* directly returns the object descriptors of the retrieved storage objects. They are listed in an array, and the order of the descriptors corresponds to the access and execution order of the complex storage object in KIOSK described in the following. During the execution of the operator, the complex storage object is internally processed in *levels*. Starting with the root storage object, first, the directly referenced storage objects are loaded from disk. Object descriptors are created for these storage objects and are marked as the first elements of the return value. The order of object descriptors equals the order of the references in the root object.

Starting from the newly loaded storage object of the first level, the storage objects of the second level are accessed. Therefore, the references of the first level storage objects are read, the referenced storage objects are loaded and their object descriptors are created. In this manner, every level of the complex storage object is processed until the complete complex storage object is loaded. As an identifier to the same storage object can exist several times within one complex storage object, before loading, KIOSK examines the references of each level in order to check if a given referenced object has already been loaded into main memory. If a storage object already exists in the buffer, the second reference is ignored. Therefore, cycles in the references are dissolved. Furthermore, it is guaranteed that retrieval of a complex storage object terminates.

As a result of the access to a complete complex storage object, all storage objects are loaded into the buffer (i.e. both the server and client buffer as KIOSK has client/server architecture, see chapter 3), the relevant pages are locked and fixed. By using the object descriptors, the client can now directly access the storage objects and continue with further processing.

2.2.2 *Accessing Layers of Complex Storage Objects*

KIOSK also allows clients to load complex storage objects *layerwise*. The root object constitutes layer 0 of a complex storage object and consists of a single storage object. Layer 1 contains all storage objects that are referenced by the layer 0 storage object. Similarly, layer 2 consists of all storage objects that are referenced by layer 1 storage objects, and so on.

Using the operator *RetrieveComplexObjectLevels()*, the client specifies the number of layers that are to be loaded. The operator is internally processed in a similar fashion as the operator *RetrieveComplexObjectAll()*, i.e. all levels are processed iteratively, and multiple references and cycles are dissolved. The operator returns an array that contains the object descriptors of the loaded levels of the complex storage object. The object descriptors are ordered as in the case of *RetrieveComplexObjectAll()*, i.e. the return value contains the descriptors of the storage objects referenced by the zero level object, continuing with those referenced by first level objects, and so on.

2.2.3 *Accessing Dynamically-Defined Parts of Complex Storage Objects*

The processing of a complex object can be made more efficient if only the necessary storage objects are loaded from secondary storage. One should avoid the application of a fixed access strategy in which a complex storage object is always loaded in its entirety, since the cost of loading and converting object parts that are not needed significantly reduces performance. On the other hand, it is not always predictable which parts of a complex object are needed in DBMS applications. Due to different query types and combinations of object specific operations, varying access patterns for complex objects exist. Queries and object-specific methods are processed and optimized in the query execution component of a DBMS. If this component is supported by the introduction of flexible operators provided by the storage object server, I/O of complex objects can be optimized significantly.

KIOSK provides the operator *RetrieveComplexObjectParts()* to allow a client to navigate through a complex storage object and specify the parts that are actually needed. *RetrieveComplexObjectParts()* permits access to dynamically-defined parts of a complex storage object by using *paths*. A path defines a branch of a complex storage object that starts in the root storage object[2]. For example, Figure 3 depicts a complex storage object that contains a path starting at the first reference of the root object (reference to storage object B), continuing in reference 0 of B (reference to storage object E) and containing reference 0, 1 and 2 of of storage object E. The complex storage object branch defined by this path is enclosed in the polygon.

Paths are the input parameters of *RetrieveComplexObjectParts()* and are represented as strings with the following format: an *integer* represents the position of a reference in the reference array while *points* indicate the change to the next level and *brackets* are used to select several references on the same level. For example, a simple path is represented by the string "1.0.0", while "1.[0,1].0" represents a path which contains two references at the first level of the hierarchy (in the example references to storage objects E and F). The KIOSK operator *RetrieveComplexObjectParts()* accepts any number of paths and loads the relevant set of storage objects.

The input parameter for the access to the encircled storage objects depicted in Figure 3 is the string "1.0.[0,1,2]". The object descriptors for the storage objects are returned in the order B, E, I, J, K.

---

[2]Note, that it is not necessary to start "deeper" as the root object in a hierarchy, as the "deeper" storage object is directly accessed.

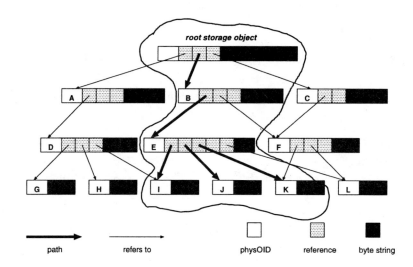

Figure 3: Accessing Dynamically-Defined Parts of a Complex Storage Object

2.3 Structural Reorganization of Complex Objects

Traditional object manipulation operations are the creation, update, and deletion of objects in a DBMS. Regarding complex objects, another important operation exists which relates to the organization of complex objects. Complex objects consist of subobjects which may be independent or dependent objects and are complex objects themselves. Typically, applications manipulating complex objects generate requests to the DBMS to exchange, delete or insert subobjects, i.e. complex objects are *structurally reorganized*.

KIOSK supports the structural reorganization of complex objects by allowing to mirror the structural changes on the storage level. Storage objects can be inserted in complex storage objects, and they can be exchanged or deleted. Newly inserted storage objects automatically take part in operations on complex storage objects. The structural reorganization is performed in KIOSK by exchanging the values of the relevant references. Therefore, KIOSK supports the following operators:

- *UpdateReference()*:

  The operator *UpdateReference()* supports the exchange of referenced storage objects by overwriting a reference value with a new value. The input parameters are the new storage object identifier, and the number of the reference that is updated. A reference can also be updated with a null value.

- *InsertReference()*:

  The operator *InsertReference()* is used to create and insert new references at any position in the reference array of a storage object. All references following the inserted reference change their position from n to n+1 (see figure 4). On the contrary to *UpdateReference()* which does not change the number *InsertReference()* actually adds new references to the storage object.

- *DeleteReference()*:

  The operator *DeleteReference()* is used to delete a reference, i.e. the value and the reference itself. This operator shrinks the reference array, and all references following a deleted reference change position from n to n-1.

212

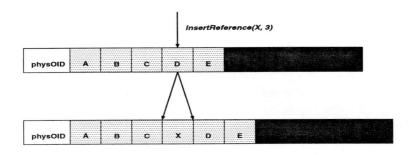

Figure 4: Inserting a Reference

Another typical manipulation operation on complex objects is the deletion of a complete complex object. For this operation it is necessary that all relevant storage objects are identified and loaded efficiently so that they can be deleted afterwards. However, care must be taken in order to not delete storage objects that are shared with other complex storage objects, unless this would effect the described scenarios.

KIOSK supports the deletion of complete complex objects using the following scheme: the operator *RetrieveComplexObjectAll()* is used to load the complete complex storage object. Using the returned object descriptors, the storage objects can then be directly deleted. KIOSK does not provide support for the analysis which of the storage objects should not be deleted. If KIOSK would keep track of the storage objects that are shared with other complex storage objects, backward references are needed to all referring storage objects. We considered this solution being too complex and restrictive. Instead, the KIOSK user is free to use references for managing backward references if necessary.

3 Implementation Issues

Compared to storage systems providing unstructured storage objects only, KIOSK performs additional tasks like management of references and operations on complex storage objects. These functions can be provided using two additional layers implemented on top of a storage system providing unstructured storage objects. The first additional layer supports storage objects with references while the second layer implements operators for complex storage objects.

KIOSK provides a client/server architecture, i.e. the databases are stored at a central KIOSK server, and if a storage object is required, all pages containing parts of it are sent to the local KIOSK clients. This kind of processing is efficient if the required storage objects are contained on as few pages as possible. Complex storage object, however, tend to be spread over many storage pages. Therefore, it can be inefficient to send all those pages which might contain just a single relevant storage object per page.

To avoid this effect, we introduce *transport pages*. Transport pages are temporary, volatile pages which are used to store the storage objects of a complex object for transport to the client. A request for a complex storage object is sent to the server that loads the relevant pages from secondary storage. Based on a cost function, the server decides if these pages are directly sent or if it is more efficient to extract the relevant storage objects from the pages and place them onto transport pages. The cost function is based on a calculation of the number of requested storage objects, their spreading over pages, the size of the storage objects, and the cost to send a page. Transport pages are sent like "normal" data pages to the client. They are buffered at the client and are directly used for updates. Updated pages are sent back to the server which installs changed storage objects onto the original pages and writes them back to disk. In this way, the amount of data sent between a KIOSK server and a client can be significantly

Parameter	Small	Medium
NumAtomicPerComp	20	100
NumConnPerAtmoic	3/6/9	3/6/9
NumCompPerAssm	3	3

Table 1: OO7 Benchmark Parameters

reduced.

The prototype implementation of KIOSK is based on the storage system EOS [3]. Complex storage objects and their access methods have been implemented. However, as EOS is a "black box" for us, transport pages are not implemented in our recent prototype. To provide this facility, the underlying storage system has to be extended. Yet, such an extension can be integrated in a modular manner.

4   Performance Results

In this section, we present a subset of the benchmark we performed to analyze the influence of the KIOSK complex storage objects on processing complex objects in non-standard DBMS. Therefore, we compared the KIOSK complex storage objects against the conventional approach of using unstructured storage objects, as e.g. used in storage systems like Exodus or EOS. For the comparison, we used the EOS storage server.

4.1   Measurement Approach

For modelling complex objects, we used the OO7 benchmark [5] since it defines the most complete notation of a complex object, i.e (m:n), (1:n) and (1:1) relationships among objects. The OO7 benchmark represents a simplified version of a typical application in the CAD/CAM or CASE area. Benchmark aspects that were not relevant for our analysis were left out (e.g. large objects, bidirectional relationships, associative queries).

We constructed the small and medium database according to the benchmark parameters shown in Table 1. These parameters correspond, beside the number of atomic parts per composite part in the medium sized database, to the original benchmark parameters.

The 007 Operations

We used a subset of the OO7 benchmark operations, i.e. two variants of a read-only traversal (T1) operation and a structural reorganization operation (SM2). Each of the test operations was run "cold", i.e. the buffer cache was flushed between runs.

Traversals:

Operation T1 traverses a complex object hierarchy and visits every subobject of the complex object. We used two versions of the T1 traversal operations. With the first version (T1.complete) a complete complex object[3] is retrieved in its *entirety*, while with the second version (T1.parts) only the private composite parts of a base assembly are retrieved and traversed. We measured the time taken to load the complex objects from secondary storage, reconstruct them in main memory, traverse the objects, and write them back to disk.

Structural Modification:

The test operation SM2 is used to perform a structural reorganization of a complex object[4] by deleting half of its subobjects, creating new subobjects and inserting them back into the complex object.

KIOSK and the OO7 Benchmark

How can we use the OO7 benchmark for a storage object server? To simulate the higher-level DBMS components, we implemented a rudimentary object manager that manages logical object identifiers (OID), and data model objects. The object manager keeps the information about a logical object's OID and the related storage object in a hash table. This information is used to load a complex object. In case of the unstructured storage object, the hash table is used to load all subobjects; for KIOSK, only the root object's storage object is loaded via the hash table. Besides the object loading and reconstruction strategies, the object manager was implemented identically for both, KIOSK and EOS.

The loading and reconstructing strategies of complex objects were realized according to the tested storage object concepts.

- Using KIOSK, references between objects were implemented as storage object references: thus, complex storage objects were created. These were used to load complex objects.

- Using EOS, references between objects were also represented by their OID, but were stored as uninterpreted values in the byte sequence of an unstructured storage object.

We considered and tested different clustering strategies for this benchmark. However, object clustering and the use of containers does not have effects on the measurements of the *RetrieveComplexObject()* operator, if container access means that data pages are left at secondary storage until storage objects are accessed. In both cases, container access and access via the *RetrieveComplexObject()* operator, the relevant data pages are brought into main memory.

As KIOSK is a prototype realizing a layer on top of EOS, the KIOSK implementation can not be as efficient as building the concepts directly into a storage system. Since our interest was to measure the influence of the KIOSK concepts directly on a storage system without having to consider the influence of other storage system components, we implemented a second version of KIOSK (i.e. the layer on top of EOS) that is identical to the original KIOSK but does not contain references and corresponding operators. Thus, it was possible to directly compare the influence of references and the *RetrieveComplexObject()* operator on complex object processing. We still refer to the compared system as EOS.

4.2 Results

The testbed configuration consisted of a Sparc1 workstation and a Sun server 690MP running SunOS 4.1.3. The Sparc1 was used as the server machine and was configured with 40 MByte main memory,

---

[3]Regarding the OO7 benchmark the operation is performed on a *BaseAssembly*.

[4]The operation is performed on a *CompositePart*.

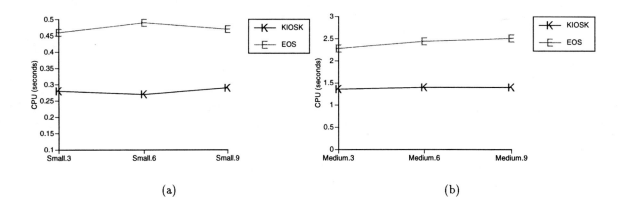

Figure 5: Benchmark results for T1.complete: (a) small database; (b) medium database

a 105 MByte disk drive (Quantum 105S) and a 240 MByte-disk drive (Quantum LPS 240S). The 105 MByte disk drive contained the system software, the swap space and the log information of the recovery management. The 240 MByte disk drive was configured as a raw disk device and was used to store the databases.

The Sun server was used as the client machine and was equipped with 144 MBytes of main memory, a 1.3 GByte disk drive (Sun IPI) and a 1.8 GByte disk drive (Seagate ST43400N). The 1.3 GByte disk drive held the swap space. The 1.8 GByte disk drive was used NFS mounted and stored the system software.

All tests were run in single user mode. The CPU time taken to perform a transaction served as performance measure. All times are in seconds.

4.2.1 Loading and Saving Complex Objects

In the first part of the benchmark, we tested the influence of the KIOSK operators for complex storage objects, i.e. the access of a complete complex storage object or selected parts in a single operation, on loading and saving a complex objects from and to secondary memory.

Traversal T1.complete:

The *T1.complete* traversal was used to measure the effect of the *RetrieveComplexObjectAll()* operator on the loading time of a complex object from secondary storage to main memory. In KIOSK, all storage objects belonging to a complex object were loaded by a single access using the operator *RetrieveComplexObjectAll()*. The returned handles were directly used to read the storage objects and to reconstruct the complex object in main memory. In EOS, the storage object representing the root of the complex object was loaded first. The object identifiers representing the referenced objects stored in the byte sequence of the storage object were read, the corresponding physical identifiers were looked up in a hash table, and the storage objects were retrieved from the storage manager. After the remaining storage objects were retrieved in a similar fashion, the complex object was reconstructed in main memory. In both test systems, the complex object was traversed and saved back to secondary storage afterwards. The results of T1.complete are shown in Figures 5a-b.

In the T1.complete traversal, the use of *RetrieveComplexObjectAll()* in KIOSK is clearly superior to EOS in loading a complete complex object from secondary storage. In the small database, KIOSK is 1.8 times

216

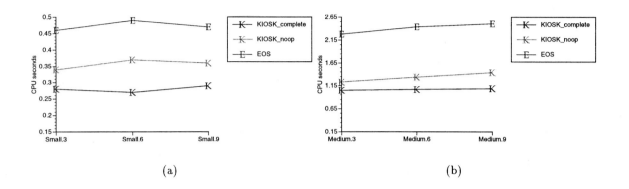

Figure 6: Use of *RetrieveComplexObject*: (a) small database; (b) medium database

faster than the conventional approach implemented on top of EOS (KIOSK 0.28 - 0.29 sec, EOS 0.46 - 0.47 sec). The performance gains are due to the fact that all relevant storage objects are retrieved with one access from KIOSK, i.e. all relevant storage objects are brought into memory, and the returned handles are used directly to read from storage objects representing subobjects; thus, reconstruction of subobjects in main memory is significantly faster. In the medium sized database, KIOSK is about 2.4 times faster than the conventional approach (KIOSK 1.05 - 1.09 sec, EOS 2.28 - 2.51 sec). These tests cases elucidate the fact that as the number of subobjects composing a complex object increases, the time required to load the complex object becomes a limiting factor to DBMS performance; loading the complex object in a single access and using object handles directly is a clear benefit. The medium database contains five times more subobjects in a complex object than the small database. Compared to the small database, the processing time for the medium database grows by a factor of 9 or 10 in EOS. In both systems, the processing time increases linearly with the number of subobjects per complex object (database size), however, KIOSK is doing slightly better.

Additionally, we tested the influence of the KIOSK *RetrieveComplexObjectAll()* operator vs. not applying this operator, and loading each subobject separately by reading its reference in the root storage object, and loading the necessary storage object directly from KIOSK. The results of this part of the benchmark are shown in Figures 6a-b. The results show that application of the *RetrieveComplexObjectAll()* provides for a 25 % improvement of loading and object conversion time compared with loading KIOSK object separately in the small database (KIOSK 0.28 - 0.29 sec, EOS 0.34 - 0.36 sec). In the medium-sized database, the same factor of performance improvement is shown when the *RetrieveComplexObjectAll()* operator is applied (KIOSK (operator) 1.05 - 1.09 sec, KIOSK (no operator) 1.23 - 1.44 sec).

Traversal T1.parts:

In the T1.parts traversal, we measured the effect of the *RetrieveComplexObjectParts()* operator where just a subset of a complex object is processed. In KIOSK, the requested subset of the complex object is retrieved with one access from secondary storage, while in EOS all relevant storage objects are retrieved separately. All other execution steps are performed as described in T1.complete. The results of T1.parts are presented in Figures 7a-b.

This traversal shows the ability to load the relevant storage objects in a single access and directly process them is clearly superior to retrieving the storage objects individually. In the small database, KIOSK is about 2 times faster than the conventional approach implemented on top of EOS (KIOSK 0.14 - 0.20

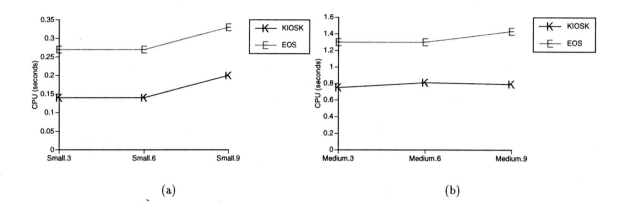

Figure 7: Benchmark results for T1.parts: (a) small database; (b) medium database

sec, EOS 0.27- 0.33 sec). The medium sized database testcase also demonstrates this fact. In this case, KIOSK is about a factor of 2 times faster than the conventional approach (KIOSK 0.75 - 0.81 sec, EOS 1.26 - 1.43 sec). As in T1.complete, by using KIOSK, the processing time increases linearly with the growth of the database (by a factor of 5).

4.2.2 Structural Modification of Complex Objects

The results of the test operation SM2 which deletes and creates subobjects of a complex object are presented in Figures 8a-b. This test operation shows that KIOSK accelerates the structural reorganization of complex objects by a factor 20 % faster for the small database (KIOSK 0.78 - 0.79 sec, EOS 0.91 - 1.08 sec). For the medium database, KIOSK is 27 % times faster than the conventional approach (KIOSK 4.52 - 4.92 sec, EOS 6.23 - 6.68 sec). As the loading time is just a part of the overall processing time of this test operation, the performance gains of KIOSK can be assumed the same as in T1.complete while the main part of the processing (around 0.5 seconds in both cases for the small database) are consumed for the reorganization of the complex objects. This shows an overall performance improvement of around 20-25 % by the application of the complex object operator while the creation and deletion of storage objects with is as efficient as the management of unstructured storage objects.

4.2.3 Summary of Results

Several observations on storage support for complex objects can be made based on the benchmark results:

- The benchmark clearly demonstrates that making the structure of complex objects known to the storage system and providing operators that allow higher-level DBMS components to directly retrieve the relevant storage objects speeds up the loading process by a reasonable factor. Performance gains are achieved for two reasons: first, the relevant storage objects can be loaded by one storage system access, i.e. communication overhead is reduced; second, higher-level DBMS components do not need to incrementally analyze which storage objects have to be loaded next as the structural interrelations are now known to and managed by the storage system.

218

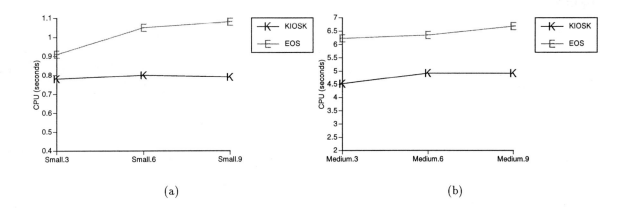

Figure 8: Benchmark results for SM2: (a) small database; (b) medium database

- Due to the support of flexible operators to complex storage objects, performance improvements are achieved for all kinds of operations on complex objects, i.e. a complete complex object access or access of a complex object's parts.

- Performance gains are even more significant when complex objects are large, i.e. contain a large number of subobjects. Using KIOSK, the performance increases linearly with the size of complex objects while using the conventional approach slows down performance overproportional to the object size (at a factor 2).

5   Related Work

In recent years, it has become obvious that storage system support is necessary to improve the overall applicability of complex objects and non-standard DBMS. Orion [11, 12] was one of the first systems that introduced storage techniques specialized for complex objects in a two-level DBMS architecture. The Orion storage server supports storage objects with field types for arrays, sets, and variable-sized data values. A similar approach was taken in DAMOKLES [8] and O_2 [22], but here the field types are simpler. Performance analysis showed that employment of storage objects with diverse field types provides higher efficiency for processing associative queries on complex objects, but is an impediment if complex objects are processed in their entirety as the highly structured storage structures impose significant overhead during loading and storing complex objects [12]. The goal of KIOSK is to provide high efficiency on the overall spectrum of operations on complex objects and, thus, does not support specialized storage structures.

Storage object servers like EOS [1], Exodus [6] and non-standard DBMSs like DASDBS [19] or Prima [9] have taken a different approach. These systems support unstructured storage objects, i.e. storage objects that consist of a variable-sized byte sequence which is not interpreted at the storage level. This approach is favored today, as it provides necessary flexibility for the storage of different data model types and provides good overall performance.

Systems such as Mneme [16] and EOS version 2.2 [4] also support the concept of references in storage objects. However, Mneme's object references are only valid within a single file, which corresponds to a cluster in KIOSK. For a reference to an object stored in another file, a surrogate object containing its file and object identifier must be stored in the original file. Both systems only support operators on the reference itself. In contrast to the systems mentioned above, KIOSK explicitly supports the *structural aspect* of complex objects at the storage level which is not further exploited by other storage systems. By using references between storage objects, it is possible to make the structure of complex objects known to the storage system by forming *complex storage objects*. In this way, KIOSK is able to support specialized operators that are cognizant of the structure of complex objects.

6   Conclusion

In this paper, we presented the concepts of the KIOSK storage object server designed to efficiently load complex objects from secondary storage. KIOSK introduces the notion of *complex storage objects* that facilitates modelling the structural aspect of complex objects at the *storage level*. KIOSK provides operators to load a complex storage object in its entirety from disk by one access and additionally allows clients to retrieve dynamically-defined portions of a complex storage object. Benchmark results presented show that using complex storage objects accelerates the processing of complex objects in a DBMS by approximately a factor of 2 or 3 due to minimized load and store time.

Acknowledgements

We want to thank Edmond Mesrobian, Eliot Moss, and the anonymous referees for their comments that helped to improved the presentation of the paper. We also thank Thimios Panagos for the excellent EOS support. Furthermore, we want to thank Edmond Mesrobian for helping to set up the benchmark environment at UCLA again.

References

[1] A. Biliris. An Efficient Database Storage Structure for Large Dynamic Objects. In *Eighth International Conference on Data Engineering, Tempe, Arizona*, pages 301–308. IEEE Computer Society, 1992.

[2] A. Biliris. The Performance of Three Database Storage Structures for Managing Large Objects. In *International Conference on Management of Data (SIGMOD), San Diego, California*, pages 276–285. ACM Sigmod Record, 1992.

[3] A. Biliris and E. Panagos. The EOS User's Guide, Release 2.0. Technical report, AT&T Bell Laboratories, Murray Hill, NJ, 1993.

[4] A. Biliris and E. Panagos. The EOS User's Guide, Release 2.2. Technical report, AT&T Bell Laboratories, Murray Hill, NJ, 1995.

[5] M.J. Carey, D.J. DeWitt, and J.F Naughton. The OO7 Benchmark. Technical Report Technical Report, Computer Science Department, University of Wisconsin-Madison, 1994.

[6] M.J. Carey, D.J. DeWitt, J.E. Richardson, and E.J. Shekita. Object and File Management in the EXODUS Extensible Database System. In *Twelfth International Conference on Very Large Databases*, pages 91–100. IEEE Computer Society, 1986.

[7] K.R. Dittrich, A. Geppert, V. Goebel, S. Nittel, and S. Scherrer. A Declarative Approach to DBMS Construction. In *Conference of Database Research in Switzerland, Lausanne*. SI, 1991.

[8] K.R. Dittrich, W. Gotthard, and P.C. Lockemann. DAMOKLES - A Database System for Software Engineering Environments. In *Conradi*, pages 353–371, 1986.

[9] T. Haerder, K. Meyer-Wegener, B. Mitschang, and A. Sikeler. PRIMA - a DBMS Prototype Supporting Engineering Applications. In *Thirteenth International Conference on Very Large Databases, Brighton*, pages 433–442. IEEE Computer Society, 1987.

[10] A. Kemper and D. Kossmann. Adaptable Pointer Swizzling Strategies in Object Bases. In *Ninth International Conference on Data Engineering, Vienna, Austria*, pages 155–162. IEEE Computer Society, 1993.

[11] W. Kim, E. Bertino, and J.F. Garza. Composite Objects Revisted. In *International Conference on Management of Data (SIGMOD), Portland, Oregon*, pages 337–347. SIGMOD Record, 1989.

[12] W. Kim, H.-T. Chou, and J. Banerjee. Operations and Implementation of Complex Objects. In *Third International Conference on Data Engineering, Los Angeles, California*, pages 626–633. IEEE Computer Society, 1987.

[13] C. Lamb, G. Landis, J. Orenstein, and D. Weinreb. The ObjectStore Database System. *Communications of the ACM*, 34(10):50–63, 1991.

[14] P.C. Lockemann and J.W. Schmidt. Datenbank-Handbuch. *Springer Verlag*, 1997.

[15] J. Eliot B. Moss. Working with Persistent Objects: To Swizzle or Not to Swizzle. *IEEE Transactions on Software Engineering*, 18(8):657–673, 1992.

[16] J. Eliot B. Moss and S. Sinofsky. Managing Persistent Data with Mneme: Designing a Reliable Shared Object Interface. In *Advances In Object-Oriented Database Systems:Second Int. Workshop on OODBS, Bad Münster, Germany*. Computer Science Lecture Notes 334, Springer Verlag, New York, 1988.

[17] S. Nittel. Einsatz und Nutzen von objektorientierten Betriebssystemen fuer die Implementierung von Datenbanksystemen. In *1. GI-Workshop Datenbanksysteme und Betriebssyteme, Heidelberg, Germany*. GI Datenbank-Rundbrief, Ausgabe 11, 1993.

[18] S. Nittel. The KIOSK Interface Description. Technical Report Technischer Bericht 93.24, Institut für Informatik, Universität Zürich, Switzerland, 1993.

[19] H.-B. Paul, H.-J. Schek, M.H. Scholl, G. Weikum, and U. Deppisch. Architecture and Implementation of the Darmstadt Database Kernel System. In *International Conference on Management of Data (SIGMOD)*. SIGMOD Record, 1987.

[20] E. Shekita and M. Zwilling. Cricket: A Mapped, Persistent Object Store. In *Fourth International Workshop on Persistent Object Systems*. Morgan Kaufmann Publishers, 1990.

[21] V. Singhal, S.V. Kakkad, and P.R. Wilson. Texas: An Efficient, Portable Persistent Store. In *Fifth Int'l Workshop on Persistent Object Systems, San Miniato, Italy*, 1992.

[22] F. Velez, G. Bernard, and V. Darnis. The O_2 Object Manager: an Overview. In *Thirteenth International Conference on Very Large Databases, Amsterdam*, pages 357–366. IEEE Computer Society, 1990.

Higher-order Distributed Computation over Autonomous Persistent Stores

Miguel Mira da Silva and Malcolm Atkinson

Dept of Computing Science, University of Glasgow
Glasgow G12 8QQ, Scotland
{mms,mpa}@dcs.gla.ac.uk

Abstract

The traditional approach for building distributed applications is by calling a procedure in another store using an RPC mechanism. However, an RPC requires a round-trip network delay for every call and makes each store dependent on the availability of other stores. A solution to this problem is to migrate the remote objects needed to the client store, and in particular the remote procedures themselves.

After building an initial higher-order RPC we observed that in a persistent programming language the transitive closure of references for many objects includes large parts of the store, creating significant problems in efficiency and semantics. In this paper we present a refined programming model based on two new mechanisms: *migration by substitution* to avoid migrating the entire transitive closures; and *persistent spaces* that help with preserving object sharing both within and between stores.

1 Introduction

The construction and maintenance of large-scale, long-lived persistent applications requires improved support [AM95]. Models for distributed programming — in particular those that support an incremental approach and preserve store autonomy — are essential for building such applications. We propose a high-level, distributed computation model based on moving values of arbitrary type between autonomous stores.

Researchers in the persistent community have extended persistence towards distribution by hiding as many aspects of distribution as they could. We call this approach *transparent distribution* if it attempts to deliver the illusion of a "one world model". Persistence abstracts over the locality of data "vertically", i.e., programmers do not need to know whether objects are on disk or memory. The *one-world model of distribution* extends this abstraction but now "horizontally", i.e., programmers do not need to know whether objects are local or remote.

For example, DPS-algol [Wai88] was an experiment that produced a distributed version of the persistent programming language PS-algol. DPS-algol extended PS-algol and its abstract machine so that the location of objects could be made invisible at the language level. (In addition programmers could also control the placement of computations for performance reasons.) Others have attempted to implement transparent distribution at the persistent store level [LJGS90, GADV92] or even to build a distributed persistent operating system itself [KSD⁺90, DdBF⁺94].

Transparent distribution is a step towards more scalable architectures and offers a simple programming model. However, transparent distribution cannot be made to scale indefinitely [MdSAB96]. The main reason is that the many inter-store references needed to support transparent distribution run into difficulties with communication delays and with failures increasingly as the number of machines grow. Transparent distribution has a role in smaller sub-domains, but other models of distribution are required for assembling these into larger applications.

The other extreme approach for distribution is to present the application programmer with primitives to meet the challenge of handling all of the cost, delay and failure issues. In the *federated model of distribution* we compromise on transparency and simplicity to afford autonomy, availability, and scalability. Object locality, movement and consistency are now exposed and under programmer control. Real persistent applications may benefit with this model [AE90]. It is also fundamental if we want to scale persistence beyond the local area network and towards the global computing network represented by the Internet. In short, application programmers may have application specific knowledge that can be applied to reduce costs and latency, and may also need specific responses to failures.

When a federated model makes distribution visible to application programmers, there must be suitable abstractions with which to present distributed aspects of the computation. An example is the binding mechanism to match clients with servers; other abstractions are needed because of security and recovery reasons, and for engineering optimisations. These distributed abstractions can be integrated into a purpose-built persistent programming language [Lis88] or offered on top of an existing persistent language [Mun93, MdS95a, MMS96].

We seek to develop and validate useful distribution abstractions which balance the trade-off between: *simplicity* with details of distribution automated; and *control* so that application programmers can specify aspects of the distributed computation. These abstractions will be useful if they encapsulate frequently required patterns of behaviour. Once validated, they may later be given linguistic support. Validation involves demonstration of feasibility, scalability and utility.

The rest of the paper is organised as follows. In section 2 we present the distribution abstraction of an initial programming model, together with an example application and performance measurements. This initial abstraction is not appropriate for automating the movement of all persistent objects. A refined abstraction including two novel techniques is then presented in section 3, again with examples and measurements. Related research work is then presented in section 4. We conclude with a summary of the main contributions of the paper and a list of future research issues in section 6.

2   Initial Programming Model

We base our abstractions for building federated distributed applications on the remote procedure call (RPC) model [BN84]. There are many RPC mechanisms for traditional (i.e., non-persistent) programming languages (see [TA90] for a survey) and a few for persistent ones, e.g., [MdS95a, MMS96]. Our research work differs from other proposals because we aim to consistently support the following, sometimes conflicting, goals.

1. *Programming Model* — Both general to support a large class of distributed persistent applications and easy for application programmers to understand and use.

2. *Data Type Completeness* — We seek to transmit values of any type, including all compound values. Particularly challenging in a persistent environment are values that contain code which may refer to variables in its context, such as procedures, abstract data types and objects; these should be as capable of being passed between stores as any other data type, like base types and their constructors.

3. *Add-on and Portable* — Support distribution in an existing strongly-typed persistent programming language without over-dependence on its particular implementation.

4. *Realistic* — The mechanism has to operate efficiently under real conditions (workloads, networks and computers) so it can be used and tested in a number of persistent applications which will give us feedback.

To facilitate adoption, disruption to the existing programming model for local computations should be minimised. Existing safety nets provided to support programming within a node — such as strong type checking and encapsulation — should be accommodated so that similar support is given to programmers writing distributed applications. We also want to take advantage of existing knowledge, practice and tools.

As an example, let us compare the above goals with a well-know distributed persistent system based on the federated model. Argus [LS83, Lis84, Lis88] proposed a well-defined programming model with a notion of guardians (stores) that communicate using distributed transactions. Our work is different because Argus required a new language and implementation, and it does not transmit values that include bound code. (Instances of abstract data types can migrate between guardians, but only if their type definition and implementation already exist in the target.)

2.1   Design

In order to achieve the goals outlined above, we have designed and built a *type-safe persistent RPC* mechanism [MdS95a] for Napier88 [MBC+94]. Here we summarise its characteristics.

1. *Synchronous RPC* — The client (caller) is halted after the call, pending the response from the server (callee).

2. *Add-on* — Built on top of Napier88 with RPC calls looking like local procedure calls.

3. *Automated stub generation* — Both the server and client stubs are generated automatically from the standard definitions of procedure signatures in Napier88 using reflection [Kir93] meaning that programmers are not required to learn an additional interface description language.

4. *Passing arguments by copy* — Like Sun/RPC [Sun93], it restricts the types of its parameters and results to base types and types composed by the recursive application of simple constructors (records, unions and arrays). These are passed by copying their values across the network. Each value is transmitted (marshaled and un-marshaled) independently of the others.

5. *Automatic type-safety* — The mechanism (unlike Sun/RPC) guarantees type-safe remote calls by a type handshake before calls commence. These *type sessions* amortise the cost of type checking over a number of remote calls. Type-safety is automatic because type sessions *start* and *end* without any user intervention.

Initial experiments suggested improvements to this first RPC prototype, which and summarised below but presented in more detail in the Napier/RPC 2.2 user manual [MdS95b]. The abstraction offered is still very similar to local procedure calls.

6. *Type-completeness* — The RPC now supports *arguments of any type*, including procedures, still by deep copying. (Although there are restrictions to the remote procedure itself, which, for example, cannot be polymorphic.) Copying all objects reachable from the arguments makes sure the object can be reconstructed remotely with its run-time context.

7. *Failure model* — Many common failures are now detected and returned to the calling program, for example "server not responding" and "remote procedure not supported at the server". Programmers can now write code to handle these failures taking into consideration the knowledge they have about the application.

8. *Call timeout* — If the result of a remote call does not arrive in a number of seconds (specified by the application programmer) the call is aborted and an appropriate failure is returned instead.

9. *Call optimisation* — The socket connection is maintained active for sometime because many successful remote calls are immediately followed by another remote call to the same server.

This version of the persistent RPC was considered stable and robust enough to be used. An example is given in the next section.

2.2   Application Example

Napier/RPC has been used to build a client/server version of the Library Explorer [Bro93], a tool for retrieving information from the Glasgow Libraries [WWP+95]. It was also used for communication between stores in a multi-player card game built to demonstrate and test the mechanism.

The *Library Explorer* is a persistent application that accepts free-text queries (specifying software components required by the user) and using information retrieval techniques returns a list of matches (procedures that offer approximately that functionality). The user can then request documentation for a particular procedure to be retrieved and displayed. The client/server version of the Explorer is divided into two programs: one running on a *Definitive Library Server* that maintains everything related with Glasgow Libraries (a database of procedures and documentation about them) and a light-weight Explorer running in the client store that accesses the Definitive Server using Napier/RPC to retrieve the information.

The remote version of the Library Explorer was implemented by converting three internal procedures into remote calls (see figure 1). These were already used to communicate between the user interface and the database parts of the normal Explorer.

The remote Explorer first checks the Library Server. If `indexIsEmpty` returns `false` (see figure 2) the query is passed as an argument to `searchResult` which returns a vector of name/score pairs ordered by score value. When the user selects a name, `retrieveDoc` is called to obtain the documentation.

We have observed that application programmers usually encapsulate in a procedure the code needed for failure treatment when calling a remote procedure. In this way, aspects of distribution (latency, failures, etc) are separated from the rest of the application. This is the reason why the remote operation presented later in figure 4 has an interface similar to a local procedure call.

```
type resultEntry is structure( name: string; score: real )

indexIsEmpty: proc( null -> bool )
searchResult: proc( string -> *resultEntry )
retrieveDoc: proc( string -> string )
```

Figure 1. Remote Procedures in the Library Explorer

```
let test = explorerClient(callRemProc)("indexIsEmpty",any(nil))

if test is error then
    !* error treatment
else
    project test'ok as ok onto
        bool : empty := ok
        default : !* error treatment
```

Figure 2. Calling a Remote Procedure

2.3   Performance

We aim to measure the behaviour of systems and applications under typical working conditions. For this reason, all measurements in this paper are taken "warm", i.e., after all set-ups have been made, indexes built, and caches primed. The measurements do not include hand crafted optimisations based on knowledge of the implementation of Napier88 and our RPC; they are based on code written by the implementor of the Explorer, which we hope is typical of normal application programmers.

The machines are the same DEC Alphas with OSF/1 that are normally used to run Napier88, connected via the departmental Ethernet. These times are taken after the normal working hours but the network still had other users. Numbers are in seconds. "User CPU" means the time spent executing the operation in the user address space; "O/S CPU" is the time spent in the operating system; and "Elapsed Time" the total wall-clock time. The observed performance is disappointing, but provides some useful provocation.

2.3.1   Minimal Remote Calls

Table 1 shows an experiment with minimal remote calls using Sun/RPC and of *equivalent* local calls in C, whereas table 2 presents similar measurements for Napier/RPC and Napier88 respectively.

Procedure	Elapsed time		
	User CPU	O/S CPU	Total time
Local (nanoseconds)	143	zero	143
Remote (milliseconds)	0.0623	0.20	1.76
Ratio	*436*	—	*12,300*

Table 1. Performance of Sun/RPC

The results show that a C program could make 12 thousand minimal local calls in the time taken to do one RPC, whereas Napier88 could make 43 thousand. (The tables also show the current Napier88 implementation is slow, but that issue is not part of our research.) In an attempt to disregard the relative speeds of the two languages, we could identify this as Sun/RPC having approximately the same *normalised* speed as Napier/RPC. However, while communication dominates the performance for Sun/RPC, CPU time is the bottleneck in Napier/RPC.

From the tables above we conclude that the absolute performance of Napier/RPC is clearly problematic. This can be because Napier/RPC has not been optimised, e.g., the packed arguments and results are transmitted in packets with 4 bytes each whereas

Procedure	Elapsed time		
	User CPU	O/S CPU	Total time
Local (microseconds)	38.8	2.47	58.6
Remote (seconds)	1.61	0.198	2.50
Ratio	*41,500*	*80,000*	*43,000*

Table 2. Performance of Napier/RPC

a minimal remote call in Napier/RPC transmits 108 bytes to the server program. Figure 3 shows that, although packets with 4 bytes are approximately 9 times slower than the alternative of sending a single packet with 108 bytes, the time on transmitting the byte array (0.00587 seconds) is not relevant to the total time for a remote call (2.5 seconds).

Array size	Elapsed time (seconds)		
	User CPU	O/S CPU	Total time
4 bytes	0.00330	0.00160	0.00587
108 bytes	0.000451	0.000113	0.000664
Ratio	*7.32*	*14.2*	*8.84*

Table 3. Time to Transmit 108 bytes in Napier88

The remaining question now becomes: if it is not spent on communication, where is the time going ? Since most of the time is being spent on local operations at the user level, even when the client is blocked waiting for the result, this may suggest Napier88 is executing in the background (e.g., to implement the timeout). However, since there is no facility to analyse the execution of a program (a profiler, as provided by many C compilers) it will be difficult to progress much further in our performance analysis.

2.3.2 Library Explorer

The second experiment measured the execution times of the client/server Library Explorer (see section 2.2 above) for three different user requests for software. The number of matches is limited to the first 10 ordered by score (the total number of matches is shown in parenthesis). Each request was repeated 5 times for each of the local and remote versions of the Explorer, and the elapsed time is reported as the minimum and maximum times achieved.

Task Requested		Local Server	Remote Server
Query	Matches	Elapsed time	Elapsed time
"View slides"	1 (1)	1–1 secs	3–8 secs
"Display an image"	10 (55)	1–2 secs	5–10 secs
"Write a string"	10 (279)	2–3 secs	6–11 secs

Table 4. Performance of the Local and Remote Library Explorer

The results presented in table 4 show that a remote call is approximately the sum of the local processing time (1 to 3 seconds) plus the time for the remote call itself (2.5 seconds, see table 2). They also show the performance degrades quickly with the data volume being transferred between stores. In the Library Explorer there are no semantic problems with copying values between stores as these are just used for displaying snapshots.

3 Refined Programming Model

The initial programming model with its type-safe type-complete RPC passing arguments by deep copy is useful for such traditional applications like the Library Explorer. These require data migration between autonomous stores, but not higher-order

226

objects such as those that include code. For these complex objects, the initial RPC attempts to deep copy the entire transitive closure, which sometimes may reach the entire store [MdSAB96].

But copying large parts of the store not only creates efficiency problems. It also creates semantics problems, as many of these objects in the transitive closure are shared by other objects. This sharing relationship is lost when they are copied to other stores and replicas created remotely. Furthermore, in an environment with completely disconnected stores there is no simple way to share objects between stores.

So we now add to our previous goals of: simple and general programming model, automatic type-safety, passing by copy for store autonomy, run-time generation of stubs, server evolution on-the-fly, and a failure model; the following three goals:

1. *Make type-completeness affordable* — By reducing the amount of data being copied between stores to a reasonable level for all data types. Investigate which objects cannot migrate for semantic or engineering reasons.

2. *Preserve intra-store sharing* — Arrange that the relationships between successive parameters, which prevail for sequences of local calls, be available for remote calls.

3. *Help with inter-store coherence* — Offer application programmers primitives for sharing object values between stores without compromising too much on autonomy and availability.

This extended set of goals presents challenging research issues. So far we are only able to propose a solution suitable for a sub-set — although a large one — of all distributed persistent applications, based on the following assumptions.

1. The number of object servers is much smaller than the number of clients of these objects. Servers have usually far more computing resources (disk space, processing power, broadband networks) and human resources (for building and maintaining the system) than clients. The number of objects that migrate from servers to clients is small relatively to the total number of objects in the whole system — though not necessarily very small in absolute terms.

2. Objects made available for clients by servers have usually reached a relatively stable state before they migrate to other stores. Clients may not always require the latest version of all objects, but they need a facility to check if objects have changed and fetch the most recent copy if they want.

3. Networks are slow, unreliable and expensive relative to the costs of computation and data movement within computers. There is no indication these differentials will be reduced.

However, we recognise that for some objects in some applications these assumptions will not hold. These objects will require a more general mechanism that may be more expensive and more difficult to use than ours, but seldom needed. On the other hand, application programmers can always use the basic RPC mechanism to fetch the most up-to-date version of an important and rapidly changing, relatively simple, object — the canonical example being a stock market value.

Our new abstraction is based on RPC with two additional mechanisms — migration by substitution and persistent spaces. These have been built, used and measured and the new features are presented below.

3.1   Migration by Substitution

In this section we propose a novel semantics for passing parameters to a remote procedure called *migration by substitution*. We have described elsewhere a variety of semantics for parameter passing in a type-complete persistent RPC [MdSAB96]. Our model of passing by substitution lies somewhere between pure deep copy and passing only a remote reference that points to the original object.

The value of an object migrating by substitution is not really copied itself, but instead only a *surrogate* identifying the object is sent to the target store. On arrival at the target the surrogate has to be substituted by an equivalent object with the same type — though not necessarily with the same value — as the original object.

It is up to application programs in both stores to register the required objects for substitution. Because the equivalent objects at the source and the target have different (local) identities and probably different values, *the equivalence is defined by a logical name agreed between the source and the target store.* As usual we verify that the original and final values have equivalent types.

The substitution tables are persistent. Consequently, separate application programs can set-up these tables before other programs execute, thus removing the registration load from normal operation. Indeed, standard utilities supply the entries for the Napier88 Standard Library [KBC+94] and Glasgow Libraries [WWP+95] in the experiments described below. Then, application specific substitutions can be added.

Avoiding to copy values that already exist in the target is not a new idea. *Ubiquitous resources* have been proposed before as objects that should exist — or are supposed to exist — in all stores. For example, in Facile [Kna95] these ubiquitous resources are identified *at compile-time* by the programmer using a different keyword. In Tycoon/RPC [MMS96] substitutable values are also defined at compile-time, or at run-time without guarantee of type-safety.

These approaches provide a restricted form of substitution where values originating from the same compilation can be defined equivalent between stores. The novelty of our model of substitution is that substitutable objects are defined: *dynamically* while the program is running; *by name* agreed between programmers; and *type-checked* between source and target stores. Other examples of substitution are described in section 4, but they all fail to provide one or more of these characteristics.

3.1.1 Programming Interface

The flexibility provided by substitution can only be fully described with a concrete example. Figure 3 illustrates how to create a procedure called `error` in order to migrate it later to the target program. This procedure `error` simply prints a message of type `string` to the screen and aborts the current execution. Both `writeString` and `abort` belong to the Napier88 standard library [KBC+94].

```
let error := proc( msg:string )
    begin
    writeString( "ERROR: [ " ++ msg ++ " ]'n" )
    abort()
    end
```

Figure 3. Source Code of `error`

Figure 4 shows how the application programmer can register at run-time the *names* for `writeString` and `abort` at the source program (similar statements are required at the target). The *values* of these procedures will then be accessed by following the path indicated in the name. The registration makes these procedures to be substituted in further migrations to the `target` program.

```
substitute( target, "/Library/writeString" );
substitute( target, "/System/abort" );

migrate( target, any(error) )
```

Figure 4. Migrating `error` Using Substitution

When the marshaled value of `error` arrives at the target, the un-marshaling algorithm replaces these two names by the local equivalent values of these procedures.

3.2 Persistent Spaces

Migration by substitution decreases the amount of data being copied between stores but offers no help with *sharing objects* after the remaining objects have been copied. We are concerned here with a particular aspect of object sharing which affects the semantics of transfered objects with common mutable sub-structures.

Suppose A and B share a third object C, which is a common mutable sub-structure in the source store. Then if a program in the source store makes *two successive calls* to the target store — first passing A, then passing B, arbitrarily separated in time — a typical RPC system (including the previous version of Napier/RPC) will produce *two copies of C* in the target. (Some RPC mechanisms will produce this, even if A and B were separate parameters in the same procedure call.)

There are several problems with creating multiple copies of an object in the same store.

1. *Semantic decay* — Programs in the target store will behave differently from programs in the source store. If a program updates C via A, the result is seen when C is examined via B in the source store but not in the target store.

2. *Transmission and space wastage* — C is transferred twice and stored twice. A combinatorial explosion occurs if C is large and shared by many other objects.

3. *State ambiguity* — If many updates or separate program executions occur between the call that sends A and the one that sends B. In the above regime it is difficult to predict the original state of C, particularly as remote copies of C may in the interim have been updated by programs in the target store.

The traditional solution for sharing objects between stores is based on *remote references* to the object being shared [DC93], for example, by remote references requiring all operations to refer to the original store [Wai88] or cache coherency of copies requiring update propagation [KSD+90]. However, remote references force sharing to be highly dependent on the availability of the store in which the object resides, and thus precludes autonomous stores, availability and scalability [MdSAB96].

We propose the concept of *persistent spaces* in which *publishers* release objects that can later be fetched by *any number of subscribers*. Persistent spaces provide an abstraction which enables the application programmer to maintain object sharing in the target store.

Suppose again that A and B share C. If all belong to the same persistent space, and A and B migrate in succession to the target store, then only one copy of C will be created in the target store. This is valid no matter how many times A or B are transmitted, or if A, B or C are updated between migrations.

The explicit *release* and *fetch* operations allow state ambiguity to be controlled. Thus persistent spaces not only maintain sharing relationships between migrations but they also help to resolve the coherence between the copies of C in the source and the target stores.

3.2.1 Programming Interface

The following operations, all of which only access the local store, are available to the *publisher* of objects. (An application example will be described in section 3.3.)

- `publishSpace( name -> space )` — Stores can publish multiple spaces simultaneously. Because spaces do not share common sub-structures between them and thus duplicate local information (see below) we expect few spaces per store. The space name is unique only within the store, so two or more stores may publish spaces with the same name (the ambiguity is resolved by the store address).

- `putInObject( space, objname, objvalue )` — The object name is put in the *publication table* and its value marshaled and copied into the space. This permits the publisher to put objects in the space when they reach a stable value and continue working on the original versions (hidden from clients).

- `changeObject( space, objname, objvalue )` — Similar to `putInObject` but only updates the value in the persistent space, without changing its identity.

- `removeObject( space, objname )` — The object name is removed from the publication table so it cannot be fetched to the clients anymore. However, this has no immediate effect on previously fetched objects in the clients.

These operations have equivalents for subscribers:

- `subscribeSpace( server, name -> space )` — The space is made visible to the client but no objects are fetched at this time. This confirms that the server exists and that it supports a persistent space of that name. Any number of clients can subscribe to the same space. Subsequent calls with the same parameter reconfirm the existence of publisher and space, but otherwise have no effect.

- `fetchSpace( space )` — Fetches the most recent versions of the already fetched objects and fetches any additional objects put in the space that have not been fetched yet. The client has no access to the object value at this time — that is, no marshaling is made — to reduce connection time to the minimum.

There are also a number of local operations at the subscriber that do not require a remote connection to the publisher.

- `lscanSpace( space -> List[objname] )` — Returns all object names already obtained from the publisher.

- `existsObject( space, objname -> bool )` — Checks if an object with that name has already been fetched from the publisher.

- `readObject( space, objname -> objvalue )` — Reconstructs (that is, un-marshals) this object from the space and returns a local reference to its value.

Other (costly) operations can be implemented on top of these or incorporated into the model if experience shows the need. For example, there could be primitives to stop and start periods of strict consistency during which, for a specified publication space, updates would be propagated to the subscribers that applied the primitive. This can be made automatically every time the publisher puts a new object in the space or changes the value of an already published object.

The only operation that is truly remote is `fetchSpace`. Because it does not involve any marshaling or un-marshaling, connection time is much reduced (see table 7). (Although we will not develop further this idea here, persistent spaces are indicated for unreliable environments with low bandwidth, such as the Internet and mobile computing.)

3.3 Application Example

The remote version of the *Library Explorer* has been extended so that its index can be published in a store and fetched in a number of other stores. This permits one *Definitive Library Server* to maintain all the documentation for Glasgow Libraries, create the index and publish it (see figure 5). The index uses two procedures for string `equalTo` and `lessThan` tests, and these procedures migrate by substitution.

```
! creates a new persistent space
let explorer = publishSpace( "Explorer" );

! declare the procedures as substitutable
substitute( explorer, "/equalTo" );
substitute( explorer, "/lessThan" );

! publishes the index but not the procedures
putInObject( explorer, "exploreridx", any(index) );
```

Figure 5. Publishing the Explorer Index

Other stores can fetch the index so that most queries become local (see figure 6). Only the documentation for a specified procedure requires a remote procedure call, and we expect documentation requests to be at least an order of magnitude less frequent than free text queries. The index itself is small (500 KB) when compared to Glasgow Libraries and its documentation (a few tens of MB).

3.4 Performance

In this section we present and explain measurements for migration by substitution, persistent spaces and a new version of the Library Explorer using these techniques.

230

```
! creates a handle for the space
let explorer = subscribeSpace( server, "Explorer" )

! copies the space to the local store
fetchSpace( explorer )

! makes the index visible to the target program
let index = readObject( explorer, "exploreridx" )
```

Figure 6. Subscribing to the Explorer and Fetching the Index

3.4.1 Migration by Substitution

Table 5 shows an experiment conducted to compare the transfer times of a data structure with and without the substitution afforded by the new version of Napier/RPC. The data structure transferred is an empty Map[int,string] — a standard Glasgow Libraries map with integer equalTo and lessThan tests.

Value fetched	Procedures	Objects	Bytes	Time
Simple empty map	transferred	15	404	13 secs
Map[int,string]	substituted	8	300	7 secs

Table 5. Performance of Migration by Substitution

The results show that a substantial gain in performance is achieved by substituting the two procedures by surrogates. This gain is achieved both by not transmitting their values (including marshaling and un-marshaling) but especially by avoiding to compile their hyper-programs at the target [MdSA96].

We expect dramatic performance improvements for large objects migrating by substitution. In addition, for objects that cannot be copied, only substitution will make feasible migration of other objects referring to these.

3.4.2 Persistent Spaces

Table 6 shows measurements for migrating the same Map[int,string] that now contains 10 entries (the procedures migrate by substitution). The first measurement shows the cost to migrate the map the first time. The second measurement publishes and migrates exactly the same map. The numbers show how persistent spaces use *incremental migration* to reduce the amount of data being copied if large parts of common data structures remain with the same value between publications.

Value fetched	Objects	Bytes	Time
New map with 10 entries	93	3,144	10 secs
Same map (with same entries)	4	164	6 secs
Same map with another 10 entries	37	1,400	9 secs
Same map with another 20 entries	67	2,372	17 secs
Same map with another 40 entries	126	4,308	20 secs

Table 6. Performance of Incremental Migration

Interpretation of the third, fourth and fifth measurements requires understanding an aspect of the map implementation. A map has organisational data, which varies only slowly as entries are added. In this case the organisational data was about 2,000 bytes. It then has data representing the entries, in this case about 130 bytes per entry. Taking this into account, the transfers are proportional to the volume of *new* data published each time, although incremental migration also means that performance degrades with the amount of data copied in earlier migrations (e.g., compare the first with the third row).

231

3.4.3 Library Explorer

Table 7 shows measurements for the revised version of the remote Library Explorer described above in section 3.3. We refer to the user-interface program as the Explorer and to the program providing data as the Library Server. The index of the Library Server used for this experiment has 3,389 entries.

The "create index" and "publish index" (marshaling) operations are local to the Library Server. *Only the "transmit bytes" operation is remote.* After being transmitted, the index can then be reconstructed and used locally by the Explorer without the user paying the price of a remote operation for each query.

| Task | Transfer | | Elapsed Time | Place of |
Requested	Objects	Bytes	Time	Operation
Create Index	—	—	38 mins	On Library Server
Publish Index	10,486	—	18 mins	On Library Server
Transmit Bytes	—	500 KB	4 secs	Remote Operation
Reconstruction	10,486	—	37 mins	On Explorer
Typical Query	—	—	1–3 secs	On Explorer

Table 7. Performance of the New Remote Library Explorer

The numbers in the table above show that the advantage of caching the index outweighs the cost of transmitting it only if the index remains stable for a period greater than a few hundred queries. However, when the index is updated and published again, the persistent space will only transmit the *difference* between the old and the new index (incremental migration). Marshaling costs at the server are still proportional to the original index plus the difference, but both transmission and un-marshaling on the clients are only proportional to the difference.

4   Related Work

Our work addresses RPC and higher-order migration in a persistent environment. In this section we describe related research work in each of these areas.

4.1   RPC Mechanisms

Sub-contract [HPM93] lets programmers customise marshaling and un-marshaling to suit their own requirements. It is possible to implement something similar to our substitution mechanism by replacing these operations with custom-built marshaling code, but this task may require from the programmer extensive knowledge about distribution and how RPC systems work. Network Objects [BNOW93] also lets programmers to specify *custom procedures* for pickling particular data types, but details on how this can be achieved are not presented in that paper.

Although CORBA [OMG95] itself is a design, not an implementation, there are many CORBA-compliant products that implement that design. Usually, CORBA implementations are extensions to traditional RPCs and support existing non-persistent languages like C++. While data structures can be copied between different programming languages, object passing is by reference only. The OMG is preparing a *call for proposals* for object migration (in which we have been involved) but first-class procedures are not included in the CORBA object model. None of the CORBA implementations to our knowledge support an orthogonal persistent language, and the restrictions posed by CORBA may not encourage that approach.

4.2   Code Migration

Java [GM94, GM95] is an interpreted language similar to C++, but unlike C++, type-safe and portable across diverse machine architectures. In Java, entire programs — called *Applets* — can migrate as byte code between parts of the application. Java is not persistent and what migrates are self-contained programs using only standard libraries with very limited access to the local environment. The only state carried with these programs is in the static variables associated with classes. We do not know of any implementation of persistent Java that is operational at time of writing [AJDS96].

In Facile [Kna95] procedures can migrate between independent programs, provided they were declared as such at compile-time. Bindings to *ubiquitous resources* are cut and rebuilt when the procedure arrives at the destination. However, these resources have always the same value since they must originate from the same compilation. (Tycoon is described below.)

Obliq [Car95] is a purpose-built distributed programming language, although it can be used from within Modula-3 as a scripting language. Obliq is interpreted and has first-class procedures, but *is not persistent*. Initially, object migration in Obliq was only by reference, but recently Obliq also started to support deep-copy object migration and a restricted form of substitution for user-interface applications [BC95]. It offers a simple programming model but no support for sharing apart from remote references.

4.3   Persistent Systems

Argus [LS83, Lis84, Lis88] was a research programming language that supported persistence and distribution. Stores — called *guardians* in Argus — could exchange objects, including abstract data types but *excluding procedures* (which are not first class citizens in the language). Argus was explicitly designed for distribution, unlike our work which attempts to support distribution on top of an existing language.

The first attempt for migrating procedures in a persistent environment was *remote execution* [DRV91]. Every store supports a procedure rx which can be called remotely with two arguments: a data structure and a procedure. However, the paper provides no description how the transitive closure of the procedure is migrated: if it is by lazy copy, then the stores are not autonomous; and if it is by deep copy, then it suffers from the same problems as our first type-complete RPC. This may be the reason why the implementation is described as "slide ware" in the paper, whereas we are not aware of any future implementation.

A technique designed explicitly for manipulating bindings in a type-safe persistent environment is Octopus [FD93]. Octopus allows type-unsafe operations only in meta-space, but type-safety must be obtained before objects are dropped into the value space again. Although it was originally designed with distribution in mind, it does not explicitly support distribution abstractions. Both the meta-space concept and lack of distribution support may make it unsuitable for direct use by application programmers. We are unsure of its present implementation status.

The work that most closely relates to ours is that on Tycoon/RPC [MMS96, MMS95]. Tycoon/RPC is a type-complete RPC — including first-class procedures and threads — for Tycoon, a persistent programming language. Like our Napier/RPC, Tycoon/RPC is also an add-on to an existing language and it uses a technique similar to migration by substitution. However, there is no support for maintaining sharing semantics between successive migrations or to help with coherence between replicas in different stores.

5   Summary and Future Work

The requirements for distributed computing are becoming more challenging in two ways: 1) the applications attempted are becoming larger, more sophisticated and more dispersed; and 2) the number of applications of distribution is rising rapidly as computer and network costs fall. The first of these means that application programmers are expected to tackle much more complex problems. The second means that many more programmers are required to do this. Without improved technology for the application programmer this will lead to resource and reliability problems, not enough programmers competent to work on these systems and erroneous implementations.

This paper is a first step towards more general and flexible computation models to allow normal application programmers to build elaborate distributed persistent applications. In order to achieve this goal we have extended the basic concept of RPC in several ways in an attempt to meet the challenge above, while retaining as much as possible of the regular and simple concepts that characterise persistent programming. In particular we have:

1. described a general, yet simple programming model for higher-order, type-safe distributed computation that respects store autonomy;

2. presented a technique (migration by substitution) that reduce copying by letting the application programmer register objects that already exist in the other store;

3. provided a new abstraction (persistent spaces) that preserves shared data structures between successive migrations and makes mutable data available in remote stores;

4. built, used and measured an implementation in Napier88, an existing persistent programming language; and

5. developed practical distributed persistent applications to validate its usability and measured our mechanism with real work loads.

The development of Napier/RPC and its example applications have resulted in a number of issues requiring further investigation.

- *Generality and flexibility* — There are a few types which are not yet accommodated by our implementation. For example, we are still developing migration technology for abstract data types, and threads in particular. We are also establishing links with other research communities that share the same basic problems and may benefit from persistence, for example on mobile agents [MdSA96].

- *Extensions to the failure model* — Further research is required to accommodate the case when the transitive closure of an object being put into a persistent space includes objects that cannot migrate. Their resistance to migration may result from types not supported, special objects in the language, or engineering constraints. For example, is it appropriate to migrate an object visibly bound to the local screen ? If it is not, how should the application program be informed so it can take remedial action ?

- *Measurement and evaluation* — We plan to extend a number of existing persistent applications with support for distribution, such as the programming workshop [SWA+96], and to build new distributed persistent applications that take advantage of higher-order migration and persistent spaces.

- *Improved construction technology* — The present implementation depends on circumvention of the type system by the RPC provider and we have found unsatisfactory to work without the type-safety provided for application programmers. We will therefore attempt to identify new primitives that localise this dangerous code. The hope is that — utilising the reflection system which almost satisfies our requirements and a very precise probe below the type-safe interface — we may be able to build programs with type and representation dependencies in a much safer and more convenient way.

- *Better performance* — We anticipate significant performance gains from new versions of Napier88. Nevertheless, the absolute performance needs major improvement beyond that which may be obtained in this way. The exact sources of the present computation costs must be identified and the RPC implementation must then remedy the performance deficiencies.

In parallel, research work is needed on a high-level programming model for distributed computation. Although this issue is not directly related to our research work — at least for the time being — it is fundamental for a good use of the mechanisms we are investigating.

Acknowledgements

The authors would like to acknowledge Peter Dickman, Andrew Black, Stewart Macneill, Quintin Cutts, Graham Kirby, Fritz Knabe, and Bernd Mathiske. The research environment in Glasgow has been partially supported by projects $FIDE_2$ and IMIS, and is now supported by DRASTIC, PJava and ZEST. Miguel Mira da Silva is also partly supported by JNICT.

References

[AE90]   M.P. Atkinson and A. England. Towards new architectures for distributed autonomous database applications. In J. Rosenberg and J.L. Keedy, editors, *Security and Persistence. Proceedings of the International Workshop on Computer Architectures to Support Security and Persistence of Information (Bremen, West Germany, 8–11 May 1990)*, Workshops in Computing, pages 356–377. Springer-Verlag in collaboration with the British Computer Society, 1990.

[AJDS96]   M.P. Atkinson, M. Jordan, L. Daynès, and S. Spence. Design issues for persistent Java: A type-safe, object-oriented, orthogonally persistent system. In *Proceedings of the Seventh International Workshop on Persistent Object Systems (Cape May, New Jersey, USA, May 29-31, 1996)*. Morgan Kaufmann Publishers, 1996.

[AM95]   M.P. Atkinson and R. Morrison. Orthogonal persistent object systems. *VLDB Journal*, 4(3):319–401, 1995.

[BC95]   K. Bharat and L. Cardelli. Migratory applications. In *Proceedings of ACM Symposium on User Interface Software and Technology '95 (Pittsburgh, PA, Nov 1995)*, 1995.

[BN84]   A. Birrel and B. Nelson. Implementing remote procedure calls. *ACM Transactions on Computer Systems*, 2(1):39–59, February 1984.

[BNOW93]   A. Birrell, G. Nelson, S. Owicki, and E. Wobber. Network objects. In *Proceedings of the 14th ACM Symposium on Operating Systems Principles*, pages 217–230, December 1993.

[Bro93]   J.C. Brown. A library explorer for the Napier88 Glasgow Libraries. Master's thesis, Department of Computing Science, University of Glasgow, September 1993.

[Car95]   L. Cardelli. A language with distributed scope. *Computing Systems*, 8(1):27–59, January 1995. A preliminary version appeared in Proceedings of the 22nd ACM Symposium on Principles of Programming Languages.

[DC93]   J. Daniels and S. Cook. Strategies for sharing objects in distributed systems. *Journal of Object-Oriented Programming*, January 1993.

[DdBF+94]   A. Dearle, R. di Bona, J. Farrow, F. Henskens, A. Lindström, and J. Rosenberg. Grasshopper: An orthogonally persistent operating system. *Computer Systems*, 7(3):289–312, 1994.

[DRV91]   A. Dearle, J. Rosenberg, and F. Vaughan. A remote execution mechanism for distributed homogeneous stable stores. In P. Kanellakis and J.W. Schmidt, editors, *Database Programming Languages: Bulk Types and Persistent Data*. Morgan Kaufmann Publishers, 1991. Proceedings of the Third International Workshop on Database Programming Languages (Nafplion, Greece, 27th–30th August 1991).

[DSZ90]   A. Dearle, G.M. Shaw, and S.B. Zdonik, editors. *Proceedings of the Fourth International Workshop on Persistent Object Systems, Their Design, Implementation and Use (Martha's Vineyard, USA, September 1990)*. Morgan Kaufmann Publishers, 1990.

[FD93]   A. Farkas and A. Dearle. Octopus: A reflective mechanism for object manipulation. In C. Beeri, A. Ohori, and D.E. Shasha, editors, *Proceedings of the Fourth International Workshop on Database Programming Languages: Object Models and Languages (Manhattan, New York City, USA, 30th August–1st September 1993)*. Springer-Verlag in collaboration with the British Computer Society, 1993.

[GADV92]   O. Gruber, L. Amsaleg, L. Daynès, and P. Valduriez. Eos, an environment for object-based systems. In J. Rosenberg, editor, *Proceedings of the Twenty-Fifth Hawaii International Conference on System Sciences, Volume I, Emerging Technologies, Architectural and Operating System Support for Persistent Object Systems*, pages 757–768, 1992.

[GM94]   J. Gosling and H. McGilton. *The Java Language — A White Paper*. Sun Microsystems, 1994.

[GM95]   J. Gosling and H. McGilton. *The Java Language Environment — A White Paper*. Sun Microsystems, May 1995.

[HPM93]   G. Hamilton, M.L. Powell, and J.G. Mitchell. Subcontract: A flexible base for distributed programming. Technical Report SMLI TR-93-13, Sun Microsystems Laboratories, 1993.

[KBC+94]   G.N.C. Kirby, A.L. Brown, R.C.H. Connor, Q.I. Cutts, A. Dearle, V.S. Moore, R. Morrison, and D.S. Munro. The Napier88 standard library reference manual version 2.2. Technical Report FIDE/94/105, ESPRIT Basic Research Action, Project Number 6309 — FIDE$_2$, 1994.

[Kir93]   G.N.C. Kirby. *Reflection and Hyper-Programming in Persistent Programming Systems*. PhD thesis, University of St Andrews, 1993.

[Kna95]   F. Knabe. *Language Support for Mobile Agents*. PhD thesis, Carnegie Mellon University, Pittsburgh, PA 15213, USA, December 1995.

[KSD+90]   B. Koch, T. Schunke, A. Dearle, F. Vaughan, C. Marlin, R. Fazakerley, and C. Barter. Cache coherency and storage management in a persistent object system. In Dearle et al. [DSZ90].

235

[Lis84] B. Liskov. Overview of the Argus language and system. MIT Programming Methodology Group Memo 40, MIT, February 1984.

[Lis88] B. Liskov. Distributed programming in Argus. *Communications of the ACM*, 31(3):300–312, March 1988.

[LJGS90] B. Liskov, P. Johnson, R. Gruber, and L. Shrira. A highly available object repository for use in a heterogeneous distributed system. In Dearle et al. [DSZ90], pages 255–266.

[LS83] B. Liskov and R. Scheifler. Guardians and actions: Linguistic support for robust, distributed programs. *ACM Transactions on Programming Languages and Systems*, 5(3):381–404, July 1983.

[MBC+94] R. Morrison, A.L. Brown, R.C.H. Connor, Q.I. Cutts, A. Dearle, G.N.C. Kirby, and D.S. Munro. The Napier88 reference manual release 2.0. Technical Report FIDE/94/104, ESPRIT Basic Research Action, Project Number 6309 — FIDE$_2$, 1994.

[MdS95a] M. Mira da Silva. Automating type-safe RPC. In O.A. Bukhres, M.T. Özsu, and M.C. Shan, editors, *Proceedings of The Fifth International Workshop on Research Issues on Data Engineering: Distributed Object Management (Taipei, Taiwan, 6th–7th March 1995)*, pages 100–107. IEEE Computer Society Press, 1995.

[MdS95b] M. Mira da Silva. Programmer's manual to Napier88/RPC 2.2. Technical Report FIDE/95/133, ESPRIT Basic Research Action, Project Number 6309 — FIDE$_2$, 1995.

[MdSA96] M. Mira da Silva and M. Atkinson. Combining mobile agents with persistent systems: Opportunities and challenges. In *Proceedings of the 2nd ECOOP Workshop on Mobile Object Systems (Linz, Austria, July 8-9, 1996)*, 1996. To be published.

[MdSAB96] M. Mira da Silva, M.P. Atkinson, and A. Black. Semantics for parameter passing in a type-complete persistent RPC. In *Proceedings of the 16th International Conference on Distributed Computing Systems (Hong-Kong, May, 1996)*. IEEE Computer Society Press, 1996.

[MMS95] B. Mathiske, F. Matthes, and J.W. Schmidt. On migrating threads. In *Proceedings of the Second International Workshop on Next Generation Information Technologies and Systems (Naharia, Israel, June 1995)*, 1995.

[MMS96] B. Mathiske, F. Matthes, and J.W. Schmidt. Scaling database languages to higher-order distributed programming. In Paolo Atzeni and Val Tannen, editors, *Proceedings of the Fifth International Workshop on Database Programming Languages (Gubbio, Umbria, Italy, 6th-8th September 1995)*, Electronic Workshops in Computing. Springer-Verlag, 1996.

[Mun93] D.S. Munro. *On the Integration of Concurrency, Distribution and Persistence*. PhD thesis, University of St Andrews, 1993.

[OMG95] OMG — Object Management Group, Inc. *The Common Object Request Broker: Architecture and Specification (CORBA)*, 1995.

[Sun93] Sun Microsystems. *RPC Programming Guide*, 1993.

[SWA+96] D.I.K. Sjøberg, R.C. Welland, M.P. Atkinson, P. Philbrow, C.A. Waite, and S.D. Macneill. The persistent workshop — a programming environment for Napier88. In *Proceedings of the 7th Nordic Workshop on Programming Environment Research (Aalborg, Denmark, 29-31 May, 1996)*, 1996.

[TA90] B.H. Tay and A.L. Ananda. A survey of remote procedure calls. *ACM Operating Systems Review*, 24(3), July 1990.

[Wai88] F. Wai. *Distributed Concurrent Persistent Programming Languages: An Experimental Design and Implementation*. PhD thesis, University of Glasgow, April 1988.

[WWP+95] C.A. Waite, R.C. Welland, T. Printezis, A. Pirmohamed, P. Philbrow, G. Montgomery, M. Mira da Silva, S.D. Macneill, D. Lavery, C. Hertzig, A. Froggatt, R.L. Cooper, and M.P. Atkinson. Glasgow libraries for orthogonally persistent systems — philosophy, organisation and contents. Technical Report FIDE/95/132, ESPRIT Basic Research Action, Project Number 6309 — FIDE$_2$, 1995.

Data Mining Using Light Weight Object Management in Clustered Computing Environments*

R. L. Grossman[†], S. Bailey and D. Hanley

Laboratory for Advanced Computing
University of Illinois at Chicago

Magnify, Inc.
Oak Park, Illinois

Abstract

In this note, we describe the design, implementation and our initial experience with an object warehouse specifically designed for selecting, computing and filtering very large collections of objects, each of which has a large number of attributes. The object warehouse is built on top of a persistent object manager. We are especially interested in persistent object managers which are monotone, that is designed for data which is read-mostly, occasionally appended, and infrequently updated. These operations and access patterns are common when data mining large data stores, which provides the main motivation for our current work. For object warehouses to prove useful, they must scale as the number of objects increase, as the selectivity of queries increases, and as the computational complexity of queries increases. We show that our implementation scales in each of the dimensions over three orders of magnitudes: from queries taking seconds touching all the attributes on megabytes of data to queries taking hours touching a small fraction of the data on stores approaching one hundred gigabytes.

Keywords: persistent object stores, data mining, data warehouses, scientific computing, numerically intensive queries

1 Introduction

We are interested in the class of scientific and engineering applications which consist of numerically and statistically intensive queries on large amounts of data in which the access pattern consists of frequent reads, occasional appends, and infrequent updates. Examples include searching for new particles in high energy physics data [ARA], uncovering evidence for global climate change from satellite sensor data [DOZ], searching collections of radar images for military threats [LAD], looking for similarity patterns in large amounts of time series data [AGR], and searching for patterns in large amounts of textural data [DAM].

The problem is difficult due to 1) the large amounts of data, and 2) the numerically and statistically intensive queries. On the other hand, the problem is made simpler due to the access patterns: the full

---

*This research was supported in part by DOE grant DE-FG02-92ER25133, and NSF grants IRI-9224605, CDA-9303433, CDA-9413948, and the National Scalable Cluster Project. Please send correspondence to Robert Grossman, Laboratory for Advanced Computing, University of Illinois at Chicago, 851 South Morgan Street, Chicago, IL 60607, USA, 312 413 2176, 312 996 1491 (fax), grossman@uic.edu

[†]The author is also a member of the technical staff at Magnify, Inc. This work was also supported in part by the Massive Digital Data Systems Program through a contract to Magnify, Inc.

functionality of a database is not needed, since the data is by and large read only, except when additional data is being added.

To be specific, consider a persistent object store containing high energy physics data consisting of objects representing particle collisions, which are called events. Data analysis requires analyzing from several thousand to several million events. Assume that each event has several hundred attributes and is about 0.5 megabytes in size. Some of the attributes are object-valued, such as leptons in the example below, and some are collection-valued. A typical query consists of the following steps:

Select. Look through all events and select those having two leptons such that the charge of the two leptons is equal but of opposite sign.

Compute. For each event selected, compute the energy of the event that the leptons contribute.

Filter. Collect those events such that the energy contributed by the leptons is within a specified range.

Aggregate and Analyze. Compute a histogram of the lepton energy of those events passing through the filter.

These types of queries are becoming common in a variety of disciplines. As another example, consider a persistent object store containing laser radar images which are tagged with attributes and a query which *selects* those images in a specified region during the past two hours, *computes* the number of military threats in each image using a feature extraction algorithm, *filters* the results and retains those posing the greatest threats, and *analyzes* the results to provide a current estimate of the location of the threats [LAD].

Since these types of applications involve *Selecting, Computing,* and *Filtering* (SCF) large collections of objects, for lack of a better term, we say that these applications are all concerned with *SCF data mining.*

The purpose of this paper is to describe our experience designing, implementing and operating an object warehouse for SCF-queries built over a persistent object manager. We report on our experiences using the object warehouse with both synthetic and real data. We also identify some design elements which make persistent object stores useful for these types of queries and describe our preliminary work developing SCF benchmarks related to scalability.

We conclude this introduction with a brief summary of the paper. Section 2 contains background material and a description of related work.

Section 3 describes some of the characteristics of persistent object stores relevant to data mining. We call a persistent object store *monotone* (the term is due to Peter Buneman) in the case that it is designed to work with large amounts of read-only data, to which data is occasionally appended, but infrequently updated. We call a persistent object store *optimistic* in the case that it assumes that processes which access the data have information about how the data is physically laid out. Most persistent object stores and databases are optimistic, while most distributed object systems and wide area object systems are not. To further improve performance we exploited *parallelism* and *precompute* and *index* as much of the data as possible. These characteristics lead to the acronym MOPPI which we use to describe *Monotone, Optimistic* object stores supporting *Parallel* selection, computing and filtering of *Precomputed* and *Indexed* data. We view MOPPI Stores as a type of object warehouse.

The experimental results in this paper use a MOPPI Store we designed and implemented as an object warehouse called PTool. The PTool used for this paper is the third generation in a series of systems sharing the same name. The first PTool (Version 0.4) was designed to work for single networked workstations [GRO94] and was used for applications in aeronautics and high energy physics. The second PTool (Version 0.6) was designed for high performance shared nothing multi-computers, such as the IBM SP-2, and was mainly used for mining high energy physics data [ARA] and [GRO95b]. The current PTool (Version 2.0) is designed for local, campus, and wide area workstation clusters, and has been used for a variety of applications, including high energy physics [BAI], complex systems [GRO93], and computational fluid dynamics [GRO95d]. Section 4 contains a brief description of Version 2 of PTool.

An important goal of this work was to understand issues affecting the scalability of SCF-queries when using object warehouses. The model we used to investigate scalability issues is described in Section 5. In this model we identify size, parallelism, selectivity and complexity as key factors limiting the scalablity of SCF-queries. Section 6 describes our experimental results involving these factors. In this section we report on SCF-queries on tens of Gigabytes of data. Using these results we are currently experimenting on scaling our system to work with hundreds of Gigabytes of data. Section 7 contains a discussion and our conclusions.

Although this work is very preliminary, we feel that it is a challenging and important problem to understand the critical issues affecting the scalability of persistent object stores to the Terabyte range.

We feel that this paper makes two contributions to the field of scientific data mining: 1) We have identified a variant of persistent object stores—MOPPI—which are useful for scientific data mining. 2) We have designed, implemented and used MOPPI stores for several scientific data mining applications demonstrating the practicality and scalability of approach. In particular we have demonstrated numerically intensive queries on synthetic and real data on persistent object stores ranging in size from megabytes to sizes approaching one hundred Gigabytes.

2 Background and Related Work

The focus in this paper is on systems appropriate for selecting, querying, filtering and mining scientific data. The data is complex in that attributes may be elementary data types, object-valued, or collection valued.

Recall that objects are called *persistent* in the case that their existence is orthogonal to the process which creates them. This means that the creating process writes them to disk or other permanent media in a format in which other processes can later access them; otherwise, objects are called *transient*. In other words transient objects are coterminal with the process that create them.

There are a variety of systems in use for working with persistent collections of objects.

Persistent Object Managers. Persistent object managers support persistence for objects and can be viewed as extensions to, or replacements to, file systems. The collections [DEA] and [ATK] provide a variety of perspectives on persistent object managers.

Object-oriented Databases. An object-oriented database provides a variety of functionality for persistent objects, such as a transactions, back up and recovery, concurrency control, and a query language. Object-oriented databases arose to manage the data for a variety of complex applications such as computer-aided design CAD, computer-aided software engineering (CASE), scientific databases, and knowledge bases. Object-oriented databases are generally designed to support transactions involving frequent updates on relatively small collections of objects, while object warehouses are designed for numerically intensive queries on relatively large collections of objects.

Object-Relational Databases. Support for user-defined objects and user-defined functions can be added to traditional relational databases. Object-relational databases are extensions to relational databases supporting some of the most important features of object-oriented databases.

Distributed Object Systems. Distributed object systems are designed to manage objects in heterogeneous environments. Examples include OMG's CORBA in the UNIX environment and COM/OLE for Win-32 environments. The central issue for these types of systems is how a heterogeneous system can access an object without necessarily knowing its object id (OID), where it is stored or how it is stored. To support this type of complexity incurs an added overhead.

Wide Area Object Systems. Wide area object systems are designed to manage objects in internet and intranet environments. Sun's Java is an example. Security is an overriding concern for this category since clients can easily access objects from untrusted hosts.

Object file systems. As traditional file systems evolve, their files are beginning to take on some of the attributes of objects, such as supporting attributes, hierarchical structures, and embedded files.

3 MOPPI Stores

Our goal was to design, implement and gain some experience with an object warehouse designed for scientific data mining. The system had five main requirements:

R1. *Large data sets.* The most important goal was to support very large data sets, ranging in size from tens to thousands of gigabytes, consisting of objects, each of which had a large number of attributes. It was important that our system scale transparently from small stores to very large stores.

R2. *Low overhead access to the data.* Another goal was to provide access to the data with very low overhead. This was essential since most interactions with the database were numerically or statistically intensive queries.

R3. *Support for parallel queries.* Another goal was to support processing, computing and filtering of objects in parallel together with returning, and merging a *fixed object* return type.

R4. *Transparent access to the data.* It was also important that access to the data be transparent in that the application programmer should not need to worry explicitly about transforming the data from one format to another just because the data set was large or involved a large number of attributes. For example, to gain efficiency with distributed object systems one often imports the data in one format and works with the data in another.

R5. *Simple Design.* In addition, as a practical matter, our interest was to simplify the design of the system as much as possible in order to make our goal of scaling, maintaining and using the system to manage Terabytes of data as easy as possible.

By an object warehouse we mean a system designed for numerically and statistically intensive queries on persistent collections of objects. We now describe some of the strategies which are commonly used to improve the performance of these types of queries.

Precomputed. The easiest way to lower the cost of numerically or statistically intensive computations is to precompute as many queries as possible.

Indexed. Another easy way to improve performance is to provide a variety of indicies to the objects in the warehouse so that there is as direct access as possible to the underlying data.

Monotone. In mathematics, a function is called monotone in case it is non-decreasing (or non-increasing). Following a suggestion of Peter Bunemann, we use the term monotone to refer to persistent object stores in which objects are appended, but not deleted. With monotone object stores, it is easier to cluster the objects in order to improve access times. Without this property, attributes which need to be analyzed together might not be stored together. Clustering data to improve access is easier for monotone object stores. Monotone object stores are also easier to design. There are several variants: For some applications, updates to objects may be accomplished by versioning: the updated object is appended and a link added to the prior version. When necessary, the warehouse as a whole may have to be rebuilt to make room for additional data.

Optimistic. Both object warehouses and object-oriented databases typically store their objects in a format particular to a specific environment. This means that little or no reformatting is required when accessing objects from that environment. On the other hand, there may be a significant cost incurred when accessing the objects from a heterogeneous environment.

The goal of these strategies is to obtain higher performance access to objects in the warehouse. Pre-computing involves the trade off of obtaining higher performance by increasing the (one-time) cost required to populate the warehouse. Both precomputing and indexing involve the trade of off of obtaining higher performance by increasing the size of the store, since the derived data which is precomputed must be stored as must the indices. Storing the data in an optimistic fashion involves the trade off of incurring additional costs when accessing the data from heterogeneous environments.

The acronymn MOPPI is derived from the initial letters of these characteristics: the warehouses are designed to be *Monotone*, are *Optimistic* about data layout, support *Parallel* access, computing and filtering, and contain *Precomputed* data which is *Indexed*.

4   Design and Implementation

As described more fully in [GRO95b], PTool Version 0.6 provides persistence for instances of C++ classes through an application program interface (API) and class libraries. Persistent objects are grouped together into persistent container classes provided by the class libraries. This is one of the standard approaches to provide persistence to C++ objects.

To provide scalability, PTool Version 0.6 organizes physical collections of objects into segments, as is usual, and organizes physical collections of segments into larger units which we call folios. Segments are simply contiguous extents of virtual memory which are moved or mapped between disk and memory. Folios are moved between disks or between disks and tertiary storage devices. Folios are implemented as files to facilitate interfacing PTool with hierarchical and distributed storage systems [GRO95a]. In PTool, there are separate managers for objects, segments, and folios. For additional details, see [GRO95b]. The current Version 2 of PTool contains an ODMG93 compliant API and organization into object managers, segment managers and folio managers.

In addition, Version 2 is designed to work with local, campus, and wide area clusters of workstations, as well as high performance clusters of workstations. The logical model is of a distributed collection of nodes with one or more PTool processes running on each of the nodes. Nodes may run i/o, compute or query processes. The distinction between these different types of processes is discussed further in the next section. Physical data management and data transport in PTool Version 2 is divided into four layers:

Collection Layer. PTool client processes access collections of objects, supporting application specific storage and access structures.

Object Layer. Methods for creating, accessing, and updating objects are here. This is actually the simplest part of PTool and remains largely the same as in Version 0.6.

Container Layer. This layer manages segments and folios on single nodes, collections of nodes in high performance switching fabrics, nodes within a local area networks, and nodes within a wide area networks. Collective i/o is supported in this layer. This is the most complex part of PTool and is new in Version 2.

Transport Layer. This layer abstracts the process of communicating between nodes independent of whether sockets, circuits, message passing, RPCs, or some other protocol is used.

5   Computational Model

In this section, we describe a model for costing SCF-queries and for understanding their scalability. Input to these queries consists of a selection criterion and a filtering criterion. The output consists of a collection of objects or aggregated attributes of objects.

We assume that we have a collection of objects and that each object has one or more attributes. We assume that objects are stored on one or more nodes in a network. We distinguish between three types of nodes: i/o nodes, compute nodes, and query nodes, which we describe below. The model we use is illustrated in Figure 5. This section is based in part on [GRO96a].

Select. In this phase, objects satisfying a specified criterion are selected. There are two selectivities which arise in this phase. The first is called the *input-output selectivity* σ_{io}. The objects may have hundreds of attributes and not all of them may be required to determine whether the object satisfies the specified selectivity criterion. The input-output selectivity may be measured using either the ratio m_0/m, where m_0 is the number of the total number m of attributes used in criterion, or by s_0/s, where s_0 is the amount of space in bytes occupied by the attributes used in the criterion and s is the total size in bytes of the object. The second selectivity is called the *selection selectivity* σ_s and denotes the percentage of the total number of objects N in the store satisfying the specified criterion.

Compute. In this phase, derived data is computed for each object. There are two types of derived data computed: The first type simply requires using data from a single object's attributes. The second type may, in addition, require data from other objects. In the latter case the computation would access certain global meta-data.

Filter. In this phase, those objects satisfying a criterion for filtering are retained. The combined cost of the compute and filter phase of a query is denoted κ and has units seconds per object.

Aggregate. In this phase, all the objects satisfying the filter criterion are collected.

Define the *i/o throughput* τ_{io} of a node as the amount of data that can be accessed, which is measured in bytes per second. We have immediately from the definitions above that the cost of the query, which is measured in seconds, is approximately equal to

$$\max\left\{S \cdot \sigma_{io}/\tau_{io}, N \cdot \sigma_s \cdot \kappa\right\},$$

where S is the total size of the store, measured in bytes and N is the total number of objects in the store.

The effective size of the store, which is dependent upon the particular query is $S \cdot \sigma_{io}$, where σ_{io} is the i/o-selectivity. The effective number of objects, which is again dependent upon the query, is $N \cdot \sigma_s$, where σ_s is the selection selectivity. The query cost is then a simple function of the effective size of the query and either the i/o-throughput or the cost per query per object. The computation is input-output bound in the case that the first term is dominant and compute-bound in the case that the second term is dominant.

Scalability. We can now return to the primary purpose of this paper. Specifically, this paper is concerned with our experience designing, implementing and working with object warehouses built using persistent object managers which scale over three orders of magnitude as the size, selectivity, and complexity of SCF-queries vary. Specifically:

1. Does the object warehouse scale as the size S increases?

2. Does the object warehouse scale as the complexity κ of the query increases?

3. Does the object warehouse scale as the selectivities σ_{io} and σ_s increase? The *apparent i/o throughput* τ_{io}/σ_{io} provides a measure of this scale-up.

4. Does the object warehouse scale as the number of nodes n increases? Ideally, for i/o-bound queries, we expect the *total i/o throughput* to equal $n \cdot \tau_{io}$, where n is the number of i/o-nodes. A similar formula holds for compute-bound queries.

In addition, we are interested in the scalability of the system as the number of attributes of an object increases, as the individual size of an object increases, and as the number of objects in a collection class or store increases. For this preliminary work, we have concentrated on the four measures above.

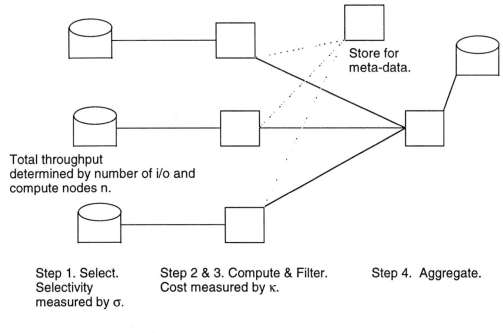

Store for
meta-data.

Total throughput
determined by number of i/o and
compute nodes n.

Step 1. Select.
Selectivity
measured by σ.

Step 2 & 3. Compute & Filter.
Cost measured by κ.

Step 4. Aggregate.

Apparent throughput determined
by selectivity σ.

Figure 1: The computational model we use.

6 Experimental Results

6.1 Synthetic Data

Experiments were conducted on a cluster of eight workstations connected with Asynchronous Transfer Mode (ATM) technology. Each workstation is a Hewlett-Packard Apollo 9000 Model 725/100 with 128 Megabytes of RAM, and a 9 Gigabyte, external, Fast-Wide, single-ended, SCSI disk. The workstations are connected by a FORE Systems ASX-200 ATM switch utilizing Hardware version 1.0 and Software version ForeThought 3.4.2 (1.3). Each workstation is connected to the switch via a Hewlett-Packard J2802B EISA/ATM adapter card rated at OC-3 (155Mbps) and two multi-mode fibers. The communication protocol was HP implemented TCP/IP over ATM (i.e. Classical IP).

All of our experiments involved a simple Event class consisting of an event header and an event body containing five hundred attributes. Size was varied by using more events. Selectivity was varied by selecting events using more of the attributes. Computational cost was varied by executing a fixed series of floating point operations from one (complexity one) to a thousand times (complexity one thousand). For further details, see [GRO96c].

Database Size. In this experiment we varied the database size between 4 and 40 Gigabytes while fixing the selectivity at 5% and the query complexity at 1. Five different database sizes where chosen: 4 Gig, 12 Gig, 20 Gig, 32 Gig, and 40 Gig. Six trials were run for each database size; the mean results of the experiment are summarized in Figure 6.1. This experiment showed that query times increase in a linear fashion as database size progresses from 4 Gigabytes to 40 Gigabytes. This is as expected since the overhead of the PTool management scheme does not increase in proportion to the database size.

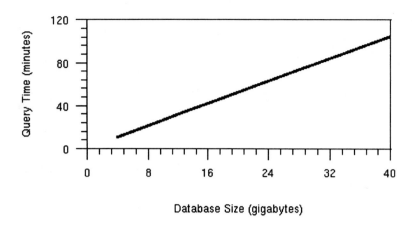

Figure 2: This graph shows the result of varying the size S of the store using synthetic data.

Selectivity. In this experiment we varied the selectivity of the query between 0.2% and 100% while fixing the database size at 4 Gigabytes and the query complexity at 1. Seven selectivities were chosen: 0.2%, 1%, 5%, 20%, 50%, 85%, 100%. Six trials were conducted at each selectivity. The mean results of the experiment are summarized in Figure 6.1. The results show an increase in query time as selectivity approaches 100% from 0%.

Further analysis shows a non-linear increase in query time as selectivity progresses from 0% to around 40% and a linear increase as selectivity continues to progress from around 40% to 100%. This dual characteristic of the query time increase is a signature of the impact of PTool's fetching and caching scheme. When selectivity is low, each Event Body that is pulled for computation is relatively far apart from the next. At extremely low selectivities this is not a factor since very few Event Bodies are fetched. However at moderate selectivities (between 5% and 40%), only a relative few selected Event Bodies are present in each PTool segment. This causes many caching misses and creates a quickly increasing overhead. However, at around 40% selectivity, the cache misses decrease as the data selected is closer together and this results in lower order increase in query time.

Complexity. For this experiment, complexity was scaled from 1 to 1000. This represents relative number of floating point operations on each object "selected." Six trials were conducted for each of 12 different complexities; the mean results are indicated in Figure 6.1. As is evident from the graph, the query time scaled linearly to a complexity rating of 1000. It is important to note that the query becomes compute bound (i.e. the query time depends on the computational performance of the machine) almost immediately (somewhere around 100).

Parallelism. To test parallelism, we created 8 i/o-nodes containing 6 gigabytes of data each. The same 8 nodes were also used as compute nodes for the compute and filter portion of the SCF-query. One of the 8 nodes was also used as the query node. The i/o-throughput τ_{io} was approximately 2.3 megabytes per node. We worked with low complexity queries so that the queries were i/o-bound. The total throughput scaled linearly from 1 to 8 nodes, provided a total throughput of approximately 19 megabytes per second over a total store size of 48 gigabytes. One does not expect this scale up to continue indefinitely since the query node which collects the returned objects will eventually create a bottleneck. Unfortunately, our experimental facility did not allow us to measure the total throughput provided by parallel SCF-operations over a greater range.

Query Time vs. Query Complexity for Database Size: 4.034 GBytes and Selectivity 5%

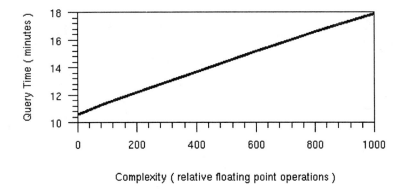

Figure 3: This graph shows the result of varying the complexity κ of the query using synthetic data.

Query Time vs. Selectivity for Database Size: 4.034 GBytes and Query Complexity: 1

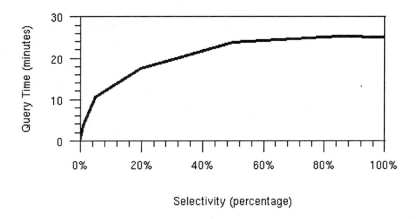

Figure 4: This graph shows the result of varying the selectivity σ_{io} of the query using synthetic data.

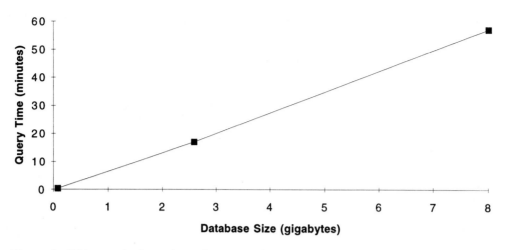

Figure 5: This graph shows how the query time scales linearly with the size of the store using high energy physics data. Some of the data for the last two points are estimates. This graph is from [GRO96b], where additional details can be found about this work.

6.2 Experimental Data

This section summarizes the results from [GRO96b]. For this series of experiments we used data from the CDF experiment at Fermi National Accelerator Laboratory. We created 3 PTool stores using four i/o-nodes. Each i/o-node was allocated 2 file systems of 2 Gbytes each. We used about 10.6 Gbytes for these 3 stores. The analysis used one PTool compute and query node running on the least loaded workstation of the SP-2 system (with a TB0 switch) at the University of Pennsylvania.

A prototype physics SCF-analysis, representing the particle decay $Z^0 \rightarrow e^+ e^-$ was coded in C++. We achieved an i/o-throughput τ_{io} of approximately 2.9 Mbytes/seconds, while the production code at Fermi Laboratory (written in Fortran) delivered approximately 0.88 Mbytes/seconds when reading the corresponding data in the legacy file format in which it was stored.

7 Discussion and Conclusion

In this paper we have described the design, implementation and usage of a specialized object warehouse for data mining queries which is built using a persistent object manager. Our interest is in using these object warehouses to support data mining queries involving numerically and statistically intensive analyses on large data stores, containing large numbers of objects, each of which has large numbers of attributes.

We focused on data mining queries involving *selecting* objects based upon a selection criterion involving one or more of their attributes, *computing* additional derived data, *filtering* to retain those objects satisfying a filtering criterion, and aggregating the results for further analysis. We call these types of queries SCF-queries. They are common in scientific data analysis, scientific computing, and related areas.

More precisely our interest was designing, implementing and operating an object warehouse in which SCF-queries scale as the data size, selectivity, and complexity of the queries range over three orders of magnitude. Specifically, we desired the ability to execute transparently queries lasting seconds on megabytes of data touching all of the attributes to queries taking hours on tens to hundreds of gigabytes of data touching 0.01% of the data. In this paper, we reported on results using actual data over most of this range and using synthetic data with the same structure over the entire range.

To provide this range of scalability we worked with persistent object stores with the following characteristics:

246

Monotone. We assume that the stores are read-mostly, with data appended, and infrequently updated.

Optimistic. We assume that the persistent object manager can provide low overhead access to data by exploiting knowledge about how the data is laid out on disk.

Parallel Access & Computing. We assume that the object warehouse supports parallel access, computation, and filtering. To simplify the design we assume that the return type of a computation is a collection of homogeneous objects.

Precomputed and Indexed. To further gain performance object warehouses precompute and index as much information as possible.

We use the acronym MOPPI to describe object stores with these characteristics.

It is usually sufficiently difficult to work with large data sets of actual data, much less to test different object store designs using real data. Although we have done so in this paper, we also have relied heavily on synthetic data having the same structural characteristics and have not been able to test as many alternate designs as may have been ideal.

In this work, we have provided a brief description of a MOPPI store we designed and implemented called PTool and uncovered some short-comings in our current implementation (Version 2). We mention two of the most important:

First, although read-only access works well for numerically and statistically intensive data access during data mining queries, it is much less satisfactory when populating persistent object stores that may be hundred gigabytes in size. For this reason, we are currently exploring a variety of means of supporting back up, recovery, and concurrency during populating very large object stores.

Second, with one hundred gigabytes of disk spread over a few dozen nodes managing the physical resources of the system becomes an important problem. Nodes, disks, and other peripherals may come and go. Distributing i/o-processes, compute processes, and filtering processes over the appropriate nodes is also a problem. For this reason, we are experimenting with different resource management algorithms, strategies and tools for handling these and related problems.

In this paper, we feel that we 1) have made the case for using MOPPI stores for data mining queries which involve selecting, computing and filtering large collections of objects, each of which has a large number of attributes, and 2) presented evidence that this approach scales over a wide range of data sizes, selectivities, and query complexities.

References

[AGR] R. Agrawal, C. Faloutsos, A. Swami, "Efficient Similarity Search in Sequence Databases," *Lecture Notes in Computer Science,* Volume 730, Springer-Verlag, pp. 69–84, 1993.

[ARA] N. Araujo, R. Grossman, D. Hanley, W. Xu, S. Ahn, K. Denisenko, M. Fischler, M. Galli D. Malon and E. May, "Some Remarks on Parallel Data Mining Using a Persistent Object Manager," *Proceedings of the Conference on Computing in High Energy Physics 1995,* to appear.

[ATK] M. P. Atkinson, V. Benzaken and D. Maier, editors, *Persistent Object Systems (Proceedings of the Sixth International Workshop on Persistent Object Systems),* Springer-Verlag and British Computer Society, 1995.

[BAI] S. Bailey, R. Grossman, and D. Hanley, D. Benton and B. Hollebeek, "Scalable Digital Libraries of Event Data and the NSCP Meta-Cluster," *Proceedings of the Conference on Computing in High Energy Physics 1995,* to appear. *Laboratory for Advanced Computing Technical Report,* Number LAC 96-R3, University of Illinois at Chicago, 1995.

[CAT] R. G. G. Cattell, editor, *The Object Database Standard ODMG-93,* Morgan Kaufmann Publishers, San Francisco, California, 1994.

[DAM] M. Damashek, "Gauging Similarity with n-Grams: Language-Independent Categorization of Text," *Science,* Volume 267, pp. 843–848, 1995.

[DAY] C. T. Day, S. Loken, J. F. MacFarlane, E. May, D. Lifka, E. Lusk, L. E.Price, A. Baden, R. Grossman, X. Qin, L. Cormell, P. Leibold, D. Liu, U. Nixdorf, B. Scipioni, T. Song, "Database Computing in HEP — Progress Report," *Proceedings of the International Conference on Computing in High Energy Physics '92,* C. Verkerk and W. Wojcik, editors, CERN-Service d'Information Scientifique, 1992, ISSN 0007-8328, pp. 557-560.

[DEA] A. Dearle, G. M. Shaw, S. B. Zdonik, editors, "Implementing Persistent Object Bases: Principles and Practice," Morgan Kaufmann Publishers, Inc., San Mateo, California, 1991.

[DOZ] J. Dozier, "Access to Data in NASA's Earth Observing System," in *Proceedings of the 1992 ACM SIGMOD, SIGMOD Record,* Volume 21, ACM, New York, 1992, page 1.

[GRO93] R. L. Grossman, D. Valsamis and X. Qin, "Persistent stores and hybrid systems," *Proceedings of the 32nd IEEE Conference on Decision and Control,* IEEE Press, 1993, pp. 2298-2302.

[GRO94] R. L. Grossman and X. Qin, "Ptool: a scalable persistent object manager," *Proceedings of SIGMOD 94,* ACM, 1994, page 510.

[GRO95a] R. L. Grossman D. Hanley, and X. Qin "Caching and migration for physical collections of objects: Interfacing persistent object stores and hierarchical storage systems," in *Proceedings of the 14th IEEE Computer Society Mass Storage Systems Symposium,* S. Coleman, editor, IEEE, 1995, pages 127-135.

[GRO95b] R. L. Grossman, N. Araujo, X. Qin, and W. Xu, "Managing physical folios of objects between nodes," *Persistent Object Systems (Proceedings of the Sixth International Workshop on Persistent Object Systems),* M. P. Atkinson, V. Benzaken and D. Maier, editors, Springer-Verlag and British Computer Society, 1995.

[GRO95c] R. L. Grossman, D. Hanley, and X. Qin, "PTool: A Light Weight Persistent Object Manager," *Proceedings of SIGMOD 95,* ACM, 1995, page 488.

[GRO95d] R. L. Grossman, A. Lifschitz, and Z. Likoudis, Persistent Object Stores of Two-Dimensional Point Vortices, *Laboratory for Advanced Computing Technical Report,* Number LAC 96-R4, University of Illinois at Chicago, 1995.

[GRO96a] R. L. Grossman, "A Computational Model for Data Mining Queries," *Magnify Technical Report,* Number 96-R6, February, 1996.

[GRO96b] S. Bailey, D. Benton, R. L. Grossman, D. Hanley, B. Hollebeek, R. Oliveira, "Mining Persistent Object Stores of High Energy Physics Data: A Case Study Using PTool," *Laboratory for Advanced Computing Technical Report,* Number LAC 96-R6, University of Illinois at Chicago, 1996.

[GRO96c] R. L. Grossman, S. Bailey, and D. Hanley, "Selecting, Computing and Filtering Large Object Stores, in preparation.

[LAD] J. G. Verly and R. L. Delanoy, "Model-based Automatic Target Recognition (ATR) System for Forwardlooking Groundbased and Airborne Imaging Laser Radars (LADAR), *Proceedings of the IEEE,* Volume 84, pp. 126–163, 1996.

[QUA] D. R. Quarrie, C. T. Day, S. Loken, J. F. Macfarlane, D. Lifka, E. Lusk, D. Malon, E. May, L. E. Price, L. Cormell, A. Gauthier, P. Liebold, J. Hilgart, D. Liu, J. Marstaller, U. Nixdorf, T. Song, R. Grossman, X. Qin, D. Valsamis, M. Wu, W. Xu, A. Baden, "The PASS Project: A Progress Report," *Proceedings of the Conference on Computing in High Energy Physics 1994,* edited by S. C. Loken, pp. 229–232, 1995.

Multicomputer object stores: the Multicomputer Texas experiment

Stephen M Blackburn and Robin B Stanton*

Department of Computer Science
Australian National University
{Steve.Blackburn,Robin.Stanton}@cs.anu.edu.au

Abstract

The paper is about design of object stores for distributed memory computers. Problems of distribution within such stores are described through the design of Multicomputer Texas, a system derived from the Texas store [SKW92] and implemented on a scalable multicomputer (a Fujitsu AP1000). Problems discussed include creating a single image of an object space across multicomputer architectures, tradeoffs between page-based and object-based granularity, the distribution of store level services and the management of concurrency and persistance within those distributed services. Problems of building layered software on multicomputers pervade these issues. Preliminary scalability performance figures for Multicomputer Texas are also presented.

Keywords: multicomputer, object store, distributed shared memory, parallel systems, persistence.

1   Introduction

1.1   Multicomputer Object Stores

This paper reports the design and outcome of an experiment in scalable object stores. The context of the experiment is the longer term goal of creating a software development workbench within which high performance distributed memory computers can be readily integrated as server nodes into networked computer systems. Object stores play an central role in the software architecture envisaged for the workbench and the distributed memory challenge arises because of the major role that multicomputer architectures play in scalable high performance computing.

Over the past decade object orientation in software architectures has evolved to the point where it is now the system construction paradigm of choice for a wide range of applications. Along with this development, support for object oriented programming styles has become a major theme for language designers and the "object store" or "object space" has become a major focus at the implementation level.

The focus on object stores in their own right has been sharpened by the advent of object databases which now stand alongside their relational counterparts for some kinds of complex data-modelling.

The insights of the persistence research community form another framework within which object stores can be viewed. Their work focusses on persistence as a fundamental property of values independently of their types [AM95]. The breadth of the computing issues which arise within that framework is indicated by the following:- type safety, orthogonal persistence, version control, mappings between persistent and process spaces, crash recovery, movement of values between stores, coherence across multiple stores, concurrency control, granularity of persistent program points, referential transparency and garbage collection.

Relative to the broad sweep of issues which fall within the persistency framework, the experiment reported in this paper has modest objectives concerned with the efficiency of mappings from persistent identifiers to process addresses under a distributed memory implementation of a store, and with control and coherency problems which arise from multiple processors launching concurrent store operations. These issues are particularly important in the design of scalable object stores.

For the purposes of this paper, scalability refers to the extent to which larger problems within a particular application can be handled by commensurate increases in hardware capacity. It can be a difficult concept to pin down in the abstract but an easy property to measure in particular cases. In the high performance object store case the objective is to design the store so that it does not become a bottle neck for otherwise scalable applications, assuming that increases in problem size is matched by increases in the number of nodes in a multicomputer. Although multicomputers do not represent all high performance architectures, at some point in the performance spectrum distributed memory machines appear to be unavoidable and multicomputers provide a refined testbed for the problems that distributed memories generate.

---

*Work supported by CRC for Advanced Computational Systems (ACSys), Fujitsu, and Object Technology International

1.2 Structure of the Paper

With the objectives outlined above in mind, the experiment was designed around Texas [SKW92] as an example of recently developed object store technology and the Fujitsu AP1000 [IHI+90], a machine with a typical multicomputer architecture. Although coherency, concurrency and address mapping problems in scalable object stores can readily be abstracted away from particular implementations, the choice of Texas and the AP1000 had a significant effect on the design of the resultant system and accordingly section 2 of the paper reviews the design of the imported store and the multicomputer architecture.

Section 3 describes major design issues for Multicomputer Texas along with the associated implementation decisions and key algorithms. The background to the design derived from high performance considerations includes the need to support both loosely and tightly coupled parallel operations over the store. The consequent need for efficient distribution of objects and the maintenance of coherence among multiple object copies argues strongly for a design based on a single virtual store across a multicomputer rather than for a scheme based on store-to-store operations between independent stores sited on each node. The decision to base Multicomputer Texas on a persistent virtual shared memory is a major one in that much of the design flows directly from that aspect of the architecture.

Section 4 describes the performance of the system from a benchmark taken from the oo7 suite [CDWN93]. Lessons from a port of a parallel application to Multicomputer Texas are also described. Although the oo7 benchmarks served to build confidence in the system they to not cover the kind of sophisticated tests needed to explore the behaviour of high performance object stores where a prime concern is to calibrate the effectiveness of enabling and exploiting concurrency opportunities.

2 Context

2.1 The Texas Object Store

The Texas object store was developed by Singhal, Kakkad and Wilson from the University of Texas [SKW92]. The store allows persistent objects to be created and retrieved by C++ programs. The design of the store is based on swizzling pointers at page fault time [WK92].

Texas groups persistent objects on pages and uses standard hardware memory protection mechanisms to detect references to objects that are not currently in memory. Hardware memory protection is also used to detect writes to pages, allowing dirty pages to be flagged for writing to store at checkpoint time. When a page of objects is faulted into memory via this mechanism, persistent address pointers are detected and replaced by pointers into virtual memory according to a map of persistent to virtual addresses. If a persistent address is not in the map, virtual address space is allocated for the page containing that address and the new entry inserted into the (persistent, virtual) address map. The newly allocated page in the virtual address space is access protected to trap the first attempt to access the data, at which point the persistent data is paged in.

The dependence on page-based memory protection hardware enforces a page-fault based granularity of interaction between the user-level program and the store. By contrast, virtual machine based stores have the virtual machine instruction as their granularity of interaction. Coarse grained interaction reduces the computational overhead of the store to zero between each of the points of interaction, but also limits the store behaviour. Consequently, Texas exhibits excellent performance when "hot" (all data is in memory), but 'blind spots' between each point of interaction make the implementation of fine grain store features difficult or impossible.

The Texas store has no in-built concurrency control and does not support concurrent access to the store. Applications must be single threaded and only one application may work on the store at a time.

Data is flushed to the store only by calls to a `checkpoint()` function. Checkpointing is implemented in a "stop the world" manner as a blocking call that flushes all dirty pages to the store. A logging scheme is implemented to guarantee atomicity.

Persistence in Texas is selective. It is introduced via `pnew()` (a persistent variant on the `new()` operator) and removed with `free()`. This can be contrasted with the 'persistence by reachability' model, where the persistence of an object is defined in terms of its reachability from a root of persistence. While the explicit denotation of persistence (expressed with `pnew()` and `free()`, for example) introduces problems of referential integrity, it is controlled in the sense that the only objects in the persistent store are those specifically designated through `pnew()` rather than all those in the reference closure.

Texas is implemented as a C++ library. Debugging information in the application binary is used by Texas to extract type and VFT[1] names used in the implementation of persistent type and VFT data. Consequently, all Texas applications are compiled with debugging turned on. Texas maintains various meta-data in order to implement persistent addresses, types and VFTs (see section 3.3.5/3.3.6).

---

[1] Virtual Function Table

Much of the Texas store is implemented by five modules responsible for page faulting and swizzling, type mappings, VFT mappings, address mappings and heap management respectively. The implementation of Multicomputer Texas is based on distributed versions of these modules (figure 3).

Texas does not provide a mechanism for memory re-use. Such a mechanism would have to detect *all* pointers into the store, a difficult task in a language such as C++ where pointer arithmetic and casting are possible. This limitation on memory reuse can have a major impact due to Texas's use of address space for all *potential* page accesses. The limitation is particularly expensive in Multicomputer Texas, where address space is consumed globally for all potential page accesses in the distributed system. Further, the problem is more acute in machines which do not have virtual memory support, such as the AP1000.

2.2 Multicomputer Environment

The platform used for Multicomputer Texas is a 128 node Fujitsu AP1000 multicomputer [IHI+90]. Key characteristics of this platform, and the influence they had on the design of Multicomputer Texas, are described in the following sections.

2.2.1 Distributed Memory

The AP1000 is a distributed memory machine, consisting of a number of processing units connected by a high speed, low-latency network, each node having local memory and possibly other resources such as disks. Access to remote resources such as memory or disk can only be made indirectly, through the host processor. Figure 1 characterises this architecture.

The need to design for a distributed memory architecture introduces many programming challenges. In large measure, the Multicomputer Texas experiment has been the about how the distributed memory can be used efficiently to present an image of a single store.

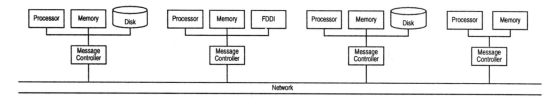

Figure 1: Typical distributed memory multicomputer architecture.

2.2.2 Message Passing

Fundamental to the distributed memory architecture is the capacity for processors to communicate via messages. An AP1000 implementation of MPI [Sit95], the emerging message passing standard, was used as the communication protocol for Multicomputer Texas.

MPI provides send and receive operations, in both blocking and non-blocking forms. Tags are used to label message types, each send being tagged, and each receive either specifying a tag or a wild-card. MPI also offers a particularly powerful "communicator" mechanism whereby multiple, non-interfering, communication channels can be established, allowing isolation of library level and application level messaging. Each MPI communication operation specifies the communicator over which the operation takes effect.

Asynchronous message handling, a proposed enhancement to MPI, was implemented to improve the performance of Multicomputer Texas. Asynchronous message handling allows a function to be associated with a message receipt. On receipt of a matching message, the associated function is asynchronously invoked in much the same way as a signal handler. The mechanism supports the creation of virtual daemon threads to run as servers inside client processes, providing functionality similar to pre-emptive threads. It it seems unlikely that MPI will become a broadly based standard without incorporating functionality of this kind.

2.2.3 Parallel file system

The AP1000 configuration included disk option boards on 32 of the 128 nodes allowing scalability tests up to 128. Each option board supports a 512Mb disk with a peak throughput of 2MB/sec, giving an aggregate 16Gb with 64Mb/sec theoretical peak throughput.

The AP1000 environment includes the HiDIOS parallel file system [TW95], a system which provides all nodes with a single file system image, the distribution of the disks being transparent to the user. Files are striped across the 32 disks in 128Kb stripes. Reads or writes that span multiple stripes can exploit the parallelism of the file system, with multiple disks serving the request in parallel. Interestingly, on machines of this type, DMA and network bandwidth can be faster than the bandwidth of local memory to memory copy, leading to the counter intuitive situation where reads from a remote disk may be faster than reads from the local disk.

2.2.4 Throughput, Speedup and Scalability

The high performance end of the computing spectrum is mostly about parallelism. Hardware architectures provide for increased parallelism when increased performance is required. Scalable software systems are, notionally at least, designed to follow the potential of hardware systems by exploiting any increases in parallelism. It is not difficult to meet this scalability goal for embarrassingly parallel problems, or for throughput problems consisting of sets of largely independent subproblems. In both cases strong isolation properties hold across processor nodes and Multicomputer Texas will exhibit reasonable scalability.

In cases where isolation across parallel nodes is weak, scalability for object stores such as Multicomputer Texas is more difficult to pin down. The objective can be thought about in terms of applications written with and without a scalable store and requiring that the former not be seriously handicapped as a scalable system by being realised as the latter. Essentially the objective is to make applications simpler and more robust by layering parallel code onto a multicomputer object store. It follows that operations and data movements within the store would have to be supported by a rich set of concurrency and coherency mechanisms, mechanisms which in turn would be controlled by application semantics.

3 Multicomputer Texas

3.1 Multicomputer Texas Architecture

Multicomputer Texas implements a single store model, each node within the distributed environment seeing the same persistent address space. The single persistent address space can be seen as a persistent distributed shared memory (DSM). However, while the key focus of DSM research is on efficient coherency that is fine grained both spatially and temporally [CKK95], the emphasis in this experiment was on engineering a uniform distributed persistent environment. This focus is in contrast to the coarser grained coherency problems which characterise the Multicomputer Texas challenge.

Architecturally, there are a number of approaches to building a distributed single store system – three of these are illustrated in figure 2. In the classic client-server model, all operations with respect to the persistent space are undertaken at a server (or servers). Client processes operate on copies of objects from the server, sending the objects back after modification. Under the distributed, single process model (DSP), processes share data through explicit requests which result in the movement of data amongst the processes. With the distributed, multi-process model (DMP), some processes may be more tightly coupled than others, for example they may reside on the same processor and share parts of the same virtual address space.

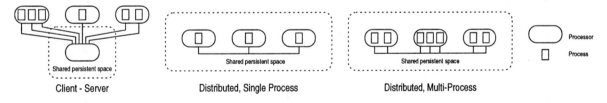

Figure 2: Three architectural approaches to implementing a shared object space.

The DSP model was adopted in the design of Multicomputer Texas. This contrasts with other distributed stores, such as Exodus [CD86], which adopt the classic client-server model. Compared with the client-server model, the DSP model's more tightly coupled nature is better suited to a multicomputer with a high speed, low latency communications network than to the loosely coupled distributed environments envisaged for stores like Exodus. A property of the DSP approach is that each process is responsible for both client and server duties. This demands a mechanism for some sort of daemon server threads, as discussed in section 2.2.2. Implementation concerns relating to VFT and type information (which are derived at compile time from the application binary), lead to a restriction whereby each process must execute the same binary image.

The DSP model does not offer the same degree of inter-process resource sharing of the DMP model, however the DMP model was not appropriate for the Multicomputer Texas experiments because the target platform does not support multiple processes per node at the hardware level. However, even with appropriate hardware support for inter process data sharing, the DSP model has advantages. For example the DMP model complicates the coherency model with problems such as the need for a process to lock a physically shared page against writes by the other sharing processes while maintaining write access for itself.

So Multicomputer Texas takes the form of a persistent distributed virtual memory. An important property of the design is that object images can be moved from node to node without modification because every node maps a given persistent address to the the same virtual address and visa versa. Pointers passed from node to node via message passing need not be remapped for the same reason and the considerable swizzling overheads which would otherwise be incurred are avoided.

3.2 Multicomputer Texas Design

Adoption of the restricted symmetric distributed architecture outlined above supports the modular implementation of distribution on top of the existing Texas implementation (see figure 3). Distribution is implemented through client sub-modules within each of the five key functional modules of the original Texas implementation (see section 2.1). These client sub-modules ensure that their parent modules see globally consistent meta data. They achieve this by making consistency checks with corresponding servers when necessary. There are therefore servers corresponding to each of the five clients which are responsible for orchestrating global consistency of the meta-data.

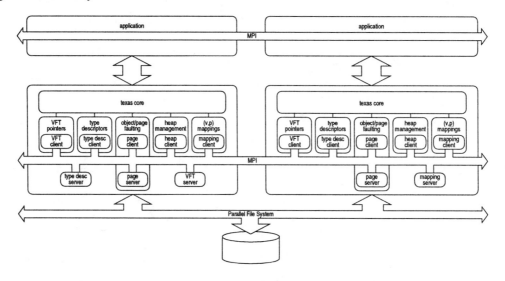

Figure 3: Multicomputer Texas architecture, showing two nodes.

Each node has a page server which serves requests for pages held by that node. Other servers, such as those for address mappings and VFT, may be be distributed across multiple nodes. Alternatively servers may be set up to operate on single nodes. In this sense Multicomputer Texas is flexible with respect to distributable services, with runtime options allowing distribution or localisation to be specified for each server.

Figure 3 illustrates the three levels of communication in a Multicomputer Texas architecture: application level, library level, and the parallel file system level. Thus there are two distinct layers of communication at the application level: direct communication through MPI; and communication through the shared persistent space as implemented by the two lower levels of communication.

3.3 Key Algorithms

3.3.1 Concurrency Control

Concurrency control is a major issue in object store design and has led to a number of quite different architectural solutions (for example, Exodus [CD86] and Flask [MCM+94]). However, control mechanisms for concurrency were not a major focus for the Multicomputer Texas experiment, partly because they also fall outside of the Texas work. As is clear from the major Texas papers, [WK92] and [SKW92], the Texas store is a comprehensive working out of the "swizzle at page fault time" mechanism, leaving concurrency control to be realised in a higher level layer.

Of course, some level of concurrency control is required to manage parallel access to the store, and to this end Multicomputer Texas implements a simple lock–based concurrency control system.

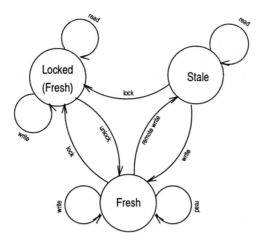

Figure 4: Page coherency state transition diagram

Under this coherency scheme, while an object is locked by a given node, normal read-write semantics are guaranteed with respect to that object for that node. If an object is not locked, reads may return stale values. Figure 4 illustrates the possible coherency states for a page under this scheme. A property of the scheme not borne out by the figure is that where the sequence of operations inside a locked region includes trailing reads, the lock may be released after the last write without altering the semantics of the sequence of operations (ie LxyU ≡ LxUy, where x = (rw)*wr*, y = r*, and r, w, L, and U denote read, write, lock and unlock respectively).

The concurrency control scheme is page–based, in keeping with the Texas framework. Memory resident pages are either *master* (mutable) or *copy* (immutable) pages. For each page in the global persistent address space, there exists at most one master page and zero or more copy pages. When a node writes to or locks an object, the node obtains the master page for that object. The node retains the master page until the object is unlocked *and* the master page is required by another node.

This behaviour guarantees the read-write semantics outlined above. An undesirable side affect of the page based locking mechanism is "false sharing" – the unintended locking of objects sharing one page. The problems of false sharing, which include including unnecessary contention and additional complexity in deadlock detection, are well documented in the literature [BCZ90].

3.3.2 Distributed Heap Management

Texas maintains two heaps, one for persistent data and one for transient data. A call to new() will allocate space for an object on the transient heap, while a call to pnew() will allocate space on the persistent heap (or the transient heap if the store argument is null). The Texas implementation interleaves the two heaps in memory with a page granularity. The allocation of space on either heap is done using a standard memory allocation strategy; if free space is available, it is reused, otherwise the heap is extended and new space used. Whenever the persistent heap is extended, the persistent address space must be extended to accommodate the new pages and the resulting (PA,VA)[2] mappings must be added to the (PA,VA) map.

The implementation of a distributed persistent heap involves distributed free list management, coherent heap extension, and distributed (PA,VA) map management (distributed (PA,VA) map management is the focus of section 3.3.3). Because the transient address space is not shared, the only special requirement of transient heap space management in Multicomputer Texas is that it use the virtual address space in sympathy with the requirements of the persistent heap. Figure 5 illustrates global address space allocation up to some point in time, transient space allocation for the same period, and the contributions made by three clients to the allocation of persistent space.

The distributed free list is implemented by each node maintaining a free list independently. A side effect of the isolation of each free list is that when a node's free list is unable to sustain a request, the node is forced to extend the persistent address space

---

[2]The (PA,VA) notation is used to refer to a Persistent Address, Virtual Address pair.

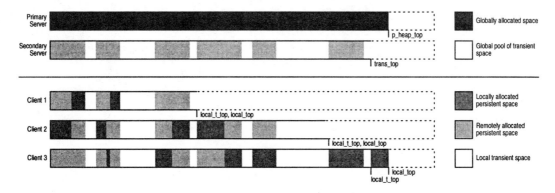

Figure 5: Global persistent and transient heaps.

despite the possibility of free lists on other nodes having suitable memory available. In order to avoid leakage of persistent memory between sessions, the free lists persist (as does the free list in Texas). Ideally the persistent free lists would be evenly redistributed between each of the participating nodes at the start of each new session, however this refinement has not been implemented.

Coherent concurrent persistent heap extension is managed by persistent heap extension requests going through a distributed heap server. Whenever a node needs to extend the persistent heap, it sends a request to the primary heap server and the primary heap server responds with an address range corresponding with an extension to the global address space sufficient to accommodate the request (see figure 6). On receiving a response from the server, the client node extends its heap space, access protecting any space between its former top of heap and the base of the newly allocated space. Such space will have been allocated to other nodes by the server. Access protecting the space allows accesses into that space to be trapped so that the relevant data can be paged in. To reduce the number of requests to the server, request are made in integral numbers of eight-page "chunks".

A secondary server exists for transient memory. The transient memory server maintains a pool of memory allocated for transient use, and draws from that pool to satisfy clients requests. This provides an effective way of allowing transient address

```
/* Extend heap (persistent) */
extend_p_heap(size){
    send(size, p_server);
    receive(base, p_server);
    protect(local_top, base);
    local_top = base + size;
    return base;
}

/* Extend heap (transient) */
extend_t_heap(size){
    send({size, local_t_top}, s_server);
    receive({temp_list, local_t_top}, s_server);
    while ((next = pop_contiguous(temp_list)) != NULL) {
        add_to_free_list(next);
        if (base(next) > local_top) then {
            protect(local_top, base(next));
            local_top = base(next) + size_of(next);
        }
    }
    /* Free list can now satisfy request for size */
}
```

Client

```
/* Grow the primary heap */
grow_p_heap() {
    receive(size, client);
    old_top = p_heap_top;
    p_heap_top = p_heap_top + size;
    send(old_top, client);
}

/* Grow the secondary heap (transient) */
grow_s_heap(){
    receive({size, client_top}, client);
    temp_list = diff(global_s_list, client_top);
    if does_not_contain(size, temp_list) then {
        send(size, p_server);
        receive(temp_base, p_server);
        trans_top = temp_base + size;
        add_to_list (global_s_list, temp_base);
        temp_list = diff(global_s_list, client_top);
    }
    send({temp_list, trans_top}, client);
}
```

Heap Servers

Figure 6: Persistent and transient heap extension algorithms

256

space to be re-used by each node (transient memory is *not* shared). The transient memory server makes requests to the primary heap server whenever the transient memory pool needs extension.

3.3.3 Address Mappings

Each node maintains a table of persistent address and virtual address (PA, VA) pairs. The task of the distributed address map server is to ensure that all nodes have consistent (PA, VA) maps. Each node's map grows when the node generates new (PA, VA) mappings as a result of extending the persistent heap, or when the node discovers a new (PA, VA) pair through the map server.

```
/* Get or set virtual address */
get_va(pa) {
    send(pa, server, GET_VA);
    receive(va, server, GET_VA);
    if (va == NULL) {
        va = malloc(PAGESIZE, persistent);
        send({pa, va}, server, SET_MAP);
    }
    return va;
}
```
Client

```
/* Get a virtual address */
get_va() {
    receive(pa, client, GET_VA);
    map = get_map(pa, NULL);
    if (map.pending)
        enqueue (client, map.queue);
    else {
        if (map.va == NULL)
            map.pending = true;
        send(map.va, client, GET_VA);
    }
}

/* Set a virtual address */
set_map() {
    receive({pa, va}, client, SET_MAP);
    map = get_map(pa, va);
    map.va = va;
    map.pa = pa;
    while (not_empty(map.queue))
        send(va, pop(map.queue), GET_VA);
    map.pending = FALSE;
}
```
Map Server

Figure 7: Coherent (persistent, virtual) map generation

When a node encounters a persistent or virtual address that is not in its local (PA, VA) map, it queries the map server. If the map server responds with a (PA, VA) pair, the pair is inserted in the node's local (PA, VA) map, and the node is able to continue. The server will respond with a null mapping if it is unaware of the address in question. The server may be unaware of an address because the address is erroneous, or because the the address is a previously unswizzled persistent address.

If a node is the first to swizzle a particular persistent address, it allocates virtual address space for the page in question (or in the case of a multi-page object, space for the object). The node must then inform the map server of the new (PA, VA) mapping. In the case where multiple nodes request the same previously unknown (PA, VA) mapping, the map server arbitrates, ensuring that only the first node creates the new mapping, the other nodes are blocked until the mapping has been established.

Multicomputer Texas supports two different map server modes. In one mode serving is concentrated on a single node, while in the other serving is distributed across all nodes. The map server mode may be set at run time, a flexibility that may be used to avoid possible bottlenecks. Distribution of the map server incurs the overhead of implementing both VA to PA and PA to VA maps, as a (PA, VA) pair will not, in general, hash to the same server. There is also a small overhead in keeping both maps coherent.

3.3.4 Page Faulting

In the Texas object store, any access to a page not in memory is trapped by ensuring that for any swizzled pointer, the corresponding page is initially access protected. Attempts to write to pages are detected by initially giving in-memory pages read access only. Once a write fault has occured on a page, the page will have read-write access until the page is checkpointed, at which time it reverts to read-only permission so that any attempt to write to it can be trapped and flagged as a dirty page for the next checkpoint.

In Multicomputer Texas, the implementation differs, with read and write faults handled by a client sub-module that, together with its corresponding server, ensures that the Multicomputer Texas concurrency control protocol is adhered to (section 3.3.1). This is implemented by managing the movement of *master* and *copy* pages. The map server (section 3.3.3) keeps page ownership information for each (PA, VA) pair.

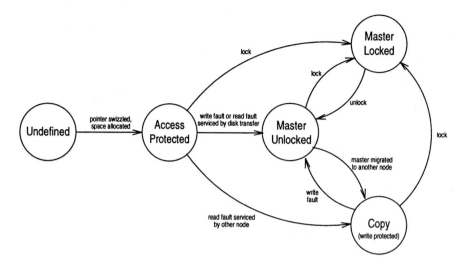

Figure 8: Page fault state transition diagram

When a read fault occurs, a request is sent to the map server for a copy of the relevant page. If the page is in memory, the map server forwards the request on to the owner to the master. The owner of the master responds to the original requestor by passing on a *copy* of the master. If the page is not in memory, the map server marks the requestor as the owner of the master and responds to the requestor with a message indicating that the requestor should read the page from store and swizzle it.

When a write fault occurs, a request is sent to the map server for the master page. If the page is in memory, the map server marks the requestor as the new owner of the master and forwards the request on to the last owner to the master. The owner of the master responds to the original requestor by passing on the master, keeping a *copy* for itself. If the page is not in memory, the map server marks the requestor as the owner of the master and responds to the requestor with a message indicating that the requestor should read the page from store.

A result of this protocol is that a node may receive a request for a page while it is waiting for the master page, or while it has the master locked. Consequently, nodes queue requests for page copies and set a `next_master` field if a request for the master arrives before the page is available. As soon as a master page is available, the copy queue and `next_master` field are checked and requests serviced.

To ensure efficient and correct checkpointing, master pages are tagged with an update bit. At checkpoint time, in addition to committing all dirty pages, each node commits any clean master pages which have their update bit set.

3.3.5 VFT Mappings

Virtual function tables allow dynamic binding of functions to instance objects in C++ by establishing pointers to relevant executable code on instantiation of the object. VFTs must be persistent in order that persistent objects with virtual functions can bind to executing binaries.

VFT pointer management involves mapping of three types of interrelated data, as illustrated in figure 9; compile-time generated string identifiers (SIDs), runtime identifiers (RIDs), and persistent identifiers (PIDs). SIDs are compiler generated function identifiers, RIDs are pointers into the application binary, and PIDs are four-byte persistent replacements for RIDs, guaranteed to be unique by the VFT server.

A (SID, RID) map is generated from the application binary at compile time[3], a persistent (SID, PID) map exists as part of the store, and a (PID, RID) map is constructed at run time. The (SID, RID) map contains mappings for all virtual functions in the application binary, the persistent (SID, PID) map contains mappings for all virtual functions pointed to by objects in the store, and the (PID, RID) map contains mappings for the set of all VFT pointers swizzled at a point in the current execution of

---

[3]The map is generated using a tool based on a standard debugger.

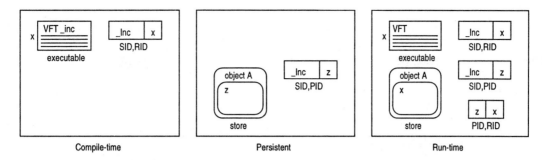

Figure 9: The role of SID, RID and PID mappings in persistent VFT management.

the application. The role of the VFT manager is to maintain the (SID, PID) and (PID, RID) maps as VFT pointers are swizzled and unswizzled.

In the distributed implementation, each node has its own copy of the three maps. The role of the VFT server is to ensure that PIDs are generated consecutively and that (SID, PID) and (PID, RID) maps are one to one.

Clients may request an update to their local maps, passing an indicator of the state of their maps and optionally passing a PID or RID which is not in their local map. On receiving a request, the server will add to the maps if necessary, and respond to the client with any part of the (PID, RID) map that the client does not have. The client can then update its (SID, PID) and (PID, RID) maps. Clients are responsible for checkpointing the (SID, PID) map, and must ensure that their map is consistent prior to each checkpoint.

3.3.6   Type Mappings

Type information is used by Texas to locate and swizzle pointers in the body of objects, and must persist for as long as any objects of that type persist. Texas uses SID, PID and RID mappings to manage types in a very similar way to its management of VFTs. A PID identifies the type of a persistent object by an index into a persistent type description table. An RID identifies the type of an in-memory object by an index into a transient type description table, and a SID is a compier-generated string used to match entries in the persistent type description table with compile-time generated type information associated with the executing binary.

The similarity of VFT and type management allows a common implementation of their distributed management.

4   Testing, Performance and Use

4.1   Testing and Benchmarking

Multicomputer Texas has been successfully implemented on both the Fujitsu AP1000 multicomputer and a network of work-stations. A number of simple applications have been tested on the system, including a port of the oo7 benchmark and oort, an object oriented ray tracer.

The tests proved to be fruitful sources of feedback on system performance and brought to light a number of the system's performance attributes. The oo7 benchmark was simply adapted to the Multicomputer environment by having each node simultaneously run the same test (query, traversal or update) against the store. While this benchmarking approach revealed many of Multicomputer Texas's performance characteristics, a benchmark specifically designed for parallel object stores may have shed more light on issues of concurrency, however, to our knowledge such a benchmark has not been produced.

4.2   Performance

Benchmark testing brought out the best and worst of the Multicomputer Texas architecture. Each node simultaneously running the same test against a single store inevitably leads to a high level of data sharing and consequently, data contention.

Caching effects (section 3.3.4) led to good performance on the read only tests, such as the non-committing traversal and query tests. On cold runs, the cost of reading the pages from disk was amortised across all participating nodes, with read contention for the master page only slowing the system slightly (figure 10). The hot runs were even better suited to the caching scheme, completion times scaling perfectly with the lack of any distribution or page faulting overhead. The good scalability results for read-only tests suggest that the distributed management of the heaps, address mappings, page faulting, and VFT and type maps where not significant bottlenecks.

Tests that wrote or committed (for example, "Hot-Commit", figure 10) brought out bottlenecks in the Multicomputer Texas architecture. The concurrency protocol ensures that there exists only one mutable copy of any page. Consequently, bottlenecks arise whenever there is heavy demand for write access to a given *page*, whether or not there is actually contention for a particular object. The "Hot-Commit" results in figure 10, where no updates are made, but a commit is called, illustrate that even contention for pages holding store meta-data can be a serious problem.

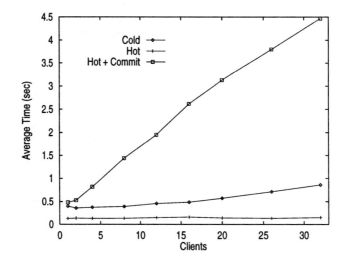

Figure 10: oo7 "Traversal 1" results

4.3   Use of Multicomputer Texas

The porting of applications to Multicomputer Texas was the source of considerable feedback on the usability of the programming model it provides. Broadly speaking, the environment is comfortable for those with experience with C++ and message passing programming on a multicomputer. However, the concurrency model was not particularly easy to work with and the lack of support for optimistic computation limited opportunities for exploiting concurrency.

Another problem with the programming model was the ease with which referential integrity violations can be introduced. This is a characteristic common to Texas. Each time a persistent object is instantiated, care must be taken to ensure that any objects instantiated by that object's methods are also made persistent. This makes the use of existing class libraries problematic. A common approach to solving to this problem is the use of a macro such as the following:

```
#define new(x) pnew(obj_store_of(this), x)
```

This ensures that new objects inherit their persistence from the object that created them (`this`).

5   Conclusions

The following observations and conclusions are supported by the Multicomputer Texas experiment.

Layered software architectures on multi-computers.   Central to the challenge of creating effective programming workbench for multi-computers is the extent to which standard layering techniques can be preserved. At present multicomputer programming is dominated by models based on communicating processes with very weak layering above the communications level. Multicomputer Texas is one of a number of experimental systems aimed at building confidence in taking distributed memory program models to higher levels in this sense.

In the context of a transactional model of computation and object level granularity data management results from Multicomputer Texas are encouraging if not definitive. The system exhibits reasonable scalability without any aspect of distribution management within the store layer being visible. This outcome is qualified to some extent by the limitations of the benchmarks used in evaluating Multicomputer Texas.

Multicomputer Texas functionality. Although the design of Multicomputer Texas followed Texas in the way application bindings are established and in the way persistent to virtual mappings are managed, the distribution based problems of data coherence, migration and stabilisation are new. The solutions presented to these problems of distribution are satisfying in so far as they do not introduce additional constraints.

The relatively unsophisticated mechanism whereby local copies survive non-local lock operations, combined with system wide serialisation of writes, gives rise to quite good performance, at least under the benchmark limitations mentioned earlier. In addition the distributed services model proved effective for ensuring consistent persistent address spaces across the distributed memories and global serialisability of "transaction" styled computations across processor nodes. However as isolation between transactions is weakened it is clear that bottlenecks will arise and that some degree of optimistic computation could become profitable. At that point the interaction between a concurrency control layer and the coherence mechanisms in Multicomputer Texas would require close attention with possible major revisions to the latter.

Asynchronous communications. Distribution mechanisms for a distributed store tend to reside in their own layer sitting on top of system communications services. In the Multicomputer Texas case those services were provided through an MPI service. While MPI elegantly supports layering through domains, it does not support priorities of the kind often handled with preemption of threads or equivalent schemes. Of course MPI is not alone in this respect. In any case without support for relative priority and preemption at processor nodes, the performance of Multicomputer Texas would be unacceptable.

Objects and pages. Many object stores work at the page, rather than object level of granularity. The problems of phantom locking and reduction in potential concurrency are traded off for performance improvements that flow from the use of uniform units of storage derived from virtual memory and disk technology. Very little is understood about this tradeoff for shared memory stores and even less is known about it in the distributed memory case. It is an important open question which Multicomputer Texas does not address. However as an observation, it seems likely that object serving among processor nodes is not entirely at odds with the use of pages as the key unit of data management.

Persistence. Texas assumes that at any one time, only one program is bound to the persistent store and further that only one processor is involved. Consequently there is no provision for concurrency. The introduction of multicomputing forces consideration of the management of concurrency and the simultaneous binding of multiple programs, including multiple versions of the one program, to the store. Under these circumstances the mechanism that Texas uses to validate bindings between programs and objects in the store would have to be replaced with one which respected identity and subtype relations between programs.

This issue raises deep problems in complete, type safe stores under a number of program evolution scenarios. It is mentioned here as an important point of departure from the Multicomputer Texas system rather than as a criticism of the Texas mechanism. Clearly that mechanism can be adapted to multiple versions of the one program in a safe way by accommodating differences across processes in the location of VFTs and associated binary entry points, however in general a much stronger run-time type analysis mechanism would be required.

6 Acknowledgements

We wish to acknowledge the contributions to this work from the St Andrews University persistence group, the Australian National University CAP project (`http://cap.anu.edu.au/`), and the Herod group in the CRC for Advanced Computational Systems. We also wish to acknowledge the valuable feedback provided by anonymous reviewers, their comments have been thought provoking and have led to improvements to this paper.

References

[AM95]   Malcolm P. Atkinson and Ronald Morrison. Orthogonally persistent systems. *The VLDB Journal*, 4(3):319–402, July 1995.

[BCZ90]   John K. Bennett, John B. Carter, and Willy Zwaenepoel. Adaptive software cache management for distributed shared memory architectures. In *Proc. 17th Annual Symp. Computer Architecture (SIGARCH)*, Seattle, May 29-June 2 1990.

[CD86]   Michael J. Carey and David DeWitt. The architecture of the EXODUS extensible DBMS. In *Proc. Int. Workshop on Object-Oriented Database Systems*, pages 52–65, Pacific Grove, CA (USA), September 1986. IEEE.

[CDWN93]   Michael J Carey, David J. De Witt, and Jeffrey F. Naughton. The oo7 benchmark. In *Proceedings of the 1993 ACM-SIGMOD Conference on the Management of Data*, Washington D.C., USA, may 1993.

[CKK95]   John B. Carter, Dilip Khandekar, and Linus Kamb. Distributed shared memory: Where we are and where we should be headed. In *Proceedings of the Fifth Workshop on Hot Topics in Operating Systems*, pages 119–122, May 1995.

[IHI⁺90]   H Ishihata, T Horie, S Inano, T Shimizu, and S Kato. CAP-II architecture. In *Proceedings of the First Fujitsu-ANU CAP Workshop*, Kawasaki, Japan, November 1990. Fujitsu Laboratories Ltd.

[MCM⁺94]   David S. Munro, Richard C.H. Connor, Ronald Morrison, Stephan Scheuerl, and David W. Stemple. Concurrent shadow paging in the Flask architecture. In Malcolm Atkinson, Véronique Benzaken, and David Maier, editors, *Sixth International Workshop on Persistent Object Systems*, pages 16–37, Tatascon, France, September 1994.

[Sit95]   David Sitsky. Implementing MPI using interrupts and remote copying for the AP1000/AP1000+. In *Proceedings of the Fourth Parallel Computing Workshop*, London, September 1995. Fujitsu Laboratories Ltd.

[SKW92]   Vivek Singhal, Sheetal V. Kakkad, and Paul R. Wilson. Texas: An efficient, portable persistent store. In *Fifth International Workshop on Persistent Object Systems*, San Miniato, Italy, September 1992. Morgan-Kaufman.

[TW95]   Andrew Tridgell and David Walsh. The HiDIOS file system. In *Proceedings of the Fourth Parallel Computing Workshop*, London, September 1995. Fujitsu Laboratories Ltd.

[WK92]   Paul R. Wilson and Sheetal V. Kakkad. Pointer swizzling at page fault time: Efficiently and compatibly supporting huge addresses on standard hardware. In *1992 International Workshop on Object Orientation in Operating Systems*, pages 364–377, Dourdan, France, 1992. IEEE, IEEE Computer Society Press.

Author Index